ASPECTS OF TOURISM 2
Series Editors: **Chris Cooper**, *University of Queensland, Australia*
and **Michael Hall**, *University of Otago, New Zealand*

Tourism Collaboration and Partnerships

Politics, Practice and Sustainability

Edited by

Bill Bramwell and Bernard Lane

CHANNEL VIEW PUBLICATIONS
Clevedon • Buffalo • Toronto • Sydney

Library of Congress Cataloging in Publication Data

Tourism Collaboration and Partnerships: Politics, Practice and Sustainability
Edited by Bill Bramwell and Bernard Lane
Aspects of Tourism: 2
Includes bibliographical references
1. Tourism–Planning. 2. Tourism–Management. 3. Tourism–Government policy.
I. Bramwell, Bill. II. Lane, Bernard. III. Series.
G155.A1 T58957 2000
338.4′791–dc21   99-088695

British Library Cataloguing in Publication Data

A CIP catalogue record for this book is available from the British Library.

ISBN 1-873150-22-9 (hbk)

Channel View Publications
An imprint of Multilingual Matters Ltd

UK: Frankfurt Lodge, Clevedon Hall, Victoria Road, Clevedon BS21 7SJ.
USA: 2250 Military Road, Tonawanda, NY 14150, USA.
Canada: 5201 Dufferin Street, North York, Ontario, Canada M3H 5T8.
Australia: P.O. Box 586, Artarmon, NSW, Australia.

Printed and bound in Great Britain by Short Run Press.

Contents

Preface

Back in the late 1980s, both editors of this book worked with local and national groups to try to establish sustainable tourism action plans. Those groups were – though we did not fully realise it at the time – forms of collaborative tourism planning. The discussion then, however, was not about collaboration and partnership. It was about the validity of sustainable tourism itself – as a paradigm rather than as a practice. Now that at least the concept of sustainability in tourism is quite widely accepted, the discussion has moved on. Practice and implementation have become the new critical questions of the day, along with the evaluation of practice and implementation. This volume is a contribution to that new discussion. It looks at issues and case studies in collaboration and partnership development, in particular as tools for sustainable tourism.

The book began as a special issue for the *Journal of Sustainable Tourism*. The call for papers for that special issue (Vol. 7, Nos. 3&4, 1999) was remarkably successful. The issue was expanded from its regular 96 pages to a double issue of 192 pages, and then more. But there were still too many valuable contributions for the theme issue. And so the book was born. It brings together fifteen chapters by researchers and practitioners across the world. In addition, the book has a substantial introduction to the subject, and a conclusion that looks forward to further developments in research, debate and practice. The decision to produce a book on collaboration and partnerships in tourism also opens the wealth of experience, advice and discussion contained within its pages to a wider audience than those who subscribe to an academic serial.

The production of the book has only been possible with the help of many people. Our authors have worked long and patiently on succeeding drafts of their work. Unlike many books, every chapter has been refereed by the editors and then blind refereed, usually by four experts in the field. This detailed review process has helped the authors to add to the value and clarity of their contributions. We are much indebted to the referees as well as to our contributors. The editors must also thank those many members of partnerships across England and in other parts of the world with whom they have worked on collaborative experiments and experiences over the years. We have learned a very great deal from their efforts. Finally, we must thank Mike and Marjukka Grover at Channel View Publications. They have had faith in this project from its beginnings in a Manchester bar over two years ago, and they have backed it unstintingly with advice and resources over that long gestation period.

Bill Bramwell
Tourism Centre, Sheffield Hallam University, UK

Bernard Lane
Rural Tourism Unit, University of Bristol, UK

The Contributors

Madeleine Boyd holds an environmental science degree from Griffith University. She worked as research officer with the Australian Cooperative Research Centre for Sustainable Tourism, a partnership between industry, universities and governments to enhance the environmental, economic and social sustainability of tourism. She and her partner are currently biking around the world gaining first hand experience of sustainable tourism.

Bill Bramwell is Reader in Tourism Management at the Centre for Tourism at Sheffield Hallam University, UK. He has published widely in the field of tourism policy and planning and is co-founder and co-editor of the *Journal of Sustainable Tourism*. He has extensive experience of working with tourism partnerships through his former post at the English Tourist Board.

Alison Caffyn worked in development and research for Regional Tourist Boards in England and Scotland before moving to the Centre for Urban and Regional Studies at the University of Birmingham, UK. She directs the postgraduate programme in Tourism Policy and Management and conducts contract research in Britain and abroad. Her research interests include public policy in tourism, partnership approaches, rural tourism and regeneration.

Terry de Lacy is chief executive of Australia's Cooperative Research Centre for Sustainable Tourism, Professor of Environmental Policy at the University of Queensland, and Chair of the Management Board of Green Globe Asia Pacific Pty. Ltd. His personal research work focuses on sustainable development with an emphasis on protected areas: his geographical focus covers both Asia and Australia.

Donald Getz is Professor of Tourism and Hospitality Management at the University of Calgary, Canada. He has expertise in event management, destination planning and marketing, family business and entrepreneurship, rural tourism, impact assessment, and special-interest travel. Recent books written and edited include *The Business of Rural Tourism* (1997), *Event Management and Event Tourism* (1997) and *Wine Tourism Management* (2000).

Michael Hall is Professor at the Centre for Tourism, University of Otago, New Zealand and Visiting Professor at Sheffield Hallam University in the UK. He has written widely on tourism, heritage and environmental history and has a long-standing interest in tourism policy and rural and regional development issues. He is currently researching second home development, and cool-climate wine and walnut growing related to rural diversification.

Tazim Jamal is Assistant Professor in the Department of Recreation, Park and Tourism Sciences at Texas A&M University, USA. She had several years of industry experience before becoming a University teacher and researcher. Her main interest areas lie in strategic destination management and planning for the sustainability of natural and sociocultural resources, together with the enhancement of the quality of life for community residents.

Margaret Johnston is a polar enthusiast whose research explores the regulation of tourists and the tourist industry in both the Arctic and Antarctic. Other interests include sustainable communities and special event volunteering. She received her doctorate in Geography from the University of Canterbury, New Zealand, and is now Director of the School of Outdoor Recreation, Parks and Tourism at Lakehead University, Canada.

Bernard Lane is Director of the Rural Tourism Unit at the University of Bristol, UK. With Bill Bramwell he co-founded and co-edits the *Journal of Sustainable Tourism*. He lectures and acts as consultant on sustainable rural tourism development on a global basis and has helped create and manage a range of tourism partnerships.

Philip Long is a senior lecturer at the Centre for Tourism, Sheffield Hallam University, UK. Before embarking on an academic career, Phil worked in the tourism industry, including a period in southern Africa. As well as working on partnerships and collaboration in tourism, his current research interests include the relationships between tourism and culture, the arts, and the media.

Lindemberg Medeiros de Araujo is a geographer. He has worked for over 14 years in the field of environmental planning and is a teacher at the Department of Geography of the Federal University of Alagoas State, Brazil. He is currently completing his PhD in tourism management at Sheffield Hallam University, UK.

Peter Mason is Reader in Tourism within the Business School at the University of Luton, UK. He worked previously at the University of Plymouth, UK, and from 1996–1999 at Massey University in New Zealand, where the contribution to this book was written. His research and publications cover tourism impacts, tourism planning and management, tourism education, heritage interpretation and polar tourism.

Steven Parker is an Associate Professor of Political Science at the University of Nevada in Las Vegas, USA. The main focus of his research has been on the nexus between marine tourism and public policy. He has recently completed sabbatical fieldwork on this subject in Papua New Guinea and Queensland, Australia.

Maureen G. Reed is an Associate Professor in the Department of Geography at the University of British Columbia, Canada. Her research is focused on sustainability and community development, particularly on the politics of rural resource communities that are experiencing changes in environmental conditions and policies, and associated issues of economic and social restructuring.

Brent Ritchie holds the Professorship of Tourism Management in the Faculty of Management, and is Chair of the World Tourism Education & Research Centre at the University of Calgary, Canada. He has published extensively in leading journals, co-authored two definitive tourism texts, and is associate editor of the *Journal of Travel Research*. He has been consultant to numerous private and public sector groups, and has won awards and recognition nationally and internationally for his contribution to the study of travel and tourism.

Lesley Roberts is a consultant and lecturer in rural tourism development in the Leisure and Tourism Management Department of the Scottish Agricultural College. Her work in Romania and Bulgaria reflects her focus on innovative approaches to rural development throughout Europe. She is currently researching factors influencing the development of tourism micro-businesses.

Mike Robinson is Reader in Tourism Studies and Director of the Centre for Travel & Tourism at the University of Northumbria at Newcastle. His work involves him in research and consultancy project management, international conference management, and publishing. Personal research interests include the impacts of tourism on cultures and society, the role of tourism in local community economic and cultural regeneration, and tourism and the arts.

Steve Selin is an Associate Professor in the Division of Forestry at West Virginia University, USA. He has had a long-standing professional interest in collaborative processes in the tourism, recreation, and natural resource fields. His work on partnerships has been published in the *Annals of Tourism Research, Tourism Management, Society and Natural Resources, Journal of Forestry, Journal of Sustainable Tourism* and the *Journal of Park and Recreation Administration.*

Fiona Simpson is an environmental planner, based in the Glasgow office of Land Use Consultants in Scotland. She has been involved in consultancy and related research projects in Bulgaria, Czech Republic, Estonia, Slovakia and the UK. Her research interests include planning, institutional and community capacity building, tourism, and integrated rural development.

Dallen Timothy is Assistant Professor in the Sport Management, Recreation and Tourism division of Bowling Green State University, Ohio, USA. His research interests in tourism include political boundaries, planning in developing countries, ethnic communities, heritage and peripheral/rural regions. He is co-author of forthcoming books on *Tourism and Political Boundaries* with Geoff Wall and *Heritage Tourism* with Stephen Boyd.

Pascal Tremblay is senior lecturer at the Northern Territory University in Darwin, Australia. His research interests include industrial organisation and evolutionary economics of tourism, sustainable tourism and wildlife management, information technologies and strategic management. His PhD dissertation (University of Melbourne, 1997) was on 'Information and Organisation: the Economic Coordination of Tourism'.

Dave Twynam is Associate Dean at the School of Tourism, University College of the Cariboo, BC, Canada. His research focuses on ecotourism opportunities and market segmentation, principles and codes of conduct for Arctic tourism, and the motivations of special event volunteers. In addition to researching Arctic tourism guidelines, he has worked with the Ecotourism Society's project on Caribbean marine ecotourism principles.

1. Collaboration and Partnerships in Tourism Planning

Bill Bramwell
Centre for Tourism, Sheffield Hallam University, UK

Bernard Lane
Rural Tourism Unit, University of Bristol, UK

Introduction

Tourism, like so many modern industries, is essentially an assembly process. In few situations does one company or organisation control all the components, or all the stages and decision-making processes in the creation and delivery of the tourism product. Vertical integration is not a hallmark of most tourism operations. Equally, horizontal integration is relatively rare: single ownership of all the airlines, hotels or other forms of tourism product is unusual, even in one region.

The diffuse and fragmented nature of tourism development has long been recognised. Ways of overcoming the problems caused by fragmentation have also been long sought. Over the last fifty years, local tourism associations have promoted intra-industry cooperation, and national tourism offices have represented the enterprises of their country to the market (Pearce,1992). Internationally, groupings such as the Pacific Asia Travel Association (PATA) and the World Travel and Tourism Council (WTTC) typify cross-border tourism alliances.

Few or even none of the above is, however, a collaborative arrangement or partnership in the sense discussed in this book. The term partnership is used here to describe regular, cross-sectoral interactions between parties based on at least some agreed rules or norms, intended to address a common issue or to achieve a specific policy goal or goals. All the collaborative arrangements examined in this collection of papers are concerned with issues or policies that go beyond basic tourism questions, and have broader economic, social and environmental dimensions. The cross-sectoral reference is important: partnerships that seek to create sustainable tourism need to be holistic in outlook. A focus on cross-sectoral interactions also rules out the examination here of simplistic marketing groups or trading alliances.

Conceptual Background

The importance of involving diverse stakeholders in tourism planning and management is receiving growing recognition. This has led to increasing attention being directed to the use of collaborative arrangements or partnerships that bring together a range of interests in order to develop and sometimes also implement tourism policies. Collaborative arrangements for tourism planning involve face-to-face interactions between stakeholders who may be in the public, semi-public, private or voluntary sectors, including pressure and interest groups. Stakeholder collaboration has the potential to lead to dialogue, negotiation and the building of mutually acceptable proposals about how tourism should be developed. Partnerships involved in tourism planning usually bring together interests in the same destination but in different sectors, or else parties in different destinations but with mutual interests in one issue or related issues.

A key reason for the growing interest in partnerships in tourism development is the belief that tourist destination areas and organisations may be able to gain competitive advantage by bringing together the knowledge, expertise, capital and other resources of several stakeholders (Kotler *et al.*, 1993). Some commentators also contend that decisions about tourism development should not be left to a few politicians, government officials or tourism entrepreneurs, suggesting that a wide range of stakeholders should have opportunities to participate in decision-making that affects their interests. These commentators claim that the broadly based ownership of tourism policies can bring democratic empowerment and equity, operational advantages, and an enhanced tourism product (Jamal and Getz, 1995; Joppe, 1996; Murphy, 1985; Timothy, 1999).

Partnership approaches to tourism planning are now widely endorsed by government and public agencies in many developed countries. The UK government's tourism policy document, *Tomorrow's Tourism*, includes a commitment to 'encourage tourism management partnerships between local authorities, tourism operators and local communities' (DCMS, 1999:53). Within the UK context, Charlton and Essex (1996:178) have noted that 'A striking feature of the contemporary tourism landscape is the wealth of collaborative initiatives and partnerships'. Across the Atlantic, Selin and Chavez (1995: 844–5) suggest that 'While tourism organizations have always been involved in partnerships to a certain degree, recent economic, political, and social forces in the United States and elsewhere, have combined to make partnerships an explicit priority of these agencies'. Beyond the English-speaking world, the concept of the partnership approach is also beginning to make headway. Spain's new tourism policy document, *Spain: A Sustainable Tourism*, speaks of 'the incorporation of long-term considerations and the integration of the environmental factor, along with the participation of all parties implicated' (Ministerio de Economia y Hacienda/Ministerio de Medio Ambiente, 1999:23).

The new prominence for collaborative approaches involving diverse parties reflects changes in governance as a whole in many western countries (Harvey, 1989; O'Toole, 1997; Thomas and Thomas, 1998). Notable among these changes are a blurring of the boundaries between the public and private sectors, a shift in the public sector from direct service provision to an 'enabling' function, and, as a result of these changes, the emergence of complex networks of agencies and partnerships (Goodwin, 1998; Rhodes, 1996). Several commentators have related these developments to fiscal problems for government from the late 1970s that have encouraged resource-sharing activities, to the rise of a politically effective critique of state activity that was developed by the 'New Right', and to a significant public disenchantment with government (Kickert *et al.*, 1997). Some have also noted that political actors at the local level have themselves formed partnerships, although sometimes these have been promoted by higher tiers of government (Judge *et al.*, 1995).

A variety of terms are used to describe different collaborative arrangements in tourism, including coalitions, forums, alliances, task forces and public-private partnerships. While the term collaboration is commonly used in the academic tourism literature, in government and practitioner circles the term partnerships is especially popular, and in practice these are taken to embrace many collaborative forms (Bailey, 1995). For example, Long and Arnold (1995:5) state that in the US 'The term "partnership" has become a part of the terminology of leaders concerned with environmental quality, resource conservation, and sustainable development'. As the partnership label is so widely used it is also used in this book to denote a collaborative arrangement.

Despite increasing interest in tourism partnerships, until recently there has been little systematic research on the internal processes and external impacts of these organisational forms. Information on tourism collaboration was often restricted to accounts by practitioners, and these can be limited by a tendency to condense complex processes into simple description, to avoid analysis and criticism, and to gloss over points of conflict in order to present a project in the best possible light. This book begins to bridge this research gap by providing a collection of theoretically informed empirical studies examining tourism partnerships that bring together a range of parties to develop tourism policies. Case studies examine the processes and impacts related to these collaborative arrangements in specific contexts. The issues papers discuss thematic, operational and ethical questions arising from this critical debate. It is important to stress, however, that no examination is made here of alliances involving parties in just one sector, such as marketing alliances between tourism businesses. All the case study cross-sectoral partnerships are engaged in developing policies and planning that go beyond basic tourism questions: they also deal with broader economic, social and environmental issues. All the issues papers also consider questions related to the wider concepts of partnerships for sustainable tourism.

Specific concerns highlighted in the case studies include the scope of the issues or 'problem domain' that is addressed and the range of stakeholders that participate in the collaborative process. Are there participants from government, business and non-profit sectors, and from national, regional and local policy arenas? A key issue in several chapters is the extent to which collaborative relations are inclusive. Are all participants in a partnership fully involved in the discussions, is there mutual respect and shared learning, and are all participants equally influential in the negotiations and decision-making? Further questions relate to the extent to which agreement is reached, if at all, about how to decide or act on the problem domain. Finally, there is consideration of the outputs or achievements of the collaborative arrangements. By studying these issues in specific circumstances it is possible to enhance our critical understanding of tourism partnerships and to assist practitioners to understand how collaborative approaches can succeed and fail.

One important intention of the book is to assess the potential for partnerships involved in tourism planning to contribute to the wider objectives of sustainable development. Although sustainable development is a contested concept with many potential interpretations, particularly with respect to the relationship between sustainability and development, some core principles have long been identified (Bramwell *et al.*, 1996). Prominent among these is a recognition that the health and integrity of natural, built and human cultural resources is critical to our future well-being, and that this depends on those resources being conserved. Sustainable development is also often considered to involve concern for the welfare of future generations, so they benefit from a supply of resources, opportunities and choices at least as good as those inherited by the current generation. Another common theme is concern that there should be fairness in the distribution within society of the economic, social, cultural and environmental benefits and costs of development. Further, it is often suggested that socially equitable development depends on participation by all sectors of society in the decision-making about development options (Bramwell, 1998; LGMB, 1993). And it must not be forgotten that, in the seminal work on sustainable development, the Brundtland Report (WCED, 1987), the need for partnerships between stakeholders was identified as a key to implementing sustainable development.

In theory, at least, collaborative approaches should help to further the core principles of sustainable development. First, collaboration among a range of stakeholders including non-economic interests might promote more consideration of the varied natural, built and human resources that need to be sustained for present and future well being. Second, by involving stakeholders from several fields of activity and with many interests, there may be greater potential for the integrative or holistic approaches to policy-making that can help to promote sustainability (Jamal and Getz, 1995 and 1996; Lane, 1994). Partnerships can also reflect and help safeguard the interdependence that exists between tourism and other activities and policy fields (Butler, 1999). Third, if multiple stakeholders affected by tourism development were involved in the policy-making process, then this might lead to a more equitable distribution of the resulting benefits and costs. Participation should raise awareness of tourism impacts on all stakeholders, and this heightened awareness should lead to policies that are fairer in their outcomes. Fourth, broad participation in policy-making could help democratise decision-making, empower participants and lead to capacity building and skill acquisition amongst participants and those whom they represent (Benveniste, 1989; Roberts and Bradley, 1991).

What is Collaboration and What are Partnerships?

Collaboration involves relationships between stakeholders when those parties interact with each other in relation to a common issue or 'problem domain'. Each stakeholder controls resources, such as knowledge, expertise, constituency and capital, but on their own they are unlikely to possess all the resources necessary to achieve their objectives and to plan effectively for their future in relation to a significant tourism development issue. This is because of the complexity of tourism issues, often due to the fragmented nature of the industry and the multiple stakeholders who influence, or are affected by tourism development: both the resources and capacities to affect an issue can be dispersed among several stakeholders. Hence, a number of stakeholders may work together if they consider that their chances of realising their goals and creating new opportunities in a problem domain are greater by performing jointly rather than by acting alone. This resource dependency and stakeholder interdependence means there are potential mutual or collective benefits from stakeholders collaborating with each other (Gray, 1989; Selin and Beason, 1991). These potential mutual benefits include a collaborative process where the participants might learn from each other, learn from the process itself, develop innovative policies, and respond dynamically to a changing environment. There may be, therefore, synergistic gains from sharing resources, risks and rewards and from the prioritisation of 'collaborative advantage' rather than individual 'competitive advantage' (Edgell and Haenisch, 1995; Huxham, 1996; Lowndes and Skelcher, 1998).

Interdependency is based on the distribution of resources between various actors, the goals they pursue and their perceptions of their resource dependencies. Collaboration can lead to the exchange of information, goals and resources. Because collaborative interactions are frequently repeated, then 'processes of institutionalisation occur: shared perceptions, participation patterns and interaction rules develop and are formalised' (Kickert *et al.*, 1997: 6). Normally collaborative interaction is considered to involve face-to-face dialogue, and this is an important feature distinguishing the processes of collaboration from some other types of participation in policy-making (Carr *et al.*, 1998). This dialogue means there may also be potential for both mutual learning and shared decision-making, although one or both of these may not occur in practice.

According to Wood and Gray (1991:146), 'Collaboration occurs when a group of autonomous stakeholders of a problem domain engage in an interactive process, using shared rules, norms and structures, to act or decide on issues related to that domain'. Stakeholders are autonomous as they retain independent decision-making powers even when they agree to work with each other within a framework of rules or other expectations. Hence, mergers of formally independent organisations are excluded from this definition of collaboration, although stakeholders can agree to relinquish some autonomy to the collaborative alliance. Wood and Gray (1991:148) also suggest that 'Because a collaboration is directed toward an objective, the participants must intend to "decide or act". Note, however, that this definition does not imply that the intended objective must be reached for collaboration to occur; the collaboration may fail in its objective'. This means that interactions that are regular but do not have specific objectives in relation to addressing a problem will fall outside the definition. Regular meetings of members of a professional association would most likely fail the test. Wood and Gray's definition also suggests that participants must work within an agreed-upon set of norms and rules with at least the intention to develop a mutual orientation in response to an issue, perhaps to determine direction, organisation and action. Whether or not this mutual orientation emerges in practice needs to be established through empirical enquiry.

Wood and Gray's definition of collaboration is especially useful as it encompasses the diversity of partnership forms that are found in practice. This allows for the variety of forms of collaboration in tourism planning to be established through empirical research. For example, the breadth of the definition makes no assumptions about the scope and nature of the issue or problem domain around which the collaboration is formed. Hence, it can incorporate interactions among stakeholders working on tourism-related issues that are focused at a global scale as well as those related more to the neighbourhood or community level. It can also include partnerships that form around broad strategic issues as well as around a highly specific concern within an individual project. The definition also makes no assumptions about which stakeholders will participate, how much power they may have, how representative they may be, or about the total number of stakeholders that are involved.

Further, the definition allows for variations between different partnerships in their duration or time-scale, although collaborative processes usually need to be based on stakeholders interacting on several occasions. These structures are normally temporary arrangements that are dissolved once it is considered that the collaboration has achieved its goals. However, it might be argued that they could have a more permanent structure, although subsequently these too may change in their character or simply collapse (Dyzma, 1986). The degree of more formalised organisation will also vary from example to example, although the parties need to retain their independent decision-making powers. Selin and Chavez (1995:845) suggest that tourism collaborations 'may be highly structured, characterized by legally binding agreements, or may be quite unstructured verbal agreements between participating organizations'. The intended outcomes of collaborative arrangements can also differ, with the objective sometimes being to develop a strategic vision or a plan for a destination, and in other cases it is to implement some practical measures. However, it might be suggested that dialogues among organisations aimed solely at exchanging information do not meet Wood and Gray's requirement that there is an intention 'to act or decide on issues'.

The form of a collaborative process can vary according to many dimensions, and for analytical purposes it is helpful to conceptualise each dimension as a continuum, along which specific examples can be located. In this context, some authors place the ideas of collaboration between stakeholders within a broader conceptual framework of the network of stakeholders relevant to an issue and of the diverse relations between these parties (Amin and Thrift, 1995; Healey, 1997; Thompson, 1991). There are often complex relational webs between stakeholders that are structured around diverse economic, political and cultural forces, with some linkages in these networks being relatively more structured than others. Along a continuum from more to less formalised relations within these webs or networks, the definition of collaborative arrangements developed by Wood and Gray relates to relatively formal institutional or policy networks and their associated stakeholder relations.

Potential Benefits from Collaboration and Partnerships

There are many potential benefits when diverse stakeholders affected by tourism attempt to collaborate and to agree policies and plans about how they should proceed. For instance, it is frequently suggested that collaboration can help to avoid the long-term costs of adversarial conflicts between interest groups. Adversarial conflicts can be wasteful as stakeholders entrench their mutual suspicions, improve their confrontation skills and play out similar conflicts around each subsequent issue. Interest in collaboration between stakeholders affected by particular issues has also been encouraged by a reputedly poor record of traditional representative democratic arrangements as a means of ensuring people are involved in debates and decisions that affect their lives. These arrangements generally involve the election of local councils that oversee the working of professionals in the operation of planning and the delivery of services. This model has been challenged in recent years because its record of responsiveness and involvement has not always been impressive, and because 'it implies a standardised approach to an increasingly diversified set of issues and populations' (Pile, 1999: 329).

Some potential benefits of collaboration in tourism planning are summarised in Table 1. These benefits might result in fewer adverse tourism impacts, increased operational efficiency and enhanced equity. In a broader sense, too, both organisations and destinations may develop some form of 'collaborative advantage' from the benefits of executing a successful partnership approach (Gray, 1996; Huxham, 1996).

Table 1 Potential benefits of collaboration and partnerships in tourism planning

- There may be involvement by a range of stakeholders, all of whom are affected by the multiple issues of tourism development and may be well placed to introduce change and improvement.
- Decision-making power and control may diffuse to the multiple stakeholders that are affected by the issues, which is favourable for democracy.
- The involvement of several stakeholders may increase the social acceptance of policies, so that implementation and enforcement may be easier to effect.
- More constructive and less adversarial attitudes might result in consequence of working together.
- The parties who are directly affected by the issues may bring their knowledge, attitudes and other capacities to the policy-making process.
- A creative synergy may result from working together, perhaps leading to greater innovation and effectiveness.
- Partnerships can promote learning about the work, skills and potential of the other partners, and also develop the group interaction and negotiating skills that help to make partnerships successful.
- Parties involved in policy-making may have a greater commitment to putting the resulting policies into practice.
- There may be improved coordination of the policies and related actions of the multiple stakeholders.
- There may be greater consideration of the diverse economic, environmental and social issues that affect the sustainable development of resources.
- There may be greater recognition of the importance of non-economic issues and interests if they are included in the collaborative framework, and this may strengthen the range of tourism products available.
- There may be a pooling of the resources of stakeholders, which might lead to their more effective use.
- When multiple stakeholders are engaged in decision-making the resulting policies may be more flexible and also more sensitive to local circumstances and to changing conditions.
- Non-tourism activities may be encouraged, leading to a broadening of the economic, employment and societal base of a given community or region.

Potential Problems which can Arise from Collaboration and Partnerships

An obvious question to ask is: why is there a discrepancy between the many endorsements listed above and the limited adoption of collaborative tourism planning, despite the strong arguments for it and its intuitive appeal? In fact as indicated in Table 2 below there are significant problems with collaborative approaches to tourism planning, both in principle and in practice. These limit the number of partnerships and also mean that those that have formed have not always achieved their potential. One potential difficulty is the perceptions and misperceptions that prospective partners hold about one another. Overcoming mistrust is difficult, particularly when there are complex environmental problems related to tourism. With environmental issues, the prospective partners – non-profit sector, government and business – are different in so many ways: 'They have different core missions, employ different types of people, use different languages, and operate on different timetables' (Long and Arnold, 1995:43). Partnerships may also have difficulties as they challenge the vested interests and power of otherwise dominant organisations and businesses (Healey, 1997 and 1998; Timothy, 1999). Additionally, it must be remembered that central control in a hierarchical system has the advantage of being more predictable than is the case in more complex and fragmented systems. Hence it should not be assumed that each of the various stakeholders would automatically believe it is in their best interest to participate in a partnership.

It is suggested that we need to appreciate 'the extent to which barriers to participative systems are embedded in social, economic, and political principles deeply valued in their own right' (McCaffrey, Faerman and Hart, 1995:604). There are considerable pressures in society to maintain the status quo in inter-organisational relations. Hence the study of collaboration in tourism will benefit from close attention to how social, economic, and political structures constrain or facilitate such processes (Reed, 1997).

Importantly, collaborative arrangements may also be criticised because some social groups and individuals may find it difficult or impossible to gain access to these arrangements. Power relations are likely to influence which people join these groups and who has most influence in decisions. For example, only well organised and state-licensed interest groups may play a prominent role in policy formation by groups or agencies that exist in some policy arenas (Hall and Jenkins, 1995; Reed, 1997). A network of collaborative arrangements is also more complex and dispersed, and hence tends to be less clearly accountable than is the case with the more centralised, hierarchical systems of elected local government (Bramwell and Rawding, 1994). In addition, while government may have democratic legitimacy, its involvement in consensus building in partnerships may entail it having to compromise in its role in protecting the 'public interest', such as in conserving environmental resources for future generations. One response to these issues might be to strengthen the role of elected local government as an organisation able to facilitate, orchestrate and arbitrate in the work of partnerships, and also to mobilise debate, opinion and support where necessary (Donnison, 1998; Kickert, Klijn and Koppenjan, 1997). A government role might be to encourage research and training in the complex art of partnership creation and management.

Table 2 Potential problems of collaboration and partnerships in tourism planning

- In some places and for some issues there may be only a limited tradition of stakeholders participating in policy-making.
- A partnership may be set up simply as 'window dressing' to avoid tackling real problems head on with all interests.
- Healthy conflict may be stifled.
- Collaborative efforts may be under-resourced in relation to requirements for additional staff time, leadership and administrative resources.
- Actors may not be disposed to reduce their own power or to work together with unfamiliar partners or previous adversaries.
- Those stakeholders with less power may be excluded from the process of collaborative working or may have less influence on the process.
- Power within collaborative arrangements could pass to groups or individuals with more effective political skills.
- Some key parties may be uninterested or inactive in working with others, sometimes because they decide to rely on others to produce the benefits resulting from a partnership.
- Some partners might coerce others by threatening to leave the partnership in order to press their own case.
- The involvement of democratically elected government in collaborative working and consensus building may compromise its ability to protect the 'public interest'.
- Accountability to various constituencies may become blurred as the greater institutional complexity of collaboration can obscure who is accountable to whom and for what.
- Collaboration may increase uncertainty about the future as the policies developed by multiple stakeholders are more difficult to predict than those developed by a central authority.
- The vested interests and established practices of the multiple stakeholders involved in collaborative working may block innovation.
- The need to develop consensus, and the need to disclose new ideas in advance of their introduction, might discourage entrepreneurial development.
- Involving a range of stakeholders in policy-making may be costly and time-consuming.
- The complexity of engaging diverse stakeholders in policy-making makes it difficult to involve them all equally.
- There may be fragmentation in decision-making and reduced control over implementation.
- The power of some partnerships may be too great, leading to the creation of cartels.
- Some collaborative arrangements may outlive their usefulness, with their bureaucracies seeking to extend their lives unreasonably.

Frameworks to Understand Collaboration

Rather than simply provide yet another rationale of why partnerships may, or may not be valuable, there is a need to develop analytical frameworks that assist us to understand the processes of collaboration in tourism planning. Such frameworks can also provide practitioners in tourism with an enhanced appreciation of how partnerships might be made more effective in particular contexts.

One framework developed by Bramwell and Sharman (1999) identifies three sets of issues to consider when examining the partnership relations involved in local tourism policy-making prior to policy implementation. The first of these relate to the scope of each partnership. A key question here is whether the range of participating stakeholders is representative of all stakeholders affected by the issue or issues. In ideal circumstances there should be a balance between those with power, perhaps through their financial resources or regulatory authority, and those with limited power. A study of participants in a tourism and outdoor recreation alliance in the United States found that they frequently mentioned the diversity of the participating stakeholders as a factor in the alliance's effectiveness (Selin and Myers, 1998). Another issue is the extent to which there is an initial agreement among participants about the range of concerns that are to be tackled by a partnership, as differing or unreconciled expectations about the questions to be addressed may derail a project.

The second set of issues highlighted by Bramwell and Sharman concern the intensity of collaborative relations between relevant stakeholders. One consideration here is the frequency with which these stakeholders are involved in partnership activities. Also of importance is the extent to which there is honest and open dialogue among the participants, whether they respect and learn from each other's interests, systems of meaning and attitudes, and whether trust develops between the stakeholders (Friedmann, 1992; Innes, 1995). Are the interests, styles of dialogue and views of the less powerful parties being ignored?

A third set of concerns focus on the degree to which consensus emerges among the stakeholders in a partnership, if this happens at all. In some instances no aspects of agreement may be reached, and in others the stakeholders might consider the overall policy direction is reasonably acceptable and they support it even if it is not their preferred outcome (Gray, 1989). According to Bryson and Crosby (1992:245): 'Coalition members do not need to agree with every detail of the proposal, but they must be able to agree to support the proposal'. As tourism issues are often complex and affect stakeholders holding diverse views, then consensus building is likely to involve continuing conflict even when some convergence and harmony is achieved. A consensus might also be based on a less than thorough examination of a potentially divisive issue or a continuing underlying ambiguity. Central to Bramwell and Sharman's framework is consideration of the effects of power differentials and conflict on the relations between participating stakeholders.

Some research on tourism partnerships presents frameworks based on the suggestion that these inter-organisational forms often evolve over time in broadly similar ways. Hence, Jamal and Getz outline a three-stage model through which tourism collaborative arrangements develop. They explain that

> the first stage consists of problem setting (identifying key stakeholders and issues), and is followed by the second stage of direction setting (identifying and sharing future collaborative interpretations; appreciating a sense of common purpose). The third stage is implementation (institutionalising the shared meanings that emerge as the domain develops), which may or may not be required, depending on the nature and objective of the collaboration (Jamal & Getz, 1995:189).

The last stage includes putting the resulting policies into practice, monitoring progress and ensuring compliance with collaborative decisions. This stage model is based on one originally devised by McCann (1983) and Gray (1989). More recently, Gray (1996:61–2) suggests that not all collaborations proceed through these phases and that 'the phases are not necessarily separate and distinct in practice. Overlapping and recycling back to earlier issues that were not addressed may be necessary'.

Selin and Chavez (1995) add two extra stages to the tourism partnership model advocated by Jamal and Getz. At the start of the process they add an antecedents stage, which relates to the initial circumstances and opportunities for collaborative tourism planning. A final partnership outcomes stage is also introduced, within which is included the impacts on the problem domain, such as the creation of additional jobs, and the consequences for relations between participating stakeholders, which might include improved mutual understanding and respect. In addition, they suggest that the future course of the partnership emerges in this stage, such as whether it continues with ongoing work, is wound up or is modified. These are issues of relevance to the question of how to evaluate the success of a partnership.

The achievements of partnerships are hard to evaluate. One difficulty among many is that they can be evaluated on a number of levels. A valuable framework to identify these levels was developed by Long and Arnold (1995) to evaluate the performance of partnerships focused on environmental issues. They suggest that such partnerships be evaluated on at least three levels. First, against the environmental goals: did the partnership accomplish its objective to improve a specific element of environmental quality? Second, in relation to indirect benefits: are there other benefits not directly related to the central environmental issue? And, third, in relation to the processes of collaborative working: how well did the process of partnering work? In this context it would be inappropriate to equate partnership management or process success with success in securing environmental goals. Hence, the three levels of evaluation must be viewed as separate and distinct activities with different purposes. Evaluation at each level also needs to consider the performance of the partnership against that of other potential approaches, including regulation.

Outline of the Book

The book is divided into three sections. Following this chapter, the first section examines the processes involved in setting up and working within partnership arrangements in a variety of situations. Some patterns are also identified that may be relatively common in partnerships, with particular attention paid to features that may be found at varying stages of partnership development and also to different categories or types of partnerships. The second section focuses on the effects of the political context and of power on collaboration between stakeholders. Finally, the third section examines some emerging approaches to collaborative tourism planning, and their implications for tourism planning in general.

Processes and patterns

Chapter 2 by Timothy assesses the potential benefits and problems of collaboration between park authorities in adjacent regions in different countries. Unfortunately, boundaries of all kinds have a history of impeding the coordinated management and marketing of tourism. These issues are examined in a detailed evaluation of cross-border partnerships established for three international parks that lie across the US-Canada border. The extent to which collaborative relations exist between the authorities in these parks is related to a five-part typology that ranges from complete alienation to complete integration or merger. Consideration is given to whether the scope of the collaboration between park organisations extends to activities such as their management frameworks and their conservation and promotional work. Timothy suggests that collaborative working in all three cross-border partnerships has helped to advance the principles of sustainable tourism.

Chapter 3 by Ritchie explains the approach taken to involve stakeholder groups in developing a vision and strategy for the future of the Banff National Park in Alberta, Canada. A roundtable was set up composed of representatives of sector interests concerned with using and protecting the Park. Each representative was asked to identify in a series of meetings with their sector the main interests that had to be satisfied by the strategy. The resulting information was used in discussions among roundtable members that sought to find common ground for agreement on key issues. Interest Based Negotiation techniques were used, which focus on separating the people from the problem, interests rather than positions, inventing options for mutual gain, and using 'objective criteria' rather than the strength of will of each stakeholder. Ritchie argues that the process successfully developed a vision for the Park as a sustainable destination that provides for tourism businesses and the enjoyment of visitors within limits that are needed to preserve the Park's ecological integrity.

In Chapter 4 Parker uses a three-stage model to examine changes over the mid-1990s in the process of collaborative tourism planning on the island of Bonaire in the Caribbean. In the second or direction-setting stage of the collaborative process there was some closing of the gap between the previously conflicting commercial and environmental interest groups on the island. A policy for sustainability evolved that allowed an expansion of tourism development within a strict limit in order to generate the economies of scale and funding needed to construct a wastewater treatment plant that was seen as important by all interest groups. However, in the third or implementation stage the policy has not been put into practice. One reason for the lack of implementation was commercial concern about a recent trend for fewer tourists coming to the island than predicted. Parker also contends that it was affected by the collaboration being too informally or loosely structured to motivate the stakeholders to continue to make progress on the issue in these changed circumstances.

In 1995 the World Wide Fund for Nature (WWF) Arctic Tourism Programme began to devise proposals to promote the development of more sustainable forms of tourism in the Arctic. Chapter 5 by Mason, Johnston and Twynam reviews the collaborative relationships in the programme between WWF, the sponsoring environmental NGO, and other stakeholders. A key element of the consultation and negotiation process was a series of meetings which were open to whoever displayed an interest and where participants were involved in presenting their own material and in sharing views and experiences. According to the authors, this interactive process succeeded in giving ownership of tasks to the participants. It appears that some 'strong voices' dominated over 'weak voices', that some views were not articulated, and that there were a few problems of discontinuity of participation. However, while not everyone agreed with everything, it is suggested that a negotiated consensus emerged based on a majority rule approach. Practical outputs of the programme included separate codes of conduct for visitors to the Arctic and for operators, as well as pilot projects that are testing various aspects of the programme.

Chapter 6 examines the Cooperative Research Centre for Sustainable Tourism, an Australian partnership between industry, government and universities established to undertake research on sustainable tourism. De Lacey and Boyd describe the partnership's research programmes in planning and environmental management; technology, engineering and design; policy, products and business; training and education; and industry extension. They warn that the partnership will face the high transaction costs of overcoming the 'two cultures' of industry and researchers and of applied and theoretical research, encouraging researchers from varied disciplines to focus on solving tourism problems, securing cooperation between different industry sectors, and communicating between geographically widely dispersed parties.

Chapter 7 by Selin develops a typology of sustainable tourism partnerships in the US based on selected dimensions by which these partnerships vary or are similar. These dimensions include their geographical scale (from community to national); legal basis (from cases where partners choose to collaborate to cases that are legally mandated, authorised or compelled); locus of control (from convening agency control to stakeholder control); size and organisational diversity (from small numbers in one sector to large numbers in multiple sectors); and time frame (from temporary and often informal to more permanent and often formal). Individual partnerships can be placed within this and other potential typologies, and this may help managers to recognise the diversity of potential forms and to design partnerships that are appropriate in specific circumstances. It is argued that tourism partnerships evolve dynamically and thus their position in typologies will alter over time.

Politics and practice

In the second section of the book the analysis focuses on how collaborative relations among stakeholders involved in tourism policy-making may be affected by the power differentials between them or by the broad political context.

A central argument of Chapter 8 by Hall is that the growing interest in partnerships that engage in policy-making reflects the changing role of the state in many western countries. This changing state role involves a shift from hierarchical control to governance that is dispersed through networks of non-government agencies and collaborative arrangements. Hall recognises that collaborative approaches to tourism planning have the potential to involve a wide set of stakeholders and hence to increase political participation and social equality, and that such consequences would contribute to more sustainable forms of tourism. However, he warns that in practice the stakeholders involved in non-government agencies and collaborative arrangements may not be sufficiently inclusive. His examination of the role of interest groups in the tourism policy-making process in Australia indicates that business interests may have tended to dominate, and that this may have precluded inputs from stakeholders from environmental organisations and wider community interests.

In Chapter 9 Jamal and Getz explore a multiple stakeholder roundtable process to devise a growth management strategy for the tourist centre of Canmore in Canada. The authors adopt an interpretive approach that emphasises the everyday, lived experience of participants in the collaborative process as well as the meanings attributed to their participation. This approach offers valuable insights into the rhetorical, ideological and power-based aspects of relationships involved in the roundtable. The authors conclude that one outcome of the roundtable process was an increased capacity of the community to address local conflicts, with movement from 'destructive conflict' to 'constructive conflict' as relationships were built through learning, listening and paying respect to other views. But they also identify overt as well as covert constraints on participation. For example, some less 'visible' segments of the community and the view that there should be 'no growth' were not represented in the process. In addition, being involved in the roundtable did not mean that stakeholder views were heard equally, as this was affected by the perceived legitimacy of the views and by the aggressive gesturing and tactics of some participants. Rules to guide the roundtable process that were established in the early convening stage are also considered to have been both enabling and constraining for the consensus-building process. For example, a rule that the roundtable should end if a participant walked away from the table appears to have contributed to some participants feeling that consent became manufactured coercively. Jamal and Getz conclude that the instrumental use of rules can be a means for ideological and power domination in collaborative processes.

'Regime theory' was developed in research on US cities, and it suggests that certain public, private and voluntary sector actors in cities are able to blend their capacities within a governing 'regime' in order to achieve common purposes. Governments are seen as driven to cooperate with those who hold resources needed to achieve certain policy agendas. Such agendas are considered likely to be focused around a commitment to economic growth, since that promises long-term material gains whose benefits can also be shared locally. Regime theory recognises the importance of fluid and changing networks of power in cities and the need to consider ways of managing them dynamically. It is emphasised that society privileges the participation of more powerful interests in governing regimes, although what is at issue is depicted as not so much domination as the capacity to achieve certain goals (Stoker, 1995). Chapter 10 by Long uses regime theory in an examination of the relations between actors involved in a governing 'regime' promoting sustainable tourism in the inner-city fringe district of Islington in London, UK. It is suggested that regime theory might provide a valuable framework to evaluate how actors participating in such regimes may differ in their objectives and approaches.

While some commentators advocate the use of stage models to assess the evolution of tourism partnerships, little attention has been directed to a potential final phase for a partnership when decisions may be made about whether it should continue, take some new form or else terminate. In Chapter 11 Caffyn develops a stage model based on evaluations of several UK partnerships involved in tourism planning that are characterised by a high level of involvement by public sector organisations. She then focuses on the 'exit strategies' that partnerships may pursue or have forced on them. Key influences on the course of the collaborative arrangements are identified as the availability of core funding from a few public sector sources and the skills of the project manager that is appointed. The main funding partners are in a particularly powerful position to affect the viability and continuation of these partnerships. Caffyn argues that it may be helpful for partners to plan ahead for a positive end to a partnership arrangement in its current form so that it ends on a high note and avoids the dangers of 'organisational drift'. A number of options for partnership 'exit strategies' are suggested.

In Chapter 12 Roberts and Simpson investigate collaborative working in rural tourism in two mountain regions of Bulgaria and Romania in south-east Europe. The post-socialist context provides a number of potential obstacles to partnerships, including a lack of social and cultural acceptance of collaborative approaches and also complexities that have emerged during the 1990s in relations between the public and private sectors. While people's attitudes in Romania have been shaped by a history of top-down, 'super-centralised' control and planning, a key donor requirement was for collaborative working involving non-government organisations in the tourism development process. In both case studies the external donor organisation has required that the activities have a clear structure, prioritisation of aims and objectives and regular monitoring. Roberts and Simpson suggest that in both case studies a range of stakeholders have been involved, but that the stakeholders do not have, or are unlikely to maintain an equal influence on the work of the partnership, thereby undermining 'meaningful' participation.

Emerging approaches

The third section of the book examines some emerging thinking and approaches in relation to collaborative tourism planning. It also considers the relevance of these new ideas to tourism planning more generally. For instance, Jamal and Getz (1996:74) have called for tourism planning to adopt 'a process-based framework incorporating concepts from inter-organizational collaboration and corporate strategic planning. Such a combination would enable the planning framework to be dynamic and interactive'.

In Chapter 13 Reed argues that tourism planning will be improved by the use of collaborative approaches within a broader framework of 'adaptive management'. Both approaches potentially can emphasise responsiveness to the uncertainties, complexities and potential for conflict that are found in real planning situations. Adaptive management can embrace these conditions by introducing continuous management adjustments and modifications based on learning from the unexpected outcomes of actions. These processes of continuous learning and modification of actions can be assisted by collaborative planning when it involves listening to the views and 'local knowledges' of the multiple stake-holders who are directly affected by the consequences of tourism. Reed examines how an adaptive approach to the collaborative tourism planning process used in the small town of Squamish in Canada might have helped the participants to overcome the problems that were encountered over their own unequal power relations. She also suggests some of the characteristics and challenges of an adap-tive paradigm for sustainable tourism.

Being identified, or conversely, not being identified, as a relevant stakeholder can affect the whole process of collaborative planning. Hence, planning for part-nerships can benefit from identifying relevant stakeholders and evaluating their potential influence. In Chapter 14 Medeiros de Araujo and Bramwell review approaches to identifying the stakeholders affected by a tourism project and who might participate in collaborative tourism planning. Two such approaches are used in an assessment of stakeholders affected by the Costa Dourada project, a regional tourism planning initiative in north-east Brazil. These approaches are employed to examine whether the range of stakeholders who participated in the planning process was representative of the stakeholders affected by the project. In addition, the approaches are used to determine the extent to which the range of participants in the planning process was likely to encourage consideration of the diverse issues of sustainable development, which are social, cultural, envi-ronmental, economic and political, and relate to various geographical scales.

In Chapter 15 Robinson discusses the potential benefits of relevant stake-holders participating in the making of policies that affect the cultural dimensions of sustainable tourism. Stakeholder collaboration can help to address the diffi-cult issues of cultural consent, that is whether or not, or on what terms, a cultural group will provide the tourism industry with permission for parts of its culture to be developed, represented and sold for tourist consumption. Collaboration between stakeholders can also enhance respect for different cultural paradigms or world views, including the differences of views on identity, spiritual meaning and moral rights. Robinson suggests that when developing policies for sustain-able tourism with indigenous peoples the answer is not to attempt to make the different world-views commensurable but to recognise and respect these differ-ences and to help the indigenous peoples to address sustainable development in their own way.

In Chapter 16 Tremblay argues that tourism planning must recognise and respond to the pervasive ignorance of the consequences of any given action, this often being due to the considerable complexity of the tourism industry, its impacts, and the values attached to those impacts by community members in destination areas. This ignorance requires ways to be found for tourism planning to adapt to future environments with characteristics that cannot be predicted. For Tremblay, inter-organisational collaboration between stakeholders can help them to learn from each other's knowledge, understand each other's needs, and to work together to learn about their environment. It is suggested that the sustainable development of both tourism and the community resources on which it depends should involve a collaborative learning process which strikes a balance between a convergence of visions and also flexibility to adapt, generate new ideas and follow them through.

In the final chapter the editors highlight some key themes that run through many of the contributions. The chapter focuses on three themes. First, issues that need to be considered in order to increase the success of cross-sectoral partnerships engaged in tourism planning; second, the potential for these partnerships to contribute to the objectives of sustainable development; and, third, some potential directions for future research on collaborative tourism planning.

References

Amin, A. and Thrift, N. (1995) Globalisation, institutional 'thickness' and the local economy. In P. Healey, S. Cameron, S. Davoudi, S. Graham and A. Madani-Pour (eds) *Managing Cities. The New Urban Context* (pp. 91–108). Chichester: Wiley.

Bailey, N. (1995) *Partnership Agencies in British Urban Policy*. London: University College London Press.

Benveniste, G. (1989) *Mastering the Politics of Planning: Crafting Credible Plans and Policies that Make a Difference*. San Francisco: Jossey-Bass.

Bramwell, B. (1998) Selecting policy instruments for sustainable tourism. In W.F. Theobald (ed.) *Global Tourism* (pp. 361–379). Oxford: Butterworth-Heinemann.

Bramwell, B., Henry, I., Jackson, G. and van der Straaten, J. (1996) A framework for understanding sustainable tourism. In B. Bramwell, I. Henry, G. Jackson, A.G. Prat, G. Richards and J. van der Straaten (eds) *Sustainable Tourism Management: Principles and Practice* (pp. 23–71). Tilburg: Tilburg University Press.

Bramwell, B. and Rawding, L. (1994) Tourism marketing organisations in industrial cities. *Tourism Management* 15, 425–434.

Bramwell, B. and Sharman, A. (1999) Collaboration in local tourism policy-making. *Annals of Tourism Research* 26 (2), 392–415.

Bryson, J.M. and Crosby, B.C. (1992) *Leadership for the Common Good: Tackling Public Problems in a Shared-Power World*. San Francisco: Jossey-Bass.

Butler, R.W. (1999) Problems and issues of integrating tourism development. In D.G. Pearce and R.W. Butler (eds) *Contemporary Issues in Tourism Development* (pp. 65–80). London: Routledge.

Carr, D.S., Selin, S.W. and Schuett, M.A. (1998) Managing public forests: Understanding the role of collaborative planning. *Environmental Management* 22 (5), 767–776.

Charlton, C. and Essex, S. (1996) The involvement of district councils in tourism in England and Wales. *Geoforum* 27 (2), 175–192.

Department for Culture, Media and Sport (DCMS) (1999) *Tomorrow's Tourism. A Growth Industry for the New Millennium*. London: DCMS.

Donnison, B. (1998) *Policies for a Just Society*. London: Macmillan.

Dyzma, W.A. (1986) Success and failures in joint ventures in developing countries: Lessons from experience. In F.J. Contractor and P. Lorange (eds) *Cooperative Strategies in International Business* (pp. 403–424). Lexington, MA: Lexington Books.

Edgell, D.E. and Haenisch, R.T. (1995) *Coopetition: Global Tourism Beyond the Millennium*. Kansas City, MO: International Policy Publishing.

Friedmann, J. (1992) *Empowerment: The Politics of Alternative Development*. Oxford: Blackwell.

Goodwin, M. (1998) The governance of rural areas: Some emerging research issues and agendas. *Journal of Rural Studies* 14 (1), 5–12.

Gray, B. (1989) *Collaborating: Finding Common Ground for Multi-Party Problems*. San Francisco: Jossey-Bass.

Gray, B. (1996) Cross-sectoral partners: Collaborative alliances among business, government and communities. In C. Huxham (ed.) *Creating Collaborative Advantage* (pp. 57–79). London: Sage.

Hall, C.M. and Jenkins, J.M. (1995) *Tourism and Public Policy*. London: Sage.

Harvey, D. (1989) From managerialism to entrepreneurialism: The transformation in urban governance in late capitalism. *Geografisker Annaler* 71B (1), 3–17.

Healey, P. (1997) *Collaborative Planning: Shaping Places in Fragmented Societies*. London: Macmillan.

Healey, P. (1998) Collaborative planning in a stakeholder society. *Town Planning Review* 69 (1), 1–21.

Huxham, C. (1996) The search for collaborative advantage. In C. Huxham (ed.) *Creating Collaborative Advantage* (pp. 176–180). London: Sage.

Innes, J. (1995) Planning theory's emerging paradigm: Communicative action and interactive practice. *Journal of Planning Education and Research* 14, 83–90.

Jamal, T.B. and Getz, D. (1995) Collaboration theory and community tourism planning. *Annals of Tourism Research* 22 (1), 186–204.

Jamal, T.B. and Getz, D. (1996) Does strategic planning pay? Lessons for destinations from corporate planning experience. *Progress in Tourism and Hospitality Research* 2 (1), 59–78.

Joppe, M. (1996) Sustainable community tourism development revisited. *Tourism Management* 17, 475–479.

Judge, D., Stoker, G. and Wolman, H. (eds) (1995) *Theories of Urban Politics*. London: Sage.

Kickert, W.J.M., Klijn, E.-H. and Koppenjan, J.F.M. (eds) (1997) *Managing Complex Networks: Strategies for the Public Sector*. London: Sage.

Kotler, P., Haider, D.H. and Rein, I. (1993) *Marketing Places: Attracting Investment, Industry, and Tourism to Cities, States, and Nations*. New York: Free Press.

Lane, B. (1994) Sustainable rural tourism strategies: A tool for development and conservation. In B. Bramwell and B. Lane (eds) *Rural Tourism and Sustainable Rural Development* (pp. 102–111). Clevedon: Channel View.

Local Government Management Board (LGMB) (1993) *A Framework for Local Sustainability*. Luton: LGMB.

Long, F.J. and Arnold, M.B. (1995) *The Power of Environmental Partnerships*. Fort Worth: Dryden Press.

Lowndes, V. and Skelcher, C. (1998) The dynamics of multi–organizational partnerships: An analysis of changing modes of governance. *Public Administration* 76, 313–333.

McCaffrey, D.P., Faerman, S.R. and Hart, D.W. (1995) The appeal and difficulties of participative systems. *Organization Science* 6 (6), 603–627.

McCann, J.E. (1983) Design guidelines for social problem-solving interventions. *Journal of Applied Behavioral Science* 19 (2), 177–189.

Ministerio de Economia y Hacienda and the Ministerio de Medio Ambiente (1999) *España: Un Turismo Sostenible* (Spain: A Sustainable Tourism). Madrid.

Murphy, P.E. (1985) *Tourism: A Community Approach*. London: Methuen.

O'Toole, L.J. (1997) Treating networks seriously: Practical and research-based agendas in public administration. *Public Administration Review* 57 (1), 45–52.

Pearce, D., (1992) *Tourist Organizations*. Harlow: Longman.

Pile, S., Brook, C. and Mooney. G. (eds) (1999) *Unruly Cities? Order/Disorder*. London: Routledge.

Reed, M.G. (1997) Power relations and community-based tourism planning. *Annals of Tourism Research* 24 (3), 566–591.

Rhodes, R.A.W. (1996) The new governance: Governing without government. *Political Studies* XLIV, 652–667.

Roberts, N.C. and Bradley, R.T. (1991) Stakeholder collaboration and innovation: A study of public policy initiation at the state level. *Journal of Applied Behavioral Science* 27 (2), 209–227.

Selin, S. and Beason, K. (1991) Interorganizational relations in tourism. *Annals of Tourism Research* 18, 639–652.

Selin, S. and Chavez, D. (1995) Developing an evolutionary tourism partnership model. *Annals of Tourism Research* 22 (4), 844–856.

Selin, S.W. and Myers, N.A. (1998) Tourism marketing alliances: Member satisfaction and effectiveness attributes of a regional initiative. *Journal of Travel and Tourism Marketing* 7 (3), 79–94.

Stoker, G. (1995) Regime theory and urban politics. In D. Judge, G. Stoker and H. Wolman (eds) *Theories of Urban Politics* (pp. 54–71). London: Sage.

Thomas, H. and Thomas, R. (1998) The implications for tourism of shifts in British local governance. *Progress in Tourism and Hospitality Research* 4, 295–306.

Thompson, G. *et al.* (1991) *Markets, Hierarchies and Networks: the Co-ordination of Social Life.* London: Sage.

Timothy, D. (1999) Participatory planning. A view of tourism in Indonesia. *Annals of Tourism Research* 26 (2), 371–91.

Wood, D.J. and Gray, B. (1991) Toward a comprehensive theory of collaboration. *Journal of Applied Behavioral Science* 27 (2), 139–162.

World Commission on Environment and Development (1987) *The Brundtland Report.* Oxford: Oxford University Press.

2. Cross-Border Partnership in Tourism Resource Management: International Parks along the US-Canada Border

Dallen J. Timothy

School of Human Movement, Sport and Leisure Studies, Bowling Green State University, Bowling Green, OH 43403, USA

This paper examines cross-border partnerships in three international parks along the US-Canada border based on principles of sustainable tourism. A model of intensity of cross-border partnerships is developed, and areas of coordination examined include management frameworks, infrastructure development, human resources, conservation, promotion, and international- and local-level level border concessions and treaty waivers, all of which play a part in the sustainable management of trans-frontier resources. The findings suggest that the more integrated the two sides of an international park are in relation to the border, the higher the level of cooperation will be. Furthermore, the paper demonstrates the importance of bilateral treaties, official treaty waivers, and less formal local cooperation for laying the groundwork for sustainable management of cross-border tourism resources.

Introduction

International boundaries have traditionally been viewed as barriers to human interaction. Indeed many borders have been defined and demarcated precisely for the purpose of limiting contact between neighbouring societies or filtering the flow of people, goods, services, and ideas between countries. As a result, tourist destinations, especially those on national peripheries, have tended to develop in a manner clearly constrained by limits of national sovereignty. The world is full of examples where adjacent regions in different countries share excellent natural and cultural resources, and therefore potential for joint tourism development and conservation. Unfortunately, political boundaries have a history of hindering collaborative planning, which has resulted in imbalances in the use, physical development, promotion, and sustainable management of shared resources.

In many regions the function of international boundaries as barriers is decreasing rapidly, however, and the position of borderlands as areas of contact and cooperation between different systems is gaining in strength (Hansen, 1983; Timothy, in press). Consequently, there are increasingly more opportunities for cross-border cooperation in tourism through national and regional policies that stimulate contact and openness between neighbouring countries (Timothy, 1995a).

One global manifestation of this change is the growth in numbers of international parks that lie across, or adjacent to, political boundaries. Thorsell and Harrison (1990) and Denisiuk *et al.* (1997) identified more than 70 borderland nature reserves and parks throughout the world; some work together with their cross-border neighbours and some do not. Many other natural and cultural areas that straddle international boundaries have been identified and are currently in the process of being created or are still in the initial discussion phases (see Brown,

1988; Parent, 1990; Young & Rabb, 1992; MacKinnon, 1993; Blake, 1994; Gradus, 1994; Lippman, 1994; Timothy, forthcoming). With improvements in international relations and the growth of the conservation movement, it is likely that trans-frontier parks will continue to be designated in the future.

Conservation efforts and good relations during the twentieth century have resulted in the creation of several international parks and monuments along the US-Canada border. All of these parks have become significant tourist attractions (Timothy, 1995b). Nevertheless, they and their cross-border management have been virtually ignored by tourism scholars. Therefore, the purpose of this paper is to examine cooperative tourism management within three of these borderland parks, based on principles of sustainable tourism development.

Sustainability and Cross-border Partnerships

During the 1990s, the concept of sustainable tourism has received a great deal of attention in the academic literature. In their discourses on sustainability, commentators have emphasised a forward-looking form of tourism development and planning that promotes the long-term health of natural and cultural resources, so that they will be maintained as durable, permanent landscapes for generations to come. The concept also accepts that tourism development needs to be economically viable in the long term and must not contribute to the degradation of the sociocultural and natural environments (Butler, 1991; Mowforth & Munt, 1998; Murphy, 1998). According to Bramwell and Lane (1993: 2), four basic practices should form the essence of sustainable tourism development: (1) holistic planning and strategy formulation; (2) preservation of ecological processes; (3) protection of human and natural heritage; and (4) development in which productivity can be sustained over the long term for future generations. These practices can best be supported when the following principles are used to guide development: ecological integrity, efficiency, equity, and integration-balance-harmony (Wall, 1993).

In areas where natural and cultural tourism resources lie across, or adjacent to, international boundaries, these principles of sustainability can be upheld better through cross-border partnerships. While the general cooperation and collaboration literature is vast, focusing on many forms of partnerships, Timothy (1998) identified four types that are most essential in the context of tourism planning (Figure 1). Private–public sector initiatives (including NGOs) are vital as the public sector depends on private investors to provide services and to finance the construction of tourist facilities. By the same token, private tourism projects require government approval, support, and infrastructure development. Cooperation between government agencies is essential if tourism is to develop and operate smoothly. Coordinated efforts between agencies decrease misunderstandings and conflicts related to overlapping goals and missions, and they help eliminate some degree of redundancy that exists when parallel, or duplicate, research and development projects by different agencies occur. Furthermore, to be successful, tourism development in a region usually requires coordinated efforts between two or more levels of administration (e.g. nation, state, province, district, county, municipality), particularly when each level is responsible for different elements of the tourism system. Finally, as mentioned above, partner-

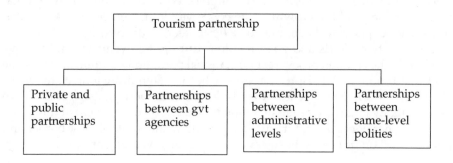

Figure 1 Types of partnerships in tourism (*Source:* After Timothy, 1998)

ships between same-level polities are particularly important when natural and cultural resources lie across political boundaries. This can help prevent the over-utilisation or under-utilisation of resources and eliminate some of the economic, social, and environmental imbalances that commonly occur on opposite sides of a border (Timothy, 1998). In a global sense, international cross-border partnerships are perhaps the ultimate form of partnership because they require more careful planning and formalisation than linkages between authorities and private institutions within one country.

Martinez (1994: 3–4) introduced a four-part typology of cross-border interaction to assess human movement between adjacent countries. First, *alienated* borderlands are those where day-to-day communication and interaction are almost entirely absent. Second, *coexistent* borderlands are found where the frontier is slightly open to minimal levels of interaction. Third, *interdependent* borderlands are characterised by a willingness between adjacent countries to establish cross-frontier networks and partnerships. Fourth, *integrated* borderlands exist where all significant political and economic barriers have been abolished, resulting in the free flow of goods and people.

Borrowing from Martinez's (1994) model, Figure 2 combines his alienation, coexistence, and integration elements with cooperation and collaboration to illustrate a five-part typology of levels of cross-border partnerships in tourism. Alienation means that no partnerships exist between contiguous nations. Political relations are so strained or cultural differences so vast that networking is not feasible or possible. Coexistence involves minimal levels of partnership. As the word denotes, neighbouring nations tolerate each other, or they coexist, without a great deal of harmony. They do not stand in the way of each other's development, but do not actively work together to solve common problems. Cooperative partnerships are characterised by initial efforts between adjacent jurisdictions to solve common problems, particularly in terms of illegal migration and resource utilisation. Collaboration occurs in regions where binational relations are stable and joint efforts are well established. Partners actively seek to work together on development issues and agree to some degree of equity in their relationship.

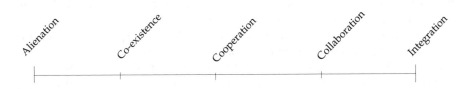

Figure 2 Levels of cross-border partnerships in tourism

Finally, integrated partnerships are those that exist without boundary-related hindrances, and both regions are functionally merged. Each entity willingly waives a degree of its sovereignty in the name of mutual progress.

While cooperation and collaboration are clearly important, not all outcomes are positive. Cross-border partnership is time-consuming and costly and often results in effects not commensurate with the efforts involved. In the case of fully integrated networks, some of the attractiveness of border resources may be dulled as they become too similar on both sides. Several scholars claim that contrasts in politics, economics, cultures, and landscapes are part of the tourist appeal in borderland attractions (Arreola & Curtis, 1993; Eriksson, 1979; Leimgruber, 1989). Furthermore, in some cases, cross-border coordination may lead to political opportunism and the reinforcement of existing power among a privileged few on one or both sides of the boundary (Church & Reid, 1996: 1299), which may result in more pronounced disparities between regional development outcomes (Scott, 1998).

Trans-frontier networks may also promote competition that is harmful to peripheral regions in that it creates rivalries between local authorities. This can ultimately result in destabilised cross-border relations (Church & Reid, 1996). Moreover, Scott (1998: 620) suggests that the formalisation of cross-border partnerships may encumber and lead to the bureaucratisation of certain processes instead of allowing them greater freedom to develop.

These criticisms notwithstanding, natural ecosystems and, in many cases, cultural areas are not restricted within human-created boundaries. When such resources overlap international frontiers, yet another twist is added to the already complex concept of sustainability. Thus, some degree of interjurisdictional networking is vital because it has the potential to reduce economic, social, and ecological imbalances that occur on opposite sides of a boundary (Kiy & Wirth, 1998) and will lead to more holistic and efficient planning as all parts of the attraction are considered as one, and the duplication of development projects may be eliminated (Timothy, 1998). Nonetheless, obstacles, such as immigration and customs restrictions, different languages, poor international relations, contrasting management regimes, and lack of authority of local administrators to make cross-boundary arrangements, may challenge, or even thwart, cooperative efforts (Blatter, 1997; Dupuy, 1982; Saint-Germain, 1995).

Administrative frameworks, infrastructure development, conservation, human resources, promotional efforts, and border concessions are of special interest to management personnel and planners in international parks because they are directly linked to contrasting political systems and issues of sovereignty. By working in concert with their cross-border affiliates, resource administrators can contribute to meeting the goals of sustainable tourism.

Special management frameworks that allow cross-frontier coordination while still respecting the sovereignty of each nation can be created. In most cases this is done by formal treaty. Funding and land ownership, as well as everyday operations, can be integrated into management systems that are appropriate for borderland locations.

Transportation standards can be upheld better with the internationalisation of infrastructure development and maintenance (Artibise, 1995). Open accessibility is hindered when governments do not collaborate on issues such as road construction, public services, and transportation. When this happens it is usually a result of the fact that national priorities tend to outweigh cross-national considerations (Naidu, 1988). Working together on matters of infrastructure can also eliminate or decrease inequitable access to shared resources (Ingram *et al.*, 1994). Also, a lack of coordinated efforts to develop the infrastructure can result in costly and needless duplication of facilities (Gradus, 1994). By working jointly in areas of physical facilities planning, both parties can create similar conditions that will appeal to visitors and contribute to a sense of harmony and integration, as well as provide opportunities for more efficient production.

Partnerships also work wonders for conservation. A lack of cross-boundary cooperation can result in the over-exploitation of resources on one side of a border, which may create severe conservation problems for neighbouring regions (Timothy, 1998). Some species of animals, for example, may be protected in one jurisdiction but hunted for sport in a neighbouring jurisdiction. Since resources are not bound by political borders, many conservation problems cannot be solved without the involvement of administrators in both regimes. In an effort to promote ecological integrity, integration, balance, and harmony, transnational networking can help facilitate the standardisation of conservation regulations and controls on both sides of a border. This is especially important when borders separate the location where problems are felt most keenly from the places where the most effective and efficient solutions can be applied (Ingram *et al.*, 1994: 9).

Different cultures may share few of the same values related to human resource management (Newman & Hodgetts, 1998), even in contiguous regions, which can be affected by the presence of a border. Also, frontier zones are sensitive areas, since illegal crossings for employment are a significant concern in some parts of the world, and borders are commonly impermeable for workers as formidable restrictions keep them on their own sides. These odds can be overcome, however. Coordination along the lines of human resources might encourage more equitable and efficient management and improve ecological and cultural integrity as ideas are shared and knowledge gained through personnel exchanges and joint training efforts.

Greater degrees of efficiency, integration, balance, and harmony will result from cross-frontier collaboration in marketing and promotion. With the publication of joint promotional literature, promotion budgets on both sides of the border can be decreased and the differences spent on other important aspects of management such as conservation, human resources, and infrastructure development. Furthermore, broadcast media spill across national borders, so that more concerted efforts to standardise campaigns would increase efficiency and would reach a larger, and perhaps more diverse, market (Clark, 1994).

Many of these management issues and opportunities can only be addressed if some degree of lenience is given by the national governments involved to eliminate or adapt some of the existing border restrictions. Border treaty waivers, or less formal concessions, contribute to a more holistic form of planning and allow management of a cross-national attraction to function more efficiently and equitably.

The following sections explore these management issues (i.e. management frameworks, infrastructure, conservation, human resources, promotion, and border concessions) within three parks along the US-Canada border (see Figure 3).

Figure 3 Locations of the three international parks

Methods

The information presented in this study is based on 27 in-depth interviews with park administrators, park personnel, and Canadian and American border officials in June and July 1998. The snowball and theoretical sampling approaches were used as interviews were arranged in the field based on recommendations by initial participants, who were employed by the parks and local immigration/customs offices. Interviews consisted of a combination of open-ended questions and semi-structured probing. Participants were asked about the principles discussed above (e.g. conservation, management, and infrastructure) in relation to each park as well as the entire Canada–US border. Customs and immigration officials were generally reluctant to participate at first, which is to be expected given the sensitive nature of border issues. However, after building rapport, all officers opened up and were willing to discuss everyday experiences, laws, and regulations pertaining to the border and cooperation across it.

Bilateral treaties between the United States and Canada that deal with the establishment of international parks along their common border were also examined to understand the nature of the agreements and to help establish a baseline for evaluating park management. Published plans, management documents, and copies of original treaties provided by park administrators were used in this exercise.

International Parks along the USA-Canada Border

There has long been a great deal of cross-border cooperation and collaboration between the United States and Canada in matters of industrial development, agricultural production, natural resource management, and tourism (Artibise, 1995), and much of this has been policy driven (Cohn & Smith, 1995). Furthermore, with the establishment of the North American Free Trade Agreement, the way has been paved for additional and stronger partnerships to be established (Randall & Konrad, 1995). One indication of this long history of trans-border coordination has been the establishment of several international parks along the US-Canada border during the twentieth century for the purpose of commemorating peace between the two countries and for the joint protection of shared resources. Three of these parks – the International Peace Garden, Roosevelt Campobello International Park, and the Waterton-Glacier International Peace Park – are examined in the sections that follow.

The International Peace Garden

On 14 July 1932, the International Peace Garden (IPG) was formed straddling the border between North Dakota (USA) and Manitoba (Canada). The Garden was strategically placed in the centre of the continent half way between the Atlantic and Pacific coasts and only 49 km north of the geographical centre of North America. In 1931, the state of North Dakota and the province of Manitoba donated adjacent tracts of land totalling 930 ha for the purpose of establishing the international park. At the time of its inception, the US portion of the park was under agricultural production, while the Canadian side was still in a relatively pristine state as a Manitoba forest reserve (Mayes, 1992).

The primary purpose of this botanical garden was to commemorate the peaceful relationship between the two countries and to stand as a monument to worldwide peace. Each summer more than 150,000 flowers are planted in the gardens and ceremonies are held that commemorate peaceful international relations. The Garden also includes the peace chapel, which straddles the border with half of the building in each country, walkways and bicycle paths, campgrounds, a cafeteria, souvenir shop, and interpretive centre. Since its early days, the IPG has taken on a significant conservation role in the region as it has become a reserve for various forms of wild vegetation, fluvial ecosystems, and wildlife, including deer, moose, and a wide range of birds.

The IPG is now a significant tourist attraction in both Manitoba and North Dakota and is featured prominently in the tourism literature of both regions (Ministry of Industry, Trade and Tourism, 1999; Tourism Department, 1999). Approximately 200,000 people visit the Garden every year from all parts of North America and overseas (see Table 1). Furthermore, the Royal Canadian Legion Athletic Camp and the International Music Camp take place each summer in the park and attract hundreds of young people from around the world.

Table 1 Annual visitation at the International Peace Garden

Year	Visitors
1985	177,300
1986	183,600
1987	187,400
1988	186,000
1989	191,580
1990	197,327
1991	203,247
1992	209,345
1993	215,625
1994	222,093
1995	218,036
1996	211,495
1997	205,151

Source: Statistical records, IPG

Management framework

The IPG is privately owned by International Peace Garden Incorporated (IPG Inc.) and administered through a 20-member board of directors. Management and operation responsibilities lie with the executive director, who in turn delegates responsibilities to six committees. These include the personnel, buildings and grounds, publicity, membership, planning, and finance committees (Figure 4). Bound by treaty, membership of the board of directors is divided equally between Canadians and US citizens, with the exception of one, who may be of either citizenship. Board meetings are held once a year to discuss management issues and problems.

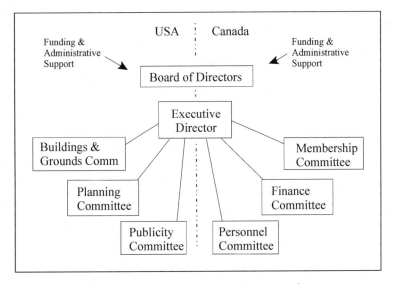

Figure 4 International Peace Garden Management Framework

The status of land ownership within the park is unique. The title of US lands is held by the state of North Dakota in trust for the express use of IPG Inc. On the Canadian side, lands were allocated from Manitoba's Turtle Mountain Forest Reserve. The 1932 International Peace Garden Act charged IPG Inc. with the control and management of 587 ha of crown land for use in the Garden. Terms on both sides stipulate that if the lands cease to be used as the IPG, the rights of IPG Inc. will be revoked and land, buildings, plants, public works, and improvements will revert to Manitoba and North Dakota.

The IPG is funded from a variety of sources. Grants are generally received from state, provincial, and local governments on both sides and the Canadian federal government. Gate receipts, camping fees, youth camps, concessions, and building rentals are examples of other sources of revenue for the IPG. To avoid currency exchange problems, Canadian funds are kept in Canadian banks and US funds in American banks. Every effort is made by management to assure that supplies and services are purchased equally on both sides of the border, although this is not always possible.

The IPG is loosely affiliated with the US National Parks Service (USNPS). It is not under the control of the USNPS, but owing to its use of federal assistance, it is officially known as a National Park System Affiliated Area. Most of the aid received from the USNPS is in relation to management plan formulation and other administrative support. The IPG is not affiliated with Parks Canada.

Infrastructure

The park has its own water and sewage treatment plants, but electricity on the north side is provided by Canada and on the south by the United States. The same is true for telephone services, although administrative offices, which are located on the US side, are equipped with Canadian and American telephone lines. There are about 16 km of roads in the IPG. On the Canadian side, parking lots, roads and traffic signs are maintained by the Province of Manitoba. In the United States, these are maintained by the North Dakota Department of Transportation. Park signs and walkways on both sides are maintained by the Peace Garden. Several tourism services exist in the park, including a souvenir shop, cafeteria, vending machines, and interpretive centre. These are all owned and managed by the IPG regardless of which side of the border they lie. Owing to the economic importance of the IPG to North Dakota, all of the park's service vehicles are donated and maintained by the state's Department of Transportation.

Conservation

In terms of conservation, the primary difference between the two sides is that the land surrounding the park on the Canadian side belongs to the Turtle Mountain Provincial Park, so that vegetation and all wildlife are protected. On the US side, hunting is permitted in areas around the park and few protective measures are taken. Within the park, however, on both sides of the border, no hunting is permitted and all forms of wildlife are protected. Administrators work diligently to assure that conservation measures are taken throughout the park regardless of what is permitted in surrounding lands.

Human resources

The entrance gate to the IPG is located between the Canadian and US immigration and customs posts. Upon departure from the park, people are required to report for either US or Canadian inspection, depending on which country they are entering. This situation, often referred to as being in 'no-man's land', or a neutral zone, creates a unique situation for IPG employees. Every effort is made to ensure that there is an equal balance of Canadian and American employees in the park. Staff members are allowed to work in either section of the park without having to obtain work visas from the other country. This is facilitated by the fact that the park lies between the countries' border stations, so that American workers do not pass through Canadian formalities to get to work and Canadians do not have to pass through American formalities. Each employee is paid and taxed based upon his or her country of residence. For example, Canadian staff are paid in Canadian dollars and are taxed with Canadian and Manitoba provincial income taxes. Insurance issues, such as workers' compensation, health, and unemployment, are also dealt with based on country of residence.

Promotion

Since the park functions as a single business that straddles the border, promotional efforts are geared towards building awareness of the park as one entity. Over 44,000 visitor guides were produced in 1998, as well as 8000 other promotional flyers. North Dakota and Manitoba both include images and elaborate descriptions of the IPG in their promotional literature. There does not appear to be a great deal of cross-border cooperation between the two regions in terms of promotion, but within the park both sides function as one.

Border concessions

Several border concessions have been made for the International Peace Garden in the form of treaty waivers. The US-Canada borderline is marked with cement, stone, and steel posts set periodically along the boundary, which are used for surveying purposes. It is also marked with a seven-metre wide cleared swath, or vista, that allows surveyors and maintenance crews to access the border markers more easily. Law requires this swath to be maintained free of vegetation and human structures higher than one metre or so. The International Boundary Commission (IBC) is a joint body with commissioners from both countries, whose purpose is to maintain the border monuments and vista. Concessions were made by the IBC in the Peace Garden to allow construction of the peace chapel directly on the borderline. The survey marker for IBC is located on the roof of the building so that the next marker down the line is in view. Similarly, the IPG successfully petitioned the Boundary Commission recently to permit the erection of a new welcome sign and fountain that exceed IBC size specifications precisely on the borderline at the entrance to the park.

Recent treaty waivers have also facilitated more efficient management of the park. For example, it is unlawful to transmit radio waves across the border intentionally. In 1998, a treaty waiver was granted that now allows park employees to communicate across the boundary within the park on radios for the purpose of dealing with everyday issues and business functions.

Another significant border concession is the tax-free status of products brought into the park for park use. In common with the human resource issue of a neutral zone, because the entrance to the park lies between the customs stations of both countries, goods brought into the IPG from the United States or Canada never pass through the other country's inspection procedures. Therefore, all goods that enter the park are free of customs duties, and can be used freely on both sides of the border within the park.

Several local-level cooperative efforts are also made in terms of border concessions. In North Dakota, the legal drinking age is 21. In Manitoba it is 18. The IPG has adopted 21 as the drinking age within the park, and the province of Manitoba has agreed to uphold the decision within this small section of the province.

Law enforcement is a tricky issue that requires some border concessions. The Royal Canadian Mounted Police (RCMP) has legal jurisdiction over the park's 587 ha that lie in Canada. On the American side, the Rolette County sheriff is in charge of legal matters. Generally, when crime and accidents occur on the Canadian side of the park, the RCMP is called to officiate. On the other side, the sheriff is summoned. However, a great deal of local-level cooperation occurs between the two law enforcement agencies. For example, during the summer of 1998, three American teenagers broke into, and stole money from, the cafeteria, which lies on the Canadian side of the park. After being caught by US customs and immigration officers, the adolescents were immediately taken to jail in North Dakota by the local sheriff. Because the crime was committed on Canadian soil, the RCMP had a vested interest and were invited to participate in the investigation. According to park management, these kinds of occurrences usually result in local cooperation.

Roosevelt Campobello International Park

Roosevelt Campobello International Park (RCIP) was established in 1964 by treaty between the United States and Canada. The park, totalling 1133 hectares, lies entirely within Canada, just across the border from the United States on Campobello Island, New Brunswick. As with the International Peace Garden, this park was built to commemorate the peaceful relations between the two countries. It is also a joint memorial by Canada and the United States to President Franklin D. Roosevelt, who played an important role in both countries' histories, and who spent many summers at the Roosevelt family vacation home on the island.

In contrast to the other two examples in this paper, the primary theme of this park is cultural heritage. However, the park also includes large tracts of natural areas. These were purchased by the park Commission in an effort to protect the Roosevelt cottage and other features of the built environment from commercial development (Roosevelt Campobello International Park Commission, n.d.). The natural areas are now preserved in a similar condition to what was on the island when the Roosevelts vacationed here earlier this century. Picnic areas, walking trails, scenic vistas and observation areas, and park drives are all part of the attraction base within the park's natural areas.

Tourism is an important component of Campobello Island's economy, most of it centred around the RCIP (Clarke, 1991). The island offers a number of accommodations and restaurants for tourists and is also well known for its coastal scenery. Annual visitor numbers at the park range from 110,000 to 150,000 (see Table 2), which is a significant number given the fact that the park is open to the

Table 2 Annual visitation at Roosevelt Campobello International Park

Year	Visitors
1985	131,477
1986	148,678
1987	153,939
1988	160,369
1989	162,881
1990	144,678
1991	151,327
1992	138,950
1993	135,842
1994	132,551
1995	122,682
1996	111,431
1997	121,530

Source: Statistical records, RCIP

public only 20 weeks per year from May to October. The majority of tourists are residents of the United States and Canada and travel by private automobile to the island. However, non-US and non-Canadian tourists are also common, but they generally visit the park as part of a group tour in conjunction with other destinations in the region.

Management framework

Figure 5 illustrates the management framework of the RCIP. Ownership of the park lies with the RCIP Commission, which received the Roosevelt property as a gift from its owners in 1964. The Hammer family donated the Roosevelt cottage and surrounding grounds to the two countries to be used to commemorate the life of President Roosevelt. Adjacent natural lands and cottage properties were purchased from private owners by the Commission shortly after the park was operationalised in 1964. In one sense, the park can also be viewed as a quasi-public entity, responsibility shared equally between the US and Canadian governments, since all funding for the park comes from federal grants on both sides. However, as mentioned above, the park is located entirely on Canadian soil and, therefore, Canada has sole sovereign authority over the territory enclosed within it.

The RCIP Commission was formed by treaty and is comprised of three Canadian representatives, three American representatives, and three alternates from each country. The Governor General in Council, on the recommendation of the Secretary of State for Foreign Affairs and International Trade, appoints Canadian representatives to the Commission, one of which is nominated by the government of New Brunswick. The American commissioners are appointed by the president of the United States. One of these is nominated by the government of Maine. The role of chairperson of the commission alternates every two years between Canadian and US representatives.

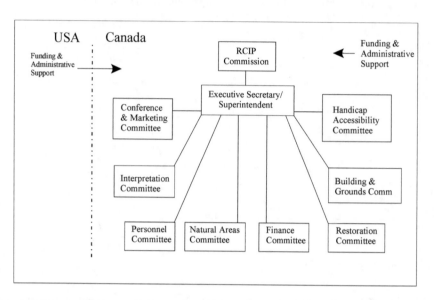

Figure 5 Roosevelt Campobello International Park Management Framework

Members of the Commission meet twice a year to discuss pertinent issues and problems facing the park and to direct ongoing programmes and projects. In an effort to increase efficiency and provide timely feedback, eight subcommittees have been formed among members of the commission to address various management needs. These committees are: finance; personnel; Roosevelt restoration, which is charged with the care of the Roosevelt home; interpretation; conference and marketing; buildings and grounds; natural areas; and handicap accessibility. Each of these committees has clear responsibilities that contribute to the overall success of park operations. To assist the Commission and sub-committees, the park is managed by an executive secretary and other officials, who are given authority to oversee everyday operations in such areas as personnel management, budgeting, landscaping, security, and facilities.

As part of the 1964 treaty, the Commission has the right to obtain, without reimbursement, legal, engineering, architectural, accounting, financial, maintenance, and other services from government agencies in both countries. This arrangement allows park officials to bypass many of the bureaucratic measures that government-owned entities are required to endure. The Commission received a great deal of assistance from the US National Park Service and Parks Canada when it was founded. Both agencies were assigned responsibility to assist the Commission in the development of the park. According to administrators, the Commission took the best of both park services and devised its own system. In common with the International Peace Garden, today the RCIP Commission is only loosely affiliated with the two park services in terms of federal grants and administrative assistance.

Unlike the International Peace Garden, RCIP is almost entirely financed by the two federal governments. As mentioned above, funding for the park is received equally from both countries. This is done indirectly through federal agencies. For example, on the US side, operating funds are directed through the Department of the Interior and the National Park Service to the RCIP Commission. The park budget, including payroll, is based on a US dollar system, but administrators make every effort to assure that funds are spent equally between the two countries, in terms of supplies, personnel, and other administrative costs.

Infrastructure

Because RCIP is located completely within New Brunswick, telephone and electric services are provided by that province. Also, New Brunswick's Ministry of Transportation is charged with maintaining the main road that passes through the park. As the island is only accessible by wheeled traffic through the state of Maine, Campobello Island and RCIP are dependent on Maine officials to keep that state's roads in good condition. Cooperative efforts assure the maintenance of the FDR Memorial Bridge, which connects the island with the town of Lubec, Maine. Roads, trails, and parking lots within the park, however, are the responsibility of RCIP in terms of both finances and labour. Road and walkway signs are maintained by RCIP. The visitor centre includes a museum where artefacts and photographs related to the Roosevelt family are on display. The centre also focuses on cooperation between the two countries as it attempts to educate visitors about Canadian and American interests in the park. No additional funding or assistance, such as the provision of vehicles, is provided by either government. All infrastructure development directly related to the park is done from the park budget.

Conservation

Again, the primary focus of RCIP is cultural heritage. However, the natural areas within the park function as a nature preserve. One of the conservation goals of park officials is to maintain the areas surrounding the Roosevelt buildings in a relatively pristine state, much as it would have been when the Roosevelts vacationed on the island. As part of this goal, camping is not permitted, although it is allowed in the adjacent Herring Cove Provincial Park. Most of the cottages have been restored and are maintained with period furnishings, and since education is known to be a useful conservation tool, interpretive tours are given to educate visitors about the park and experiences of the Roosevelt family.

Human resources

Human resource management in border areas can be particularly sensitive, but the issue related to foreigners (i.e. citizens of the United States) employed by the Commission working entirely within Canada has the potential to become even trickier. However, so far major problems have been avoided. According to the RCIP treaty, the Commission may employ both Canadians and United States citizens. The government of Canada has taken measures to allow Americans to accept employment with the Commission in Canada by eliminating the need for them to secure a work visa and enabling them to obtain a work authorisation. Employees are taxed and insured depending on where they live. Nevertheless, American personnel are still subject to Canadian customs and immigration inspections on the way to work, as well as US inspections on their way home. As mentioned earlier, salaries and wages are divided as equally as possible between the two countries to eliminate any form of favouritism.

Promotion

The RCIP Commission produces brochures and other literature that emphasise the international nature of the park. The views expressed in the literature are neutral, rather than being biased towards one country or the other. The RCIP dominates the local literature on Campobello Island, and is featured prominently in Maine and New Brunswick's tourism literature. In addition, all literature produced by the Commission provides both a Canadian and an American address for contact information.

Border concessions

Administrators describe the park as a sort of '"neutral zone" with special customs and immigration policies' that are different from other communities along the border. The primary frontier concession is the waving of border taxes on the importation of goods and services by the Commission. According to the RCIP treaty, 'all personal property imported or introduced into Canada by the Commission for use in connection with the Park shall be free from customs duties'.

Relatively few local-level border concessions are made in this context, owing to the fact that the park is located entirely within Canada. On a somewhat local level, however, in March 1964, New Brunswick also agreed to uphold the tax-free status of the Commission. The Commission, therefore, is exempt from property, income, and sales tax on all its holdings and goods purchased. Provincial sales tax is not levied for goods imported from the United States, which is not the case for residents of New Brunswick who shop in Maine.

Waterton-Glacier International Peace Park

Waterton-Glacier International Peace Park (IPP) is located on the United States-Canada border in the province of Alberta and in the state of Montana. As a result of intense lobbying by residents on both sides of the border to unite Glacier National Park (USA) and adjacent Waterton Lakes National Park (Canada), both governments enacted a bill to connect the two parks symbolically as the IPP in 1932. The two primary aims of the international park were to promote peace between neighbours and to conserve the natural environment on both sides of the international boundary. This effort did in fact link the two parks together symbolically, but each retains its individuality and each country retains full sovereignty over each section (Scace, 1978). Together the two parks form the 4450 km^2 Waterton-Glacier International Peace Park, which is home to a wide variety of plants, animals, and natural scenery. In 1995, UNESCO designated the Waterton-Glacier IPP a World Heritage Site.

Prior to 1932, the two parks were essentially isolated from each other, connected only along the seven-metre wide cleared vista that marks the international boundary. Construction of a road linking the two parks began in 1932 and was completed three years later. Customs stations were erected at the border in both parks to ensure that legal requirements were met by travellers (Lieff & Lusk, 1990).

As early as 1932, it was recognised that establishing the joint park would likely attract more tourists and increase the flow of rail traffic to southern Alberta and northern Montana (Lieff & Lusk, 1990). Today, the IPP is one of the most important tourist destinations in the region, drawing about two million visitors to the

Table 3 Annual visitation at Waterton Lakes and Glacier National Parks*

Waterton Lakes N.P.				Glacier N.P.			
Year	Visitors	Year	Visitors	Year	Visitors	Year	Visitors
1985	n/a**	1992	345,662	1985	1,580,620	1992	2,199,767
1986	n/a	1993	344,453	1986	1,579,191	1993	2,141,704
1987	n/a	1994	389,510	1987	1,660,737	1994	2,152,989
1988	n/a	1995	364,740	1988	1,817,733	1995	1,839,518
1989	338,157	1996	346,574	1989	1,821,523	1996	1,720,576
1990	353,908	1997	370,733	1990	1,987,000	1997	1,708,877
1991	344,028			1991	2,096,966		

* Numbers are presented separately because each park enumerates visitors separately, and some people visit both sides of the IPP.
** Prior to 1989 a different counting system was used in Waterton N.P.
Source: Statistical records, Waterton Lakes and Glacier National Parks.

American side and nearly 400,000 visitors to the Canadian side each year (see Table 3), although many tourists visit both parts of the IPP on the same trip. For example, according to one study (Parks Canada, 1996), approximately half of the visitors to the Canadian park also visited the American side on the same trip in 1994.

Management framework

As mentioned above, Waterton Lakes National Park and Glacier National Park are owned and managed independently of each other under the jurisdiction of each country's park service (see Figure 6). This has resulted in two different management systems working side by side along an international boundary, although a great deal of informal cooperation goes on between them. In the United States, Glacier Park is managed by a superintendent who relies on four sub-divisions to assist in a variety of matters. The divisions include interpretation, resources management, administration, and facility management. The superintendent is under the direction of the intermountain regional director, who reports to the national park service director. The national parks service director works under the direction of the US Department of the Interior.

The management system in the Canadian park is slightly more complex. The Department of Canadian Heritage oversees the work of Parks Canada. Parks Canada is divided into five subdivisions, most of which have some direct interest in Waterton Lakes National Park in one form or another. Next in the hierarchy is the executive director of mountain parks, followed by the superintendent of Waterton Lakes National Park. The superintendent is assisted by five sub-committees, which together with the superintendent, form the park's executive committee, charged with policy making. These sub-committees include historic sites, front country, town site and client services, warden services and ecosystem secretariat, and finance and administration.

Waterton receives all of its funding from Parks Canada, while Glacier receives its funding in full from the USNPS. Owing to the different management frameworks, there is little in the way of cross-border funding and administrative support between the two countries.

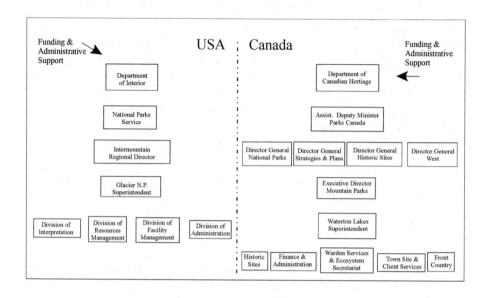

Figure 6 Waterton-Glacier International Peace Park Management Framework

Infrastructure

Waterton and Glacier both function as any community would within the boundaries of each respective country in terms of utilities and provision of public services. The highways leading to Waterton Lakes National Park are maintained by public agencies in Alberta, and in Montana the state maintains the highways leading to the park. Within the parks, however, as with nearly all national parks in North America, roads are maintained by each park service.

Although some of Waterton's back country signs are made by Glacier and match Glacier's signage (Lieff & Lusk, 1990), the erection of universal trail and distance signage throughout both sides of the park is not feasible at this time, since Canadian law requires that signs in national parks be printed in English and in French. Signs on the US side are marked in metric measurements for the benefit of Canadian and other international visitors.

Conservation

Each park is under the jurisdiction of its respective national, provincial, and state government regarding issues of nature conservation. Some natural features, such as Cameron Lake and Upper Waterton Lake, lie across the international border, which has the potential to create conservation problems. For example, bull trout, a protected species in Alberta, if caught in Alberta, must be released. In Montana, however, the fish is not protected and does not have to be released. This has not created much of a problem in the lakes that straddle the frontier because Glacier officials have agreed to enforce the Canadian regulations on the US end of the lakes to avoid confusing visitors with two sets of regulations (Lieff & Lusk, 1990) and to promote the preservation of a common natural resource. Similarly, wolves are protected in Montana, but are controlled as a nuisance species in Alberta. However, on both sides of the IPP, wolves are protected. Even though the parks protect the species, the polities in which the parks are located are at odds with regard to wolves (Glacier National Park, n.d.). Although natural resource management legislation is slightly different on opposite sides of the border, administrators coordinate their efforts to work through the differences.

The primary border-related conservation problem is the border itself. The IPP is not exempt from the International Boundary Commission regulation of clearing the border vista of all natural and cultural obstructions. Public sentiments about this cleared swath of land are not positive, especially within the park. The common view is that this practice is working against the IPP's conservation goals. According to one former Glacier Park superintendent, 'Maintenance of this artificial scar between the two parks is incongruous with the concept of an International Peace Park and hinders the goal of preserving a naturally functioning ecosystem' (quoted in Gilbert, 1996: 26).

Human resources

Park personnel are employed by each government on their respective sides of the border, and no special concessions have been made to change this. However, park personnel exchanges are one area of networking that has been instituted in recent years. Canadian interpretation staff commonly spend their summers working in Glacier National Park, while some American personnel spend their summers working in Canada. It is believed that this arrangement contributes to a wider public understanding of the international peace park concept. Interpreters are still paid by their own park service while working abroad, thereby avoiding the need to obtain work permits.

Every year, management staff from both sides meet together to discuss issues of overlapping interests, and to update each other on significant events affecting the parks. The location of the meeting alternates between Waterton and Glacier (Lieff & Lusk, 1990). Furthermore, staff uniforms on both sides of the boundary include a common Peace Park insignia that was designed as part of the 50-year anniversary of the IPP.

Promotion

The USNPS and Parks Canada work cooperatively to produce high-quality promotional and interpretative brochures and maps that are distributed to visitors equally on both sides of the border. Much of the literature produced by Montana and Alberta extols the virtues and beauties of the IPP and encourages people to visit both sides, and community organisations in both areas work together to produce several newspapers, which inform visitors of current events and issues affecting the park.

Joint special events that enforce the IPP concept are also part of ongoing cooperative efforts. For example, joint warden meetings are held on alternate sides of the border; the annual Hands Across the Border Ceremony is well attended; and weekly hikes led by naturalists and wardens from both countries departing from Waterton Town to the international boundary and back are popular during the summer.

Border concessions

Although memorandums of understanding are in place between the two parks to promote informal cooperative efforts, few border-related concessions have been made between the two countries to facilitate such efforts. As one administrator put it, 'we have to work within the confines of border restrictions'. Each section of the park purchases goods on its respective side, and special arrangements are not in place to allow the duty free importation of items from either country. Tourists are required to report to customs and immigration when travelling between the two sides of the IPP by road and by hiking trail. The passage of staff and administrators is also restricted by border regulations.

Recent petitions to the International Boundary Commission to waive the 1925 requirement to clear the border of vegetation and other obstructions within the IPP have been unsuccessful. According to activists, 'the border swath is a symbol of division, not unity' (Gilbert, 1996: 27), but the Boundary Commission sees the importance of maintaining this line of sovereign authority between the two countries.

Boat transportation on Upper Waterton Lake began in 1927 and is still one of the most popular attractions in the IPP. A US-registered boat carries passengers several times a day across the international boundary to the US end of the lake where they disembark for approximately 30 minutes to see a visitor centre with exhibits on park history, plants, and wildlife. In this case, frontier restrictions have been eased somewhat by both countries' immigration services. Passengers are not required to pass through US customs and immigration for their short stay on the US side of the lake, and they are not required to pass through Canadian formalities upon their return to the dock in Canada. Hikers wishing to continue their excursion further into Glacier National Park, however, are required to report at the nearby USNPS ranger station for immigration and customs procedures.

The international peace park designation allows the two sides to work together to promote common goals. This has resulted in the establishment of several local border concessions within the IPP, such as the annual personnel exchanges and joint meetings discussed earlier. Other local cooperative efforts that require some degree of border concessions include joint firefighting efforts, search and rescue operations, and constant communication regarding public safety warnings, weather conditions, and trail closures. Informal arrangements have also been made between superintendents for reimbursement of funds to each side for fuel costs for firefighting and search and rescue, as well as for the passenger boat on Upper Waterton Lake, which is registered in the US but docked in Canada. A new memorandum of understanding between the USNPS and Parks Canada was recently (May, 1998) put into place, which will hopefully strengthen cross-border ties between the two parks and emphasise the international nature of the IPP. While not geared specifically towards the IPP, the new agreement aims to increase partnerships in management, research, protection, conservation, and presentation of national parks and historic sites near the border. In other words, this new document is expected to strengthen the types of local cooperation that already exist between Waterton and Glacier but now with full support of both countries' park services. Because they are out of the range of authority of the park systems, however, official border concessions or treaty waivers are not a part of the agreement.

Conclusions

This paper has examined the situations of three international parks along the Canada-US border. Each one is different in its spatial relationship with the international boundary – one lies directly on the borderline (International Peace Garden), another lies only in Canada but adjacent to the border (Roosevelt Campobello International Park), and the third is effectively two contiguous parks on opposite sides of the border that function as individual entities (Waterton-Glacier International Peace Park).

Although limited in scope, this study demonstrates that the more desegregated the two sides of an international park are in relation to the border, the higher the level of partnership will be. Size and ownership no doubt affect this as well and deserve additional research attention. According to the terms set out in Figure 2, the International Peace Garden is at an integrated level of partnership, wherein both sides are functionally merged and managed as one entity, and the border has relatively few effects on everyday functions. The management framework of Roosevelt Campobello International Park also demonstrates characteristics of integration although, in practice, border restrictions – which have a significant bearing on operational issues such as human resources and transportation – create a collaborative relationship. Waterton-Glacier International Peace Park clearly demonstrates attributes of a cooperative relationship owing to restrictions created by the international boundary and lack of a joint management framework.

It is clear from this study that levels of cross-border partnership are largely based on at least three forms of trans-frontier actions: international treaties; official border concessions, or treaty waivers; and locally or regionally based, less-formal agreements. Integrated relationships occur when all three forms are present. Collaboration exists when one form is weak or does not exist at all. Cooperative networks occur in boundary regions where only one or possibly two forms of action are practised. And, while beyond the empirical scope of this paper, it can be assumed that coexistent relations exist when only rudimentary coordination occurs in any form.

In all three cases, cross-border partnership, whether official and binational, or informal and inter-local, has been instrumental in advancing the principles of sustainable tourism along the US-Canada border. Infrastructure development within the parks has increased efficiency and equity. Joint budgets have been created in two of the parks, which translates into higher levels of efficiency. If integration in this sense were not to occur, infrastructure development would likely mean lengthy and drawn-out negotiation processes between the two sides. More equitable conditions have been created as access to both sides of the border is guaranteed in the International Peace Garden, and in Waterton-Glacier, highways and trails allow access to both sides of the park.

Conservation has benefited from the cooperative, collaborative, and integrated relationships within the three parks. Ecological harmony and balance are encouraged as both sides work together in Waterton-Glacier IPP to protect the depletion of natural resources and wildlife. Within the IPG, conservation measures have been standardised on both sides of the border, and natural and cultural resources in the RCIP are being protected through collaborative and integrated efforts between both countries.

Equity is mandated within the management frameworks of IPG and RCIP in terms of human resources. Every effort is made to employ an equal number of Americans and Canadians, and outside the parks, products are purchased equally from communities in both countries. Work visas are unnecessary for either nationality, which makes park management more efficient. In Waterton-Glacier IPP, staff exchanges have been instrumental in cross-educating wardens and other park employees in areas of ecological conservation and cultural sensitivity.

Promotional efforts in all three parks have resulted in a more efficient production of literature, as well as balance and harmony. Joint tourism literature and Internet sites have been developed that provide a balanced view of both sections of each park. This is particularly important in the case of Waterton-Glacier because each section is administered separately. Even within the literature of each individual park, the other is promoted and visits encouraged.

While cross-border partnerships may help advance the cause of sustainable development in terms of infrastructure, human resources, conservation, and promotion, it might be that partnerships themselves do not necessarily lead to greater levels of sustainability. Rather, they may simply lay the ground rules for action. In fact, it might be that partnerships in some instances delay action as participating parties have to muddle through complex partnership procedures. Levels of tourism certainly have not been very sustainable in recent years as is evident from the data in Tables 1–3, particularly the recent drops in tourist numbers in Roosevelt Campobello and Glacier National Park.

In the context of these three international parks, there is little evidence to suggest that cross-border partnership has resulted in problems of cost, political opportunism, and harmful competition, although more research is needed to confirm this. However, in accordance with Scott's (1998) assertion, the formalisation of cross-border partnership in this context has led to the bureaucratisation of processes. Seeking waivers on boundary restrictions, for example, can be very time consuming and arduous. Power struggles exist between levels of government and between residents and officials as local-level efforts are hindered by national laws pertaining to the border.

In general, the Canada–US experience with international parks has been positive and has contributed to a binational understanding of sustainability and peace. Dozens of international peace parks are in the process of being established in many parts of the world, including areas where conditions of alienation have long existed. Given this change, and as the broader process of globalisation continues, cross-border partnerships will become all the more essential in managing international resources. Perhaps government officials and managers of new and other established borderland parks could learn from these examples in North America, and maybe cross-border partnerships will thus help establish the groundwork for sustainable tourism development in other parts of the world as well.

Acknowledgement

The author gratefully acknowledges the generous financial support for this study by the Canadian Government through its embassy in Washington, DC, and valuable information from the executive directors and superintendents of the borderland parks examined in this paper.

Correspondence

Any correspondence should be directed to Dr Dallen J. Timothy, School of Human Movement, Sport and Leisure Studies, Bowling Green State University, Bowling Green, OH 43403, USA (dtimoth@bgnet.bgsu.edu).

References

Arreola, D.D. and Curtis, J.R. (1993) *The Mexican Border Cities: Landscape Anatomy and Place Personality*. Tucson: University of Arizona Press.

Artibise, A.F.J. (1995) Achieving sustainability in Cascadia: An emerging model of urban growth management in the Vancouver-Seattle-Portland corridor. In P.K. Kresl and G. Gappert (eds) *North American Cities and the Global Economy: Challenges and Opportunities* (pp. 221–250). Thousand Oaks, CA: Sage.

Blake, G.H. (1994) International transboundary collaborative ventures. In W.A. Gallusser (ed.) *Political Boundaries and Coexistence* (pp. 359–371). Berne: Peter Lang.

Blatter, J. (1997) Explaining crossborder cooperation: A border-focused and border-external approach. *Journal of Borderlands Studies* 12 (1/2), 151–174.

Bramwell, B. and Lane, B. (1993) Sustainable tourism: An evolving global approach. *Journal of Sustainable Tourism* 1 (1), 1–5.

Brown, W. (1988) A common border: Soviets and Americans work to create a joint park in the Bering Strait. *National Parks* 62 (11), 18–22.

Butler, R.W. (1991) Tourism, environment and sustainable development. *Environmental Conservation* 18 (3), 201–209.

Church, A. and Reid, P. (1996) Urban power, international networks and competition: The example of cross-border cooperation. *Urban Studies* 33 (8), 1297–1318.

Clark, T. (1994) National boundaries, border zones, and marketing strategy: A conceptual framework and theoretical model of secondary boundary effects. *Journal of Marketing* 58, 67–80.

Clarke, J. (1991) On Campobello, Roosevelt was always on vacation. *Boston Globe* 28 April, 61.

Cohn, T.H. and Smith, P.J. (1995) Developing global cities in the Pacific Northwest: The cases of Vancouver and Seattle. In P.K. Kresl and G. Gappert (eds) *North American Cities and the Global Economy: Challenges and Opportunities* (pp. 251–285). Thousand Oaks, CA: Sage.

Denisiuk, Z., Stoyko, S. and Terray, J. (1997) Experience in cross-border cooperation for national park and protected areas in Central Europe. In J.G. Nelson and R. Serafin (eds) *National Parks and Protected Areas: Keystones to Conservation and Sustainable Development* (pp. 145–150). Berlin: Springer.

Dupuy, P.M. (1982) Legal aspects of transfrontier regional co-operation. *West European Politics* 5, 50–63.

Eriksson, G.A. (1979) Tourism at the Finnish-Swedish-Norwegian borders. In G. Gruber, H. Lamping, W. Lutz, J. Matznetter and K. Vorlaufer (eds) *Tourism and Borders: Proceedings of the IGU Group, Geography of Tourism and Recreation* (pp. 151–162). Frankfurt: Institut für Wirtschafts- und Sozialgeographie der Johann Wolfgang Goethe Universität.

Gilbert, R. (1996) Growing down a wall: One barrier yet divides Waterton-Glacier International Peace Park. *The Rotarian*, March, 26–27.

Glacier National Park (n.d.) Waterton-Glacier International Peace Park. Unpublished manuscript in possession of the author.

Gradus, Y. (1994) The Israel-Jordan Rift Valley: A border of cooperation and productive coexistence. In W.A. Gallusser (ed.) *Political Boundaries and Coexistence* (pp. 315–321). Berne: Peter Lang.

Hansen, N. (1983) International cooperation in border regions: An overview and research agenda. *International Regional Science Review* 8 (3), 255–270.

Ingram, H., Milich, L. and Varady, R.G. (1994) Managing transboundary resources: Lessons from Ambos Nogales. *Environment* 36 (4), 6–38.

Kiy, R. and Wirth, J.D. (eds) (1998) *Environmental Management on North America's Borders.* College Station: Texas A&M University Press.

Leimgruber, W. (1989) The perception of boundaries: barriers or invitation to interaction? *Regio Basiliensis* 30 (2), 49–59.

Lieff, B.C. and Lusk, G. (1990) Transfrontier cooperation between Canada and the USA: Waterton-Glacier International Peace Park. In J. Thorsell (ed.) *Parks on the Borderline: Experience in Transfrontier Conservation* (pp. 39–49). Gland: IUCN.

Lippman, T.W. (1994) Israel, Jordan agree to plan joint ventures. *The Washington Post,. 8 June, 28.*

MacKinnon, J.R. (1993) An Indochina tri-state reserve: The practical challenges. In A.H. Westing (ed.) *Transfrontier Reserves for Peace and Nature: A Contribution to Human Security* (pp. 77–85). Nairobi: UNEP.

Martinez, O. (1994) The dynamics of border interaction: New approaches to border analysis. In C.H. Schofield (ed.) *World Boundaries Vol. 1: Global Boundaries* (pp. 1–15). London: Routledge.

Mayes, H.G. (1992) The International Peace Garden: A border of flowers. *The Beaver* 72 (4), 45–51.

Ministry of Industry, Trade and Tourism (1999) *Manitoba Explorer's Guide, 1999.* Winnipeg: Manitoba Ministry of Industry Trade and Tourism.

Mowforth, M. and Munt, I. (1998) *Tourism and Sustainability: New Tourism in the Third World.* London: Routledge.

Murphy, P.E. (1998) Tourism and sustainable development. In W.F. Theobald (ed.) *Global Tourism* (2nd edn) (pp. 173–190). Oxford: Butterworth-Heinemann.

Naidu, G. (1988) ASEAN cooperation in transport. In H. Esmara (ed.) *ASEAN Economic Cooperation: A New Perspective* (pp. 191–204). Singapore: Chopmen.

Newman, D.R. and Hodgetts, R.M. (1998) *Human Resource Management: A Customer-Oriented Approach.* Upper Saddle River, NJ: Prentice Hall.

Parent, L. (1990) Tex-Mex Park. *National Parks* 64 (7/8), 30–36.

Parks Canada (1996) *1994 Waterton Lakes National Park: Exit Survey Final Results.* Calgary: Parks Canada, Western Region.

Randall, S.J. and Konrad, H.W. (eds) (1995) *NAFTA in Transition.* Calgary: University of Calgary Press.

Roosevelt Campobello International Park Commission (n.d.) *Roosevelt Campobello International Park.* Campobello Island, NB: RCIPC.

Saint-Germain, M.A. (1995) Problems and opportunities for cooperation among public managers on the U.S.-Mexico border. *American Review of Public Administration* 25 (2), 93–117.

Scace, R.C. (1978) *Waterton-Glacier International Peace Park, Story Line Document.* Calgary: Parks Canada Western Region.

Scott, J.W. (1998) Planning cooperation and transboundary regionalism: Implementing policies for European border regions in the German-Polish context. *Environment and Planning C* 16 (5), 605–624.

Thorsell, J. and Harrison, J. (1990) Parks that promote peace: A global inventory of transfrontier nature reserves. In J. Thorsell (ed.) *Parks on the Borderline: Experience in Transfrontier Conservation* (pp. 3–21). Gland: IUCN.

Timothy, D.J. (1995a) International boundaries: New frontiers for tourism research. *Progress in Tourism and Hospitality Research* 1 (2), 141–152.

Timothy, D.J. (1995b) Political boundaries and tourism: Borders as tourist attractions. *Tourism Management* 16 (7), 525–532.

Timothy, D.J. (1998) Cooperative tourism planning in a developing destination. *Journal of Sustainable Tourism* 6 (1), 52–68.

Timothy, D.J. (in press) Tourism planning in Southeast Asia: Bringing down borders through cooperation. In K.S. Chon (ed.) *Tourism in Southeast Asia: Opportunities and Challenges*. Binghamton, NY: The Haworth Press.

Timothy, D.J. (forthcoming) Tourism and international parks. In R.W. Butler and S.W. Boyd (eds) *Tourism and National Parks: Issues and Implications*. Chichester: Wiley.

Tourism Department (1999) *North Dakota: Discover the Spirit!* Bismarck: North Dakota Tourism Department.

Wall, G. (1993) Towards a tourism typology. In J.G. Nelson, R.W. Butler, and G. Wall (eds) *Tourism and Sustainable Development: Monitoring, Planning, Managing* (pp. 45–58). Waterloo, ON: Department of Geography, University of Waterloo.

Young, L. and Rabb, M. (1992) New park on the bloc. *National Parks* 66 (1/2), 35–40.

3. Interest Based Formulation of Tourism Policy for Environmentally Sensitive Destinations

J.R. Brent Ritchie
Faculty of Management, University of Calgary, Calgary, Alberta, Canada T2N 1N4

The Banff-Bow Valley Study (BBVS), a major, two-year, $2.4 million study, sought to identify a common ground between the enduring and deeply held views of citizens espousing the maintenance of ecological integrity and those supporting continued freedom of access and enjoyment, as the country plans the future of the 'Crown Jewel' of Canada's National Park System. This article provides a review of a consensus-building approach that has been relatively neglected in tourism. The approach employed, Interest Based Negotiation (IBN), appears to have succeeded in improving understanding of the issues involved, in arriving at a common vision for the future of the region, and in facilitating the first steps towards implementation of consensus-based recommendations. Nearly two years following the submission of the Task Force's final report and its over 500 recommendations, the majority of stakeholders involved in the process remained optimistic that the IBN approach had indeed proven useful in finding a common ground for ensuring the well-being of a magnificent tourism destination within a highly sensitive ecosystem.

Introduction

A Tourism Policy Forum held at George Washington University (GWU) nearly a decade ago identified a number of major trends that participants believed would shape the future of tourism policy in the 1990s. Two of the top policy trends identified by the group of approximately 100 experts (Hawkins *et al.*, 1991) were:

(1) that the physical environment is taking 'centre stage' in tourism development and management; furthermore, there is recognition that there are finite limitations to tourism development in terms of both physical and social carrying capacity of destinations;

(2) that resident responsive tourism is the watchword for tomorrow; community demands for active participation in the setting of the tourism agenda and its priorities for tourism development and management cannot be ignored.

Since the forum, the attention paid by both scholars and practitioners to the relationship between tourism and the environment has grown dramatically (Nelson *et al.*, 1992; Rohter, 1992; McIntyre *et al.*, 1993; Lindberg & Hawkins, 1993; Cater & Lowman, 1994; Burns & Holden, 1995). Also, a large number of publications have demonstrated just how seriously both scholars and the public have taken the call for more active collaboration in community socio-economic planning (Chrislip & Larson, 1994; Jamal & Getz, 1995; Huxham, 1996). Finally, the Local Agenda 21 (LA21) process developed at the 1992 Rio Conference represents yet another very significant indication of the growing commitment of decision-makers to meaningful public consultation in the formulation of policies affecting the environment and tourism. The recent adoption of the LA21 initiative confirms official level commitment to the philosophy of public consultation in policy formulation.

The present article provides another concrete example, not only of concern for the environment in tourism planning, but also for the desire to involve citizens in consensus-based tourism planning in a very meaningful way. It is felt particularly significant that it documents a major example as to how the confluence of policy trends predicted almost ten years ago has been realised.

In addition to reporting on a large-scale, long-term study regarding concern for the environment that involves extensive community participation in long-term strategic planning for tourism (Pearce *et al.*, 1996), the present article adds a further dimension that should be of considerable interest to readers. More specifically, it describes the use of a planning approach referred to as 'Interest Based Negotiation' (IBN) (Fisher & Ury, 1991). While the technique is certainly not new, it represents an alternative approach to the consensus-based methods that have been reported to date in the tourism literature on collaborative planning (Jamal & Getz, 1995; Ritchie, 1985, 1988). In this case, the technique was found to be a highly valuable catalyst for strategic destination planning within a high visitation, environmentally sensitive region. The region in question was Banff National Park, in Alberta, Canada.

In brief, the present study provides tourism scholars with an additional framework for consensus policy formulation that can be generalised to most settings. While the details of the application reported are by necessity linked to the destination in question, the use of Interest Based Negotiation, and the planning framework developed around this approach, have been presented in a way which it is hoped will make them of general value to others involved in tourism policy and planning.

Consensus Planning for Tourism Destination Development/Management

Strategic planning for destination management

Following the end of the Second World War, and particularly with the introduction of long-range aircraft, the tourism sector has grown steadily, and often dramatically. As a consequence, many areas have achieved considerable success as tourism destinations. For many of these destinations, success has been a matter of good luck rather than good management. Expanding populations, rapidly rising incomes and a minimum of alternatives have meant that many destinations derived substantial economic benefits from tourism without extensive investments, and without allocating significant efforts or resources to ensuring the quality of tourism-related facilities or to promoting the destination to potential visitors. In effect, market affluence and lack of competition, combined with minimal concern for environmental protection, have allowed many well-endowed destinations the luxury of ignoring the need for professional management of their tourism resources.

As we approach the new millennium, however, we find that the realities facing the tourism sector have, as the GWU Forum predicted, changed radically. General market affluence has been replaced by highly specific market niches, each having very individualistic characteristics, incomes and behaviours. Societal concerns for environmental protection have placed new constraints on both the development and operation of destination facilities. At the same time, the emergence of many new highly attractive destinations, often having considerable cost advantages, has dramatically altered the intensity of competition in the marketplace. As a consequence, destinations that have failed to take a proactive stance regarding the management of their tourism industry have risked stagnation and a decline in their ability to compete.

Recognition of the foregoing realities has been described by certain authors as the arrival of a 'new tourism' (Poon, 1993). Other authors have identified a broad range of opportunities that are emerging as a result of these 'new realities' (Ritchie, 1992). However described, the many changes occurring in tourism have created massive pressures to enhance destination competitiveness; that is, the ability, through more effective destination management, to appeal to the marketplace, to provide high quality visitor experiences, and to deliver these experiences in a cost-efficient manner.

At the same time that the level of competition has been growing on a global basis, there has been a parallel emergence of an almost universal pressure for an increased democratisation of governing processes at all levels. In the tourism sector, this pressure has translated itself into a movement demanding greater involvement of the citizenry in the broad range of decisions associated with virtually all forms of tourism development and promotion. These demands have become particularly forceful in relation to those forms of tourism development and promotion that have a significant potential to harm the environment, host communities or indigenous cultures (Getz & Jamal, 1994).

It is the foregoing set of forces, as they apply to one particular situation, which gave rise to the study on which this article is based. To be specific, the present article reports on a situation in which international competition, growing levels of visitation, and pressures for environmental protection were the primary forces that incited the Canadian Government to commission a high-profile, two-year, $2.4 million study to address growing public concern for the long-term well-being of Canada's most treasured conservation and tourism icon, Banff National Park. In addition, the recent incorporation of the Town of Banff had created a situation in which local residents (or 'Permanent Tourists' as they are sometimes referred to) represent a significant percentage of 'person days' in the Park – and as such are becoming an increasing environmental threat in their own right.

The study, formally known as the 'Banff-Bow Valley (BBV) Study', was directed by a five-person Task Force comprised of individuals appointed by the Minister for their expertise in the fields of the environmental sciences, public policy and tourism. Highly specialised assistance was provided to the Task Force by a permanent secretariat and a number of consultants.

The Banff-Bow Valley Study: A 'satellite' overview

As can be surmised, the reporting of a complex, contentious study that took two years to complete at a cost of over $2.4 million (CDN), and which resulted in some 500 specific recommendations, was a demanding task. Aside from sheer size (over 425 pages), it was essential that all assertions and recommendations be as well justified as humanly possible by other existing facts/knowledge, or by especially commissioned pieces of research.

Since the purpose of this article is not to describe the total study, but rather to focus on one essential aspect of the methodology utilised to foster collaboration, only a brief overview of the study is provided here. Readers wishing to gain a greater understanding of the total study process are referred to an overview by Ritchie (1999a), or more ideally, to the complete final report itself (Banff-Bow Valley Study, 1996). For the immediate needs of the present discussion, readers are referred to the composite Figure 1 (comprising (a) and (b)). This attempts to provide a 'capsule' or 'satellite' overview of the key components of the study process, namely Public Input and Information Gathering (A), Research and Analysis (B), Round Table Deliberations (C), Task Force Deliberations (D), and Final Report Preparation and Submission (E).

Each of these major components of the study process involved its own distinct set of activities. The present paper is intended to focus on the subsets of activities that comprise the process referred to as 'Interest Based Negotiation' (IBN). However, before turning to an in-depth review of IBN, it is important to fully comprehend the 'Round Table' context within which IBN was pursued.

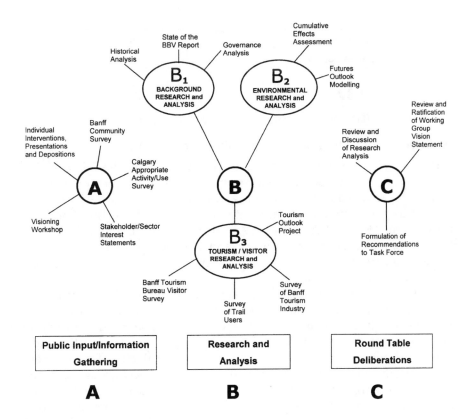

Figure 1(a) The Banff-Bow Valley Study: A 'satellite' overview

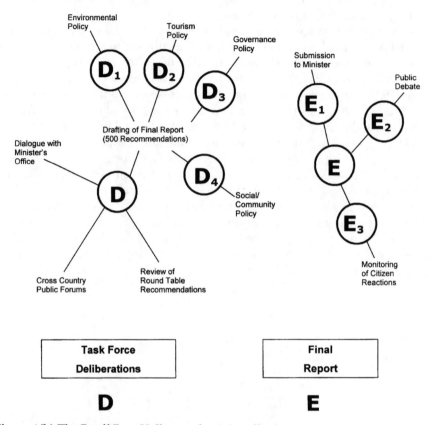

Figure 1(b) The Banff-Bow Valley study: A 'satellite' overview

The Round Table: Structure, composition and process

The Task Force made an early decision that the study should be explicitly driven by all stakeholder groups having an active and proven interest in ensuring the environmental, economic, and social well being of the Park. In order to turn this philosophical commitment into hard reality, the Task Force established a formal Round Table process. As will be seen, this Round Table served as the heart of the consultation, advisory, and analytical processes that provided the Task Force with the information, ideas, insights, and understanding used to formulate its recommendations.

The Round Table (see Figure 2), was composed of some 14 'interest sectors'. Each of these sectors, as the name implies, was established to represent the interests of its constituents within the process designed to plan the future of the BBV region. A sector was loosely defined as a grouping of stakeholders (individuals and/or organisations) having a common, yet distinctive set of interests concerning the protection and usage of the region. Each sector was comprised of a Chair, a working committee, and a supporting constituency. The Round Table information sharing and IBN process was facilitated by a technical expert who worked with Round Table members to develop procedural rules, to formulate a vision, principles, and goals for the future of the region, to analyse the major

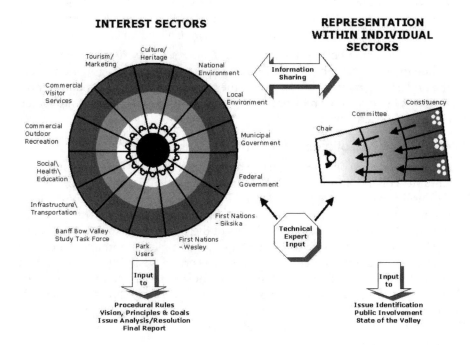

Figure 2 Banff-Bow Valley Round Table: Stucture, composition and process

issues involved, to reach consensus, and to put forth recommendations from the Round Table to the Task Force. The Round Table met monthly between February 1995 and March 1996.

Interest Based Negotiation

As previously noted, the distinguishing characteristic of the consensus based planning process used by the Round Table was its reliance on the process of IBN. This process, largely attributed to Fisher and Ury (1991), was developed to provide a negotiation process where, in contrast to traditional *'positional bargaining'*, the process focuses on *'basic interests'* and seeks to achieve a *'wise'* agreement. Fisher and Ury argue that the method:

> permits you to reach a gradual consensus on a joint decision *efficiently*, without all the transactional costs of digging into positions only to have to dig yourself out. And, separating people from the problem allows you to deal directly and empathetically with the other negotiators as human beings, thus making possible an *amicable* agreement. (Fisher & Ury, 1991: 14)

To summarise, the IBN approach rests on four main principles:

- separate the people from the problem (i.e. depersonalise the negotiators);
- focus on interests, not positions (i.e. the desires and concerns that moti-vate people rather than a statement describing 'what has been decided upon');

- invent options for mutual gain (i.e. identify all available answers);
- insist on using objective criteria (i.e. settle differences of interest on the basis of objective criteria rather than *'strength of will'* of each side).

While the distinction between *'positions'* and *'interests'* may require some familiarisation in practice, the basic idea is to attempt to ensure that negotiations focus on the underlying motivational needs of the parties involved, rather than simply on a stated position which may or may not be the only way of meeting the underlying needs of each party.

Interest Based Negotiation as a Form of Collaborative Planning

From a theoretical perspective, it can be argued that IBN is simply a form of (a) community collaboration (Gray, 1989; Himmelman, 1992; Jamal & Getz, 1995), of (b) group-based consensus decision-making (Delbecq & Van de Ven, 1971; Johnson & Johnson, 1987) or, of (c) conflict resolution (Potapchuk & Polk, 1993). In retrospect, it may well be that members of the Task Force chose to emphasise the Fisher and Ury approach to collaborative planning for pragmatic rather than theoretical considerations (the 'method' had a certain 'visibility'). As well, they were undoubtedly influenced by the consultant selected to facilitate the Round Table process. Regardless, the formal utilisation of IBN and its associated methodologies did provide what most have judged to be a successful approach within the setting in question. As a result of this success, others may also wish to consider its merits.

Operationalisation of Interest Based Negotiation (IBN)

This section of the paper now focuses on providing as much insight as possible into the actual functioning of the IBN process – without it is hoped, overwhelming the reader with excessive detail of primarily local interest.

Setting the stage: Instructions to Round Table participants

In the present study, as part of the Public Input/Information Gathering phase, each of the 14 sectors of the Round Table were first asked to formally identify the main sector interests that they felt had to be satisfied by the overall study process (see Figure 1(a), Component A). A three-part format was suggested to each sector as the basis for the structure and content of their interest statements. These suggestions/directions are summarised in Table 1.

Initial input: Submission of sector interest statements

Based on the facilitator's guidelines, the members of each sector held a series of meetings at which they reached consensus on a series of statements that they felt reflected both their immediate and more long-term interests. Selected examples of the interests stated by different sectors are given in the Appendix. The original interest statements have, for purposes of brevity, been selectively edited. However, an attempt has been made to preserve as much as possible of the *'feeling'* of the original documentation. This has been done so as to provide destinations wishing to adopt the IBN model with a better understanding of the nature of interest statements from an *'on the ground'* perspective.

Table 1 Facilitator suggestions/directions to sectors regarding the format (structure and content) of their interest statements

---

Part 1 – Authority and Accountability

This is a specific requirement of the procedural rules. Its importance is obvious. People need to know who you represent and how you are generally accountable to those you speak for. You should answer the following questions:

(1) who do we represent?

(2) who sits on our sector steering committee?

(3) how do we communicate with their constituency?

(4) what authority do we have to make decisions on behalf of constituents? and

(5) how will we ratify agreements with constituents?

Part 2 – Sector Interests

Before the table as a whole can explore interests, it is important for each sectoral steering group to have catalogues its own. A thorough consideration of 'what is important to our sector and why' will be most helpful to each sector representative in educating the rest of the table. To help define sector interests, you may wish to consider the following questions:

(1) Identifying principal interests:
   - What are our sector's several most important interests?
   - Can we prioritise them?
   - How much do we care about each?

   Other questions which may help identify principal interest include:
   - What are we doing this negotiation for?
   - What do we hope to gain from this?
   - What could we lose if this process does not succeed?
   - What are the key factors of success for us?

(2) Elaboration of Interests:
   - Can we make our interests more easily understood by sorting them into needs, desires, fears, and hopes?

(3) Measuring success:
   - How will we know if our interests have been achieved?
   - Can they be qualified or measured?
   - If so, how?

(4) Other sectors' interests:
   - What do we think other sectors' interests might be?
   - Can we prioritise them?
   - What sector(s) share some sets of interest with us?

Part 3 – Sector Interests (long-term interests)

The first phase of the Banff-Bow Valley study requires the development of goals and a vision for the Bow Valley in the Banff National Park that bring together ecological, social, and economic value.

A vision attempts to answer such questions as:

Table 1 (cont.)

---

(1)   What do we want the Banff-Bow Valley to look like in 10, 50, 100 years?

(2)   What kind of place do we want to leave for our descendants?

In the context of this discussion, a vision can perhaps best be defined as the *longer-term* interests or aspirations of a sector. If presented in this way, your interest statement could provide a useful departure point for the vision-building phase of your work. The question you may wish to consider is 'what is important to our sector *in the longer term* and why' or, put another way, 'what needs or hopes must a vision for the Banff-Bow Valley take into account?'

Essentially, the format being suggested will allow you to describe your short- or mid-term interests in Part 2 and your long-term interest in Part 3 – giving you a head start on the visioning process.

Source: Adapted from the Facilitator's Reports to the Round Table.

Summarising the detailed interest statements

Following the submission of detailed individual sector interest statements, the professional facilitator for the IBN process prepared a 'Summary of Interests' in which he:

(a)   consolidated the range of interests submitted; and
(b)   classified the main ideas captured by the various interest statements into three main categories: Environmental, Economic and Cultural/Community Governance (see Table 2). The primary purpose of this summary was to help identify complementary interests, common interests, and interests apparently in conflict. Interests apparently in conflict then became issues for resolution.

As such, the information in Table 2 was then utilised as the basis for discussion among Round Table members. During these discussions, the facilitator sought to find common grounds for agreement on key issues. The conceptual nature of this process is given in Figure 3. The figure attempts to demonstrate how positions that are initially far apart, may, through the discussion of interests, arrive at a common ground in which options for agreement, acceptable to both parties, can be agreed upon.

Evolution of interest statements and the development of a negotiation agenda

During the period following the presentation of initial interest statements and a subsequent summary, the facilitator reviewed the interest statements in greater depth and prepared a 'positions of interest' pyramid based on Figure 3 – a format intended to put the interest statements into a form more suitable for ongoing development and reference. More specifically, participants were asked to review this information for the purpose of:

- identifying issues (subjects participants wanted to see on the negotiation agenda – bearing in mind the scope of the process); and

Table 2 Summary of sector interests

Cultural/community/ governance	Economic	Environmental
Generate a will to work together for the overall benefit of the BBV Improve the public image of BBV communities Preserve small town and rural character Build community trust, communication and partnerships Build pride in community preserve community values Maintain quality of life – residents Re-establish sense of 'connectedness' in community	Create predictable policy and regulatory environment to support long-term business planning Clarify the role and function of national parks Ensure a predictable regulatory environment Accommodate need for operational flexibility Maintain the ability of business to adapt to market changes Ensure that parks legislation is understood, accepted and applied consistently Ensure predictability and consistency in application of park policy	Acknowledge 'non-human' uses in BBV
Build shared responsibility and cooperation at all levels of government	Recognise the economic and public safety benefits derived from well–maintained and appropriate transportation and telecommunication corridors	Determine appropriate future use
Protect the positive attributes of BNP for future generations Enhance national parks experience for residents Set a world class example Maintain/restore profile and prestige of BNP Protect and resurrect culture Protect historic buildings, sites and structures	Acknowledge historic use and development in the BBV Account for unique character of BNP in reconciling social, economic and environmental interests	Encourage deeper public understanding and awareness of environmental and national park values Build support and understanding of all Canadians for the importance of national parks Build respect for ecological integrity Recognise the relationship between economic viability and environmental protection
Enhance opportunities for citizen participation in public decision-making	Balance impact of marketing, the cost of maintaining a saleable experience and revenue generation	Maintain ecological integrity and restore natural processes where required Recognise the importance of wilderness
Recognise 'human factor' in sustainability relationships	Alleviate seasonal pressures on the community Sustain the regional economy Maintain economic viability of local business Build year round economic viability	Ensure opportunities for people to experience nature Ensure public access to wilderness perimeters

Table 2 (cont.)

Cultural/community/ governance ←→	Economic ←→	Environmental
Manage growth accounting for emotional, economic and environmental costs Not 'kill the goose' Define and maintain community health and well-being Ensure adequate housing for community residents	Determine development thresholds in designated townsites	Maintain wildlife populations, habitat, corridors, safety
Maintain safe communities (emergency services, highways, railways, dams and reservoirs)	Remain competitive in global markets Enhance and improve safety, competitiveness with other destinations and overall physical attractiveness Ensure high quality, safe tourism and recreation	Make decisions based on reliable information and scientific interpretation
Maintain opportunities for outdoor recreation	Accommodate adequate and appropriate services and facilities Build infrastructure to support tourism growth	Mitigate ecological problems Protect against environmental degradation Restore major ecological corridors and avoid habitat fragmentation
Maintain the commemorative (cultural and historical) integrity of the BBV	Build cooperation and partnerships with community	Provide leadership in environmental initiatives
Recognise competing demands on community, provincial and national tax base	Sustain traditional recreation activities consistent with protection Support nature-based activities which do not impair nature's function (nature-related tourism)	

Source: Facilitator's Report to Round Table.

- moving from position statements (participants' preferred solutions to the issues) to interests (the factors that motivate the preferred solutions of participants).

In addition, participants were asked to identify any 'open questions' they felt might assist in the negotiation process. Guidelines suggested by the facilitator for the formulation of these 'open questions' are summarised in Table 3. These 'Open Questions' were intended to 'help the parties to move away from a fixed position on something'. These 'Open Questions' were of four types: Probing, Clarifying, Justifying, and Consequential. Greater detail concerning the precise purpose and nature of each of these types of questions is also given in Table 3.

Focusing the process: From common interests to a common vision

Once Round Table members had achieved a common understanding of each other's major interests and had the opportunity to fully probe and explore the nature of each sector's interests, a second important process was initiated. The

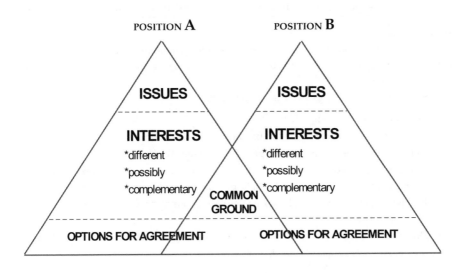

ISSUE	The subject matter of a dispute, i.e. 'what we are here to talk about?'
POSITIONS	Positions are the solutions that each party thinks will satisfy their interests. That is, each party's 'preferred outcome'. Positions are negotiable.
INTERESTS	The factors (needs, wants, fears or concerns) that motivate the parties to reach positions. Interests may be substantive, procedural or psychological. Interests may be negotiable at the margins.

Figure 3 Moving from positions to interests to agreements

process attempted to build on the understanding of each other's interests to develop a consensus based *'Vision'* or *'Roadmap for the Future'* for The Banff-Bow Valley Region. This effort sought to meet the first formal objective of the Banff-Bow Valley Study, namely 'to develop goals and a vision for the Bow Valley in Banff National Park that bring together ecological, social and economic values'.

Those wishing to examine the complete BBV Vision Statement are referred to the Final Report itself (Banff-Bow Valley Study, 1996: 21). Those desiring a more detailed understanding of both the vision and the visioning process are referred to (Ritchie, 1999b). For present purposes, readers should note that the *Core Vision* consisted of a brief statement that consolidated all key dimensions of the desired future for the region. It was, in effect, the heart of the visioning document; a portrait describing how the Task Force hoped the region would evolve as it moved into the next century. The 'Core Vision' read as follows:

> The Bow Valley in Banff National Park reveals the majesty and wildness of the Rocky Mountains. It is a symbol of Canada, a place of great beauty, where nature is able to flourish and evolve. People from around the world

Table 3 Guidelines for the formulation of 'open questions' by participating sectors

---

The Open Question

Open questions are questions that cannot be answered with a 'yes' or a 'no'. They have the effect of opening up discussion, expanding issues, broadening, perspectives, and encouraging inductive thinking.

Open questions may be very useful to do the following:

- Open up the options when parties seems stuck;
- **Help parties to move away from a fixed position on something;**
- Help parties to see things from the perspective of the other;
- Help explain the broad context in which a behavioural choice was made, making it easier to understand the behaviour and enhancing trust among the parties;
- Function as an agent of reality by asking the party to look at the practical effect of his or her expressed view.
- Slow down the process where parties are engaged in a heated back and forth exchange.

There are several kinds of open questions:

- Probing Questions ask for more information
- Clarifying Questions seek to sharpen the listener's understanding of what has been said;
- Justifying Questions ask the speaker to given some evidence for the view expressed;
- Consequential Questions are used for reality testing; to ask about potential solutions or look at possible consequences. At times, and in certain cultural settings, some questions may be considered intrusive, disrespectful, and inappropriate. Be aware of the cultural context you are working in and move forward with care.

Probing Questions

These questions ask for more information. They seek to identify what it is about something that make it important to a party e.g. 'You mentioned a moment ago that when his aunt left the room, you felt you had lost an opportunity. Can you tell me more about what you hoped would happen while his aunt was there?'

Way to phrase probing questions:

- What is it about this that concerns you the most?
- When was it that you realised how much the entire service was going to cost?
- How did you come to decide to choose another place for the next course?
- Please let me more about how you came to feel/think that?

Clarifying Questions

These questions seek to sharpen the listener's understanding of what has been said e.g. 'So, it was not so much the loss of the contract that concerned you as it was the loss of the relationship?'

Ways to phrase clarifying questions:

- When you say 'the meeting', which time are you referring to?
- You said a few minutes ago that you thought it was possible to recover part of what had been lost. Can you tell me what you meant by the word 'recover'?
- You spoke of immigrants. Did you mean people who are recent arrivals, or some other group?

Table 3 (cont.)

Justifying Questions

These questions ask the speaker to give some evidence for the view expressed. They are useful when there is some incongruence between what the speaker has said on different occasions, or when there is incongruence between what the speaker has said and his or her body language. Use these questions with caution when dealing with parties from a hierarchical culture or organisation. They may incite defensiveness or alienation e.g. 'Mary, You said a few minutes ago that you had written Bob off. Now you are talking about a continuing business relationship. Can you tell me how those might fit together?'

Ways to phrase justifying questions:

- Earlier you said … and just not I thought I heard you say that … Can you tell me how you plan to move forward?
- When you said you were going out of town, I thought I heard a note of finality in you voice. Just now you used the world 'maybe' when I asked about your plans to travel out of town. Could you help me with my confusion?

Consequential questions

These are questions to 'reality test'; to ask about potential solutions, to look at the possible consequences of a position taken or a solution e.g. If you go on as planned, who do you think will be most affected?

Phrasing for consequential questions:

- How do you think the sequence will change the plan you had earlier?
- Have you thought about the down side for you if the market turns before the units are built?
- What do you think your response might have been if this suggestion were made by Sally two months ago?

Source: Adapted from Facilitator's Report to Round Table

participate in the life of the valley, finding inspiration, enjoyment, livelihoods, and understanding. Through their wisdom and foresight in protecting this small part of the planet, Canadians demonstrate leadership in forging healthy relationships between people and nature. The Banff-Bow Valley is, above all else, a place of wonder, where the richness of life is respected and celebrated. (Banff-Bow Valley Study, 1996)

The Core Vision described here stressed the majesty and wilderness of the Rocky Mountains, and their importance as a symbol of Canada. It emphasised that people from around the world are invited to participate in the life of the valley, thereby finding inspiration, enjoyment and understanding. As well, the Vision reminds us that the Banff-Bow Valley is but a small part of the planet and one where Canadians demonstrate leadership in forging healthy relationships between people and nature.

This 'Core Vision' was in turn rendered more meaningful through the identification of eight specific subthemes – or Elements – of the Vision. These elements/subthemes are shown in Table 4. Each of the elements was intended to provide an operational focus for the implementation, or 'realisation' of the total Vision. With this concern clearly in mind, the next critical step was to identify very specific policies, and supporting actions, that would translate the agreed-upon vision (including its supporting elements) into eventual reality.

Towards this end, each of the policies and action recommendations that resulted from the information gathering, research/analysis, and subsequent Round Table discussions, were examined to determine how and where they related to various components of the vision, and their eventual realisation. In effect, the vision served as an 'inspirational framework' within which, and against which, all proposed actions were assessed for both relevance and acceptability. Because the number of recommendations (most of which related to the maintenance of ecological integrity), exceeds the scope of the present discussion, attention will now focus only on those recommendations that provide guidance for the future of tourism in Banff National Park, and for the new tourism destination model that the country seeks to develop in this region.

Providing a focus for tourism within the overall vision

An examination of the eight supporting elements of the total vision (as shown in Table 4) reveals that several of these elements infer a future tourism vocation for the Banff-Bow Valley – but only indirectly. For example, the second element addresses the issue of visitation by 'Canadians and international guests'. Element 3 talks about 'understanding the value of National Parks ... where services are provided ... within and beyond the boundaries of the Park. Introduction to this knowledge is a fundamental part of each visitor's experiences'. And finally, Element 5 directly refers to 'A healthy economic climate ... [that] contributes to national, provincial, and local economies', plus the fact that, 'Businesses evolve and operate ... when providing services including ...'

Thus, although the Vision for the BBV clearly indicates a role for tourism, it does not provide an explicit framework for the future of tourism. In light of this ambiguity, it was felt essential to develop a very specific model for tourism that would not only be consistent with the overall Vision, but also elaborate on it from a tourism perspective.

With ongoing guidance from the Round Table, the Task Force then formulated a 'refocused model' of tourism for the Banff-Bow Valley. This model was entitled the 'Touchstone for the Canadian Rockies' (see Figure 4). The term 'Touchstone' was meant to convey the hope that Banff National Park will set a standard that will be judged worthy both today, and by the next generation.

The Touchstone Tourism Destination Model has, as its primary emphasis, the theme of learning, education, understanding and appreciation of nature and the Rocky Mountains. This theme will pervade the management philosophy of the whole destination; it is intended to be the 'glue' that binds the efforts of all who seek to realise the tourism potential of the Banff-Bow Valley.

In examining the Touchstone Tourism Destination Model, the reader is asked to remember that the Vision of the Banff-Bow Valley recognises that visitors, the essence of tourism, are fundamental to the long-term success and sustainability of the region. It also recognises that preserving the beauty and ecological integrity of the Park is essential to its appeal as a sustainable tourism destination. In return, those in the tourism sector who truly understand the current social and

Table 4 Vision for the Banff-Bow Valley Region

Core vision

The Bow Valley in Banff National Park reveals the majesty and wildness of the Rocky Mountains. It is a symbol of Canada, a place of great beauty, where nature is able to flourish and evolve. People from around the world participate in the life of the valley, finding inspiration, enjoyment, livelihoods and understanding. Through their wisdom and foresight in protecting this small part of the planet, Canadians demonstrate leadership in forging healthy relationships between people and nature. The Banff-Bow Valley is, above all else, a place of wonder, where the richness of life is respected and celebrated.

Key supporting themes

- The Bow Valley in Banff National Park is a living example of the way in which ecological values are protected while appropriate kinds and levels of human activity are welcomed.
- Within the valley, natural systems and all their component native species are free to function and evolve. The Bow Valley supports and is supported by the natural systems of the region around it.
- The Bow Valley in Banff National Park is available to all Canadians and international guests, who wish to participate in a diverse range of appropriate activities. They treat the park with respect. The quality of the natural environment is fundamental to the visitor experience, which is enriched by the quality of services provided.
- Understanding the value of our National Parks is a part of being Canadian. Education and awareness about National Park values, ethics, natural and cultural heritage, and services are provided both within and beyond the boundaries of the Park. Introduction to this knowledge is a fundamental part of each visitor's experiences.
- A healthy economic climate, based on the heritage values of the Park, contributes to national, provincial and local economies. Businesses evolve and operate along aesthetically pleasing and environmentally responsible lines. Innovative ideas, designs and technology are emphasised when providing services including education, transportation, waste management, and other infrastructure.
- Federal, provincial and municipal authorities cooperate in protecting and managing the National Park and regional ecosystem. To achieve this, they nurture cooperation with businesses, organisations, and individuals. Public participation processes contribute to open, accountable, and responsible decision-making. Principles of precaution are exercised when the effects on the ecosystem are uncertain.
- Laws and regulations affecting the economy and the environment are consistent and predictable. Enforcement of regulations is consistent for all.
- Communities in the Bow Valley are healthy and viable and are leaders in the quest for environmental and cultural sustainability. Residents are hospitable and pride themselves in accepting their responsibility for protecting and sharing this natural and cultural heritage for the benefit of present and future generations.

Source: Banff-Bow Valley Study, 1996: 21.

economic dynamics of the country, appreciate the need to provide leadership in the overall process of maintaining the ecological integrity of the Park. This leadership acknowledges the need for tourism to provide a fair financial contribution for the privilege of operating in the Park. Conversely, the tourism industry

Tourism in the Banff-Bow Valley has as its Foundation, the:

Values and Diverse Interests of Canadians and Shared, Open Decision Making

Its Goal, Above All, Is To Facilitate And Enhance:

Learning – Understanding – Appreciation of Nature and The Rocky Mountain Culture

While Providing Visitors With:

High Quality, Authentic Experiences – A Hospitable Ambiance – Fair Value

In Doing So, It Will Maintain:

Ecological Integrity – Fair & Equitable Access

While Contributing To:

Regional Economic Vitality – National Pride & Unity

As It Respects The Rights Of :

Tourism Operators – All Canadians – Community Residents

While In Return Making:

A Fair Contribution To Park Well-Being

Figure 4 Touchstone for the Canadian Rockies Tourism Destination Model
Source: BBV Study (1996)

should have the opportunity to realise a fair return on its investment and its efforts. In recognition of this commitment and support, the industry also has the right to public respect from both visitors and the environmental community, and to development policies that assist them, wherever possible, to compete effectively in the constantly evolving tourism marketplace.

In assessing the Tourism Destination Model, it is important to understand what development means in the context of sustainable tourism. There is a difference between development that results in more facilities and more people, and development that changes aspects such as:

- the physical structure of facilities;
- the quality of facilities;
- nature of the experience; and
- the ability to compete and at the same time protect ecological integrity and the quality of the visitor experience.

The Tourism Destination Model for the Banff-Bow Valley also recognises that the protection of the Park cannot be carried out in isolation from the surrounding ecological, social and economic reality. Ecosystem management demands that the ecological island be integrated with the physical environs. Similarly, social and economic realities require that tourism activity in Banff National Park both support, and be supported by, tourism activity in the surrounding regions – and indeed, in the rest of Canada, Banff National Park is not merely an important tourism destination in Canada; it also serves as an enduring icon for the marketing of Canada internationally.

The goal of the Tourism Destination Model is to provide unique and memorable, nature based experiences for Canadians, and for guests from around the world. It seeks to do this in a manner that respects the ecological integrity of the region, while laying the foundations for a lasting, sustainable tourism destination in the Valley.

Supporting Principles for the Sustainable Tourism Destination

Banff National Park has been a major Canadian tourism destination for many years. As such, the BBV Study faced the very significant challenge of redefining and refocusing Banff National Park's role as a tourism destination for the next 50 years. To achieve this goal the Task Force felt it was important to formally define the principles that would underlie this future role. These are:

- It is recognised that the Town of Banff was created as a tourism destination, and still today, the primary reason for its existence is to provide essential and basic services for visitors to the Park.
- Because Banff is a national park, all Canadians must have fair and equitable access to the experiences it has to offer. To fulfil this role, the policies related to Banff National Park as a tourism destination should attempt to make the Banff experience available to as many Canadians as possible, while ensuring that the ecological integrity of the Park is maintained.
- Banff National Park has historically provided Canadians with a broad range of recreational experiences. Those experiences that do not undermine ecological integrity, and that are judged appropriate, will continue to be allowed and supported.
- The newly defined Banff National Park will place a greater emphasis on education and learning related to Park values.
- It is important that Banff National Park as a tourism destination be economically sustainable.

In summary, the Tourism Destination Model first acknowledges the reputation and great tourism strengths of Banff National Park as it exists today; second, it then accepts the need for selected changes and limitations on future growth of infrastructure so as to preserve both the ecological integrity and the competitive market appeal of the destination; and third, it proposes a refocusing of the destination's development and marketing strategy. This refocusing will maintain those current dimensions of destination development and marketing that take advantage of Banff National Park's magnificent scenery and its constrained ability to provide a range of nature-based recreational experiences. In parallel, it will add a strong emphasis on providing visitors with an equally broad range of opportunities to learn about, better understand, and more fully appreciate the value of the natural wonders and the mountain culture that are unique to the Banff-Bow Valley.

As noted earlier, the theme, 'Touchstone for the Canadian Rockies', seeks to convey to Canadians, and to all citizens of the world, the desire that Banff National Park set a clear standard for the way tourism can support and enhance ecological integrity within an environmentally sensitive tourism destination. In somewhat different terms, the objective is to create a very special kind of tourism destination. More specifically, it is intended that Banff National Park be a destination that:

(1) fully respects the ecological integrity of its unique setting;
(2) reflects the values of Canadians;
(3) is accessible to all Canadians on a fair and equitable basis, regardless of income, age, physical ability or place of residence;
(4) seeks to inspire and enable visitors to learn about, understand and better appreciate nature and the mountain culture in the Canadian Rockies;
(5) within the constraints of ecological integrity, allows and encourages visitors to enjoy recreational experiences that are judged appropriate (Simpson, 1995; Ritchie, 1998);
(6) recognises its importance to the economic vitality of the local region and to the economy of Canada;
(7) recognises its very special role in Canada as a vehicle for inspiring and fostering national pride and national unity;
(8) recognises that nature is not free, and that pricing must reflect Banff's obligations as a national park;
(9) acknowledges the diverse interests of Canadians; and
(10) provides authentic rather than artificial experiences.

In addition to respecting each of the foregoing dimensions, the Tourism Destination Model stresses the strong need to create a holistic and pervasive atmosphere of respect for learning regarding nature and the Rocky Mountain culture. Creating this atmosphere requires the commitment of all Canadians, all organisations and all individuals in the Valley, to the principles and basic tenets of the Tourism Destination Model. The goal is a powerful and memorable experience for visitors; one that is perhaps unique in the world.

Realising the Touchstone Model

In efforts to realise the Touchstone Tourism Destination Model, the Task Force recognised that we must seek to provide visitors with a range of experiences, each of which should in some way contribute to learning, understanding, and a better appreciation of nature and culture in the Banff-Bow Valley. Once again, this is the core of the Tourism Destination Model.

In addition to offering these specific Bow Valley experiences, the promotion of Banff National Park will place an emphasis on attracting visitors who seek these experiences. Despite this focusing of promotional efforts, the Park experience will continue to mean different things to different visitors.

Specific recommendations for realising the new model of tourism in Banff

The Touchstone Tourism Destination Model represents an ambitious and challenging refocusing of Banff National Park's tourism experiences so as to satisfy the interests of all major stakeholders. The successful implementation of the model will require the implementation of a number of recommendations involving specific objectives, actions, initiatives and programmes covering a broad range of areas of responsibility. The 13 major areas where actions to implement the tourism model were recommended are summarised in Ritchie (1999a). Those wishing to comprehend the true depth and scope of the changes proposed to realise the Banff-Bow Valley tourism destination model should examine the total set of recommendations within the context of the complete final report of the Task Force (Banff-Bow Valley Study, 1996).

The transition from today to tomorrow

The Task Force recognised that the Tourism Destination Model cannot be fully realised overnight. At the same time, it hopes that it will become a reality well before the 50-year horizon of the report.

The Task Force also appreciated that refocusing the current tourism model will involve changes to existing facilities and services, and adaptations by the front-line staff on which the tourism sector depends.

These changes will take time and will involve a certain level of investment. The Task Force was optimistic, however, that members of the tourism sector will agree that these changes and these investments will enhance both the attractiveness and the profitability of the destination, while contributing to the maintenance of ecological integrity. The immediate challenge is to manage the transition from today to tomorrow. This will require an ongoing consensus among all stakeholders – a consensus that was only initiated by the IBN process.

Achieving an ongoing consensus

Banff National Park has been many things to many people. While the diversity of its meanings to Canadians will continue to vary, it will become increasingly important that the major groups wishing to see a healthy future for the Park each make a greater effort to contribute to the common vision of Banff National Park as the 'Touchstone for the Canadian Rockies'.

The new vision for Banff National Park as a sustainable national and international destination seeks to attract visitors who are interested in the unique heritage experiences the Park can provide. It also expects visitors to accept and appreciate the many dimensions of the experience which reflect Park values.

At the same time, visitors must recognise that the tourism industry provides a complex and expensive support system. For investors and employees who establish, maintain and operate this support system, there must be the opportunity to realise a fair return for their investment and their efforts. This implies the need to charge appropriate fees.

In addition to acknowledging this need for economic sustainability, visitors must accept their responsibility to maintain the ecological integrity of the region. In return for the privilege of enjoying the many wonders of the Park, they must understand the necessity for restrictions on their behaviour and on their numbers.

In a similar vein, persons who have the privilege of living in the Park must acknowledge their special obligations to sustain the ecological integrity of the Park and create a hospitable environment for Canadians and international visitors.

To summarise, the renewed vision of Banff National Park as a national and international tourism destination is one in which both visitors and residents seek to maintain a destination which provides high quality hospitable experiences and enjoyment to as many citizens as is feasible without endangering the ecological integrity of the region. The pursuit of this ideal requires that each major group recognise its responsibilities to make very special contributions.

The contribution of the environmental movement

While pursuing ecological integrity, those interested in environmental protection must acknowledge both the legitimacy and desirability of tourism in the Banff-Bow Valley. Because this contribution is clearly essential, the environmental community should willingly welcome tourism as an integral partner in preserving ecological integrity in Banff National Park. To offer less is considered hypocritical and unacceptable by those who toil daily in an effort to provide high quality visitor experiences in Banff National Park.

The contribution of Parks Canada

Park managers must recognise the realities of human existence in the Park. Banff National Park cannot be viewed as a virgin territory in which all the ideals of ecological integrity will always be realised. While residency in the Park is clearly inappropriate in today's terms, it is a reality that will continue for the foreseeable future. Similarly, the national transportation corridor is an essential social and economic reality that affects the ideal of ecological integrity. Despite the problems it creates, it must be accommodated. And finally, visitors must not be seen as an imposition to be tolerated. While clearly secondary, enjoyment of national parks is critical to furthering the goal of improved understanding and appreciation of Park values.

The contribution of visitors: Changing our concept of the Banff-Bow Valley

Just as environmentalists must modify their view of tourism, Canadians, and others, must accept, and indeed endorse, the idea that visiting Banff National Park is not like visiting any other destination. To visit Banff National Park is to enhance one's understanding and enjoyment of the especially sensitive characteristics of this unique wonder of nature. Visitors must not arrive with expectations that this ecological jewel can or should provide all the conveniences or range of facilities found in a more traditional destination. Rather, Canadians must willingly embrace the idea that to visit Banff National Park is to visit a very special tourism destination and behave accordingly when doing so.

Contribution of the tourism sector: Changing our expectations of the visitor experience

The tourism sector must endorse this modified view of Banff National Park in its international promotions. It must also demonstrate support in day-to-day operations. Both the industry and visitors must recognise that nature is not free. Pricing policies that place a premium on the nature and quality of experience are fundamental to the new Vision of Banff National Park as a national and international tourism destination.

Some Concluding Observations

The uniqueness of the Banff-Bow Valley Study

From the author's perspective, the Banff-Bow Valley Study represented a once-in-a-generation opportunity to truly explore the many complex relationships that must be managed if we are to create unique, high quality, natural tourism destinations that are sustainable while remaining competitive in a constantly evolving marketplace.

The Round Table process, which served as the primary vehicle for soliciting public and community input, was an approach that is unprecedented in the history of National Parks in Canada – and one that many believe will have a profound effect on how Parks are managed in the future. The use of the Round Table (along with traditional methods) for obtaining public input, represents a shift from consulting the public, to asking them to share in the responsibility for making decisions about their national parks – based on their 'interests' rather than their 'positions' (Fisher & Ury, 1991). This approach to consensus planning has been labelled 'Interest-based Negotiation'. In contrast to a number of other approaches for obtaining public input and consensus that have been reported in the tourism literature (Simmons, 1994; Getz & Jamal, 1994; Haywood, 1988; Ritchie, 1988; Keogh, 1990), the IBN model not only sought consensus from participating stakeholders, it transferred a meaningful percentage of actual decision-making from the Task Force to members of the Round Table.

The inevitable impact of the ballot box; the need for awareness, education, understanding and equity

As environmentalists, tourists, residents, industry investors and operators modify their views of Banff National Park as a sustainable tourism destination for next century, a number of reactions can be expected. Because these reactions will be diverse, broad-scale public support is needed. If the vision is unacceptable to most Canadians, then it will be unrealisable. Should the 'new' Banff National Park frustrate Canadians, become the preserve of the elite, or become inaccessible for financial or other reasons, then the electorate will ultimately redefine Banff National Park's fate. Clearly, a strong, well-articulated vision, that engages all Canadians as to the future of this great national park, is essential to its continued existence.

While the management of Banff National Park certainly requires strong scientific and professional guidance, this guidance must be conveyed in a manner that is sensitive to the interests of all Canadians. In order to maintain the support of all Canadians, we must continue to inform and educate.

In conclusion: Did we get to yes?

While there was considerable scepticism at the beginning as to whether the IBN process would prove any more useful than previous approaches, the Final Report of the Task Force concluded by saying, 'They [*IBN participants*] sought common ground and used it as a foundation for the vision, principles and values that will guide the management of The Banff-Bow Valley into the next century. They looked at issues from each other's point of view, and recommended innovative and practical solutions.' (Banff-Bow Valley Study, 1996).

No doubt, as in any final report of this type, there was an interest and a desire to portray the outcomes in as positive a light as possible. Nevertheless, from the standpoint of both a Task Force member, and a sometimes scholar in tourism studies, it is fair to report that in comparison with other approaches, the process did appear to facilitate the breaking down of strongly held positions, to promote the seeking of positive outcomes, and to enhance a genuine commitment to shared decision-making. Perhaps most important, since the report has been issued, the IBN planning process has definitely appeared to facilitate the implementation of those recommendations that require meaningful compromise on the part of all key stakeholders.

From a strictly tourism perspective, there has been some meaningful action to implement the new tourism model in Banff National Park. While its name has now changed (to the Heritage Tourism Model), most of its premises and initiatives have been adopted. It is particularly rewarding to note the members of the private sector who have taken an important lead in attempting to enhance visitor understanding of the Park within their own establishment. Whether or not this initial enthusiasm is maintained in the light of future economic performance remains to be seen. For the present, it appears that most stakeholders have found common interests that they wish to actively pursue. To the extent that the process of 'Interest Based Negotiation' has helped, it merits serious consideration by those seeking to create collaborative relationships within environmentally sensitive regions.

The author wishes to express his sincere appreciation to fellow members of the Banff-Bow Valley Study Task Force for their contributions, commitment, and collegiality throughout the study process. Other Task Force members were Dr Robert Page (Chair, The University of Calgary), Dr Suzanne Bayley (University of Alberta), Mr Douglas Cook (Taurscale Consultants Ltd) and Mr Jeffrey Green (AXYS Environmental Consulting Ltd). Appreciation is also extended to Mr Doug Hodgins (Executive Director) and to other members of the Secretariat that provided invaluable support to the Task Force, to Mr Craig Darling (Facilitator for the Study Round Table), and very especially to all participants in the Banff-Bow Valley Study, on which this paper is primarily based.

Correspondence

Any correspondence should be directed to Professor J.R. Brent Ritchie, Faculty of Management, University of Calgary, Calgary, Alberta, Canada T2N 1N4 (britchie@mgmt.ucalgary.ca).

References

Banff-Bow Valley Study (1996) *Banff-Bow Valley: At The Crossroads*. Technical report of The Banff-Bow Valley Task Force (Robert Page, Suzanne Bayley, J. Douglas Cook, Jeffrey E. Green, and J.R. Brent Ritchie). Prepared for the Honourable Sheila Copps, Minister of Canadian Heritage, Ottawa, Ontario.

Burns, P. and Holden, A. (1995) *Tourism: A New Perspective*. Prentice Hall: New York.

Cater, E. and Lowman, G. (1994) *Ecotourism: A Sustainable Option?* New York: John Wiley.

Chrislip, D.D. and Larson, C.E. (1994) *Collaborative Leadership: How Citizens and Civic Leaders Can Make a Difference*. San Francisco: Jossey-Bass.

Delbecq, A.L. and Van de Ven, A.H. (1971) A group process model for problem identification and program planning. *Journal of Applied Behavioral Science* 7 (4), 466–492.

Fisher, R. and Ury, W. (1991) *Getting to YES: Negotiating Agreement Without Giving In* (2nd edn). New York: Penguin Books USA.

Getz, D. and Jamal, T.B. (1994) The environment – community symbiosis: A case for collaborative tourism planning. *Journal of Sustainable Tourism* 2 (3), 152–173.

Gray, B. (1989) *Collaborating: Finding Common Ground for Multi Party Problems*. San Francisco, CA: Jossey-Bass.

Hawkins, D.E., Ritchie, J.R.B., Go, F. and Frechtling, D. (1991) *Global Tourism Policy Issues for the 1990s Special Feature in World Travel and Tourism Review*. Wallingford: CAB International.

Haywood, M.K. (1988) Responsible and responsive tourism planning in the community. *Tourism Management* 9 (2), 105–118.

Himmelman, A.T. (1992) *Communities Working Collaboratively for a Change*. Minneapolis, MN: Himmelman Consulting Group.

Huxham, C. (1996) *Creating Collaborative Advantage*. Thousand Oaks, CA: Sage Publications.

Jamal, T.B. and Getz, D. (1995) Collaboration theory and community tourism planning. *Annals of Tourism Research* 22 (1), 186–204.

Johnson, D.W. and Johnson, F.P. (1987) *Joining Together, Group Theory and Gray Skills* (3rd edn). Englewood Cliffs, NJ: Prentice-Hall.

Keogh, B. (1990) Public participation in community tourism planning. *Annals of Tourism Research* 17, 449–465.

Lindberg, K. and Hawkins, D.E. (1993) *Ecotourism: A Guide for Planners and Managers*. North Bennington, VT: The Ecotourism Society.

Local Agenda 21 (1992) *Summit on the Environment and Economic Development*. Rio de Janiero.

McIntyre, G., Hetherington, A. and Inskeep, E. (1993) *Sustainable Tourism Development: Guide for Local Planners*. Madrid: World Tourism Organization.

Nelson, J.G., Butler, R. and Wall, G. (1992) *Tourism and Sustainable Development: Monitoring, Planning, Managing*. Heritage Resources Centre Joint Publication, No. 1. University of Waterloo, Ontario.

Pearce, P.L., Moscardo, G. and Ross, G.F. (1996) *Tourism Community Relationships*. New York: Pergamon.

Poon, A. (1993) *Tourism, Technology and Competitive Strategies*. Wallingford: CAB International.

Potapchuk, W.R. and Polk, C.G. (1993) *Building the Collaborative Community*. Washington, DC: National Institute for Dispute Resolution.

Ritchie, J.R.B. (1985) The Nominal Group Technique – An approach to consensus policy formulation in tourism. *Tourism Management* 6 (2), 82–94.

Ritchie, J.R.B. (1988) Consensus policy formulation in tourism – measuring resident views via survey research. *Tourism Management* 9 (3), 199–212.

Ritchie, J.R.B. (1992) New realities, new horizons: Leisure tourism and society in the third millennium. *The American Express Annual Review of Travel* (pp. 11–26). New York: American Express Travel Related Services Company.

Ritchie, J.R.B. (1998) Managing the human presence in ecologically sensitive tourism destinations: Insights from the Banff-Bow Valley Study. *Journal of Sustainable Tourism* 6 (4), 293–313.

Ritchie, J.R.B. (1999a) Policy formulation at the tourism/environment interface: Insights and recommendations from the Banff-Bow Valley Study. *Journal of Travel Research* 38 (2), 100–110.

Ritchie, J.R.B. (1999b) Crafting a value-driven vision for a national tourism treasure. *Tourism Management* 20 (3), 273–282.

Simpson, A.M. (1995) An analysis of appropriate activities assessment mechanism in protected areas. Master's thesis, School of Resource and Environmental Management, University of Waterloo.

Rohter, I. (1992) *A Green Hawai'i: Sourcebook for Development Alternatives*. Honolulu, Hawai'i: Kā Kāne O Ka Malo Press.

Simmons, D.G. (1994) Community participation in tourism planning. *Tourism Management* 15 (2), (98–108).

Appendix: Selected examples of the formal interest statements of various sectors participating in the Banff-Bow Valley Study Process of 'Interest Based Negotiation' process[1]

(a) Interests of the Banff-Bow Valley Task Force Sector

Highest Priority

- to ensure that the Task Force supports the involvement of individuals, organisations, communities and Canadians in the Study;
- to provide a final report to the Minister of Canadian Heritage in June, 1996;
- to fulfil its obligations as set out in the Terms of Reference in such a way that builds support for a long-term vision and strategy among Valley constituents that is acceptable to and will be supported by Canadian taxpayers;
- to fulfil its obligations within its designated budget;
- to respect the geographic scope of its study;
- to work in collaboration with the constituency of Banff National Park and the Banff-Bow Valley;
- to respect the Statutory obligation of Parks Canada as set out in the National Parks Act, and other national and international agreements;
- to respect the different values and perspectives of the participants while facilitating a common, task-oriented agenda;
- to work effectively with the Round Table without imposing on the Table or compromising the Task Force's mandate, independence and impartiality;
- to put in place a management structure that can assist and participate in the implementation of the recommendations;
- to provide guidance in integration of environmental, social and economic interests.

In addition

- to support a shared decision-making approach to achieve its goals in keeping with the widely accepted principles of Interest Based Negotiation;

- to make participants aware of the goals, opportunities and challenges associated with a shared decision-making approach to land use planning;
- to ensure that all affected interests have an opportunity to be heard and to 'own' the decisions made;
- to respect and response to the financial and other constraints faced by participants;
- to acknowledge the commitment demonstrated by all participants;
- to deliver to the Minister and the public a consensus set of recommendations generated by the participants;
- to reflect the varying legitimate roles of the Banff-Bow Valley in a way that respects the National Park goals of achieving and maintaining ecological integrity while also achieving commemorative integrity and economic vitality;
- to leave in place a framework to resolve future issues through interest based negotiations;
- to support the development of 'sustainable' relationships among participants which will allow them to work together to accommodate the interests of all;
- being inclusive, open and transparent in fulfilling our task mandate and in delivering support for the Round Table negotiation process;
- to encourage the participants to make optimal use of the mediator, facilitators and other support services in order to help realise an interest-based outcome;
- to learn from the process, as a basis for future initiatives undertaken by Parks Canada or other protected areas management agencies;
- to disseminate its knowledge from this process as widely as possible so that others may learn from the experience.

(b) Park Users Sector

Our interests are:

- to protect a region where it is possible to experience a sense, or an appreciation, of wilderness;
- to ensure that the type of wilderness we desire is as near as possible to its original natural state;
- to understand our impacts on the wilderness areas, and agree to curtail our activities if we are spoiling the experience of wilderness – we err on the side of preservation;
- recognising that outdoor recreation in wilderness areas is fundamental to our spiritual health, to ensure that opportunities remain for a broad range of appropriate activities;
- to ensure The Banff-Bow Valley is not a sacrifice zone – the wilderness would be near to where we live;
- to ensure access to the wilderness is not rationed on the basis of who has money;
- to ensure that appropriate activities are available to disabled persons;

- to ensure types and levels of activities that are not appropriate to a wilderness area and that will spoil the experience of wilderness for others are curtailed. An 'appropriateness' standard is necessary to govern/evaluate and limit activities within the Banff-Bow Valley;
- that the telling of the history of the exploration of the wilderness areas of the Banff-Bow Valley enriches the experience of the modern- day explorer (visitor);
- that the national transportation corridor is valued as a means of access to the Banff-Bow Valley. In managing, maintaining, and planning transportation corridors through the Banff-Bow Valley, the primary consideration should be environmental protection, followed closely by public safety;
- that a healthy and stable community is maintained. Such a community is better able to provide basic services to support our visits to the Banff-Bow Valley, and also enriches our experience;
- that fair, open and consistent regulation of the activities within the Banff-Bow Valley ensures that all those who derive a benefit from The Banff-Bow Valley pay their fair share of the cost of maintaining the amenities of the Banff-Bow Valley.

(c) Local/regional environment sector

Our sector has not assigned priorities to our interests since we believe they all are important. Our principle interests in the Banff-Bow Valley are that the following conditions prevail:

- respect for ecological integrity, its maintenance, and its restoration where necessary;
- protection of biological diversity – our definition of sustainability includes all species;
- the National Parks Act and Policy are understood, accepted, and applied in a consistent manner;
- Park management adheres to its central mandate to maintain ecological integrity while allowing appropriate human use without impairment;
- decisions in national parks are free of political interference and not subject to political whims;
- decision-makers are qualified to understand, interpret and implement their mandate;
- the Bow Valley and Banff National Park are managed as part of the protected core of a larger ecosystem;
- the Bow Valley is recognised as the ecological heart of the park;
- decisions in national parks reflect the national public interest;
- the mountains are seen as living landscapes, not merely scenery;
- genuine long-term thinking and planning replaces short-term political expediency;
- environmental assessment is fully integrated at the front end of decision-making as an independent tool, free from manipulation;
- decision-making errs on the side of environmental protection in the face of uncertainty with respect to potential impacts;

- the vital role of national parks as protected areas is recognised in the context of a diminishing natural land base world wide;
- local communities embrace their responsibilities as stewards of the park and their part of the Bow Valley;
- the quality of the visitor experience as it relates to nature (national park values) is much more important than the quantity of visitors;
- education leads to a deeper understanding and awareness of national (natural) park values, which translates to a greater caring for the life of the Planet.

(d) Tourist sector

The principal interests of our Sector can be summarised as follows:

- effective long term protection of the Park's natural resources in accordance with the general principles espoused by the National Parks Act is essential;
- a balance must be struck between the demand to use the Park and the need to ensure these protected areas be preserved unimpaired for the enjoyment of future generations;
- the profile and prestige of Banff and the Park as a world class/renowned destination resort must be maintained and promoted;
- traditional recreation activities within the Park should be permitted to continue and allowed to prosper;
- a distinction must be made between the land use issues facing the Town of Banff and the balance between protection and enjoyment needed for the balance of the Park. The Bow Valley use of the Park is not subject to the same pressures as Banff for these controls. Banff is not representative of the Park and vice versa. There are controls, plans and vision statements in place for the Town of Banff including the Land Use Bylaw, Architectural Controls and the Town Plan, all which have already received public input and have been approved by the Minister;
- the spirit of cooperation and partnership that has been fostered between parks and management and the commercial tourism industry should continue to be fostered;
- the fact of the Park containing two national transportation corridors and its historical development as a world class destination resort must be recognised in any vision or management plan that is adopted;
- the quality and planned activities in the areas surrounding the Park should be considered and encouragement should be given to proposals that would be mutually beneficial to the interests of protection and enjoyment; and
- increasing demands on the government's fiscal resources can no longer be relied on and other sources of funding must be found to ensure a positive future for the Park.

Health and safety:

- good emergency service coverage throughout the Bow Valley;
- a safe Trans Canada highway;

- minimise wildlife hazard;
- a safe railway – we want to ensure well-planned railway crossings and good protection from and prevention of disasters such as toxic spills;
- safe dams – we are concerned about the status of the many dams in our area – how well they are maintained, whether they are safe.

Long-term vision:

- to aid other Round Table participants in understanding the municipal sector's long-term vision, we have attached the approved vision statements of the Town of Canmore, the Town of Banff, and the MD of Bighorn.

(e) Municipal sector

Within our steering committee, we have agreed that our sector shares the following interests:

Political

- to convince the provinces to join the Round Table – we believe that the work of the Table will be easier to do and to implement if the Provinces are full members of the discussion;
- authority must go with responsibility – municipalities and similar structures within the national park cannot carry out the responsibilities they are given unless they have typical municipal authority as well;
- democratic representation – whether people live inside or outside the national park, they need to be able to exercise a meaningful vote in local issues;
- conservation buffer – neighbouring municipalities have a problem with being the place where activities that are not allowed in National Park 'spill over'. They would rather extend some of the national park values and qualities into their jurisdictions;
- continued and better cooperation between jurisdictions – we want to encourage more efficient and effective operation through working together, and identify and eliminate procedural barriers to doing so;
- efficient/effective use of federal tax dollars – we are at the bottom of the 'pass the buck' downloading. Therefore, we want to be sure that Round Table decisions are cost-conscious;
- consistency in federal regulations and enforcement – for our long-term planning and that of all residents, we need to know that a decision made in one place or time will be reasonably consistent with a decision made in another.

Economic

- year-round economic viability for all communities – several of our communities experience major economic swings during the year. This has a negative effect on our residents and our ability to maintain stable communities;
- don't kill the goose – all of our communities take their economic livelihoods from the beauty of our natural surroundings. We want to make sure that those surroundings are maintained;

- utilities available – we have a responsibility to maintain basic power, water, gas, and sewer services to our communities;
- Trans Canada and Highway 93 – major economic importance – keeping these routes accessible is fundamental to our economic survival;
- improve public relations image – we believe that recent news coverage has hurt our image – we want to improve that image;
- fair park fees and user fees – all residents in the area have an interest in seeing equitable and reasonable fees.

Environmental

- air quality – we are concerned about the maintenance of our present good air quality and perceive the major potential threats as coming from the changes at Exshaw;
- water quality – we have a responsibility to leave the Bow River water quality as good downstream of our communities as it is upstream. We are also concerned about maintenance of good water quality in the underground system that supplies wells;
- wildlife corridors (based on solid science) – we want to protect wildlife corridors through good planning practices, but we need to know that the information provided is reliable;
- enhance National Park experience for residents and visitors – we want people who come here and live here to know that they're in a national park – not just because of the signs, but because the whole surroundings and quality of life reflect that status.

Social

- preservation of community values – all of our communities are in danger of being obliterated by the juggernaut of the mass tourism that supports us all. We want to maintain a sense of community in the midst of destination resorts;
- sustainable community / social viability – we want our communities to continue to be home to families, young people, seniors – the whole normal demographic range. We think that this mix is what gives any community its social framework and social support;
- preserve small town and rural character – in appearance, safety and friendliness, we want our communities to continue to be like small towns, even when their visitor population vastly exceeds their resident population;
- affordable housing – we want to explore every option that will help guarantee the supply of affordable housing in our communities;
- fair land rent/taxes – we think that people in a national park should still pay equitable and reasonable costs for services, whether those costs are in the form of taxes, land rent, or some mix of the two.

(f) National Environmental Sector

We are interested/believe in the following:

- that the management of Banff, as Canada's oldest and most famous national park, has implications for Canada's entire national park and protected area system, Canada's sustainable development commitments and other commitments like the World Heritage Convention and the Biodiversity Convention agreed to in Rio de Janeiro;

- in Banff National Park being managed as a national park and World Heritage Site;
- national parks are first and foremost protected areas where ecological processes are maintained and people come to experience nature – the Angus Reid Poll of 1994 confirms that the vast majority of Canadians share this view;
- certain activities are appropriate and others are inappropriate to a national park experience. Those activities that are nature based, or which support nature based activities, are appropriate as long as they do not impair nature's function. We recognise Banff has a history of a townsite and of some fixed tourist development including ski hills;
- the level of development that existed in 1980 reflected that history and was acceptable. We believe things have gotten seriously out of hand since than. We believe the Government of Canada has failed in its duty to the Canadian people to maintain Banff National Park unimpaired for future generations and to maintain its ecological integrity;
- that Banff National Park is being exploited for commercial tourism pursuits that are not nature-based (e.g. golf courses, mini golf, shopping for non-essential services, second residence housing). Opportunities for wilderness experiences in the Bow Valley are compromised even in the backcountry due to permanent horse camps, lodge developments and road and railway noise;
- the Bow Valley contains an important part of the montane eco- region that is critical to the ecology of the central Canadian Rockies, not just Banff National Park. Major ecological corridors should be restored by closing and rehabilitating areas;
- that the viability of large mammal populations (e.g. moose, grizzly, and black bear) is in serious jeopardy in the Bow Valley even though the Valley provides critical habitat. We believe this is due to habitat fragmentation through human development and road and railway kills. We also believe that native fish species should be restored;
- Banff and adjoining parks should be a protected core surrounded by carefully managed buffer zones with connecting wildlife corridors extending north to British Columbia's Northern Rockies and south to the Crown of the Continent ecosystem as part of a Yellowstone to Yukon Biodiversity strategy (see attached article);
- the highways and railways that traverse the park are already a major ecological problem that must be mitigated. We are not yet persuaded that twinning the Trans Canada highway is appropriate, although if some of the problems created by the first phase were fixed, and good solutions found for the next phase, we might be persuaded;
- the Canadian Rockies are the last great, wild mountain range on earth – the Alps have been seriously degraded by tourism development; the Andes are

heavily inhabited and developed; the Himalayas are heavily populated and are being denuded of their forest cover;

- our vision is of Banff National Park as a centrepiece in one of the last places on earth where wild nature can be experienced while ecological processes continue unimpaired.

(g) Commercial Visitors Services Sector

Political

- have guidelines in place that Parks can administer without the need for lobby group interference. Ideally business should be able to develop their business as changes occur in the marketplace. A set of agreed upon guidelines would certainly be a great benefit for everyone;
- our sector would like to see Parks focus their efforts on interpretation, preservation, maintenance, and education with minimal time spent on administration. We encourage the privatisation of as many Park assets (e.g. pools, campgrounds, entrance gates, etc.) in order that Parks manpower can be allocated to areas of greater importance.

Economic

- as it is vital that Parks generate appropriate levels of revenue to maintain and develop programs, it is also essential that business be able to maintain economic viability by upgrading and improving its operations;
- our sector believes that in order to be able to support the Round Table recommendations, a series of user fees must be implemented. Our feeling is we presently give the National Park experience away at little or no charge. Anyone who enters the Park is a user and should be willing to pay for the experience. Our suggested user fees are as follows:
  - $100/truck
  - $200/tour bus
  - $30/auto (summer)
  - $10/auto (winter)
  - $150 annual auto and family pass
  - $100 seven day vehicle and auto pass
  - $2/rail car
  - Backcountry fees $20/person/night
- the money generated from vehicle and person admittance fees would be used for:
  - educating all visitors who use the Park, whether at an entrance orientation centre, guided hikes, information areas. Emphasis will be placed on the Park's history, where we were in 1995, and where we expect to be in the future;
  - the implementation of a wildlife program that is the most advanced of its kind
  - rehabilitation of a historical balance of nature
  - rehabilitation of lakes and streams

- the development of wildlife corridors that work – if we need over-passes/underpasses that cross the highway or railway, we will develop ones that will set a world standard;
- increased controlled burns or other recommended methods of creating healthy new forests.

Environmental/Educational

- our sector supports the pursuit towards clean water through conservation and efficient sewage treatment;
- we support the desire to develop an effective plan that sees animal populations such as the moose and grizzly brought back to historic levels;
- we support the sectioning of the Park into user zones – high use (service zone – Banff, Front country), medium use, low use, and no use;
- our sector would support a program whereby all visitors would go through an orientation program before they entered the Park;
- our sector would support any reasonable deterrent that would effectively reduce 'road kill';
- we support the philosophy of controlled burns – if they have proven effective should the frequency be increased;
- we believe the elk population in and around Banff is adversely affecting other animal populations – we would like to see the populations reduced and maintain properly each year thereafter;
- our sector would recommend that bus diesel motors be turned off when buses are not in motion.

Social

- our sector would like to see Banff residents develop a sense of pride about its vision of the future – we feel that our town has unlimited potential and can become a world leader in terms of how a town can be an integral park of a National park that has its roots based in recreation, education, and preservation;
- proper housing for all workers and residents is essential – where possible, more land should be made available for housing – another alternative would be to allow for higher density in some areas.

Health and Safety

- our sector encourages the development of good emergency coverage throughout the Bow Valley;
- we encourage the twinning of the highway if it is the best method of reducing accidents and road kill. As an alternative, we would also support a reduction in speed limited, or using the 1A highway as a route for motor-homes and trailers (slower traffic), and highway 1 for trucks and cars;
- proper sewage treatment for all public facilities in the Park.

Summary

- the Commercial Visitors Service Sector's prime interest is to maintain the ability to adapt its business to changes in the marketplace. Replacing an old building, lift system, staff house, etc., according to guidelines that encourage conservation, tasteful aesthetics, and user friendliness are essential if we are to offer effective service to Park visitors. We believe the existing guidelines currently in force, inside and outside the Town, are reasonable and fair and would like to be able to plan future investments knowing they will not change or be subjected to outside interference;

- with an eye to the future, our sector believes that all Park visitors should leave with the feeling that their expectations have been exceeded – whether it is the beautiful ski hill lodges, the innovative wildlife overpasses, the recycling and composting programs, the orientation and education programs, the great service and meals in a restaurant, the hiking programs, or the rehabilitation programs, Banff National Park should be a world leader. By being innovative, cost-effective and having all visitors leave feeling their expectations have been exceeded, the Banff-Bow Valley will have a bright future.

Note to Appendix

1. *Source*: Extracted summaries from Sector Interest Statements, as submitted to BBV Study Round Table.

4. Collaboration on Tourism Policy Making: Environmental and Commercial Sustainability on Bonaire, NA

Steven Parker
Department of Political Science, University of Nevada, USA

This paper applies Gray's model of collaboration to deliberations concerning sustainable tourism on The Island Territory of Bonaire in the Caribbean. It examines stakeholder logic and strategy in attempting to coordinate three policy areas during the period 1993–98: those relating to hotel-room inventory, airline capacity and water pollution abatement. Relying on in-depth interviews with key participants, the paper analyses how Bonaire stakeholders attempted to pursue both economic and ecological approaches to sustainability by combining these three. It also examines why this effort has not yet been successful, an examination that emphasises a decline in tourist demand and an approach to collaboration that was unsystematic and lacking in institutionalised structure. Implications for collaboration theory include the findings that there is vulnerability in informal modes of organisation and that progress from one stage of deliberation to the next does not necessarily require closure at the earlier stage. Implications for sustainable tourism include the confirmation of hypotheses concerning the critical role played by economies of scale and policy interdependence.

Introduction

Because of its inherent complexity and multi-dimensional nature, the quest for sustainable tourism provides a singular example of what students of collaboration term a 'problem domain' (Getz & Jamal, 1994), a system-level challenge composed of numerous parts over which no single organisation or societal-sector has complete authority. Multiple stakeholders are involved with the concept yet none has the breadth of knowledge, power or legitimacy to institute the required system-wide solutions. Around the world, participants in the search for sustainable tourism include governments, NGOs, tour operators, hoteliers and conservation officials to mention only the most obvious roles. Each of these can make decisions affecting part of the equation but the breadth of control required by the nature of the problem is beyond the grasp of each, acting individually. Thus, the value of collaboration, defined by Wood and Gray (1991: 146) as what

> occurs when a group of autonomous stakeholders of a problem domain engage in an interactive process, using shared rules, norms and structures to act or decide on issues related to that domain. (Wood & Gray, 1991: 146)

According to Waddock (1989) the issues in the problem domain are more likely to be effectively dealt with by collaboration and the formation of social partnerships than by an approach emphasising confrontation and the imposition of solutions from above. While sustainability is a collaborative goal for many tourism locations, small destinations like Bonaire that depend on a single resource, are particularly in need of attention to it.

As a destination's volume of tourism grows, the difficulties experienced will frequently evolve from being small, discrete problems (congestion, air pollution, inflation, etc.) to being single but multi-dimensional and interdependent problem domains. When a domain level has been reached it is no longer possible for individual organisations to act in isolation, for each lacks the authority and ability required for concerted action. In a tourism context this would mean that as a destination grows, problems of crime and pollution, inflation and native alienation multiply and become highly salient. As this occurs, government leaders, resource planners and entrepreneurs are each unable to deal with the syndrome as long as they all continue to act in isolation. That is because it has become a domain-level problem that can only be addressed by some form of interorganisational collaboration.

Purpose and Methodology

Because of the importance of this subject it is the purpose of the current study to apply collaboration theory to a single case study in an attempt to shed some empirical light on its relevance and utility. While numerous theoretical interpretations are available (McCann, 1983; Trist, 1983; Logsdon, 1991), we will rely on the work of Barbara Gray (1985, 1989), applying her process model to decision-making on The Island Territory of Bonaire in The Netherlands Antilles. The period under investigation covered the years 1993–1998. Gray's paradigm postulates the existence of three phases in the collaborative process and examines the dynamics involved as participants move from one stage to the next. The three phases are: (1) problem-setting in which the nature of the challenge is diagnosed, (2) direction-setting wherein some type of policy consensus is achieved and (3) structuring which is concerned primarily with implementation and programming.

In point of fact, the model applied here will be a truncated one, since Bonaire has not yet dealt effectively with Phase 3. The reasons for this shortcoming will be discussed in the article's concluding section. Until then we will examine the dynamics of the first two phases which may be dated as follows: (1) problem-setting: 1993–94 and (2) direction setting: 1995–96. Our analysis will show that the Structuring phase which might have been the focus of 1997 and 1998 fell victim instead to an economic reversal and to a series of ongoing inefficiencies in the collaborative process, itself. Another focus of this study will be on the ways in which specific policies were used during the middle years to generate consensus. In fact, one of the most interesting findings of this project is that the creation of agreement on specific policies during Phase 2 may be more useful than generating an abstract consensus at Phase 1. To the extent that this finding is generalisable, it has direct implications for how collaboration might be conducted and analysed at other tourism destinations.

Field research for the study was carried out in person on the island of Bonaire during the summer of 1997 and subsequently through extended mail and telephone interviews in 1998 and 1999. Key decision-makers on the island were initially identified by their formal positions (protected-area managers, tourism promotion officers, etc.) and then each person interviewed was asked to nominate others for inclusion in the survey process. This reputational, or referral, methodology eventually resulted in the identification of 66 individuals; 48 of these were either interviewed in depth or administered a brief questionnaire. All shared a connection with tourism: government decision-makers, hoteliers, tour operators, NGO officers, resource managers, etc. Interviews and questionnaires sought responses of two types:

- closed-ended: assessing opinions and degrees of consensus on particular issues, and
- open-ended: eliciting information on goals, processes, problems, etc.

Many of the closed-ended items asked for respondent opinions on issues, leaders and problems. Others requested that they rank-order numerous options on a list or make some type of forced-choice selection. The findings of these inquiries will be utilised frequently later because they provide insight into the perceptions of key stakeholders, and it is perceptions that drive, or inhibit, a social process like collaboration.

Tourism on Bonaire

Along with Aruba and Curacao, Bonaire is still popularly referred to as one of the 'ABC Islands'. Formally, it is part of a union with Curacao, St Maarten, St Eustatius and Saba known as The Netherlands Antilles (NA), an autonomous part of The Kingdom of the Netherlands. Aruba holds a separate status. Like many other locations in the Caribbean, The Island Territory of Bonaire has moved decisively in the direction of tourism in recent years. The 1986 figure of 25,000 visitors rose to 37,000 by 1990 and to 62,000 by 1998. For years, increasing numbers of travellers, primarily from the United States and Europe, have been journeying to this tiny desert island in the southeast Caribbean, approximately 50 miles from the coast of Venezuela, to experience its famous marine-tourism attractions (see Figure 1).

The waters surrounding this 112 square-mile dive mecca are home to an extensive system of coral reefs, and island leaders have followed a very conscious strategy of marketing this natural resource. Serving the visiting SCUBA divers, snorklers, yachtsmen and sunlovers has become the island's major source of income and employment, generating US$64m in receipts in 1996 and supporting approximately 2100 jobs (Tourism Planning and Research Associates, 1997). The proportionate size of the industry is emphasised when one considers the fact that Bonaire's total population is only 15,000. Of course, another reason for the primacy of tourism is quite simply the lack of other economic options. No agricultural sector has ever developed in the region's arid climate and, with the exception of salt, neither have mineral extraction nor manufacturing, due to the paucity of natural resources and the relatively high cost of energy.

Against such a background, the genesis of tourism on the island was ironic, for Bonaire's first hotel, which opened in 1952, was a renovated structure that had been part of a Second World War internment camp. During the 1940s the island had housed a detention centre for approximately 500 German nationals who lived in The Antilles and who were considered to be security risks. Seven years after the cessation of hostilities, a renovated version of one of the buildings was opened for guests of a different sort. From this modest start, tourism has grown to become Bonaire's primary industry.

Because of the island's natural assets, this industry was able to establish a strong dive-tourism niche by the mid-1960s, but with growth came recognition

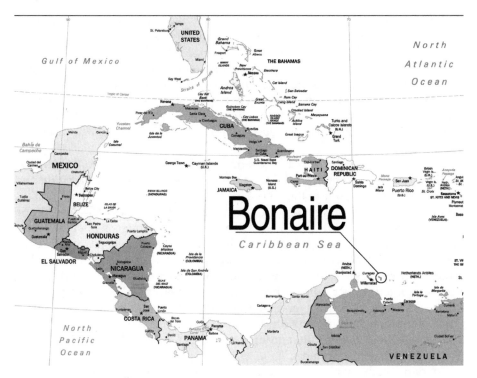

Figure 1 Location of Bonaire

of the need for management. The early days of unregulated marine tourism on Bonaire impacted the reefs heavily with spearfishing, with anchor damage to corals and with siltation caused by on-shore development. As these problems became evident, a coalition of local leaders together with The World Wildlife Fund succeeded in convincing Holland and the Antillean Government to intervene. The result was the creation of the Bonaire Marine Park (BMP) in 1979. Although the Park was funded initially by a Dutch grant, today it is self-supporting with its operating income being generated by the proceeds from a US$10 annual user fee collected from all divers. BMP's jurisdiction covers all of the waters surrounding the island from the high-water mark to a depth of 200 feet. Within these boundaries it is responsible for enforcement of Bonaire's Marine Environment Ordinance, which created a management regime of the type that Orams (1999) calls a 'no take' marine protected area. Day-to-day management of the Park was vested in an NGO known as STINAPA. This latter name is a Dutch acronym denoting The Netherlands Antilles National Parks Foundation.

In addition to STINAPA and BMP, several other organisations have played significant roles in the development of tourism on Bonaire and in the collaborative activity that will be examined below. One of these is the elected Island Government which relies heavily on the industry as a source of revenue (Fletcher, 1997), but which has intermittently pursued policies to limit its growth, as well. Another is a public corporation known as the Tourism Corporation of Bonaire (TCB). Technically an autonomous agency, it relies on both the public and private sectors for support of its main activities: tourism planning, monitoring and promotion. An additional stakeholder is the Bonaire Hotel and Tourism Association (BONHATA). With approximately 100 members drawn from the island's hotels, restaurants and other retail enterprises, it has served as the industry's main advocate since 1988 when it was formed to oppose an increase in public utility rates. Serving as a spokesman for the island's commercial interests, it pursues many of the same types of promotional activities that King (1997) described in Fiji and Queensland, Australia. These will be discussed later.

A related industry group is The Council of Underwater Resort Operators (CURO). The 12 members of CURO are the excursion operators who transport divers and snorklers out to the reefs each day. Because they are the immediate users of the reef, they have an enormous interest in the policies of STINAPA and in the operations of BMP managers. Island law gives them considerable influence with both of these entities since it has made them the user-fee collection agents for the Park. Finally, there is a group of environmental stakeholders largely drawn together by their focus on resource management and conservation: appointed, career officials housed in the government's Planning Department and the leaders of several environmental NGOs such as Friends of the Earth, Tene Bonaire Limpe (Keep Bonaire Clean) and the Save Klein Bonaire Foundation. In 1999 these latter groups created an association to coordinate their activities: The Nature Alliance.

Fundamentally, of course, there are two very different *raisons d'être* for these various organisations and constellations of interest: the promotion of tourism, on the one hand, and the promotion of conservation, on the other. In his classic analysis of this subject, Gerardo Budowski (1976) postulated three possible modes of interaction between tourism and conservation: coexistence, conflict and symbiosis. He reasoned that coexistence would be quite widespread in the early days of a country's experience with tourism, and this definitely was the case in Bonaire. In addition to the explanatory factors which he originally cited, there are numerous other reasons for the accuracy of this generalisation. In 'the early days' a great deal of growth can take place before carrying-capacity problems become obvious to decision makers (Liddle, 1997). Tourism operators, conservation officials and others can afford to minimise their interactions because initially their levels of perceived mutual threat and mutual interdependence are low. This was true of Bonaire in the 1960s and early 1970s when it was the members of CURO who managed both their businesses and the health of the reefs.

In addition, during this phase the role of government is frequently one of brokerage rather than of planning and regulation. While it is the authority mediating between two other stakeholders, these two participants are engaged in a non-zero-sum game, and thus a win for one side does not yet signal a loss for the other. Resources are more plentiful during the coexistence period. Tourism externalities are relatively small, or seem to be (Miezkowski, 1995) and thus calls for government regulatory action are minimal. Officials fortunate enough to be in office during such times have a growing number of public-sector jobs to fill and subsidies to dispense (Elliott, 1987). The industry tends to be decentralised and hard decisions about waste and resource loss are not yet on the public agenda (Elliott, 1983). Accordingly, as it was on Bonaire, the perceived need for collaboration is low.

However, as the number of tourist arrivals begins to accelerate, noticeable environmental degradation frequently sets in as does host-community disenchantment or opposition (Nash, 1989), a syndrome to which Bonaire was not immune. Ecological and social limits may soon be reached and easy coexistence is then replaced by growing conflict and resentment. At this point, the role of government may shift from brokerage to that of either planner or guardian of the status quo (Smith, 1992). The externalities generated during this phase gradually become unacceptable to resource managers and various forms of mitigation are introduced. This, of course, is a juncture at which collaboration may become a much more valued tool, as also happened on Bonaire.

Following the logic of Butler's (1980) model of a tourist area cycle, we would expect that the third mode of tourism/conservation interaction, symbiosis, would be quite rare, and that even when it occurs that it would not last indefinitely. When symbiosis does occur, however, the presence and growth of tourism can generate extra income that may be utilised for conservation purposes (Driml & Common, 1995). If this happens, then the simultaneous pursuit of both tourism and conservation may help to assure the sustainability of both the industry and the resource base on which it depends. It will be argued later that while this has not yet happened on Bonaire, the collaborative processes used on the island during the mid-1990s did orient the stakeholders in that direction.

Phase 1 – Problem-Setting

The first phase in Gray's collaboration model is termed problem-setting, and on Bonaire this phase covered the years 1993–94. Problem-setting involves the identification and acceptance of a domain's stakeholders by each other. As such, it rests on a mutual recognition of legitimacy; the idea that each participant has real concerns and interests and a right to be heard. More importantly, it also involves their search to define and acknowledge the common problems that impact them all. It is a phase that is most fundamentally about values, for as participants engage in their deliberations each normally has some set of preferred outcomes in mind, whether those emphasise the status quo or a major change in it. In a developmental, island context such value choices ultimately concern not only income, but basic questions of equity, as well (Beller, 1990).

With a problem domain as complex as sustainable tourism, an observation by Trist (1983) is especially relevant. Specifically, he noted that until the problem-setting phase has been resolved, none or few of the participants will normally be aware of the true dimensions of the domain. Instead, the attention of most will remain limited to their particular parts of it. To begin to determine whether this was the case on Bonaire, we asked interviewees to identify what they saw as the 'single biggest problem facing tourism on this island during the 1990s'. A summary of responses is presented in Table 1.

While there is a certain diversity to the items on the list, it is quite clear that when the 'DK/NAs' are eliminated all of the responses may be placed in either of two opposing categories of diagnosis:

Table 1 Biggest tourism problem

Problem	Frequency	Percentage
Too few visitors/low occupancy	8	17
Air service	7	15
People spend too little	5	10
Government taxes too high	4	8
Condition of the reef	6	13
Crime rate	6	13
Traffic/pace/congestion	4	8
Too many tourists	3	6
Don't know/NA/other	5	10
Total	48	100%

(1) those relating to visitor/business volume and the need to increase it – the first
      four lines of Table 1 (56%); or
(2) those relating to resource/social damage and the need to mitigate it – the next
      four lines of Table 1 (44%).

The first focuses on the sustainability of business and the second on the
sustainability of both the physical and social environments.

Of course, finding that such a bipolar distribution of opinion existed on
Bonaire is consistent with treatment of this subject in the literature. For example,
Jenkins (1980) assesses tourism policies in developing countries and asserts the
near inevitability of tension between conservation and tourism interests. Profitability is certainly the most significant criterion in private-investment decision-making while public policy choices may include other factors: resource
protection, attention to social and cultural impacts, etc. For businessmen in the
tourism industry, the concept of sustainability must ultimately involve
long-term earnings for no business can continue indefinitely if this concern is
ignored (McKercher, 1993). Deliberations based on economic sustainability will,
of course, emphasise such factors as return on investment, preservation of capital
and the generation of sufficient income for owners, managers and employees
(Sherman & Dixon, 1991).

However, for planning and enforcement agencies acting as the resource
guardians (Lickorish, 1991) sustainability means staying within a destination's
ecological and social carrying capacity (Ceballos-Lacurain, 1996), protecting
both cultural heritage and natural biodiversity (Dasmann & Freeman, 1973).
Here sustainability involves monitoring the impacts that visitors have on
resources and managing these impacts in ways that minimise damage. Hoteliers
and others need to maintain commercial viability while resource managers need
to maintain environmental viability. Thus it is that in tourism destinations like
Bonaire we frequently find two sets of players operating under very different
views about what is needed (Pigram, 1990; Shaw & Williams, 1990). In fact, in
places where tourism is a significant economic force, the debate over public
policy is frequently a debate between these two divergent views of the 'public

good'. Such a debate was part of the problem-setting phase of collaboration on Bonaire in the years 1993 and 1994.

Earlier, we profiled the constituent organisations that were the parties to this debate. To understand the nature of their interaction with each other, we can adapt Trist's (1983), characterisation of domains as being either 'centred' or 'networked' in design. A centred or centralised pattern for collaborating organisations involves their coordinating with one another in an evolved and highly institutionalised structure of interaction. By way of contrast, the 'network' type is far more fluid and open. For example, rather than relying on the establishment of an explicit taskforce or similar device, the networked organisation remains informal and *ad hoc*, making decisions and coordinating actions in a more implicit manner.

The Bonaire experience with collaboration displayed the characteristics of the networked rather than the centred model and, as will be discussed later, this did prove to be a major shortcoming. Roberts and Bradley (1991) have generated a complex collaboration model that includes among its main elements an emphasis on task-specialised organisation and sustained interactions among the stakeholders. Informal, episodic and personality-sensitive, tourism collaboration on Bonaire in the early and mid-1990s tended, instead, to be conducted on a far less institutionalised basis than this model would prescribe, a condition that ultimately limited its effectiveness.

Instead of establishing a system that might allow all stakeholders to meet together on an ongoing basis in some type of umbrella group or peak association, collaboration occurred primarily through the mechanisms of overlapping membership, joint participation and periodic, general meetings. Specifically, the prevailing practice was for the island's tourism and environmental groups to have members on each others' boards of directors and/or attend each others' meetings, as will be discussed later when we consider Phase 2. *Ad hoc* gatherings that focused on particular issues were also utilised as a way of bringing interested parties together to discuss their problems and coordinate their operations. Although lacking a central, authoritative structure, this approach did create a policy network capable of quick and flexible response. It thereby allowed participants to coordinate their activities and thus begin the process of collaboration. According to Trist (1983), such 'networking initiatives' constitute the first of four steps in the emergence of a domain and during the period examined in this study, that is exactly where Bonaire was: at the beginning of the process. Thus, much of this paper's relevance to the analysis of collaboration is in terms of illustrating the emergence of an inter-organisational domain. The stakeholders' inability to move beyond this point, however, constituted a substantial weakness in their joint undertaking.

While collaboration on Bonaire was limited in this and other ways, one of its countervailing strengths was its inclusive nature, for it did manage to involve almost all of the stakeholder groups referred to earlier. Leadership of their discussions was taken by participants from the TCB, BONHATA and STINAPA, a phenomenon which was quite predictable since these three groups were seen as possessing on-going and legitimate authority within the domain. The primacy of these three stakeholders was indicated in responses to the question, 'In the last

Table 2 Lead organisations

Name	Frequency cited	Percentage
Tourism Corporation of Bonaire	13	27
BONHATA (Hotel Association)	11	23
STINAPA (National Park Foundation)	7	15
Island Government	4	9
CURO (Dive operators)	3	6
Bonaire Marine Park (Management)	3	6
Friends of the Earth	2	4
Save Klein Bonaire Foundation	2	4
Don't know/NA	3	6
Total	48	100%

few years, what group has been the real leader in Bonaire on the subject of tourism?' Results are provided in Table 2.

This table lists the organisations in order of the number of citations received, and we can see that the top three organisations were also the ones that took on the leadership roles. This finding is consistent with Gray's emphasis on the deference given such groups. The other pattern that can be seen in this table is that there are two different types of leadership clusters on Bonaire: commercial and environmental. The former is made up of representatives from the TCB, BONHATA and CURO while the latter is composed of members drawn from STINAPA, BMP and the several NGOs listed. Because the great majority of collaborators were drawn from these two constellations of interest, the remainder of this paper will adopt the terms 'Commercial' (cited by 56% in Table 2) and 'Environmental' (cited by 29% in Table 2) when discussing the backgrounds and interests of the respective groups of stakeholders. Relating the responses of these two groups to the treatment of issues and problems previously presented in Table 1, we were not surprised to find that the former emphasised business problems while the latter spoke almost exclusively of ecological and social difficulties. Returning to Table 2, we may note that the Island Government was mentioned by some. However, its record has tended more in the direction of mediating rather than siding with either alliance, and accordingly we do not include it under either label.

In his work on collaboration, Trist (1983) has emphasised the activity in which participants work to cooperatively diagnose the nature of the problem(s) confronting them. However, on Bonaire these two groups had very different diagnoses, and the contradictions between them initially intensified as tourism growth rapidly accelerated a decade after the creation of the Marine Park. Stakeholders still remember and report debates during this time on such subjects as growth, crime, land use, pollution and the need for seemingly more and more tourist arrivals. Nonetheless, it was during these debates that positions began to evolve, and it slowly became clear to many that the challenges were interdependent and thus required some type of cooperative solution. However, the question that remained unanswered during most of Phase 1 dealt with what it was that needed sustaining: industry resources or natural resources. In this zero-sum formulation of the problem, participants had not yet moved beyond allegiance to their single sub-part of the domain.

This gap was partially closed by the publication of the 'Pourier Report' (1993), a document produced by a collaborative committee, reporting to the government and representing the major tourism stakeholders. The panel was established to survey the problem domain; to examine goals and, perhaps, chart a new course. Its report presented a vision of Bonaire based on slow, planned and controlled growth of the dominant sector of the island's economy: dive tourism. Even during interviews four years later, participants still referred to it as a kind of turning point, bringing stakeholders closer to a point where they could see their individual problems in terms of mutual impact, especially with the committee's emphasis on the policy connections between the condition of Bonaire's natural environment and the health of its economy. This approach may remind the reader of Weaver's (1991) assessment of policy choices in Dominica where the government has discouraged certain types of outside investment and moved to keep growth under control by such means as limiting airport expansion.

As to the scale of tourism, The Pourier Report built on an earlier development plan produced by the Caribbean Development Centre (1990) and emphatically rejected the mass-tourism approach taken by Bonaire's sister islands, Aruba and Curacao. Recognising that biodiversity can be made to pay (Pearce & Morgan, 1994). The report instead emphasised Bonaire's 'environmental product' and the need to sustainably develop it by pursuing only a very selective type of tourism: one that would cater to a small but affluent clientele. In this way, incomes could be kept high without necessarily relying on a constant increase in visitor volume. Operationally, however, the problem remained. If the numbers were too low, the hoteliers and other commercial interests would oppose the process. If they were too high, the natural-resource community would not accept the outcome because of concerns relating to carrying capacity.

Although the carrying capacity of any tourism resource may be extremely difficult to document and monitor (Innskeep, 1991), that of Bonaire's reefs had been estimated at 200,000 dives per year in a study done for the World Bank (Scura & van't Hof, 1993) early in Phase 1. However, the growth projections available to stakeholders indicated that by 1996 the island could annually be playing host to as many as 65,000 visitors who would make a combined total of some 250,000 dives. Because of the imbalance in these figures, both BMP documents and government reports (Tourism Planning and Research Associates, 1997) soon declared the reefs to be at or beyond their physical carrying capacity. This assessment was resisted by others because even during Phase 1, with visitation reaching 56,000 arrivals annually, hotel occupancy rates hovered near only 50%. Members of BONHATA and others believed that they needed better rates, with 60–70% being the consensus range cited most frequently during our interviews. Such a target would, of course, push the annual number of dives into the vicinity of 300,000, fully 50% beyond the World Bank figure. Thus, in terms of the island's primary natural resource, there were two opposing diagnoses during most of the problem-setting phase: one seeing the reefs as capable of absorbing no more growth in visitation rates and the other demanding such growth. Until another alternative was found, continued conflict seemed inevitable, given the

Table 3 Tourist arrivals (000)

Source	Year								
	1994	*1995*	*1996*	*1997*	*1998*	*1999*	*2000*	*2005*	*2010*
Economic Impact Study	57	61	66	70	74	77	80	100	119
TCB* Report									
Trend	56	59	65	69	73	78	82	103	
Low	56	59	63	64	66	67	68	70	
High	56	59	67	74	82	90	98	149	

* Tourism Corporation of Bonaire
Source: Tourism Planning and Research Associates, *Bonaire Tourism Strategic Plan*, May 1997, Appendix p. 3.

island's tourism growth statistics for the recent past and the predicted future. See Table 3.

The next section of this paper will use this table to show how such projections made possible the stakeholders' approach to dealing with these conflicting problems of hotel capacity and reef capacity. The paper's conclusion will discuss the gap that subsequently developed in the late 1990s between the predicted and the actual numbers of arrivals and how this discrepancy negatively impacted Phase 3 of collaboration.

Phase 2 – Direction Setting

Direction-setting is a collaborative activity in which the participating organisations deal with the question of what, if anything, should be done about the problem domain and discoveries made during Phase 1. Combining both agenda-setting and policy formulation, the stakeholders assess their preferred outcomes and the alternatives available for reaching them. Emphasis is on the development of mutually acceptable courses of action (Gray, 1989). On Bonaire, as we have seen, consensus on the nature of the domain was never really achieved during Phase 1. Interestingly, it was during Phase 2 that real progress was made, a fact that may lead us to speculate that a group's movement from one phase to the next does not necessarily require prior closure during the earlier phase. In fact, Phase 2 collaboration on Bonaire helped resolve certain Phase 1 issues that previously seemed intractable.

Guided by leaders at the TCB, BONHATA and STINAPA, Bonaire stakeholders shifted the focus of their collaborative efforts during 1995. Our delineation of this second phase is not predicated on a finding of any significant change in the nature of their interaction, however. It is based, instead, on an assessment of how they used their overlapping memberships and shared participation to formulate a policy agenda. Phase 2 was defined by a new vision of their shared policy preferences, not by changes in their shared, deliberative processes.

It must be remembered that Bonaire is a very small island, dominated by a single industry and that its components interlock with each other. BONHATA works directly with the TCB, and the latter holds monthly meetings with the former. A TCB representative sits on the STINAPA board as do delegates from BONHATA and the Island Government. CURO holds an organisational membership in BONHATA and serves along with several environmental NGOs on the Marine Park's Oversight Committee. Responsibility for the marine park, itself, is vested with STINAPA. Several NGO members also belong to both STINAPA and BONHATA. Ultimately this study was able to calculate that some two dozen networked individuals fill most of these key, overlapping positions. Because of their connected roles they are in frequent communication with each other and they have used their overlap to create a kind of implicit collaboration. With it, they have been able to discuss and plan numerous policies without having to create a separate layer of organisation to bring them together. While this approach has provided great flexibility, over-reliance upon it has also militated against structuring the collaborative effort into a more institutionalised form. This, in turn, has greatly limited its effectiveness.

In 1995 the attention of the interlockers shifted away from their unresolved differences about sustainability to the consideration of specific policy options of particular interest to each. The Phase 1 use of a visioning committee had produced the 'Pourier Report', but that document had been unable to generate a real consensus on values between the Commercial and Environmental groups. Rather than continue with a seemingly impossible task, the stakeholders set aside their search for common values and turned their attention instead to the question of whether there were certain things that each side wanted separately that the other could support. As they did this, their collaborative activity gradually evolved into the direction-setting phase, and three issues emerged as most salient:

- airline capacity,
- hotel capacity, and
- pollution abatement.

All three of these issues were highly interdependent, and thus extremely relevant in terms of collaboration theory. The first was concerned with demand generation for the national airline, ALM, while the second focused on both growth limits and growth incentives for hoteliers. The pollution-control question concentrated on the need for construction of the island's first wastewater treatment facility. This public-works project was seen as a way to reverse the decline that had begun on Bonaire's coral reefs. At the same time it was hoped that it would allow for an expansion in the size of the tourism industry, as will be discussed later.

For the Commercial Group the policy of augmenting airline capacity had very high priority because it was seen as the key to raising hotel occupancy rates. The Environmental Group, on the other hand, was just as committed to the idea of building the wastewater treatment plant. Their concern was based on data showing that the thousands of the divers entering Bonaire's waters each month did far less direct damage to the reefs than did the hotels' discharging of untreated effluent into the same waters (Roberts & Hawkins, 1994). Most hotels have cess pits or septic tanks, but their capacity and effectiveness are severely limited. Excess grey water is also used for landscape irrigation and often finds its way into the sea. This situation, combined with the island's porous limestone base, has resulted in serious reef damage through eutrophication (Tourism Planning and Research Associates, 1997). In this process, the additional nutrients discharged into the island's off-shore waters generate an increased production of algae. Algae, in turn, is a major factor in coral mortality.

In order to examine the fit between these reports and participant perceptions, interviewees were presented with the following statement: 'A lot of people say that the reef is not as healthy today as it was ten years ago. Do you agree or not?' There were 10 'disagrees' or 'don't knows'. The 38 individuals expressing agreement were given a forced-choice list of possible explanations for the decline and asked to rank them. Table 4 presents the distribution of frequencies for those explanations ranked highest. Significantly, a majority of those believing that the island has a problem with its marine ecology diagnosed the absence of a wastewater treatment plant as the main reason.

Still, many failed to see the problem because it was invisible for such a long period of time. For more than two decades it remained undetected, as the volume of nutrient discharge steadily grew to measurable levels. This growth was, in the eyes of many, the direct result of the government's failure to account for the environmental impact of 20 years' worth of development. A similar phenomenon has been documented with small island states in the South Pacific (Fairbairn, 1990). According to this view, what Bonaire shares in common with Fiji, Tonga and The Cook Islands is a failure to deal with the dangers of large investment projects at any time before they start to actually threaten the environment.

Once this occurred on Bonaire, there was little dispute about the need for a wastewater treatment plant – a consensus mirrored in the responses of a plurality of our interviewees, as seen in Table 4. However, a shared diagnosis could not overcome the obstacle generated by the enormous costs involved. These, in turn, created an obvious disincentive to action which initially kept the Environmental and Commercial Groups from arriving at a common ground. Unable to move forward on this issue, they shifted their attention to the subject of visitation numbers and hotel capacity, concerns not unrelated to wastewater questions. These consultations, in turn, became the key to action on direction-setting and retrospectively on problem-setting, as well. This was so because the subject of growth dealt with fundamental needs relating to both airline and wastewater planning. Hoteliers wanted to fill their rooms, and environmentalists wanted to build the treatment plant. Responding to consultant reports on airline needs, the network participants envisioned a policy of allowing the island's hotel inventory to grow to 1600 rooms (Pieters & Gevers, 1995).

Table 4 Main reason for reef decline

Reason cited	Frequency	Percentage
Sewage/lack of treatment plant	21	55
Too much shore development	6	16
Too many divers	5	13
Divers lack training	3	8
Boat pollution	2	5
Over-fishing	1	3
Total	38	100%

At first such a policy seems paradoxical. At that time there were still only 1000 hotel rooms and they were experiencing a 50% occupancy rate, a situation that raises a very logical question. If a hotelier cannot fill the number of rooms s/he has on hand, why would s/he want to build more? The answer provided by Bonaire planning officials concerned the fact that if a destination does not have enough rooms it cannot justify any extra airlift. Only by building the additional rooms would hoteliers be able to entice the airline into adding more capacity. According to the plan, such an addition would, in turn, generate enough additional passengers to increase the overall occupancy rate. Tour operators cannot work with destinations that do not have a sufficiently large pool of rooms. Lacking necessary allotments, they cannot vary their pricing in order to sell enough seats and in the absence of sold seats the airline reduces capacity and room occupancy rates tumble further. Direction-setting emphasised a policy that viewed airlift capacity and hotel occupancy as intimately related and mutually reinforcing strands in the tourism mosaic. On one side was the fact that a critical mass of room capacity was needed in order to assure adequate air service by making it profitable for the carrier. On the other side was the equally clear fact that without a certain level of air service, the existing inventory of rooms could not be filled at needed rates.

Pieters and Gevers (1995) explain that growth was also to be limited to the 1600 room figure. In other words, that number would not be just a target, but a cap as well. Once it was reached no additional rooms would be built. With an attractive, natural destination to offer and with enforceable limits on the number of visitors, scarcity rents could be raised quite high (Caribbean Development Centre, 1992, 1996). Such rates would, in turn, mean stable profits at the same time that resources were being preserved. What is fascinating for students of sustainability, however, is the fact that this figure of 1600 was initially reached by extrapolating from the capacity and profitability requirements of the airline, ALM. It was not reached by starting with estimates of the number of divers that the reefs could accommodate without degradation. In other words, commercial sustainability rather than environmental sustainability was the operative criterion, at first.

Because this was the case we must now reconstruct the other major element of Phase 2 collaboration, that concerning the wastewater treatment plant. While most stakeholders could see its value, few in the Commercial Group were willing to agree to its authorisation because of the estimated construction/implementation cost of US$14m (Tourism Planning and Research Associates, 1997: A3.3). Not only would it add enormously to the cost of operating individual properties, but it was also feared that since most of the bill would have to be passed along to guests, it would further erode Bonaire's competitive position, vis à vis other Caribbean dive destinations.

However, as the stakeholders discussed this problem during 1995 and 1996 one of the lead organisations, TCB, constantly and persuasively made the case that the plant could be made affordable if its cost was spread over a larger number of rooms. Of course, it was also an increased room inventory that had been presented as a means of addressing the airlift problem. Eventually, it was this approach to the problem domain that prevailed, for it proposed to deal with two issues (profitability and conservation) through a single growth policy that relied heavily on economies of scale. Combining numerous interview responses, we may reconstruct their collaborative reasoning as follows. If construction funds could not be found from external sources such as the European Union or the central government in Holland, then an effective way to pay for the wastewater treatment system would be through a major increase in the number of rooms. This was so because much of the funding for this project would be devoted to fixed costs such as the building of the plant itself, laying the piping to connect it to the hotel properties, constructing the pumping stations, etc. If these fixed costs were to be divided by a larger number of rooms then the per-unit cost for the entire project would be considerably lower. Exactly what this means can be seen by an examination of Table 5.

Table 5 Treatment plant cost estimates

Room inventory	Cost per room US$ total	Cost per room (30 years)
1100	$12,700	$423
1600	$8,750	$292

Here the cost of the treatment plant is presented on a per-room basis, first in terms of total cost and then, in the third column, by amortising this total over an expected life-span of 30 years. As these figures make dramatically clear, the larger pool of rooms decreases the per-unit cost by 31%. This was seen as an effective economic argument in favour of raising the number of rooms to 1600 and it also complemented the island's projected airlift requirements. If such an increase were to make the construction of the plant feasible, we would then have the seemingly paradoxical result of an increase in tourism leading to greater resource sustainability, exactly the kind of outcome postulated by Budowski (1976).

Thus it was that the direction-setting phase of Bonaire's collaborative effort emphasised economies of scale to create common ground for both of the previously conflicted groups (Commercial and Environmental). A room inventory of 1600 could make it profitable for the airline to increase its capacity. More rooms could also generate the funds needed for construction of the treatment plant. The existence of just such a dynamic regarding the size and cost-efficiency of tourism infrastructure was demonstrated years ago by Jenkins (1982). Of course, such a policy carried dangers, as well, not the least of which concerned whether the cap would be respected once it was reached. In addition, there were obvious social problems posed by the projected increase in visitor volume: inflation of land values, increased crime rates, etc. However, these have not happened because, as is discussed later, the three-part policy initiative has yet to be implemented.

Conclusion

In one sense Bonaire's attempt at collaboration was instructive, for it demonstrated how a tourism policy agenda can evolve and how stakeholders can move toward a consensus that would not have been possible previously. Participant interactions generated a convergence of airline, hotel and pollution-abatement policies. Coming together, these three were like the sides of a triangle, in that the elimination of any one of them would compromise the integrity of the whole. Collaboration is about interdependent problem solving and about decision-making at the system level, precisely what occurred in Bonaire during Phase 2. No longer were two mutually exclusive positions seen as the only ones available. Instead an approach to sustainability was visioned that created common ground and a new definition of both the problem and its possible solutions.

However, in another sense, it might be argued that collaboration on the island has been ineffective, since Phase 3's structuring process has not been completed. Structuring involves the implementation of plans made during Phase 2 and may include an acceptance of such devices as regulation, tax increases, external mandates, redistribution of power and a commitment to re-allocate resources toward the new end. Goals and timetables are set and specific tasks are assigned to organisational players. Structuring relies on the explicit ratification and execution of a practical action plan that was previously just a statement of policy intent. Its most fundamental indicator is an actual change in behaviour. Since this is so, one test of Phase 3's success quite simply involves asking whether the plans of Phase 2 were ever put into effect. On Bonaire they were not. Although the triangulated policies were interdependent, one was fundamental: that dealing with the supply of hotel rooms. As seen by Bonaire planners, this was the variable that would drive the other two. Building the additional rooms was seen as the initiative that could cause the airline to add capacity and that could also generate revenue for construction of the wastewater treatment plant.

However, none of this has yet happened and the explanation has to do with two other variables, one external to the process of collaboration and the other internal to it. The external factor involved a problem over which participants had insufficient control: visitation numbers. During most of the 1990s, Bonaire's tourism base was expanding, frequently at annual rates of near 10%. Under such circumstances, long-range plans for increasing the room inventory by some 50% were both predictable and financially defensible. However, as can be seen in Table 6, the trend in visitation numbers changed dramatically starting in 1997. The first column of this table shows the upward projections on which so much of the collaboration was based. The actual arrival numbers are presented in the second column and a very dramatic change can be seen, beginning in 1997, the year when stakeholders might have been entering Phase 3. In that year there were 6200 fewer visitors than expected, a deviation of 9%. By 1999, the discrepancy had risen to 17%, as an estimated 64,700 divers and others arrived, instead of the projected 78,000. This widening gap is presented in graph-form in Figure 2.

Due to this downturn and its associated economic uncertainty, investors were unwilling to risk substantial and coordinated levels of new development that would raise the room inventory much above its existing level. The stakeholder policy previously described had been generated in an atmosphere of economic expansion and in many ways was fundamentally dependent upon its continuation. Although initially sceptical, the commercial players had been interested in the plan of inventory expansion in order to maximise their own gains. When the situation changed and they were confronted with a contracting market at the completion of Phase 2, the same participants needed to switch to a strategy of loss minimisation, instead. Such an altering of priorities meant a loss of support for

Table 6 Tourist arrivals: projected versus actual

Year	Projected	Actual	Deviation	% deviation
1994	56,000	55,800	(200)	-
1995	59,000	59,400	400	-
1996	65,000	65,000	-	-
1997	69,000	62,800	(6,200)	(9%)
1998	73,000	61,700	(11,300)	(15%)
1999	78,000	64,700*	(13,300)	(17%)

Source: TCB
* Estimated by TCB

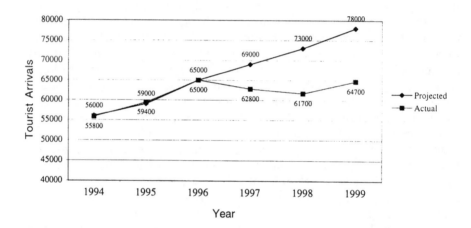

Figure 2 Tourist arrivals: projected versus actual

the plan and this, in turn, crippled the Phase 3 attempt at structuring. The target figure of 1600 rooms was also abandoned. In programmatic terms, it can be said that no coordinated progress has been possible on hotel construction, the treatment plant or the question of airline capacity since 1997.

What such a situation suggests for collaboration theory is that changes in the strategic, external environment can easily threaten what is already a fragile policy consensus. After extensive bargaining and information exchange, collaboration assumes certain external conditions and then moves forward. When the assumptions change or prove to be unfounded, retrograde movement can occur and the collaborators may be returned to earlier stages in their cooperative process. In the case of Bonaire, the main exogenous variable was tourism demand. For stakeholders, the competing definitions of the problem domain in Phase 1 were modified and softened by ever-growing demand statistics until 1997. When this situation changed, so did the prospects for success of the collaborative enterprise. Such a conclusion, in turn, raises questions about research methodology and the identification of relevant systems and stakeholders. For example, there may be a need to include institutions and processes beyond the system that is initially being analysed. In the current context, this indicates a direction for further study that would include factors such as regional/hemispheric economic conditions, market forces and Bonaire's overall competitive position, not as variables that stakeholders can control directly, but as elements that condition any collaborative process.

A second type of variable relevant to the outcome on Bonaire was internal. As has been mentioned numerous times before, the collaborative process there functioned in ways consistent with Trist's (1983) 'networked' model, rather than his 'centred' one. It was decentralised. Its communications process was informal and it relied on *ad hoc* meetings in combination with overlapping and interlocking memberships rather than creating a set of institutionalised, deliberative procedures. Lacking a durable framework, it was unable to sufficiently motivate participants to continue and redirect the problem solving when tourism numbers stagnated and the tripartite policy convergence disintegrated. These difficulties were, no doubt, exacerbated by the earlier (1993–94) lack of consensus on problem-setting, a condition discussed in Gray's (1985) writings on collaboration.

In addition, the process suffered from the fact that there was a power differential between the two groups of stakeholders, as previously indicated above in our discussion of leadership during the problem-setting phase. Thus, when the period of uncertainty began in 1997 and members of the dominant Commercial Group withdrew their support, there was little that the others could do. Such an outcome offers support for Gray's (1985) proposition that collaboration is facilitated when power is more evenly dispersed among several stakeholders. Ultimately, the mode of organisation, the process and the power discrepancies made success much less likely, especially when joined by the problems of economic contraction which occurred after 1996. In conclusion, it may be said that together, the twin variables of unexpected economic change and a collaborative process that was too informal undermined Bonaire's effort at sustainability.

Correspondence

Any correspondence should be directed to Dr Steven Parker, Associate Professor, College of Liberal Arts, Department of Political Science, University of Nevada Las Vegas, Las Vegas, Nevada, 89154-5029, USA (parkers@nevada.edu).

References

Beller, W. (1990) How to sustain a small island. In W. Beller, P. d'Ayala and P. Hein (eds) *Sustainable Development and Environmental Management of Small Islands*. Park Ridge, NJ: Parthenon Publishing Group.

Budowski, G. (1976) Tourism and environmental conservation: Conflict, coexistence and symbiosis. *Environmental Conservation* 3 (1), 27–31.

Butler, R.W. (1980) The concept of a tourist area cycle of evolution: Implications for management resources. *Canadian Geographer* 24 (1), 5–12.

Caribbean Development Centre (1990) *Structure Plan of Bonaire*. Curacao: CDC.

Caribbean Development Centre (1992) *Bonaire Tourism Investment Strategy*. Curacao: CDC.

Caribbean Development Centre (1996) *Outline Development Plan and Global Zoning*. Curacao: CDC.

Ceballos-Lascurain, H. (1996) *Tourism, Ecotourism and Protected Areas*. Caracas, VZ: The World Conservation Union.

Dasmann, R., Milton, J. and Freeman, P. (1973) *Ecological Principles for Economic Development*. London: John Wiley.

Driml, S. and Common, M. (1995) Economic and financial benefits of tourism in major protected areas. *Australian Journal of Environmental Management* 2, 19–29.

Elliott, J. (1983) Politics, power and tourism in Thailand. *Annals of Tourism Research* 10, 377–93.

Elliott, J. (1987) Government management of tourism: A Thai case study. *Tourism Management* 8, 223–32.

Fairbain, T. (1990) The environment and development planning in small pacific island countries. In W. Beller, P. d'Ayala and P. Hein (eds) *Sustainable Development and Environmental Management of Small Islands*. Park Ridge, NJ: Parthenon Publishing Group.

Fletcher, J. (1997) *The Economic Impact of International Tourism on the Economy of Bonaire*. Bournemouth: International Centre for Tourism and Hospitality Research.

Getz, D. and Jamal, T. (1994) The environmental-community symbiosis: A case for collaborative tourism planning. *Journal of Sustainable Tourism* 2 (3), 152–73.

Gray, B. (1985) Conditions facilitating interorganizational collaboration. *Human Relations* 38 (10), 911–36.

Gray, B. (1989) *Collaborating: Finding Common Ground for Multiparty Problems*. San Francisco: Jossey-Bass.

Inskeep, E. (1991) *Tourism Planning: An Integrated Sustainable Development Approach*. New York: Van Nostrand Reinhold.

Jenkins, C.L. (1980) Tourism policies in developing countries: A critique. *International Journal of Tourism Management* 1 (March), 22–29.

Jenkins, C.L. (1982) The effects of scale in tourism projects in developing countries. *Annals of Tourism Research* 9, 229–49.

King, B. (1997) *Creating Island Resorts*. New York: Routledge.

Lickorish, L. (1991) Administrative structure for tourism development: Roles of government and the private sector. In J. Bodlender, A. Jefferson, C. Jenkins and L. Lickorish (eds) *Developing Tourism Destinations* (pp. 119–46). UK: Longman.

Liddle, M.J. (1997) *Recreation Ecology: The Ecological Impact of Outdoor Recreation and Tourism*. London: Chapman and Hall.

Logsdon, J. (1991) Interests and interdependence in the formation of social problem-solving collaborations. *Journal of Applied Behavioral Science* 27 (1) 23–37.

McCann, J. (1983) Design guidelines for social problem-solving interventions. *Journal of Applied Behavioral Science* 19, 177–89.

McKercher, B. (1993) The unrecognized threat to tourism: Can tourism survive sustainability? *Tourism Management*, 14, 131–36.

Miezkowski, Z. (1995) *Environmental Issues of Tourism and Recreation*. New York: University Press of America.

Nash, D. (1989) Tourism as a form of imperialism. In V. Smith (ed.) *Hosts and Guests* (pp. 37–51). Philadelphia: University of Philadelphia Press.

Orams, M. (1999) *Marine Tourism: Development, Impacts and Management*. London: Routledge.

Pearce, D. and Morgan, D. (1994) *The Economic Value of Biodiversity*. London: IUCN & Earthscan Publications.

Pieters, R. and Gevers, D. (1995) A framework for tourism development on fragile island destinations: The case of Bonaire. In M.V. Conlin and T. Baum (eds) *Island Tourism: Management Principles and Practice* (pp. 123–32). New York: John Wiley.

Pigram, J. (1990) Sustainable tourism: Policy considerations. *Journal of Tourism Studies* 1 (2), 2–9.

Pourier, M. (1993) *Rapport van de Commissie Integrale Sociaal-Economische Aanpak Bonaire, Netherlands Antilles*. Bonaire, NA.

Roberts, C. and Hawkins, J. (1994) *Report on The Status of Bonaire's Coral Reefs*. St Thomas: Eastern Caribbean Centre, University of the Virgin Islands.

Roberts, N. and Bradley, R. (1991) Stakeholder collaboration and innovation: A study of public policy initiation at the state level. *Journal of Applied Behavioral Science* 27 (2), 209–27.

Scura, M. and van't Hof, T. (1993) *The Ecology and Economics of Bonaire Marine Park.* The World Bank, Environment Department, Divisional paper No. 1993-44.

Shaw, G. and Williams, A. (1990) Tourism and development. In D. Pinder (ed.) *Western Europe: Challenge and Change* (pp. 240–57). London: Belhaven Press.

Sherman, P. and Dixon, J. (1991) The economics of nature tourism: Determining if it pays. In T. Whelan (ed.) *Nature Tourism: Managing for the Environment* (pp. 89–131). Washington, DC: Island Press.

Smith, V. (1992) Boracay, Philippines: A case study in 'alternative' tourism. In V.L. Smith, and W.R. Eadington (eds) *Tourism Alternatives: Potentials and Problems in The Development of Tourism* (pp. 135–57). Philadelphia: University of Pennsylvania Press.

Tourism Planning and Research Associates (1997) *Bonaire: Tourism Strategic Plan.* London: Tourism Planning and Research Associates.

Trist, E. (1983) Referent organizations and the development of inter-organizational domains. *Human Relations* 36 (3), 269–84.

Waddock, S.A. (1989) Understanding social partnerships: An evolutionary model of partnership organizations. *Administration and Society* 21 (1), 78–100.

Weaver, D. (1991) Alternative to mass tourism in Dominica. *Annals of Tourism Research* 18, 414–32.

Wood, D. and Gray, B. (1991) Toward a comprehensive theory of collaboration. *Journal of Applied Behavioral Science* 27 (2), 139–62.

5. The World Wide Fund for Nature Arctic Tourism Project

Peter Mason
Reader in Tourism, Luton Business School, University of Luton, Park Square, Luton, UK

Margaret Johnston
Director, School of Outdoor Recreation, Parks and Tourism, Lakehead University, Thunder Bay, Ontario, Canada

Dave Twynam
Associate Dean, School of Tourism, The University College of the Cariboo, Kamloops, British Columbia, Canada

This article investigates the involvement of an environmental non-governmental organisation (ENGO) in a sustainable tourism initiative. The article examines the collaborative relationship between this ENGO, the World Wide Fund for Nature (WWF), and other stakeholders in this Project, which involves integrating conservation with Arctic tourism. The collaboration has included tour operators, polar scientists, tourism academics and researchers, local and national government representatives, Arctic community representatives and members of NGOs, in addition to WWF representatives. The goal of the Project was to integrate conservation ideals into tourism in Arctic locations to enable communities, tourists and operators to work towards a more sustainable form of tourism. This article discusses the aims of the Project, presents an analysis of the processes involved, particularly those of negotiation and implementation, and provides an evaluation of the outcomes in relation to the original aims.

Introduction

In recent years there has been an increase in visitor numbers to the Arctic and sub-Arctic, with in excess of a million visitors per year recorded in the mid-1990s (Mason, 1997a). There has also been growing concern about the impacts such numbers have on the Arctic environment and Arctic peoples (Hall & Johnston, 1995). Concern about tourism in the Arctic, expressed by individuals, government bodies and non-governmental organisations, has taken place within the context of more general concerns about environmental protection. The World Wide Fund for Nature (WWF), the only private environmental group with an Arctic programme covering the circumpolar Arctic, has been an active participant in debates about environmental impacts in the Arctic. In its attempt to ensure that environmental protection continues to be the main issue of circumpolar inter-governmental cooperation, WWF has promoted the Arctic Environmental Protection Strategy (AEPS) (Prokosch, pers. comm., 12 December 1998). WWF also supported the establishment of the Arctic Council, an international body comprised of member national governments and permanent participants representing indigenous peoples' organisations (Mason, 1997a). In 1995 WWF launched, through its Arctic Programme, a project focusing on tourism. The Arctic Tourism Project arose from a recommendation at a conference in St Petersburg, Russia in 1994 and was launched at a meeting in Longyearbyen, Svalbard,

Norway, in January 1996. The project's main aim was to integrate conservation ethics and activities with Arctic tourism.

This article describes the background to the WWF Arctic Tourism Project, its aims and history and the activities of the Project. An evaluation of the key processes in the Project, those of consultation, negotiation and implementation, is also provided. The analysis draws primarily upon documents produced to support the Arctic Tourism Project, personal communication with key individuals, and knowledge gained by the authors having participated at all stages of the process. From its outset the authors were closely involved with the Project, being members of a small core group who worked with WWF staff to coordinate workshops, to assist in the writing of briefing papers and other documents, and to write reports after meetings. The authors were invited by WWF to be part of this group because of their involvement in Arctic tourism research. As the Director of the Project indicated, the authors were 'the core tourism researchers who provided us with their expertise' (Prokosch, 1998: 4).

The Arctic Region and Arctic Tourism

The Arctic region is not easily defined, and attempts often separate the Arctic from the sub-Arctic on the basis of physical features (Sugden, 1982). Some definitions emphasise climatic or vegetative delineations such as the 10 degree July isotherm, or the tree line (Bone, 1992), an approach which is common in Canada and Russia. Others use a latitudinal delineation – the Arctic Circle – which is more common in Scandinavia. A political definition of the Arctic relies on the eight Arctic countries: Canada, Finland, Iceland, Norway, Denmark, Sweden, the USA and Russia. The WWF project is aimed at these countries which together form the Arctic Council, the organisation set up in 1995 to act as a forum for the discussion of Arctic issues requiring international cooperation (Mason, 1997a).

To a great extent it is still possible to view the Arctic as a resource frontier (Hall, 1987; Hall & Johnston, 1995; Mason, 1994). Resource development generally is limited in areal extent and tends to be concentrated in a few locations, although activity can be intensive (Sugden, 1990). The lack of widespread industrial development contributes to the perception of the region as a clean, unsullied wilderness, which is a major appeal for tourists (Johnston, 1995). This notion of the Arctic wilderness supports the view that the region provides great potential for recreation, adventure and enjoyment (Bronsted, 1994). The Arctic may also be perceived as being at the end of the world, both geographically and culturally, and an attractive place for tourists to escape a hectic urban existence and reflect upon links between humans, the earth and the universe (Johnston, 1995; Viken, 1993).

Given the environmental attraction of the region it is not surprising that most types of tourism activity in the Arctic are nature-based. Some forms have at their core the contemplation of nature, such as observing and photographing wildlife. Others, such as hunting and fishing, are more consumptive of resources. Snow-based activities including skiing or those involving the use of vehicles such as snow scooters (snow machines), are significant in some mountain areas and higher latitude locations (Viken, 1995).

The indigenous peoples in the Arctic are part of the region's tourist appeal. The people themselves can be the source of attraction, as are their artefacts and the manifestations of their activity, such as the reindeer herding of the Sami (Hall, 1987). Indigenous peoples are usually viewed by visitors as a part of the Arctic environment and are regarded as long-term inhabitants who have not over-exploited limited resources, but instead have lived in harmony with the environment (Smith, 1989). Hence, a number of tourism activities are culturally based, focusing on aboriginal lifestyles, crafts, artefacts, historic events or places (Hall & Johnston, 1995).

Although tourism in the Arctic is not on the scale of mass tourism in many other parts of the world, hundreds of thousands of tourists visit northern circumpolar destinations each year, with as many as half a million visiting Northern Scandinavia's Arctic regions in the mid 1990s (Johnston, 1995). However, it is difficult to provide accurate data on visitors to the Arctic, partly because of definitional problems and also because of the differing ways in which the various Arctic countries collect data on visitors. Yet, there is ample evidence of increasing numbers over the years which provides an idea of the scale of these changes. In Greenland, for example, overnight tourist visits increased from 3300 in 1987 to 16,000 in 1996 (Johnston & Viken, 1997). In Svalbard after tourism development became official government policy, bednights increased from 17,482 in 1991 to 45,100 in 1997 (Viken & Jørgensen, 1998). In 1996 approximately 12,000 visitors arrived in Svalbard by air, while about 15,000–20,000 arrived by cruise ship (Viken and Jørgensen, 1998).

Tourism numbers are likely to increase in the immediate future and the longer term (Butler, 1994; Colin, 1994). Greater disposable income and more leisure time (Mason, 1994), as well as transportation improvements (Butler, 1994; Johnston, 1995) are the main reasons for this increase. International air tourism to Greenland, Iceland, Alaska and Russia is likely to increase. Cross-border land-based and air tourism within Scandinavia and between Scandinavia and Russia, and possibly domestic tourism in Russia, will increase (Hall & Johnston, 1995).

The impacts of tourism

Irrespective of its precise nature, all tourism has an impact on local environments and local peoples. The fragility of the Arctic and its sensitivity to tourism impacts is still a matter for debate. Part of the debate reflects insufficient monitoring of tourism impacts and a need for more data (Colin, 1994). Nonetheless, Johnston (1995) stated that excessive tourism can cause major changes in the Arctic.

Damage can be caused by vehicles crossing the Arctic land surface, particularly when snow cover is thin, or by people using established sites or creating new ones. Colin (1994) stated that Arctic vegetation is fragile and recovery from damage is slow; destruction to ecosystems often occurs rapidly, but recovery may take decades. Furthermore, multiple-event or cumulative disturbances are far more damaging to Arctic ecosystems than single-event impacts (Walker *et al.*, 1987). Much tourism activity would appear to exhibit a cumulative disturbance pattern. For example, tourists tend to gravitate to the same places for activities such as hiking, photography and camping; these sites and routes may reflect this ongoing and cumulative pressure in soil compaction, plant damage, surface disturbances and the introduction of foreign substances. Tourism-related environmental damage is at present small-scale in comparison with the impacts of large industries such as oil extraction (Viken, 1995), but it has been claimed that because of the sensitivity of ecosystems, even the smallest change in some Arctic habitats could cause major long term effects in plant and animal populations (Colin, 1994).

Tourist litter and waste are becoming something of a problem in the Arctic, partly due to the lack of a system for litter removal and waste disposal and/or the unwillingness of visitors to remove their rubbish (Mason, 1994; Umbreit, 1991). As Valentine (1992) pointed out, inefficient litter disposal can create health hazards for wildlife and people, cause behavioural changes in animals and reduce the quality of the tourist experience. Tourists themselves are concerned about damage to the Arctic environment. Viken (1995) reported on a survey of over 200 visitors to Svalbard in the early 1990s in which 30% indicated that pollution and evidence of human damage to the environment were problems that affected tourism, although visitors believed these problems were not predominantly caused by tourist activities. Viken (1995) stated that although damage is currently limited, there is a consensus that ecological and cultural sustainability must be guiding principles for future tourism development on Svalbard.

It is often the claim of governments and tour operators that tourism will bring economic gain to destination regions. This argument can be particularly significant in areas where older industries are dying (e.g. coal mining in Svalbard communities) or in locations, such as Greenland, where tourism is new and there are few alternative economic activities (Johnston, 1995; Johnston & Viken, 1997). Smith (1989) states that there is a good deal of evidence to show the leakage of tourism revenue from the Arctic as much of the money paid for an Arctic visit goes to tour operators, carriers and package holiday providers outside the region itself.

The tourism industry everywhere has a reputation for packaging and commoditising indigenous cultures (see for example Krippendorf, 1987; Mowforth & Munt, 1997; Urry, 1990). Hall (1987) suggested this is happening in the Arctic and saw particular problems with the ways indigenous people are viewed and then marketed by the tourism industry, perhaps making them into objects of curiosity for adventurous tourists wealthy enough to enjoy luxury cruises. Smith (1989) hoped commoditisation could be avoided and that through local control communities could maximise economic benefits from tourism and represent accurately their culture.

Concerns such as these have been instrumental in the movement toward a comprehensive set of principles and codes for the Arctic region as a whole. The process of developing and implementing the principles and codes follows approaches common to many sustainable tourism initiatives. What must be noted, though, are the distinctions that arise from the particular geographical context and from the primary focus of WWF as the initiator of the process and its ongoing facilitator.

Regulating tourism in the Arctic

The WWF Project should be seen as an attempt to regulate Arctic tourism through the incorporation of conservation values and actions. Regulation of tourism activity takes place in a number of ways from informal rules and social norms to official policies and legislation that are ways of controlling the behaviour of people to ensure acceptable outcomes (Johnston, 1997). Prior to the commencement of the WWF work, several approaches to controlling behaviour were in existence in the Arctic. For example, in Canada regulation of tourism occurs through formal visitor management in the national park reserves in Nunavut, and in Greenland visitors to the ice cap are controlled through a licensing system operated by the Danish Polar Centre (Johnston, 1997).

A special case exists in Svalbard, Norway where regulation of tourists is comprehensive in scope and restrictive in structure. Tourism regulation here is based upon strict legislation, enforced through the governor's office and is supplemented by a 1996 management plan for tourism and outdoor recreation (Ministry of Environment, 1996; Johnston, 1997). The legislation, which is applicable to commercial operators and to all tourists, provides for sanctions, penalties and revisions to itineraries, including activities and destinations (Kaltenborn & Hindrum, 1995). This management regime was developed in order to protect the environment and wildlife, protect cultural heritage and promote visitor safety. This approach to regulation of tourists indicates that Norway places high value on protecting the Svalbard 'wilderness' and, it could be argued, provides a good model for tourism management in other parts of the Arctic. An additional component of tourism regulation on Svalbard is the self-regulation practised by the tourism industry, which has made the archipelago a fertile ground for exploring the suitability of the WWF initiative (see Viken & Jørgensen, 1998).

In addition to legislative controls and policies such as those outlined above, another approach to controlling behaviour is to develop voluntary guidelines. The Finnish Tourist Board has produced a set of guidelines aimed at the tourism industry in an attempt to promote sustainable tourism (UNEP, 1995). These guidelines focus on a number of environmental, economic and social concerns, and key principles and practical measures for attaining sustainable tourism. The measures relate to resource use, the need for conservation and recycling and disposal of litter and refer specifically to water, energy and waste (UNEP, 1995). Another example of the guideline approach is the Ten Principles on Ecotourism prepared in 1993 by WWF Sweden and the Swedish Environmental Protection Agency (Sharp, 1995).

The WWF Project falls within the voluntary guidelines approach and is intended to be implemented at the international level. The WWF initiative, however, was not the first attempt to construct guidelines for Arctic tourism. A draft visitor code for the Arctic was produced by Mason (1994). This earlier effort has the following aims: to raise awareness among visitors of environmental issues in the Arctic; to generally inform and educate visitors; to make visitors aware of environmental and cultural issues; and, to be included as part of an overall tourism management strategy for the Arctic region. The code focused on a number of environmental and cultural issues, including instructions on the use of vehicles, prevention of disturbance and damage to wildlife and habitats, the control of fishing and hunting, the proper disposal of waste and the need to respect indigenous cultures.

The key objective of the WWF Arctic Tourism Project is 'to create incentives to make tourism more beneficial for nature conservation and local communities and to decrease its negative impacts on the environment' (Prokosch, pers. comm., 12 December 1998). The major tool, used to achieve this objective, is a set of codes of conduct. Codes of conduct are often used in conjunction with guidelines, but there are important differences between regulations, guidelines and codes of conduct. Regulations usually have some form of legal status while codes of conduct, codes of practice and guidelines, although attempting to control tourism, do not generally have this standing (Stonehouse, 1990). Guidelines are usually based on well considered precepts, indicating a course of action to be followed and perhaps providing some of the reasoning behind points, while codes of conduct supply rules for behaviour in certain circumstances (Stonehouse, 1996). They are usually voluntary and are designed to act as a form of self-regulation (Mason & Mowforth, 1996). A variety of tourism codes of conduct have been existence in, for example, the UK and Canada, for at least the last 20 years.

The primary issue in relation to the use of voluntary, self-imposed regulations is their effectiveness (Mason & Mowforth, 1996; UNEP, 1995). To be effective codes must be practised as intended, but the United Nations Environment Programme (UNEP, 1995) indicated that most tourism codes tend to be poorly implemented. UNEP also suggested that assessing effectiveness will necessitate measuring the outcomes of codes. UNEP recommended that those who develop codes should monitor the effects of implementation and ensure findings are reported to appropriate bodies.

To enhance the effectiveness of voluntary codes of conduct and guidelines Mason and Mowforth (1996) proposed that, in certain circumstances, it may be necessary to have some form of external regulation. As relatively few codes currently exist in the Arctic, the issue of self-regulation or external regulation is not yet of great significance. Evidence from locations outside the Arctic (McKercher, 1993; Forsyth, 1993; Porritt, 1995) suggests that external regulation may be far more effective than self-regulation. Mason and Mowforth (1996) argued that the motivation for self-regulation either is the tourist industry wishing to appear to be acting responsibly in advance of imposed regulation, or is an attempt to stave off external regulation.

Effectiveness is also linked with the purpose and intended audience of the code. Although there are a number of discrete target groups for tourism codes – visitors, the tourism industry and members of host communities – most codes are directed at visitors (UNEP, 1995; Mason & Mowforth, 1996). Valentine (1992) argued that in any given situation it is necessary to employ simultaneously a number of codes of conduct with different target audiences. For example, a code aimed at visitors should be used in conjunction with another aimed at operators; a code for one group on its own would not be as effective. Valentine (1992) also suggested codes should be employed as a part of a wider tourism management strategy.

Tourism codes of conduct frequently fail to specify either their broad aims or more specific objectives (Mason, 1994). UNEP (1995), having reviewed several different codes, outlined a number of objectives common to environmental codes of conduct for tourism. These are: serving as a catalyst for dialogue between tourism stakeholders; creating an awareness of the need for sound environmental management; promoting awareness among tourists of appropriate behaviour; promoting environmental protection among host populations; and, encouraging cooperation between governments agencies, host communities, industry and NGOs. Beyond environmental concerns, a number of visitor codes make reference to sociocultural matters, such as respect for local religious beliefs, while codes with industry as the audience frequently refer to the need for appropriate training and honest marketing of tourism products (Mason & Mowforth, 1996).

Another aspect of the effectiveness of codes rests on the intentions of those who use them. Codes of conduct can be used as marketing devices (Mason & Mowforth, 1996). Under circumstances in which there is little monitoring of implementation or effectiveness, codes are open to abuse and could be used inappropriately to promote holiday packages. Few codes exist in the Arctic at present and there is little evidence that they are being used for this purpose; however it is vital that for the credibility and effectiveness of these codes and the WWF-inititiated codes that they actually guide behaviour and do not simply serve as tools to enable operators to gain a marketing advantage.

Despite these important concerns about code effectiveness, there are clear benefits to using codes in a region such as the Arctic. Codes are voluntary and will be adopted by those who are motivated to use them. Codes are portable from one part of a region to another; they can be transferred and altered as needed. They provide greater flexibility than laws and policies for vagaries of circumstance. They can be enacted immediately and they allow people and companies to take responsibility for their actions.

The WWF Arctic Programme and the Arctic Tourism Project

Within the context of mounting concern about environmental impacts of a number of activities, including tourism, the WWF Arctic Programme was established in 1992. Its chief aim was to act as a coordination unit for Arctic conservation issues (Pedersen, 1998). At this time WWF had national organisations in Canada, Denmark, Finland, Sweden and the USA. During the Project history, WWF also established a programme office in Russia in 1994 and linked with the Iceland Nature Conservation Association in 1997 (Prokosch, pers. comm., 12 December 1998). The WWF Arctic Programme was established to assist the promotion of governmental efforts in Arctic environmental management, particularly the Arctic Environmental Protection Strategy. The WWF Arctic Programme was also an advocate of the Arctic Council (Mason, 1997a), primarily to ensure that environmental protection was the main issue of inter-governmental cooperation of Council members (Prokosch, pers. comm., 12 December 1998)

In response to existing tourism impacts and the potential for more widespread impacts, the WWF Arctic Programme began, in 1995, to develop a proposal for tourism management in the Arctic. The goal of this Project 'is to make Arctic tourism more environmentally friendly and ... to generate support for conservation projects' (Pedersen, 1998: 3). The specific goals of the Project are:

(1) To identify common interests of tourism and conservation and use these to reduce environmental problems and maximise the advantages for the Arctic environment and the local people.

(2) To develop guidelines for Arctic tourism that not only educate tourists
     about conservation and appropriate behaviour, but that also generate polit-
     ical support from the tourism industry and tourists for WWF's conservation
     objectives.
(3) To develop competition among tour operators concerning compliance with
     the guidelines, which will require a form of evaluation/certification that can
     be used for marketing purposes, and that will be awarded to those tour
     operators who comply with the guidelines.
(4) To increase recognition of the global significance of the Arctic.
(5) To increase recognition of local needs in the Arctic and its cultural diversity
     (Pedersen, 1998).

Project history

   A catalyst for the WWF Arctic Tourism Project came at the 1994 St. Petersburg
polar tourism conference as a call for the creation of industry guidelines within a
wider regulatory framework of tourism management for the Arctic (Mason,
1996). The Director of WWF Arctic was present at this meeting and was instrumental in WWF responding to this call through the establishment of the WWF
Arctic Tourism Project (Prokosch, 1998). This section provides an overview of the
main activities and outcomes of meetings that were integral in the Project development.
   The first official meeting of the Project took place in January 1996 in the form of
a combined workshop/conference held in Longyearbyen, Svalbard, Norway.
The chief aim of this meeting was the drafting of basic principles for Arctic
tourism (Mason, 1996). Forty-three participants, covering most, but not all, of the
Arctic countries attended, including tour operators, members of conservation
organisations, representatives of indigenous peoples' organisations, government representatives and scientists. Many of those present had been specifically
invited by the WWF Arctic Programme Director on the basis of their interest and
expertise (authors' notes, 1996).
   Prior to the meeting all participants were sent briefing material which
included a number of questions about Arctic tourism and conservation issues.
These questions asked participants to:

 • consider the relationship between potential guidelines and educational
   Arctic tourism;
 • consider how guidelines should be promoted and implemented;
 • consider who could create the tourism guidelines;
 • consider mechanisms to achieve competition between tour operators;
 • suggest lessons that could be learned from Antarctic tourism management;
 • consider ways of ranking more/less ecologically friendly tourism operations; and,
 • consider whether the term Arctic ecotourism should be used in the Project
   (WWF, 1995).

Responses to the questions were discussed by a small, working group of
participants at the meeting. The results of this group's discussions were
presented to all participants at the final conference session in the form of a draft
memorandum of understanding which provided the basis for later work on

developing guidelines and codes of conduct for tourism (Prokosch, 1996). The Memorandum of Understanding contained 13 statements on Arctic tourism and closely mirrored the original 13 questions given prior to the meeting. The memorandum made reference to minimising negative impacts of tourism, optimising benefits to local communities and promoting the conservation of nature. It suggested that cooperation between tour operators, as well as competition, could be in their interests. The memorandum recommended the creation of guidelines and codes of conduct for Arctic tourism. It indicated the need for local involvement in tourism and advocated the use of a contract between local communities and tour operators. It also contained suggestions for operators to reduce the use of resources, to recycle and to minimise damage. It recommended a wide dissemination of the guidelines/codes and suggested that financing for the development of these should be sought from Arctic tour operators (see Prokosch, 1996).

The next phase of the project was a working group meeting in August 1996, held in Cambridge, UK. The group comprised a number of participants from the Svalbard conference and several new collaborators, and it transformed the Memorandum of Understanding into ten basic principles for Arctic tourism (Johnston & Mason, 1997). Working group members also produced draft codes of conduct both for tour operators and tourists, and recommendations for communities involved in tourism.

In March 1997, the WWF Arctic Program, working jointly with the Norwegian Polar Institute, and the Svalbard Tourism Board held a second workshop on Svalbard. A number of those present at earlier meetings attended this meeting. Those who attended officially or unofficially represented a variety of communities of interest and came from 12 different countries, including all the Arctic nations. The objective of the workshop was to develop a process to implement the principles and codes of conduct that had been developed at earlier meeting, and to refine those principles and codes of conduct (Mason, 1997a). Tensions evident at the meeting were resolved through the formal commitment of the participants to:

(1) use amended principles as the foundation for the future implementation process of the project;
(2) further evaluate and amend the codes of conduct developed for operators and tourists, and to develop a consultation process for the involvement of communities and local people in the project; and
(3) outline a direction for the structure of the guidelines programme (authors' notes, 1997).

To support implementation, the workshop participants decided to create an eight member Interim Steering Committee which, with the logistical support of the WWF Arctic Programme, would guide the project in the coming year (Mason, 1997b). The Steering Committee members were elected by the meeting participants to represent indigenous peoples (2), destination tour operators (1), international operators (1), local tourism NGOs (1), conservation NGOs (2), and the research community (1). Individuals were also selected to ensure geographical representation among the Arctic countries. In order to enable participation of observers, such as members of the Arctic Council or the Nordic Council of Ministers, it was intended that an accreditation procedure be established (authors' notes, 1997).

Terms of reference for the interim committee were:

- to support responsible tourism and promote the goals of the initiative;
- to develop a consultation process for the involvement of communities and local people in the project;
- to establish criteria for membership;
- to establish levels of membership and develop a membership organisation;
- to promote wide dissemination of the guidelines;
- to maintain a web site/home page on the World Wide Web;
- to coordinate the translation of the guidelines into relevant languages;
- to develop a name for the programme, a logo, and a labelling system;
- to promote communication among all parties concerned;
- to provide information to communities, tour operators, and tourists regarding the Arctic tourism guidelines;
- to address and organise monitoring of the programme;
- to establish an Arctic tourism database;
- to promote national initiatives to implement the programme; and,
- to undertake fundraising on behalf of the organisation (authors' notes, 1997).

Logistical and secretarial support for the work of the Interim Steering Committee was to be provided by the WWF Arctic Programme (Mason, 1997b). This would enable an interim secretariat to coordinate the activities of the Interim Steering Committee and prepare for the permanent structure of the organisation. The office of the permanent secretariat was to be located in the Arctic (Mason, 1997b).

It was decided that a number of pilot projects would be established to evaluate the usefulness of the various components of the guidelines project. Evaluation of the pilot projects was to take place one year later, at which point a new Steering Committee would be elected and the office of the permanent secretariat would be formalised. It was recommended that the pilot projects would:

- develop a consultation process for the involvement of communities and local people in the project;
- develop a programme name, logo, and labelling system;
- evaluate users' interpretation of the language in the guidelines and codes;
- examine issues associated with the translation of the guidelines and codes into other languages relevant to Arctic tourism;
- assess the usefulness of the guidelines and codes in a variety of pilot projects as a means of investigating their applicability to operators, tourists and destinations;
- assess the effectiveness of the codes and guidelines as tools for education and gathering support for a particular Arctic conservation project; and
- address data collection needs (authors' notes, 1997).

In December 1997, the WWF Arctic Programme published *Ten Principles for Arctic Tourism, A Code of Conduct for Tour Operators* and *A Code of Conduct for Arctic*

Tourists. These documents were the first to put this material into a widely available published form. The documents were included in *Linking Tourism and Conservation in the Arctic*, first presented as an insert in the *WWF Arctic Bulletin* (1997, No. 4). Five thousand copies of this insert were distributed to tour operators, tourist boards, environmental management organisations and government officials as well as to the general public (Pedersen, 1998). The intention was to promote awareness of the principles and codes and to encourage further discussion on their content.

In February 1998 a workshop was held in Iceland to bring together the Interim Steering Committee, interested tour operators, and tourism researchers. The purposes of the meeting included: developing methods to measure compliance with codes; developing a structure for future implementation; examining funding sources; and, identifying appropriate pilot projects to evaluate various aspects of the principles, codes and implementation (WWF, 1998). Approximately 20 pilot projects were put forward to be executed during the tourism season of 1998 with the intention that reports on each of these would be provided in 12 months' time at the next international meeting of the project. The Interim Steering Committee indicated a number of tasks to be addressed in the next year. These included: the development of a discussion paper on options for formalising the structure of the implementing body; the development of a consultation process to involve Arctic communities; the development of position papers on marketing the programme and on evaluation and monitoring operator compliance; and, the development of a plan to raise funds to support the programme (WWF, 1998).

The processes involved in the project

This section of the article discusses a number of processes involved in the WWF Arctic Tourism Project. In particular, the processes of consultation and negotiation and the factors influencing these processes are discussed. This section also provides some critical comments on the nature of the implementation of the project.

Consultation and negotiation

The main processes involved in the Project meetings were consultation and negotiation. Although activities varied from meeting to meeting, common to all was a process in which participants were involved actively in preparing and presenting their own material and, in addition, commenting on and questioning the work of other participants. Hence, this was an interactive process of consultation, and as the Arctic Programme Director indicated at the first Project meeting, the aim was to achieve a consensus of views (Prokosch, pers. comm., 5 May 1995).

This process of consultation had the advantage that it gave ownership of the tasks to participants (see Carr & Kemmis, 1986). At the early stages an individual's interpretation of the direction of the project was important as it formed the foundation for the particular activity. A consultative approach can contribute to a general feeling of involvement and the belief that one's views are significant (Carr & Kemmis, 1986). Individuals had a substantial degree of involvement in the early stages of the Project. This also worked to motivate participants and contributed to a generally high level of commitment. Allowing a high degree of control appears to have been a successful strategy as the meetings generally achieved the tasks suggested.

The consultative approach process, however, is not without problems. Participants may have had a good deal of control, but they may also have wished for clearer direction. A perceived lack of direction at an early stage of the Project was evident at the meeting held in Cambridge, at which a small group gathered to respond to particular tasks outlined in the Memorandum of Understanding. The chief task was the development of three sets of codes or guidance: one for operators, one for tourists and one for communities. At the meeting itself the first two tasks were commenced, but not completed. The third task was given over to an individual to complete so that the community code could become part of a larger working document. However, there was a lack of time at this meeting for a detailed discussion of what a community code should look like, whether one was necessary and who should be responsible for overseeing its development. This lack of context may have come about because of insufficient direction or linkage from the Svalbard meeting about what the purpose of this code was to be: the Memorandum of Understanding simply indicated that a set of management principles for communities was necessary. Another source of difficulty may have stemmed from the reliance for the operator code and the tourist code on existing codes used in the Antarctic. While in the cases of operators and tourists there may have been similarities that made such a transfer useful, there was no analog for communities. Participants at the 1996 Svalbard meeting stressed the importance of community acceptance of the principles, but how this was to be accomplished was not clearly outlined for the work that took place at the next stage. This particular issue became central at the second (1997) Svalbard meeting (the third Project meeting) with discussions about what the appropriate approach to the communities should be. Disagreement with the idea of a code was expressed by some participants, while others who supported the idea argued that it was important to gain insights from community groups around the Arctic before drafting a community code, which would take some time. Hence, this combination of factors led to the removal from the initiative of a separate community code, though there continued to be a strong commitment to seeking input from Arctic residents on the content of the draft principles and codes for operators and tourists.

Group dynamics also were important in the working groups. In these situations there were individuals with very different backgrounds, experiences, interests and concerns. Workshops were held in English, which was not the first language of many participants. This gave an advantage to some participants over others. A combination of factors contributed to varying levels of participation: some individuals expressed well articulated views while others contributed little in formal discussions. At some meetings there was evidence of what has been reported elsewhere in similar circumstances, with 'strong voices' dominating and 'weaker voices' not being listened to, as well as there being unarticulated views (see Hall, 1994 and Joppe, 1996). In relation to the Project workshops, this can be illustrated with reference to one example. One participant was a particularly 'strong voice' in a working group at the first Svalbard meeting and subsequently at the second Svalbard meeting. This individual was adamantly in support of the term 'Arctic ecotourism' being used to designate the type of tourism advocated by the project. A number of other working group members expressed concern about the use of such a term, making reference to some of the issues around such labelling raised by Mason and Mowforth (1996). These contrary views were initially ignored, seemingly in part because the view they opposed was that expressed by a strong, articulate voice. At a later meeting a number of tour operators objected more strongly to the term and it was dropped. However, this example also demonstrates another side of the group dynamics. The participant who had argued for the use of the term 'ecotourism', willingly conceded the point and accepted the majority view on the issue and continued after this event to be a very active participant in the Project.

There were a number of benefits from the sharing of experiences and ideas in a working group setting. For example, similarities between the Antarctic and the Arctic situation were noted in working groups at the first Svalbard meeting. At the Cambridge meeting there was discussion of the situations where there was potential for learning from Antarctic experience with codes and where differences were too dramatic for a useful transfer. Numerous changes to the existing Antarctic codes for operators and tourists were made to begin accommodating the specificities of the Arctic context, such as reference to communities in the operator and tourist codes.

Another issue in group work relates to timing, communication and opportunities for input. Attempting to develop consensus among a diverse and widely scattered group of individuals with varying levels of resources (such as computer access, translation services, funds for travel) has meant that some individuals' ideas were not incorporated until late in the process or were not incorporated at all. The direction taken by earlier participants formed the foundation and also informed subsequent revisions of Project work. This continues to be a factor in the development of the initiative. An example of communication difficulties is the problems which develop in transferring information between computer network programmes. A more fundamental problem arises from the inability of some participants to return to later meetings, and the complete absence throughout the process of participants from various segments of the communities of interest. The latter problem means that some views were never heard (see Murphy, 1983; Joppe, 1996; Hall, 1994) while the former means that continuity was disrupted. Both are almost inevitable in such a project, but they have important implications for the process and the final product.

Operator acceptance is a key component in the success of the Project, but there may be a reluctance on the part of some participating operators to continue their participation and on the part of some non-participating operators to become part of the process. A number of operators may have resented the possibility of the imposition of external evaluation and some may have disliked the inclusive focus on all Arctic tourism, others may have felt left out of the process, and yet others may have disagreed with the nature of the initiative. Some operators may also have taken issue with the politics of the lead organisation, although the Project Director indicated that a number of operators were very willing to be linked with the WWF panda logo, presumably for the marketing advantage it would bring (Prokosch, pers. comm., 12 December 1998). At various points during the development stages comments were made that the very involvement of WWF could hinder operator and community participation in the Project. The acceptance of WWF varies from place to place in the Arctic and by interest group, but local operators and community representatives will have at least a chance to hear the aims of the Project and make their view known in the locations involved during the community consultations parts of the Project. For example, a series of community meetings in Nunavut in 1999 brought the programme to local residents to seek their input into draft guidelines.

Another factor influencing the process was the reliance by WWF-Arctic Programme on contract-style funding in which outcomes had to result from funded activities. This meant that meetings did achieve outcomes, but the emphasis on having a product of some description to come from meetings exerted pressure on working group members. This also appeared to cause difficulties for some operators and researchers who were involved in their own work and were not always able to dedicate as much time as needed to meet the deadlines of the Project. Also, dependence on an NGO and its funding means that disruptions in its operations reverberate to the external participants. For example, personnel changes within WWF occurred and resulted in some delays and some discontinuity. This was especially evident in delays between the 1997 Svalbard meeting, when the call for pilot projects was made, and the 1998 Iceland meeting, when pilot projects were finally outlined.

Nevertheless, in summary it is possible to state that during consultation and negotiation, despite some evidence of disagreements, dissatisfaction and delays, the major aims of avoiding conflict and building consensus, were generally successful. The success reflects a number of related factors. These are as follows:

(1) having meetings open to whoever displayed an interest and attempting to advertise such meetings widely;
(2) encouraging discussion of presentations and positions papers at meetings;
(3) using working sessions to focus participation and the development of 'products';
(4) seeking input via the web for versions of the guidelines and codes; and,
(5) giving feedback to participants in the form of summaries and documents.

The processes outlined above were used in an attempt to hear people and incorporate their ideas. While it is clear that not everyone agreed with everything, it would seem that most Project participants agreed with the basic principle that a Project like this was necessary. Therefore, they were willing to have their own interests subsumed in order to keep the Project moving. Hence, this was a form of negotiated consensus building which required participants to accept a majority rule approach in the interest of moving forward. That this negotiated consensus happened should be viewed as a major accomplishment of WWF.

Implementation

A major product of the Project was the publication in 1997 of the WWF Arctic Programme entitled *Linking Tourism and Conservation in the Arctic*. This contains the code of conduct for visitors to the Arctic and the code for operators. The codes are supported in the publication by a rationale and aims, a relatively unusual occurrence in this field (see UNEP, 1995; Mason & Mowforth, 1996). Tourism codes of conduct are intended to educate as well as regulate (Stonehouse, 1990,

Mason & Mowforth, 1996), and one of the major aims of the Project was to use the Arctic codes and principles as educational tools. Some participants at early meetings thought that the document that publicised the principles and codes should contain advice and instructions as well as the rationale supporting the codes themselves. A long version can be useful for certain types of implementation, such as with small operators who can guide clients through the document, yet there are disadvantages, particularly for independent tourists who may not have any interest in reading a long document. A contrary view held that a short version of the codes would enable greater flexibility and thus enhance implementation. This suggestion was rejected as a first step on the grounds that brief codes would have less of an educational impact; however, it was recognised that as implementation progressed there might be other ways to deliver the message to the various user groups.

A key issue in voluntary compliance regulation is effectiveness (Johnston, 1997; UNEP, 1995, Mason & Mowforth, 1996). The first aspect of effectiveness that the process examined was operator adherence with an emphasis on developing a system of evaluation to measure the degree of acceptance, implementation and effectiveness. It was agreed at various stages in the process that an important component of this system would be a mechanism for providing feedback to operators in order to help them improve their practice and to recognise their achievement.

A position paper was developed to explore how best to address the issues of adherence, implementation and effectiveness for operators (Johnston & Twynam, 1998). This paper is founded upon the premise that operational indicators, or those attributes of the experience that can be controlled individually by operators, can be evaluated using specific measures and several methods of evaluation. Experience from existing evaluation programs suggests that neither operator self assessment nor client assessment of operators alone is sufficient. Rather, using a number of approaches addresses evaluation from various perspectives, enabling a more comprehensive picture of operations and their success. The position paper recommended a formal operator checklist, site visits, client surveys, and evaluation of community-level or broad-level indicators. It also recommended the formalisation of an annual feedback and follow-up process and a system of incentives and rewards for operators.

Clearly a requirement vital for the success of the principles and codes initiative is acceptance and integration into Arctic tourism activities. Operator acceptance may be hindered by a reluctance to have external formal evaluations, but may be enhanced by a certification or reward system. For operators to have confidence in the system any external reviews/evaluations need to be confidential. A number of operators in the later meetings indicated that they, in fact, wanted to share information and experiences to learn from each other. This presented opportunities for new partnerships. Commercial sensitivity and related concerns of operators about their practices seemed less important in the Project than was initially envisaged. This would seem to relate, at least in part, to the geographical diversity of the operation headquarters and their markets. Also the operators generally came from different sectors and hence were not in direct competition. Even some in the same sector – the cruise industry – were less concerned about competition and more concerned about collaboration. This probably reflects their existing collaboration in the Antarctic as members of the International Association of Antarctic Tour Operators (IAATO).

Community acceptance of the principles and codes may be helped by promotion of the program to the general public and particular interest groups. Tourist acceptance can be increased through publicity and a strong operator and community emphasis on the principles. Equally important is that the codes fit the various situations within the Arctic regions. Given that the principles and codes were developed by a specific group of individuals, it should be apparent that the philosophical framework of the program itself may limit its applicability. This suggests the need for flexibility and a process for review, requirements which have been recognised since the early stages of the Project. A further requirement is that difficulties due to inter-regional differences such as language, culture, economic resources, government regulation, access to technology and access to communication are resolved. In particular language differences could pose a major barrier to communication during promotion and evaluation. A key effort to address this issue involved the translation of *Linking Tourism and Conservation in the Arctic* (WWF, 1997) into languages used by tourists to the Arctic or by residents, such as German, Norwegian and Inuktitut.

A second component of effectiveness that the process incorporated was the implementation of pilot projects to test various aspects of the principles, codes and programme generally. The position paper recommended that prior to the implementation of the programme across the Arctic that the implementing body undertake pilot projects to address effectiveness, comprehension, usefulness and other issues (Johnston & Twynam, 1998). Outlining potential pilot projects was a key purpose of the 1998 meeting in Iceland. At that point and in the following months 23 pilot projects were initiated to examine implementation. How successful this effort has been will be determined through formal evaluations at future Project meetings.

Conclusions

Tourism has been expanding in the Arctic and with growing concerns about environmental impacts, there has been an increased awareness of the need for improved tourism management. The WWF Arctic Tourism Project is an example of an attempt at tourism management. It was established to link tourism and conservation, with the intention of using tourism to promote conservation and minimise environmental damage in the Arctic. The Project has also aimed to maximise benefits from tourism to local communities. It has involved a number of different stakeholders and has, to date, produced tourism guidelines and codes of conduct for tourists and operators. These have been distributed to a number of operators, tourists, communities and others with an interest in the Arctic. Consultation and negotiation have been key processes in the Project and WWF Arctic Programme staff have attempted to listen and take heed of a number of different 'voices'. This process has been successful in giving participants in the Project a feeling of ownership. It also has enabled the sharing of experiences and views from which the Project has benefited. Yet, as participants have a variety of experiences and concerns and do not share a common first language, communication has not always proceeded smoothly. Group dynamics have also played a part; some voices have been louder than others and some views ignored or barely noted. Maintaining continuity has been difficult in the Project as a result of WWF staff changes and the inability of some participants to attend all meetings. Despite this discontinuity of participation for some, the group as a whole has been committed to achieving the overall aims and the specific objectives of each meeting using the ideas and experiences of those present. The process of negotiated consensus has meant that the common desire to effect change has been the foundation for the progress witnessed to date.

Two key outcomes of the Project have been the publication of the principles and codes in several languages and the initiation of pilot projects in a number of Arctic locations. Evaluations of the lessons to be learned from the pilot projects was to take place at the March 1999 meeting of the group in Husum, Germany. The lessons from the pilot projects will help WWF and other parties determine future direction for implementation, including changes to language in the draft stage principles and codes, changes to facilitate use of the codes in particular settings, and development of procedures to evaluate the effectiveness of the programme itself.

This Project demonstrates an important role for environmental non-governmental organisations such as WWF in making a significant contribution to attempts at developing sustainable tourism. In this Project WWF provided its organisational skills in initiating the Project, in seeking funding to continue the Project and in conducting several international meetings to accomplish particular tasks. In bringing together individuals with differing perspectives and attempting to achieve consensus, WWF staff demonstrated a willingness to listen and respond, and also the ability to usefully inform the debate. WWF staff indicated that the Project required action, not only words, and that the organisation was committed to acting quickly to facilitate the achievement of the Project aims. The success to date of this Project also suggests that, despite some opposition, WWF had an important advantage over an industry based organisation: a genuine and credible concern for the key resource for sustainable tourism, the environment.

Correspondence

Any correspondence should be directed to Dr Peter Mason, Reader in Tourism, Luton Business School, University of Luton, Park Square, Luton, UK (peter.mason@luton.ac.uk).

References

Bone, R. (1992) *The Geography of the Canadian North: Issues and Challenges.* Toronto: Oxford University Press
Bronsted, H. (1994) Tourism activities in Greenland. In C. Kempf and L. Girard (eds) *Tourism in Polar Regions Proceedings of the Symposium, Colmar, France, April 21–23, 1992.*
Butler, R.W. (1994) Tourism in the Canadian Arctic: Problems of achieving sustainability. In C. Kempf and L. Girard (eds) *Tourism in Polar Regions, Proceedings of the Symposium, Colmar, France, April 21–23, France, 1992.*
Carr, W. and Kemmis, S. (1986) *Becoming Critical: Education, Knowledge and Action Research.* Brighton: Falmer Press.
Colin, M. (1994) Ecotourism and conservation policies in Canada. In C. Kempf and L. Girard (eds) *Tourism in Polar Regions Proceedings of the Symposium, Colmar, France, April 21–23, 1992.*

Forsyth, T. (1993) *Sustainable Tourism: Moving from Theory to Practice.* Godalming: World Wide Fund for Nature.

Hall, C.M. (1994) *Tourism and Politics.* Chichester: John Wiley.

Hall, C.M. and Johnston, M.E. (1995) Introduction: Pole to pole: Tourism issues, impacts and the search for a management regime. In C.M. Hall and M.E. Johnston (eds) *Polar Tourism: Tourism in the Arctic and Antarctic Regions* (pp. 1–26). Chichester: John Wiley.

Hall, S. (1987) *The Fourth World: The Arctic and its Heritage.* London: Hodder and Stoughton.

Johnston, M.E. (1995) Patterns and issues in Arctic and sub-Arctic tourism. In C.M. Hall and M.E. Johnston (eds) *Polar Tourism: Tourism in the Arctic and Antarctic Regions* (pp. 27–42). Chichester: John Wiley.

Johnston, M.E. (1997) Polar tourism regulation strategies: Controlling visitors through codes of conduct and legislation. *Polar Record* 33 (184), 13–20.

Johnston, M. and Mason, P. (1997) The WWF initiative to develop guidelines and codes of conduct for Arctic tourism. *Polar Record* 25 (2), 351–353.

Johnston, M.E. and Twynam, G.D. (1998) Implementation of the operator programme: Evaluating effectiveness through principles, indicators and measures. In *Linking Tourism and Conservation in the Arctic, Proceedings* (pp. 6–12). Oslo: Norwegian Polar Institute.

Johnston, M.E. and Viken, A. (1997) Tourism development in Greenland. *Annals of Tourism Research* 24 (4), 978–982.

Joppe, M. (1996) Sustainable community tourism development revisited. *Tourism Management* 17 (7), 475–479.

Kaltenborn, B. and Hindrum, R. (1995) Opportunities and problems associated with the development of Arctic tourism: A case study from Svalbard in the Norwegian Arctic. Longyearbyen, unpublished report prepared for the Arctic Environmental Protection Strategy Task Force on Sustainable Development and Utilization.

Krippendorf, J. (1987) *The Holidaymakers.* London: Heinemann.

McKercher, R. (1993) Some fundamental truths about tourism: Understanding tourism's social and environmental impacts. *Journal of Sustainable Tourism* 1 (1), 6–16.

Mason, P. (1994) A visitor code for the Arctic? *Tourism Management* 15 (2), 93–97.

Mason, P. (1996) Developing guidelines for Arctic tourism. *Tourism Management* 17 (6), 464–465.

Mason, P. (1997a) Tourism codes of conduct in the Arctic and sub-Arctic region. *Journal of Sustainable Tourism* 5 (2), 151–165.

Mason, P. (1997b) Arctic tourism: Developing and implementing guidelines. *WWF-Arctic Bulletin* 4 (2), 12–13

Mason, P. and Mowforth, M. (1996) Codes of conduct in tourism. *Progress in Tourism and Hospitality Research* 2 (2), 151–164.

Ministry of Environment (Norway) (1996) *Guidelines: Management Plan for Tourism and Outdoor Recreation in Svalbard.* Oslo: Ministry of Environment.

Mowforth, M. and Munt, I. (1997) *Tourism and Sustainability.* Routledge: London.

Murphy, P. (1983) Tourism as a community industry. *Tourism Management* 5 (4), 180–193.

Pedersen, A.O. (1998) *Linking Tourism and Conservation in the Arctic.* Oslo: WWF International Arctic Programme, Internal Report-Project Description.

Porritt, J. (1995) Education and regulation for tourism. Paper given at the conference Managing Tourism: Education and Regulation for Sustainability, Commonwealth Institute, London, 16 November.

Prokosch, P. (1996) Guidelines for Arctic tourism on the way. *WWF-Arctic Bulletin* 1, 12–13.

Prokosch, P. (1998) Introduction. In B. Humphreys, A.O. Pedersen, P. Prokosch, S. Smith and B. Stonehouse (eds) *Linking Tourism and Conservation in the Arctic.* Meddelelser No. 159. Tromso: Norwegian Polar Institute.

Sharp, H. (1995) WWF-Sweden's project 'Eco-tourism'. *WWF-Arctic Bulletin* 1 (3), 11.

Smith, V. (1989) Eskimo tourism: Micro models and marginal men. In V. Smith (ed) *Hosts and Guests: The Anthropology of Tourism* (2nd edn) (pp. 55–82). Philadelphia: University of Pennsylvania Press.

Stonehouse, B. (1990) A travellers' code for Antarctic visitors. *Polar Record* 26 (156), 56–58.

Stonehouse, B. (1996) Briefing papers for conference WWF Arctic Tourism Guidelines, held at the Scott Polar Research Institute, University of Cambridge, August.

Sugden, D.E. (1982) *The Arctic and Antarctic : A Modern Geography*. Oxford: Blackwell.

Sugden, D.E. (1990) *The Arctic and Antarctic: A Modern Geography* (2nd edn). Oxford: Blackwell.

Umbreit, A. (1991) *Guide to Spitsbergern* (3rd edn). Chalfont St Peter: Bradt Publications.

UNEP (1995) *Environmental Codes of Conduct*. Technical Report No 29. Paris: United Nations Environment Programme.

Urry, J. (1990) *The Tourist Gaze*. London: Sage.

Valentine, P. (1992) Nature-based tourism. In B. Weiler and C.M. Hall (eds) *Special Interest Tourism* (pp. 105–128). London: Belhaven.

Viken, A. (1993) The Arctic tourist experience. Paper presented at the Fifth World Wilderness Conference, Arctic tourism and ecotourism symposium, Tromso, Norway, September 24–October 1.

Viken, A. (1995) Tourism experiences in the Arctic–the Svalbard case. In C.M. Hall and M.E. Johnston (eds) *Polar Tourism: Tourism in the Arctic and Antarctic Regions* (pp. 73–84). Chichester: John Wiley.

Viken, A. and Jørgenson, F. (1998) Tourism on Svalbard. *Polar Record* 34 (189), 123–128.

Walker, D.A., Cate, D., Brown, J. and Racine, C. (1987) Disturbance and recovery of Arctic Alaskan tundra terrain. *CRELL Report* 87–11. Hanover, NH: US Army Corps of Engineers.

WWF (1995) Briefing papers for conference. Developing Guidelines for Arctic Tourism, Svalbard, January, Oslo, WWF Arctic Programme.

WWF (1997) Linking tourism and conservation in the Arctic (Supplement). *WWF-Arctic Bulletin* 4.

WWF (1998) Linking tourism and conservation in the Arctic – Workshop summary. Unpublished report prepared by WWF Arctic Programme.

6. An Australian Research Partnership Between Industry, Universities and Government: The Cooperative Research Centre for Sustainable Tourism

Terry De Lacy and Madeleine Boyd
CRC for Sustainable Tourism, Gold Coast, Australia

The Australian tourism industry has grown rapidly within the last two decades and now contributes significantly to the national economy. It is widely agreed by industry advocates that tourism development has progressed to a point where many pressing issues must be addressed to assure continued economic success and to avoid negative environmental and social impacts. At present there is a poor research basis to underpin tourism development, as well as a weak research culture. This may be attributed to: a market failure for research investment; a public research bias against service industry research; and a gulf between research providers and users. The Cooperative Research Centre (CRC) for Sustainable Tourism has the aim of overcoming these barriers by applying the Australian CRC model for cross-sectoral research collaboration to enhance the sustainability of tourism. A number of universities and private and public sector agencies are now participants. Research and development programmes for tourism are in the areas of: planning and environmental management; technology, engineering & design; policy, products and business; training and education; and industry extension. To date the CRC model is proving successful, with increasing participation from industry and researchers. However, the success of this partnership will require overcoming the 'two cultures'; between industry and researchers; between applied and theoretical; between different research disciplines; between different industry sectors; between different geographical regions; between global and local; between competing ideologies; and so on.

It is theory that dictates what we observe

Albert Einstein (quoted in Bowkett, 1996)

Tourism Research Needs

The Australian tourism industry has grown rapidly within the last decade and now contributes significantly to the national economy. In 1997 tourism earned $16 billion in exports, accounted for approximately 10.5% of gross domestic product and was directly and indirectly responsible for the employment of 1.1 million Australians (approx 12%) (Bureau of Tourism Research, 1997). It is widely agreed by industry advocates that tourism development has progressed to a point where many key issues must be addressed to assure continued success. This is driven by many factors, including: the 2000 Olympic games which will focus international attention on Australia; a competitive global market especially in developing economies; the diversification of tourism products to meet the demands of the increasingly discerning consumer; rapid changes resulting from e-commerce; increasing density of development in the coastal zone; an identified need for regional development; and greater awareness of the social and environmental impacts of tourism.

In a recent industry report to the federal government Hutchison (1997) highlighted the urgent need for a substantial increase in the information and knowledge base upon which industry policy, planning, investment and management decisions are based. In particular he indicated that:

- a sound research and statistical base for the tourism industry is critical to maintaining its international competitiveness;
- the data available to enable sound infrastructure investment, appropriate product development and effective marketing strategies is either scarce, deficient and in the case of most small businesses, non-existent;
- tourism research is desperately needed by all tourism businesses and by governments to provide satisfactory evidence of return on investment; and
- the foundation of future tourism rests with small developing businesses primarily in the regions of Australia and it is here that data was found to be significantly deficient.

Important statistical and market data is collected and analysed by the Australian Bureau of Statistics, Bureau of Tourism Research (BTR), Tourism Forecasting Council, and federal and state tourism authorities. However, little strategic work is done to understand the:

- dynamics of source markets;
- subtle and every changing motivations and desires of the postmodern tourist consumer;
- structure of particular tourist systems;
- yields, costs, benefits and alternatives for various tourism systems;
- principles of sustainable planning of destinations, natural resources, infrastructure and regions;
- development of reliable predictive models for sustainable tourism products;
- travel and tourism impact and opportunities of changing technologies; and so on.

The attractions of Australia's unique natural heritage and climate are recognised as primary industry strengths for international competitiveness (Hutchison, 1997) including, but also surpassing, icons such as Uluru, the Great Barrier Reef, and kangaroos and koalas. Even the Australian 'beach' image is dependent upon natural coastal environmental assets. Tourism, more than any other industry sector, relies on the maintenance of environmental quality. As well, ecotourism is often considered to be a viable alternative land use in sensitive natural areas, as well as a source of funding for managing rare species, threatened habitats and protected areas. However, little research has been carried out to provide a sound basis for these developments.

Thus, despite its immense value to the Australian economy, employment, environment, and regional development (in particular indigenous development), the research and development (R&D) investment in tourism by the private and public sectors is minimal (Table 1). What research is done is not based on effective collaboration between industry and academic researchers (or

indeed effective collaboration between academic researchers in different institutions) resulting in duplication of effort, poor strategy development and an
overall waste of very limited resources.

Clearly Australia lacks the tourism R & D base to drive innovation which is so
crucial for the sustainable growth of its tourism industry in an every increasingly
competitive environment.

The failure of tourism research in Australia

Table 1 clearly demonstrates a major market and public policy failure. Why?

The failure of the Australian community to provide effective strategic knowledge to its tourism industry may be attributed to:

- the systematic failure of the market to provide the required research investments;
- the historical distribution of Australian public research investment away
  from service industries; and
- the separation between research suppliers and users in many sectors of the
  Australia economy.

Failure of the market

It is estimated that 90% of the Australian tourism industry comprises small to
medium-sized businesses (Ruthven, 1998) (as tourism is not an 'official' industry
category, reliable policy data is notoriously difficult to obtain). Operators in
these size-classes lack the capacity to conduct research into anything other than
their own historical performance.

Table 1 Research and development effort by industry, 1994–95

	Industry product as share of GDP	Industry share of total exports	Govt R&D expenditure as share of		Total R&D expenditure as share of	
			Industry product	All Govt R&D	Industry Product	Total R&D
	%	%	%	%	%	
Agriculture, forestry, fishing and hunting	3.2	21.1	4.1	27.4	5.3	9.5
Mining	4.4	36.0	0.7	6.5	2.7	6.7
Manufacturing	14.8	18.4	0.4	11.3	3.5	29.2
Transport and Communications	9.1	8.3	0.2	2.8	1.8	9.2
Tourism	7.1	12.6	0.03	0.4	0.06	0.2
All Industries			0.5		1.8	

Some of the larger enterprises, such as Qantas, obviously invest heavily in research. However, many of Australia's large tourism enterprises are multinational and invest their research dollars in North America and Europe.

Beautiful but fragile natural areas are commonly sites of tourism activity, but any environmental impacts are external to the commercial success of individual operators. These externalities, which tourism has in common with other industries operating in sensitive environments, has resulted in an under- investment in associated environmental research.

Regional economies in Australia are suffering from an historical downturn in commodity prices, particularly for agricultural products. This is devastating many communities. While tourism is one of the few sectors of the economy with the potential to deliver sustainable regional development, structural impediments inhibit development outside the major gateways and cities. Consequently there is insufficient impetus to stimulate investment in producing strategic regional tourism knowledge and innovation, so essential for infrastructure, product development and marketing.

A bias against service industry research

Service industries comprise 75% of the Australian economy and account for 80% of total employment, yet it is estimated public research investment into service sector problems is only a tiny fraction of total public research investment (Mercer, 1998). This may be attributed to the historical dependence of the Australian economy on primary production, which is still reflected in public research policy. For example, agricultural research occurs in seven large university faculties; in many divisions of the Commonwealth Scientific and Industrial Research Organisation (CSIRO); through well resourced state agriculture departments (for example the Queensland State Department of Primary Industries runs over 30 well equipped and staffed research stations and laboratories); and in 14 cooperative research centres. Indeed, total public sector investment in agricultural research is several orders of magnitude greater per GDP dollar than in tourism (Table 1). In addition, the major source of federal government grants for innovation in the private sector, the AusIndustry R&D Start Program, recognises only activities developing 'physical' products for 'manufacture'. Most social and business research into human behaviour, business systems, information needs and so on are considered as 'market research' and hence ineligible for grants.

The gulf between research providers and users

It is estimated that 50% of growth in OECD economies can be attributed to the uptake by industry of research innovation (CRC Association, 1997a). However, the degree of uptake in Australia is far from optimal (CRC Association, 1997b) and industry investment in research and development is well below the OECD average. In Australia there exists a separation between the operational spheres of researchers and research users. This may be partly attributed to a view espoused in a Draft Industry Commission Review of Research that researchers 'cannot be trusted to set the research agenda' (Cullen, 1996) and a tendency towards anti-intellectualism in Australian culture. The 'ivory tower' mentality prevalent in academic institutions may serve to reinforce these views. Government and industry investors clearly expect that research will benefit socioeconomic objectives beyond simply the advancement of knowledge (Turpin *et al.*, 1996). Conversely, all aspects of the research continuum, from basic (advancement of knowledge, development of theory, diversification of concepts) to strategic and applied (practical innovation relating to a defined application), have values which might not be appreciated by those not directly involved with research (Cullen, 1996). The issue, more specifically, is that there exists a communication breakdown in which research outcomes and their value are not made clear to the potential research users, and this is partly due a limited awareness in the research community regarding the nature of issues which are relevant to the users.

In an attempt to address, in at least some small way, the chronic lack of strategic information for the tourism industry, the Australian Government established a nationally funded Cooperative Research Centre for Sustainable Tourism (crcTourism).

The Cooperative Research Centers Program

Forging collaborative partnerships

The failure of the market to invest or participate in research with long-term and strategic benefits has implications for national economic, environmental and social welfare. An essential role of government is to address such failures. One policy initiative, introduced in 1990, was to establish the Cooperative Research Centres (CRC) Program. The objectives of CRC program are to:

(1) establish internationally competitive industry sectors through supporting long-term, high quality scientific and technology research;
(2) Stimulate a broader education and training experience, particularly in graduate programmes, and enhance employment prospects of students through involvement in major cooperative, user-orientated research programmes;
(3) capture the benefits of research by strengthening the link between research and its commercial and other applications;
(4) Utilise national research effort and resources more efficiently by promoting increased cooperation and building stronger research networks.

(CRC Association, 1998)

CRCs provide a focal point for research within a nominated field by attracting funding, formulating strategic research plans and disseminating outcomes. They are generally based at universities or CSIRO, with management boards including representatives from private organisations and public sector agencies; thus linking researchers with research users. Broadly, research users and researchers jointly select research projects, which are funded by the research users in addition to a public seed grant. The research institutions receive funds to undertake the nominated projects, but also contribute 'in kind' resources, such as time and infrastructure. The unique feature of the CRC programme is that it strengthens collaboration by putting in place formal long-term strategic contractual agreements between research providers and research users in the public and private sectors (CRC Association, 1997b).

By 1997 there were 67 CRCs covering a wide range of disciplines, from agriculture, mining and manufacturing technology to information and communication technology and environmental management; and from 1997 one in Tourism.

The CRC for Sustainable Tourism (crcTourism)

Vision

In August 1997 the concerns of the tourism industry were heeded with the establishment of the CRC for Sustainable Tourism (crcTourism). Through this organisation an initial injection of $14.72 million of public funds over seven years have been committed to 'seed' the development of 'a dynamic, internationally competitive and sustainable tourism industry' by 'delivering innovation for and strategic knowledge and products to: business, community and government to enhance the environmental, economic and social sustainability of tourism'.

Structure

crcTourism is incorporated as a limited liability company. All partners (Table 2) are shareholders in the company and contribute substantial cash and in-kind (mainly university researchers' time) resources each year of the seven year initial life of the company. Industry participants, while not shareholders, contribute to individual projects and programmes. A board is responsible for the management of the centre and comprises one director from each participant plus two independent directors. Under the board, the crcTourism management structure incorporates: executive, finance and audit, management, research and industry committees, plus an industry forum. In practice crcTourism operates on a national level; while the 'headquarters' are at Griffith University, most of the sub-programme coordinators are based at participating universities. In addition, 'geographical nodes' have been established in each of the states and territories which both facilitate national coordination of research and allow a focus on local tourism problems.

The board, various committees and the industry forum are the means whereby the stakeholders have input into the research strategy. Industry committees have been established by Tourism Council Australia (TCA) to review each research programme and evaluate research proposals for industry benefit, prioritise them and suggest potential industry participants.

Programmes

Through the initial stages of collaboration crcTourism was able to broadly identify key areas for targeting strategic research. This was the basis for the three research and development and two education and extension programme areas, under which major sub-programmes and individual projects are being developed (Table 3).

International programmes

Tourism is a global industry that links Australia economically, politically and culturally to key partner countries in Asia and beyond. The international market is extremely competitive and sensitive to many economic, social and environmental variables in origin and destination countries. For example, the present

Table 2 Participants in crcTourism as of March 1999

Tourism industry association partners	*University partners*
Tourism Council Australia	Griffith University
Australian Federation of Travel Agents	James Cook University
	Northern Territory University
Government partners	University of Queensland
Tourism Queensland	University of New South Wales
Tourism New South Wales	Southern Cross University
Tourism Tasmania	Victoria University
Western Australian Tourist Commission	La Trobe University
Canberra Tourism and Events Corp.	University of Tasmania
NSW Parks and Wildlife Service	Canberra University
Tourism Victoria	Murdoch University
	Edith Cowan University
	University of Technology Sydney

Industry participants	
Qantas Airways Ltd	Touraust Corporation
Gold Coast City Council	Warner Brothers Movie World
Conrad Jupiters	American Express
Gold Coast Tourism Bureau	Restaurant & Catering Association
Cairns Port Authority	Cairns City Council
Australian Football League	Melbourne City Council
Ernst and Young	Atlas Travel Technologies

turmoil in Asian economies is currently impacting severely on various tourism sectors and destinations. crcTourism operates not only in Australia, but seeks to interact with international partners in both a commercial and research capacity. At present crcTourism is active in China, Nepal, Bhutan, Philippines and Papua New Guinea. In less developed countries, crcTourism aims to work with local people to enhance conservation and community development opportunities through sustainable tourism enterprise. In addition, crcTourism has recently been appointed as the international sustainable tourism research provider for the World Travel and Tourism Council (WTTC) and has entered into partnership with Green Globe to provide a research base for its development and deliver the new Green Globe 21 programme in Asia Pacific.

Making the Partnership Work

The summary description in the last section leaves unsaid all the interesting issues, discourse, tensions and compromises that are required to make such an ambitious operation work. Key problems have included: securing financial and time commitments from individual enterprises; getting industry to focus on stra-

Table 3 crcTourism programmes

Tourism planning and environmental management R&D (Coordinator Professor Ralf Buckley)

Aim: Develop improved ecosystem, environmental and heritage management tools and planning systems to: enhance the quality of tourism products; reduce compliance costs; ensure the sustainability of underlying ecological processes and heritage values; and deliver increased economic, social and cultural benefits to the community.

Sub-programmes:

- Tourism development and ecosystem management in the coastal zone.
- Best-practice environmental management in tourism – a crcTourism/TCA 'Green Leaders' initiative: tours; lands; and sites.
- Wildlife tourism – identify and realise opportunities for wildlife tourism and propose measures to facilitate its sustainability.
- Planning for sustainable tourism – construct principles to guide the planning and regulatory framework for tourist development.
- Mountain tourism – identify and realise opportunities for mountain tourism and propose measures to facilitate its sustainability.

Tourism information technology, engineering & design R&D (Coordinator Professor Ray Volker)

Aim: Address engineering, technological and infrastructure issues of specific relevance to the tourism industry by developing cost-effective, low- impact technologies for construction, maintenance and operation of tourist resorts; developing cost-effective, low-impact engineering solutions for coastal tourism develop ments; and enhancing the competitiveness of travel and tourism by better use and application of information technology.

Sub-programmes:

- Coastal amenities and the coastal zone.
- Waste management, water supply and associated environmental impact issues.
- Physical infrastructure design and construction.
- Travel and tourism information technology.

Tourism policy, products & business R&D (Coordinator Professor Bill Faulkner)

Aim: Provide a research foundation for the strategic development of the tourism industry through broad-based research projects covering the structure and dynamics of tourism markets, product development, impact assessment, policy and planning frameworks and strategic enterprise management.

Sub-programmes:

- Consumer behaviour, market segmentation and marketing.
- Events tourism: the role of events in destination development and marketing.
- Tourism economics, policy and planning.
- Strategic management, business planning and development.
- Regional tourism
- Indigenous tourism.

Table 3 (cont.)

Tourism training and education (Coordinator Professor Philip Pearce)

Aim: Through education, training, and developing cross institutional and industry links, (including international ones), enhance the quality of postgraduate training, improve the delivery and industry relevance of travel and tourism education and training, to facilitate a more internationally competitive tourism industry.

Tourism industry extension (Coordinator Mr Peter O'Clery)

Aim: Facilitate linkages between users and researchers to: focus research; encourage direct industry involvement in projects; commercialise IP; transfer technology into industry; and market research products nationally and internationally to grow crcTourism's research business.

---

tegic rather than tactical research; engaging researchers from a variety of disparate disciplines to focus on solving tourism problems; encouraging academics to focus on research outcomes (enhanced profits, reduced environmental impact, etc.) rather than outputs (papers, models, etc.). Tension and divisions have included those between industry demands for short-term outcomes versus researcher interest in longer-term development of theory and principle; discipline based and interdisciplinary based researchers; physical and social scientists; competing ideologies of consumption and conservation; the city and the bush; large global companies and small family run enterprises; inbound and outbound tourism operators; and so on.

The ongoing resolution of these issues and tension has to date produced the following strategies and processes.

Engaging industry

Australia has a range of effective industry organisations. Two of the largest, Tourism Council Australia and Australian Federation of Travel Agents, are core partners (shareholders) and others are participants (non-shareholders who contribute financial support for particular programmes) in crcTourism and coordinate industry involvement. Australia has very strong state (provincial) tourism commissions (boards) jointly funded by government and industry. Six of these are partners in crcTourism and have played a key role in directing crcTourism's research strategy. Thus the engagement of industry has been achieved by involving the industry associations and government tourism authorities in the broader 'public good' research and involving individual businesses in research which aims to produce intellectual property of commercial value that can be shared by crcTourism and the participating enterprises.

Developing strategic research

Following initial industry/researchers workshops, crcTourism established three broad research programmes each led by a research coordinator. These have been divided into a number of sub-programmes led by a researcher and assisted by a mainly industry-based steering committee. Each sub-programme has, or is producing, a strategy consisting of needs, gaps, objectives, partners and proposed projects, outputs and outcomes to guide research over the seven years of crcTourism.

One example of such a sub-programme is wildlife tourism, one of the fastest growing sectors of tourism worldwide, estimated to generate an annual revenue of US$47–$155 billion (Higginbottom, 1998). Further, because wildlife is often most abundant far from major urban development, wildlife tourism can provide a much needed boost to depressed economies in rural areas – an issue particularly relevant to Australia. The unique fauna of Australia is a potential tourism resource for both international and domestic markets: according to an international visitor survey (Blamey & Hatch, 1998) the most frequent factor in influencing visitors' decisions to come to Australia is wildlife/nature and more than four million Australians visit captive wildlife facilities such as zoos each year. However, this potential has not yet been systematically explored and effective marketing approaches to promote wildlife attractions have not been developed.

While having considerable economic potential, wildlife tourism based on free ranging animals has the potential to destroy the very resource on which it is based. For example, there are concerns about the impacts of whale watching and artificial provisioning of wildlife for tourism in Australia; yet there have been few attempts to assess or monitor such effects.

Research on wildlife tourism requires investigation of the interactions between wildlife and tourists; the tourism operations and operators; the wildlife species and the habitats upon which they depend; and the host communities. Such research requires an interdisciplinary approach bringing together biological, social, and economic perspectives, as befits the CRC model. The strategy for research within the crcTourism wildlife tourism sub-programme is three-staged. The first stage will involve collation and analysis of existing information and views of key stakeholders. This will provide guidance as to priority issues to be addressed by the wildlife tourism industry and to provide a direction for future research within the sub-programme. The second and major research stage will focus on field research to derive lessons for the future directions and management of wildlife tourism, but will also feed directly into product development. The final phase will use these results to develop policies and products to directly support sustainable management and development of the industry.

Determining the research portfolio

Despite the importance of effective partnerships, structure and strategies, the reality is that quality research is done by creative, experienced and technically competent scientists supported by infrastructure and funding. crcTourism has only a small fraction of the funds needed to meet the research demands placed on it by both its research users and suppliers. It allocates its funds firstly by determining the strategies described above; allocating a budget based on this strategy; calling for project applications to fit needs expressed in the sub-programme strategies; and ranking project applications on the basis of industry need and technical merit. Industry need is determined by an industry panel established for each of the three research programmes, and technical merit by the research committee (chief executive and programme coordinators) and/or referees. This is carried out on an annual basis. Priority is given to projects that exhibit strong industry collaboration including third party funding. Project management involves payment on agreed milestones and deliverables including reviews by members of the sub-programme steering committees.

Cost/benefits of the Partnership

Some of the potential benefits of crcTourism have been described above. One clear advantage of the CRC partnership model is that it provides a stable framework for sustained dialogue between the many players involved in tourism research, development and extension. The time of writing coincides with the release of crcTourism's first annual report. At this stage the organisation is undergoing a rapid expansion and there is considerable interest from many potential research users. Success, of course, can be measured in many forms. Simply by being established, bringing so many partners together, attracting significant funding, establishing a national strategic research framework and undertaking high priority research projects, is in itself a success. But to facilitate a sea change in tourism research in Australia, which is what is needed, crcTourism will have to overcome many cultural and institutional divides. Bridging all these different cultures and institutions is, to put it mildly, no small task. The 'transaction' costs are high. Considerable time of the participants in crcTourism is expended in communicating between academic institutions, state nodes, industry organisations, companies, government agencies, PhD students and others. Although crcTourism is determinedly digitising its business model (crctourism.com.au) personal and meeting communication is essential, and with Australian distances, expensive. Eight per cent of crcTourism's A$5.4 projected cash budget in 1999/00 has been allocated for administration and although the approximately A$10 annual 'in kind' budget has not estimated an allocation to administration, it is likely to be in a similar range of 8%. But the CRC partnership model has been deliberately established to foster maximum communication and establish processes to move beyond the 'divides'. Several high level government/industry reviews of the overall CRC programme have concluded that the investment in collaboration, communication, networks and industry/research institutional partnerships, is producing a significant boost to innovation in Australia's industry, economy and society.

The Cooperative Research Centre for Sustainable Tourism is an ambitious experiment to stimulate innovation in the Australian tourism industry. It should also provide a vehicle to develop, as Einstein advocated, improved theory to better observe all components of the tourism system, hence enhancing its sustainability.

Correspondence

Any correspondence should be directed to Professor Terry De Lacy, Chief Executive, CRC Tourism, Griffith University, PMB 50, Gold Coast Main Centre, Queensland 9726, Australia (t.delacy@mailbox.gu.edu.au).

References

Blamey, R. and Hatch, D. (1998) *Profiles and Motivations of Nature Based Tourists Visiting Australia*. Canberra: Bureau of Tourism Research,.
Bowkett, S. (1996) *Meditations for Busy People*. Bath: Thorsons.

Bureau of Tourism Research (1997) *BTR Research Paper No. 3, Tourism's Direct Economic Contribution 1996–97.* Canberra: Bureau of Tourism Research.

CRC Association (1997a) Mortimer misses the point. Media release 25 July 1997 from Cooperative Research Centres Association, Australia.

CRC Association (1997b) *Background Notes.* Pamphlet prepared by the Cooperative Research Centres Association, Inc. Australia.

CRC Association (1998) *Cooperative Research Centres Program: Guidelines for Applicants – 1998 Round.* CRC Association, Australia.

Cullen, P. (1996) A framework for considering collaboration. In *Managing Collaboration for Scientific Excellence.* CRC for Freshwater Ecology, Canberra.

Higginbottom, K. (1997) Wildlife tourism: Facilitating its sustainable development. A research prospectus prepared for the CRC for Sustainable Tourism, Gold Coast (unpublished).

Hutchison, J. (1997) *Tourism: Getting it Right for the Millennium.* A report from Mr Jon Hutchison, Managing Director of the Sydney Convention and Visitors Bureau, to the Hon. Jon Moore MP, Minister for Industry, Science and Tourism, providing industry input to the development of a National Tourism Plan. Canberra: DIST.

Mercer, D. (1998) Tourism a key for a national strategy. Paper presented to Australian National Tourism Convention, Tourism Council Australia, Brisbane, October.

Ruthven, P. (1998) Economics and societal trends. Paper presented to Australian National Tourism Convention, Tourism Council Australia, Brisbane, October.

Turpin, T., Garrett-Jones, S., Rankin, N. and Aylward, D. (1996) *Using Basic Research; Part 2: Socio-economic Connections to Academic Research in Australia. Australian Research Council Commissioned Report No. 45.* Canberra: Australian Government Publishing Service.

7. Developing a Typology of Sustainable Tourism Partnerships

Steve Selin
Division of Forestry, PO BOX 6125, West Virginia University, Morgantown, WV 26506-6125, USA

Partnerships and collaboration have come of age in the tourism field. However, our understanding of how partnerships form and how to build the capacity of appropriate collaborative ventures has lagged behind developments in the field. This paper first discusses how, within a United States context, partnerships are contributing to sustainable tourism development and then reviews past partnership research across several disciplines. Next, this research is extended by developing a preliminary typology of sustainable tourism partnerships, identifying dimensions by which tourism partnerships vary or are similar across time and geographic region. Representative tourism partnerships are selected and plotted along a number of dimensions including: geographic scale, legal basis, locus of control, organisational diversity and size, and time frame. By better understanding the diversity of forms partnerships take in response to societal pressures, tourism managers can begin to design partnerships that provide the appropriate response to resolving intractable problems or taking advantage of significant opportunities.

As we approach the end of the 20th century, it has become quite clear to tourism managers, planners, and academics that no one individual or organisation can dictate the future of the tourism industry. Whether the tourism objective is economic development, conservation, social justice, or protected area management, we are discovering the power of collaborative action. This integration has spawned a diverse array of new inter-organisational forms and agreements including multinational firms, coalitions formed by global accords, regional planning authorities, joint management of protected areas, and community-based cooperatives. These emerging partnerships can be defined as situations where there is a 'pooling or sharing of appreciations or resources (information, money, labor, etc.) among two or more tourism stakeholders to solve a problem or create an opportunity that neither can address individually' (Selin & Chavez, 1995).

Much of the literature describing emerging partnerships in the tourism field has been descriptive in nature (Jamal & Getz, 1995). Typically, accounts of individual initiatives identify the advantages of working together and suggest the model be applied widely. Unfortunately, like other social forms, partnerships can be a force for good or bad. Concentration of power in multinational firms may be efficient in monetary terms but may marginalise national social justice and environmental laws. Missing from the tourism literature have been science-based investigations attempting to sift through the inflated rhetoric to develop a deeper understanding of tourism partnerships and collaboration, an understanding which can then be used to enhance the capacity of partnerships which contribute to the public good. The purpose of this paper is to, first, discuss how partnerships are contributing to sustainable tourism development, primarily within a United States context. A second purpose is to develop a preliminary typology of sustainable tourism partnerships being convened or currently operating in the United States.

Partnerships and Sustainable Development

A variety of societal forces are providing powerful incentives for tourism interests to forge collective responses to industry challenges and opportunities. Rapid economic and technological change, global interdependence, and blurred boundaries between government, industry, and the voluntary sector have spawned a diverse array of collaborative responses to gain access to new technologies or spread the cost of marketing innovation over several parties (Selin, 1993). However, this assessment is focused on one genre of emerging tourism partnerships – those convened to pursue a 'sustainable' path for economic development, conservation or other mutually agreed upon tourism objective.

While there has been considerable debate within the tourism field about what 'sustainable development' is and how it applies to tourism development (Hunter, 1997), that is not the purpose of this paper. Rather, the purpose here is to illustrate how partnerships have emerged as a strategy for implementing a sustainable course for tourism development. In the United States, in 1993, President Clinton convened the President's Council on Sustainable Development to develop a national sustainable development action strategy and to follow up on recommendations made at the Earth Summit, held in 1992. In a summary document to the work of this Council, Sitarz (1998) profiles sustainable development initiatives taking root in the United States and outlines actions needed to achieve a sustainable America. In the topical areas of most interest to tourism stakeholders – sustainable natural resources and sustainable communities – the report highlights emerging partnerships and collaborative approaches to natural resource and community planning and recommends actions to institutionalise these collective forms of planning and management.

A majority of tourism partnerships described in the sustainable development literature are cross-sector initiatives that often involve representatives from industry, government, and the voluntary sectors (Sitarz, 1998). For example, the Coalition for United Recreation in the Eastern Sierras, dedicated to provide coordinated planning for outdoor recreation resources, includes over 90 members representing 50 different agencies as diverse as the USDA Forest Service, resort owners, and the Sierra Club (Selin & Myers, 1998). This is not to say that sustainable tourism development cannot result from partnerships within one sector. Examples from the tourism field abound such as recent initiatives by hotel and restaurant associations to promote environmental responsibility through recycling and other eco-efficiency measures. However, the negotiation, mutually determined goals and actions, and monitoring resulting from cross-sector partnerships make it more likely that these initiatives will result in sustainable outcomes.

Recent Partnership Theory and Research

It is tempting to assume that the emergence of partnerships and collaboration in the tourism field is unique and that little systematic research has examined this important topic. Unfortunately, this assumption would ignore a wealth of knowledge that has accumulated over the past two decades attempting to understand these new inter-organisational forms and identify strategies for enhancing their capacity. As society has become more complex and economies more interdependent, organisations are finding it increasingly difficult to act unilaterally to achieve internal objectives. Over the past two decades, collaborative solutions have emerged to problems in every sector of society – business, government, labour, and the environment (Gray, 1989). As these non-traditional forms have gained prominence, they have attracted the attention of social scientists from a number of disciplinary perspectives seeking to better understand the internal dynamics of these partnerships as well as the external forces that either facilitate or constrain the formation and growth of these collaborative and partnership arrangements.

When collaboration and partnerships began to emerge as an alternative response to societal forces in the 1980s, a cadre of organisational theorists began to take note of these new inter-organisational forms (Gray, 1985, 1989; McCann, 1983; Waddock, 1989). Through primarily case study research and analysis, these theorists broke new ground in their efforts to conceptually define and understand the common characteristics of partnerships and collaboration. Other objectives of this formative work were to better understand the stages of development partnerships evolve through. In addition, these early studies explored those external and internal factors that either serve to facilitate or constrain partnership formation and growth.

Gray's work (1985, 1989) is emblematic of this genre of research. Gray (1989: 11) defines collaboration, 'as a process of joint decision making among key stakeholders of a problem domain about the future of that domain'. Gray proceeds to identify five characteristics critical to the collaborative process: (1) stakeholders are interdependent; (2) solutions emerge by dealing constructively with differences; (3) joint ownership of decisions is involved; (4) stakeholders assume collective responsibility for the future direction of the domain; and (5) collaboration is an emergent process. Perhaps the most potent lesson for tourism managers and scholars to draw from this formative work is that partnerships and collaborative arrangements are dynamic rather than static phenomena, evolving dynamically in response to a host of internal and external forces.

Managerial and scholarly interest in partnerships and collaboration has grown steadily during the 1990s. In addition to the continued interest of organisational theorists, partnership research has gained a foothold in a number of applied social science fields including natural resource management and tourism. Case study research has been complemented by an increasing number of quantitative investigations, including several studies assessing large regional or national populations of partnerships (Selin *et al.*, 1998; Williams & Ellefson, 1996; Wondolleck & Yaffee, 1994; Yaffee *et al.*, 1996). New streams of inquiry represented in this work include assessing characteristics of successful and failed partnership efforts, identifying barriers to partnership formation and growth, understanding motives for participation, and, increasingly, outcome-based assessments of partnership accomplishments.

This has certainly been true in the tourism field. The escalating importance of tourism partnerships has prompted a rash of descriptive case studies (Howe *et al.*, 1997) assessing these new organisational forms and identifying keys to success in initiating and sustaining these collaborative ventures. As in other social science disciplines, case studies have been followed by more systematic research examining the dynamics of these new structures. Recent work has developed conceptual models describing tourism partnerships (Darrow, 1995; Jamal & Getz, 1995; Selin, 1993; Selin & Chavez, 1995) and assessed member satisfaction and effectiveness attributes of regional tourism planning partnerships (Selin & Myers, 1998). These early investigations provide a signpost for an expanded programme of research, evidenced by this special issue examining collaboration and partnerships in the tourism field. The following assessment extends this line of research by developing a preliminary typology of sustainable tourism partnerships, identifying dimensions by which tourism partnerships vary or are similar across time and geographic region. Then, selected partnerships are plotted along these various dimensions.

Methods

Typologies have a rich tradition in social science disciplines. They are essentially an organisational model that systematically illustrates how a social phenomena varies or is similar along a number of selected dimensions or attributes (Waddock, 1989). The following typology was constructed by first identifying a diverse range of partnership forms at work within the tourism field. A second stage in developing the partnership typology was to identify multiple dimensions or attributes by which these partnerships vary or are similar across time and geographic region. Finally, representative tourism partnerships were selected and plotted along these various dimensions. Theoretically, there are likely to be an infinite number of dimensions or characteristics by which tourism partnerships vary or are similar. The purpose here is not to be exhaustive but to identify several preliminary dimensions that illustrate the contextual diversity under which tourism partnerships form and evolve.

Several selection criteria were used to evaluate partnerships for possible inclusion in the typology. In keeping with the theme of this special issue, partnerships were selected if their stated purpose and activities focused on sustainable development. The investigator recognises the difficulty of reconciling stated purposes with actual sustainable outcomes. However, monitoring of partnership outcomes was beyond the scope of this study and should be recognised as a potential limitation. For practical purposes, the investigator delimited the population of tourism partnerships to those based in the United States though recognising the obvious international importance of emerging tourism partnerships. In addition, from the investigator's past research, many of the partnership examples used in this typology relate to tourism and natural resource management issues. Finally, partnerships considered for inclusion in the typology were quite diverse in their goals and objectives. In some cases, sustainable tourism development was the primary objective of the endeavour – for example, the work of the Western States Tourism Policy Council (Seal, 1997). In other cases, tourism development was one part of a larger, integrated set of partnership goals and objectives such as the goals of the Northern Forest Lands Council which also included objectives such as forest conservation, economic development, and watershed protection (Poffenberger & Selin, 1998).

The investigator used a number of primary and secondary sources to construct a population of partnerships for possible inclusion in the typology. From past research, the investigator has compiled an extensive database of partnership case studies and reviews that were helpful in constructing this typology. Several other published databases of partnership information were also consulted in preparing this typology and provided enough background to reliably chart these partnerships along various typology dimensions (Wondolleck & Yaffee, 1994; Yaffee *et al.*, 1996).

A Typology of Sustainable Tourism Partnerships

The following figures and descriptions outline a preliminary typology of sustainable tourism partnerships. Representative tourism partnerships are plotted along five primary dimensions: geographic scale, legal basis, locus of control, organisational diversity and size, and time frame. The geographic scale dimension is common to each of the typology figures presented. Thus, in each of the figures, tourism partnerships are plotted at either a community, state, regional, or national scale depending on their geographic orientation.

Figure 1 plots tourism partnerships along both the geographic scale dimension and by the legal basis for convening the partnership. At one end of the continuum are primarily grassroots partnerships, initiated voluntarily by participating partners. Many of these grassroots partnerships are community-based in their orientation, representing the best tradition of voluntary associations in the United States. They may be organised informally or under some legal form such as a non-profit organisation. Local watershed associations are an excellent example of this type of voluntary partnership. These local partnerships convene for a myriad of reasons – sometimes to fight a perceived threat to a watershed area such as either point or non-point pollution sources. Other watershed partnership objectives typically include issues such as ecological restoration, improving outdoor recreation opportunities, fish habitat, and enhancing the quality of life for both local residents and visitors (Collins *et al.*, 1998). Ecotourism associations represent another emerging voluntary partnership in the United States. Convened at various geographic scales from community through region, the membership of ecotourism associations are dedicated to promoting responsible nature-based travel in their respective area. Texas is an industry leader in this area. The Texas Natural Tourism Association has been very active in developing voluntary guidelines for nature tourism operations, assisting in the promotion of nature-based visitor opportunities, and establishing a Texas Nature Tourism Information Center (Texas Parks and Wildlife Department, 1997).

At the other end of the legal basis continuum are partnerships that are either legally mandated, authorised, or compelled. Here, some legal entity or authoritydentifies a planning process that includes a participatory component that falls within the partnership definition used for the study. Public tourism and natural resource management agencies are under intense public pressure to adopt more participatory, integrated planning approaches which incorporate partnership forms such as citizen advisory committees, task forces, and working

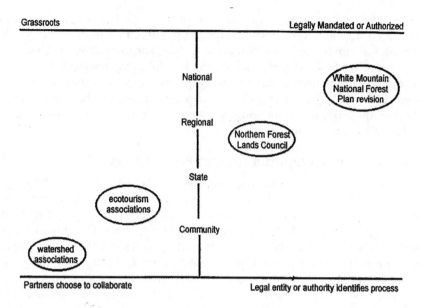

Figure 1 Geographic scale by legal basis

groups (Selin & Chavez, 1995). The examples from Figure 1 illustrate two efforts in this vein.

The Northern Forest Land Council (NFLC) was convened out of public concern in the Northeastern region of the United States over the potential large-scale transfer of land from forest to developed property. The NFLC was authorised and funded by Congress in 1990. Facilitated by the USDA Forest Service, the mission of the NFLC was to reinforce the traditional patterns of ownership by enhancing the quality of life of local residents through the promotion of economic stability, encouraging the production of sustainable yield of forest products, and protecting recreational, wildlife, scenic and wildland resources (Levesque, 1995). In developing their recommendations, the NFLC worked with citizen advisory committees from each state and held hundreds of regular public meetings and forums throughout the region. In addition, working groups were established that served in an advisory capacity for the issue areas being studied including sustainable tourism development in the region.

A second example of legally authorised partnership development are the Forest Plan Revisions currently being made within the National Forest System in the United States. While the National Forest Management Act of 1976 mandates broad public participation in national forest planning and management, some national forests have interpreted this legal requirement narrowly while others, such as the White Mountain National Forest (WMNF) in New Hampshire, have adopted more participatory and interactive approaches to forest planning (USDA Forest Service, 1997). In the current round of Forest Plan Revision, the WMNF is encouraging collaborative planning through the formation of public planning groups composed of interest groups, local working groups, and other interested individuals. Participants are engaged in joint problem-solving throughout the planning process where everyone is responsible for helping to devise solutions to vexing natural resource problems.

Figure 2 plots geographic scale by the locus of control present between public tourism or natural resource management agencies and participating stakeholder interests. The locus of control continuum is adapted from Borrini-Feyerabend's (1997) level of participation scale which ranges from complete agency control at one end of the scale to complete stakeholder control at the other end of the scale. According to our working partnership definition, most partnerships and collaborative arrangements would be positioned towards the centre of this continuum where there is more shared responsibility for decision-making and problem resolution.

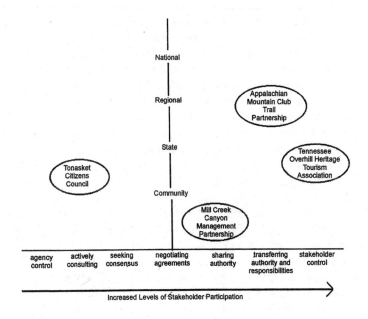

Figure 2 Geographic scale by locus of control

Advisory groups are a good example of collaborative arrangements operating towards the agency control side of the continuum. Typically, a diverse group composed of various stakeholder interests serves in an advisory capacity to the managing agency, providing input into decisions that the managing agency ultimately is legally responsible for making. The Tonasket Citizens Council, for example, operates in rural Washington State providing input into Forest Service decisions on the Okanogan National Forest (Wondolleck & Yaffee, 1994). Composed of about 40 members from diverse local groups and interests, the Council assists the Forest Service in making decisions that balance the needs of various timber, recreation and tourism, wildlife, and watershed interests.

Towards the middle of the locus of control continuum are cooperative agreements and memorandums of understanding where responsibilities and resources are negotiated and shared between a managing authority and various stakeholder groups. For example, Mill Creek Canyon is a popular recreation area about an hour's drive from Salt Lake City, Utah. Unfortunately, high-density recreation use of this National Forest land had led to high rates of vandalism causing extensive damage to picnic and trail areas and severe degradation of water quality in Mill Creek (Wondolleck & Yaffee, 1994). In an innovative response to this problem, the Forest Service forged a Memorandum of Understanding with the County Boards of Public Health and Parks and Recreation where the County administered a day use recreation fee and then donated a portion of the proceeds back to the Forest Service for rehabilitation work in the Canyon. In addition, this Memorandum of Understanding led to the organising of an Interagency Canyon Management Team to coordinate future joint projects in the Canyon.

In some partnership cases, authority and responsibility are transferred from the managing agency to some stakeholder group. One of the best examples of this in the United States is the partnership between the Appalachian Mountain Club (AMC) and the USDA Forest Service. Since 1908, the AMC, through a series of cooperative agreements, has been responsible for constructing and maintaining hiking trails within several National Forests in New England (Jacobi & Wellman, 1983). These responsibilities have expanded over the years to include constructing and operating a system of mountain huts, providing interpretive programmes, and operating shuttle services for hikers. AMC members now maintain over 1500 miles of hiking trails in the Appalachian Mountains.

At the right end of the locus of control continuum are partnerships where stakeholder groups exert primary control over decision making. Public tourism or natural resource management agencies may provide technical assistance, grant support, or serve as members of the partnership. However, the partnership itself is legally autonomous in its decision making. The Tennessee Overhill Heritage Tourism Association (TOHTA) is an example of this type of tourism partnership (McAllister & Zimet, 1994). Organised in 1990, the TOHTA is a three-county corporation whose board is composed of 34 members of diverse local stakeholder groups. According to their strategic plan, the TOHTA, 'is an alliance of communities, historic and natural sites, the public and private sector, and individuals working to share with visitors the Appalachian experience in the Overhill country by showcasing the river stories, the forests, the Cherokee experience, and company towns created by industrialisation and the coming of the railroad' (p. 19). While the TOHTA has received technical assistance and grant support from a number of federal, state, and private agencies, they exert primary control over support for projects and programmes that relate to the heritage and culture of the region.

In Figure 3, geographic scale is plotted against the degree of organisational diversity and size. At one end of the continuum, tourism partnerships are relatively homogenous with a smaller number of partners from one sector, for example, from either the commercial, non-profit, or government sectors. At the other end of the continuum are partnerships that are quite diverse, often with organisational partners from all three sectors and usually with a larger set of partners. Cooperative tourism marketing arrangements are a good example of relatively homogenous tourism partnerships. These partnerships range from community-based ventures where, for example, a downhill ski resort provides a

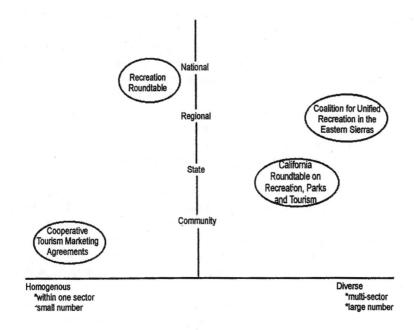

Figure 3 Geographic scale by organisational diversity and size

discounted rate if skiers arrive with a receipt from a local pizza shop to national partnerships between airline carriers, hotels, and rental car companies to provide frequent flyer miles and awards to loyal customers.

Another example of a homogenous tourism partnership, though national in scale and with a larger set of partners, is the Recreation Roundtable (Recreation Roundtable, 1998). Founded in 1989, the Recreation Roundtable is composed of Chief Executive Officers from some of the largest recreation and tourism companies in the United States including L.L. Bean, Walt Disney Attractions, Times Mirror Magazines, Recreation Equipment, Inc. and many others. The full Roundtable meets twice annually although committees and task forces are active throughout the year. The goal of the Recreation Roundtable is to influence public policy affecting outdoor recreation and to enhance recreation opportunities in America. Roundtable initiatives have led to an increase in funding for federal recreation programmes of the Forest Service and National Park Service and led to the initiation of a National Scenic Byways Program. While these tourism partnerships fall within our conceptual definition of tourism partnerships, some would question how often one sector partnerships actually result in sustainable outcomes, being driven by the values of only one sector rather than integrating the values of multiple sectors.

Two examples from California illustrate more diverse, multi-sector tourism partnerships. At a state level, the California Roundtable on Recreation, Parks, and Tourism, initiated in 1996, has about 45 members representing the tourism industry, public land agencies, user groups and environmental organisations, as well as recreation equipment manufacturers and retailers (Seal, 1997). The Roundtable is involved in a number of initiatives including advocating increased funding for state and national parks, restructuring contracts between the government and private companies, and coordinating an outreach programme to publicise outdoor recreation to the state's various ethnic and cultural groups.

The Coalition for Unified Recreation in the Eastern Sierra (CURES) is a broad-based tourism partnership dedicated to preserving the Eastern Sierra's natural, cultural, and economic resources and enhancing the experiences of visitors and residents (Selin & Myers, 1998). Comprised of over 90 members representing over 50 different federal, state, and local government agencies, tourism businesses, user groups, and environmental organisations, CURES was initiated to provide comprehensive, coordinated planning for outdoor recreation resources in the Eastern Sierra region. CURES initiatives have led to completion of a regional marketing plan, visitor information/multi-media kiosks, and several scenic byway enhancement projects. In each of these cases, the joint information search, visioning, implementation, and monitoring activities engaged in by members of diverse tourism sectors has led to a number of sustainable outcomes.

In Figure 4, geographic scale is plotted against the time frame of the respective tourism partnership. At the left end of the continuum are tourism partnerships with a short time frame. These partnerships are convened temporarily, often to solve some pressing problem or take advantage of some important opportunity, and then participants return to their respective organisations and interests. Many of these ephemeral partnerships are informal in their structure. At the other end of the continuum are tourism partnerships with a longer time frame. Many of these partnerships are institutionalised in their legal form and structure as well as their decision-making practices.

Tourism partnerships with a shorter time frame can be illustrated by the interagency steering committee convened to assist the town of Dubois, Wyoming in designing and raising funds to support the construction of a National Bighorn Sheep Center in the community just south of Yellowstone National Park (Wondolleck & Yaffee, 1994). During its operation, the steering committee included representatives from the Town of Dubois, the Wyoming Game and Fish Commission, Bureau of Land Management, and the Forest Service. After raising over $1.1 million to support the construction phase of the centre, its operation and management were turned over to the Town of Dubois.

Other community-based tourism partnerships with a short time frame have convened to manage urban growth. For example, the population of Jackson Hole, Wyoming, located within the shadow of the Teton Mountain range and Yellowstone National Park, doubled in the 1970s and early 1980s (Howe *et al.*, 1997). Many local residents were displaced by the rising cost of living – housing prices have tripled in the past 15 years. In 1995, both Teton County and Jackson Hole adopted new land-use plans to preserve the natural resources of the area and the character of the community. These plans were enacted after a series of public workshops held around the county and sponsored by 47 different community organisations. Success in implementing these plans was largely attributed to the impetus coming from the community to control the rate of community growth.

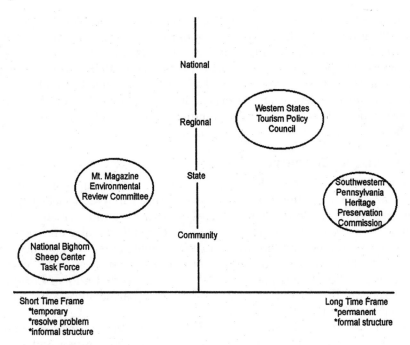

Figure 4 Geographic scale by time frame

Finally, in Arkansas, an Environmental Review Committee (ERC) convened to facilitate the construction of a new lodge at Mt. Magazine State Park which serves as another example of a partnership with a shorter time frame (Wondolleck & Yaffee, 1994). The ERC was composed of a diverse set of stakeholders including the Arkansas Natural Heritage Commission, the Arkansas Nature Conservancy, the Arkansas Game and Fish Commission and the Arkansas River Valley Area Council. The ERC provided a sounding board to both the Arkansas State Parks Authority and the Forest Service throughout the planning process and served as a liaison between these agencies and all interested stakeholder groups. The committee was dissolved once the planning process was complete.

Tourism partnerships can also have a much longer time frame and more permanent, formal structure. The Western States Tourism Policy Council is a regional partnership composed of tourism directors from eight western states (Seal, 1997). The Tourism Policy Council's goal is to influence public policy towards enhancing outdoor recreation opportunities on public lands in the West. The Council has taken on a number of initiatives including sponsoring an annual conference last attended by more than 440 participants from 13 states. The success of the Tourism Policy Council has led to ambitious plans for the future to coordinate efforts between public land managers and tourism industry officials.

One final example of a more permanent and formal tourism partnership is the Southwestern Pennsylvania Heritage Preservation Commission (SWPHPC), established by Congress in 1986 to coordinate efforts to preserve, protect, and interpret the industrial heritage of the region (National Park Service, 1992). The 21-member Commission has representatives from each of the nine counties, the

Pennsylvania Historic and Museum Commission, the National Park Service, and several Planning and Development Commissions. The SWPHPC receives federal funding to support community-based heritage preservation projects. In its mission to support community partnerships, the SWPHPC works through both Technical Advisory Groups as well as County Heritage Committees. The SWPHPC is an excellent example of a federally mandated partnership that disburses federal funds to support community-based heritage preservation projects.

Discussion and Conclusions

It is quite evident from this typology of tourism partnerships that collaboration can take on many different forms in response to a variety of societal forces. It is ironic that at a time when competitive pressures are mounting, many tourism stakeholders are choosing to engage in joint decision making and resource sharing. It is premature though simply to congratulate ourselves and move on. Tourism partnerships are still underdeveloped due to many geographic, organisational, and political constraints. It will take a concerted effort from many sectors to ensure that current and emerging tourism partnerships contribute to the sustainable future of the field.

It is also clear from this typology that tourism partnerships evolve dynamically. For example, related to the locus of control dimension, tourism and natural resource management agencies are under increasing public pressure to adopt more participatory planning and management methods (Selin & Chavez, 1995). So, in Figure 2, there is a trend within the tourism and environmental management fields to move towards the right side of this locus of control continuum, giving additional rights and responsibilities to various stakeholder groups. However, there has been a backlash against this trend towards more stakeholder control. Conservative resource managers fear collaborative initiatives will lead to a loss of agency power and influence while representatives of national environmental groups are loathe to see hard-fought environmental laws circumvented by community-based collaboration. McClosky (1996) fears that industry and small local minorities have the potential to coopt the collaborative process or veto actions that may be in the national interest. Emerging tourism partnerships must be monitored closely to ensure that their outcomes are truly sustainable and equitable in their distribution of benefits and costs.

It should be noted that this typology of tourism partnerships only captures one facet of the contextual diversity that characterises partnerships and collaboration in the field. Future typologies could integrate many other partnership attributes including diverse purposes, informal versus formal structure, partner characteristics, and initiating factors, to mention a few. Future work might also incorporate an international perspective to the geographic scale dimension. However, this emerging work does begin to identify those internal and external factors that tourism partnerships evolve in response to and seek to influence.

This work should also be useful to tourism managers interested in initiating or building the capacity of ongoing collaborative efforts. By better understanding the diversity of forms partnerships take in response to societal pressures, managers can begin to design partnerships that provide the appropriate response to resolving intractable problems or taking advantage of significant opportunities. Managers can learn from the experience of partnerships elaborated here and avoid some of the mistakes that often plague the early stages of partnership development. For example, one clear lesson to emerge from these cases is the suggestion that the way to enhance public ownership and support of partnership outcomes is to provide meaningful opportunities for public involvement throughout the planning process.

Partnerships and collaboration have come of age in the tourism field. However, our understanding of how partnerships form and how to build the capacity of appropriate collaborative ventures has lagged behind developments in the field. Hopefully, special issues like this can serve as a signpost to tourism operators, planners, and academics interested in how partnerships and collaboration can contribute to the future sustainability of tourism both globally and locally.

Correspondence

Any correspondence should be directed to Dr Steve Selin, Associate Professor, Division of Forestry, PO BOX 6125, West Virginia University, Morgantown, WV 26506-6125, USA (sselin@wvu.edu).

References

Borrini-Feyerabend, G. (1997) *Collaborative Management of Protected Areas: Tailoring the Approach to the Context*. Switzerland: IUCN.

Collins, A., Constantz, G., Hunter, S. and Selin, S. (1998) Collaborative watershed planning: The West Virginia experience. *Conservation Voices* 1 (2), 31–35.

Darrow, K. (1995) A partnership model for nature tourism in the eastern Caribbean Islands. *Journal of Travel Research* 33, 48–51.

Gray, B. (1985) Conditions facilitating interorganizational collaboration. *Human Relations* 38 (10), 911–936.

Gray, B. (1989) *Collaborating*. San Francisco, CA: Jossey-Bass Publishers.

Howe, J., McMahon, E. and Propst, L. (1997) *Balancing Nature and Commerce in Gateway Communities*. Washington, DC: Island Press.

Hunter, C. (1997) Sustainable tourism as an adaptive paradigm. *Annals of Tourism Research* 24 (4), 850–867.

Jacobi, C.D. and Wellman, J.D. (1983) Recreation management in cooperation with nonprofit organizations: Pros and cons. *Journal of Forestry* 8 (9), 589–592.

Jamal, T.B. and Getz, D. (1995) Collaborative theory and community tourism planning. *Annals of Tourism Research* 22 (1), 186–204.

Levesque, C.A. (1995) Northern Forest Lands Council: A planning model for use of regional natural resource land. *Journal of Forestry* 93 (6), 36–38.

McAllister, W.K. and Zimet, D. (1994) *Collaborative Planning: Cases in Economic and Community Diversification*. Durham, NH: USDA–Forest Service.

McCann, J.E. (1983) Design guidelines for social problem-solving interventions. *Journal of Applied Behavioral Science* 19, 177–189.

McCloskey, M. (1996) The limits of collaboration. *Harper's Magazine*, November, pp. 34–36.

National Park Service (1992) *Comprehensive Management Plan for the Southwestern Pennsylvania Heritage Preservation Commission*. Denver, CO: NPS.

Poffenberger, M. and Selin, S. (eds) (1998) *Communities and Forest Management in Canada and the United States*. Berkeley, CA: WG–CIFM.

Recreation Roundtable (1998) *The Recreation Roundtable*. Available from http://www.funoutdoors.com/rndtable.html.

Seal, K. (1997) Tourism, public-land official seek accord. *Hotel and Motel Management* 212, 3, 8.

Selin, S.W. (1993) Collaborative alliances: New interorganizational forms in tourism. *Journal of Travel and Tourism Marketing* 2 (2), 217–227.

Selin, S. and Chavez, D. (1995) Developing a collaborative model for environmental planning and management. *Environmental Management* 19 (2), 189–195.

Selin, S.W. and Myers, N.A. (1998) Tourism marketing alliances: Member satisfaction and effectiveness attributes of a regional initiative. *Journal of Travel and Tourism Marketing* 7 (3), 79–93.

Selin, S., Schuett, M. and Carr, D. (1998) Developing a model of collaborative initiative effectiveness. Unpublished manuscript, West Virginia University.

Sitarz, D. (ed.) (1998) *Sustainable America*. Carbondale, IL: Earthpress.

Texas Parks and Wildlife Department and Texas Department of Commerce (1997) *Nature Tourism in the Lone Star State, Economic Opportunities in Nature*. Austin, TX: State Task Force on Texas Nature Tourism.

USDA Forest Service (1997) *Forest Plan Revision: Fitting the Pieces of Forest Management Together. White Mountain National Forest, VT: USDA Forest Service*.

Waddock, S.A. (1989) Understanding social partnerships: An evolutionary model of partnership organizations. *Administration and Society* 21 (1), 78–100.

Williams, E.M., and Ellefson, P.V. (1996) *Natural Resource Partnerships: Factors Leading to Cooperative Success in the Management of Landscape Level Ecosystems Involving Mixed Ownership*. St Paul, MN: University of Minnesota.

Wondolleck, J.M. and Yaffee, S.L. (1994) *Building Bridges Across Agency Boundaries: In Search of Excellence in the United States Forest Service*. Ann Arbor, MI: USDA-Forest Service.

Yaffee, S.L., Phillips, A.F., Frentz, I.C., Hardy, P.W., Maleki, S.M. and Thorpe, B.E. (1996) *Ecosystem Management in the United States: An Assessment of Current Experience*. Washington, DC: Island Press.

8. Rethinking Collaboration and Partnership: A Public Policy Perspective

C. Michael Hall
Centre for Tourism, University of Otago, Dunedin, New Zealand

Issues of coordination, collaboration and partnership are now at the forefront of much tourism research on finding new solutions to resource management and destination development problems. However, despite the value of such attention in possibly improving destination management and the development of more sustainable forms of tourism, the concepts have remained relatively poorly critically analysed from a public policy perspective. The paper argues that the emphasis associated with network concepts is related to the changing role of the state in Western society and the attempt to find market or semi-market solutions to resource and production problems. However, the paper argues with reference to examples from various Western countries, and Australia in particular, that caution needs to be applied in the utilisation of these concepts because of the implications that they may have for notions of governance and the public interest. In addition, the paper argues that the predominance of narrow corporatist notions of collaboration and partnership in network structures may serve to undermine the development of the social capital required for sustainable development.

The tendency to privatise and commercialise functions that were once performed by government which has been almost universal in Western nations since the late 1970s has had substantially affected the nature of many national governments' involvement in the tourism industry (Pearce, 1992; Hall & Jenkins, 1995a, b; Elliot, 1997; Hall, 2000). According to Davis *et al.* (1993: 24) three principal economic reasons for this trend can be identified: 'governments are interested in reducing the dependency of public enterprises on public budgets, in reducing public debt by selling state assets, and in raising technical efficiencies by commercialisation'. However, the economic reasons are themselves shrouded in political rationales that relate to broader philosophical perspectives which have most often been associated with a 'New Right', corporatist or neo-conservative economic agenda which in various countries was labelled as 'Reaganism' (USA), 'Thatcherism' (UK) or 'Rogernomics' (New Zealand).

In such a political and economic climate the role of government in tourism has undergone a dramatic shift from a traditional public administration model which sought to implement government policy for a perceived public good, to a corporatist model which emphasises efficiency, investment returns, the role of the market, and relations with stakeholders, usually defined as industry. Corporatism, here, is used in the sense of a dominant ideology in Western society which claims rationality as its central quality and which emphasises a notion of individualism in terms of self-interest rather than the legitimacy of the individual citizen acting in the democratic interest of the public good (see Saul, 1995). However, in many policy areas, including tourism, the changed role of the state and the individual's relation to the state provides a major policy quandary. On the one hand there is the demand for less government interference in the market and to allow industries to develop and trade without government subsidy or assistance while, on the other, industry interest groups seek to have government policy developed in their favour, including the maintenance of government funding for promotion as in the case of the tourism industry (e.g. see Craik, 1990, 1991a). This policy issue has generally been resolved through the restructuring of national and regional tourist organisations (a) to reduce their planning, policy and development roles and increase their marketing and promotion functions; and (b) to engage in a greater range of partnerships, network and collaborative relationships with stakeholders. Such a situation has been described by Milward (1996) as the hollowing out of the state in which the role of the state has been transformed from one of hierarchical control to one in which governing is dispersed among a number of separate, non-government entities. This has there-fore led to increased emphasis on governance through network structures as a *'new* process of governing; or a changed condition of ordered rule; or the *new* method by which society is governed' (Rhodes, 1997: 43).

The implications of the restructuring of governments involvement in tourism has been documented in Australia (e.g. Craik, 1991b; Hall, 1995), New Zealand (e.g. Pearce, 1990, 1992); Canada (e.g. Hall & Jenkins, 1995a; Lovelock, 1999) and the United States (e.g. Bonham & Mak, 1996). For example, in the United States the federal government's role in tourism has come under intensive review, in part because of the perceived need to gain greater private-sector funding. In some states the role of tourism organisations has also changed dramatically. For example, in Colorado the state's tourism offices were abolished by voters, while Oregon and Virginia have privatised their state offices in the desire to gain greater levels of private sector funding (Bonhan & Mak, 1996). Similarly, in Australia and Canada, state tourism offices have been corporatised with greater emphasis being given to the establishment of partnerships with industry in joint marketing and promotional campaigns (Hall & Jenkins, 1995a).

The growing emphasis by government tourism organisations on partnership arrangements with the private sector is also related to developments in manage-ment theory. For example, strategic planning now places substantial emphasis on relations with stakeholders as part of the planning process while the emer-gence of theories of collaboration (e.g. Gray, 1985, 1989; Wood & Gray, 1991) and network development (e.g. Powell, 1990; Freeman, 1991; Cooke & Morgan, 1993) highlights the importance of the links to be made between stakeholders in processes of mediation, promotion and regional development. For example, in Australia the Federal Government has invested substantial funds into promoting business network development between businesses in a number of sectors including tourism (e.g. AusIndustry 1996), while network development is an important common element in many European Union regional develop-ment programmes such as LEADER (e.g. Zarza, 1996).

Awareness of the need for tourist organisations to create links with stake-holders is, of course, not new. The community tourism approach of Murphy (1985, 1988) emphasised the importance of involving the community in destina-tion management because of their role as key stakeholders, although in actuality this often meant working with industry and community-based groups in a desti-nation context rather than through wider public participation mechanisms. The difficulty in implementing community based tourism strategies is reflective of wider difficulties with respect to effective destination management and tourism planning (Davidson & Maitland, 1997), namely the diffuse nature of tourism phenomenon within economy and society and the problem this creates with respect to coordination and management.

The partially industrialised nature of tourism means that tourism, like the environment, should be regarded as a meta-problem which represent highly interconnected planning and policy 'messes' (Ackoff, 1974) which cut across fields of expertise and administrative boundaries and, seemingly, become connected with almost everything else. Tourism, therefore 'is merely an acute instance of the central problem of society' (Hall, 1992: 249) of creating a sense of the whole which can then be effectively planned and managed. Nevertheless, planning for tourism is still regarded as important because its effects are so substantial and potentially long standing. Indeed, concern with making tourism, along with all development, sustainable has provided even greater imperative for developing relevant tourism planning frameworks (Hall 2000). Yet despite use by tourism researchers of the evolving network paradigm in management literature (e.g. Selin, 1993, 1998; Selin & Chavez, 1994; Jamal & Getz, 1995; Buhalis & Cooper, 1998) there has been, given the central role of government in tourism promotion and development, surprisingly little reference to the public policy literature which analyses what has been, until recently, a 'neglected' aspect of contemporary administration and policy-making (O'Toole, 1997).

The present paper utilises the developing literature on network thinking in Public Policy to critically assess the roles of public-sector collaboration and partnership in tourism in relation to ideas of governance, participation and the contribution it may make to developing the social capital of sustainability. It does so with emphasis on the role of government in tourism in Western nations and in Australia in particular.

Notions of collaboration, coordination and partnership are separate, though closely related, ideas within the emerging network paradigm. Networks refer to the development of linkages between actors (organisations and individuals) where linkages become more formalised towards maintaining mutual interests. The nature of such linkages exists on a continuum ranging from 'loose' linkages to coalitions and more lasting structural arrangements and relationships. Mandell (1999) identifies a continuum of such collaborative efforts as follows:

- linkages or interactive contacts between two or more actors;
- intermittent coordination or mutual adjustment of the policies and procedures of two or more actors to accomplish some objective;
- *ad hoc* or temporary task force activity among actors to accomplish a purpose or purposes;
- permanent and/or regular coordination between two or more actors through a formal arrangement (e.g. a council or partnership) to engage in limited activity to achieve a purpose or purposes;
- a coalition where interdependent and strategic actions are taken, but where purposes are narrow in scope and all actions occur within the participant actors themselves or involve the mutually sequential or simultaneous activity of the participant actors; and
- A collective or network structure where there is a broad mission and joint and strategically interdependent action. Such structural arrangements take

on broad tasks that reach beyond the simultaneous actions of independently operating actors.

However, as Mandell (1999: 8) cautions:

> because we as professionals are eager to achieve results, we often look for prescriptions or answers as to how to solve ongoing dilemmas ...it is tempting for both academics and practitioners to try to develop a model of success that will fit this complex world. In this regard, the concepts of networks and network structures can easily become the next in line for those in the field to 'latch onto' and use wholesale. Although it may be tempting to do so, this 'one size fits all' type of modelling does not take into consideration the myriad of factors and events that must be understood before these concepts can be of much use in the 'real world'.

It is in the light of this cautionary statement that this article now turns.

Coordination, Collaboration and Integration in Tourism Planning

One of the key intellectual sources for the development of approaches to sustainable tourism (e.g. Inskeep, 1991; Wight, 1993, 1998) are the developments in resource management and environmental planning which have focused on integrated forms of resource planning (e.g. Lang, 1986; Mitchell, 1989). Integrated approaches towards *tourism planning* are neither *top-down*, 'where goals at each level in the organisation [or spatial area] are determined based on the goals at the next higher level' (Heath & Wall, 1992: 69), nor *bottom-up*, where the goals of individual units are aggregated together. Instead, integrated tourism planning may be regarded as an *interactive* or *collaborative* approach which requires participation and interaction between the various levels of an organisation or unit of governance and between the responsible organisation and the stakeholders in the planning process to realise horizontal and vertical partnerships within the planning process (Hall & McArthur, 1998).

The need for coordination has become one of the great truisms of tourism planning and policy. For example, Lickorish *et al.* (1991: vi) argued that:

> There is a serious weakness in the machinery of government dealing with tourism in its coordination, and cooperation with operators either state or privately owned. Government policies or lack of them suggest an obsolescence in public administration devoted to tourism ... Political will is often lacking. 'Co-ordination' usually refers to the problem of relating units or decisions so that they fit in with one another, are not at cross-purposes, and operate in ways that are reasonably consistent and coherent. (Spann, 1979: 411)

Coordination for tourism occurs both horizontally, e.g. between different government agencies which may have responsibilities for various tourism-related activities at the same level of governance (i.e., national parks, tourism promotion, transport), and vertically, e.g. between different levels of government (local, regional, provincial, national) within an administrative and policy system. Two different types of coordination are covered under Spann's definition: administrative coordination and policy coordination. The need for administrative coordination can be said to occur when there has been agreement on aims, objectives and policies between the parties that have to be coordinated but the mechanism for coordination is undecided or there are inconsistencies in implementation. The necessity of policy coordination arises when there is conflict over the objectives of the policy that has to be coordinated and implemented. The two types of coordination may sometimes be hard to distinguish as coordination will nearly always mean that one policy or decision will be dominant over others. Furthermore, perhaps the need for coordination only becomes paramount when it is not occurring. Most coordination occurs in a very loose fashion that does not require formal arrangement. In addition, some conflict can also be productive in the formulation of new ideas or strategies for dealing with problems (Hall & McArthur, 1998). Nevertheless, coordination is a political activity and as a result of this coordination can prove extremely difficult, especially when, as in the tourism industry, there are a large number of parties involved in the decision-making process.

Coordination therefore tends to refer to formal institutionalised relationships among existing networks of organisations, interests and/or individuals, while cooperation is 'characterized by informal trade-offs and by attempts to establish reciprocity in the absence of rules' (Mulford & Rogers, 1982: 13). Often, the problem of developing coordinated approaches towards tourism planning and policy problems, such as the metaproblem of sustainability, is identified in organisational terms, e.g. the creation of new organisations or the allocation of new responsibilities to existing ones. However, such as response does not by itself solve the problem of bringing various stakeholders and interests together which is an issue of establishing collaborative processes. Instead, by recognising the level of interdependence that exists within the tourism system (Hall, 2000), it may be possible for 'separate, partisan interests to discover a common or public interest' (Friedmann, 1973: 350). For example, moves towards the implementation of an 'ecosystem management' approach among United States government natural resource management agencies has opened up new ways of thinking about heritage management. According to the United States National Park Service (NPS) (1994: nd):

> Ecosystem management is an awareness that resources and processes do not exist in isolation. Rather, living things exist in complex, interconnected systems within a broad landscape. These interconnected communities of living things, including humans, together with the dynamic physical environment are termed ecosystems. The interconnected nature of ecosystems necessitates that NPS managers shift from a primarily park- or resource-specific approach to a wider systems and process approach to management.

An ecosystem management approach is essentially collaborative and requires the development of partnerships with stakeholders.

> The NPS has complementary roles as a direct resource steward and as advisor to others through education and assistance programs. Both roles require active partnerships. Partnerships encompass two elements: formal partnership assistance programs such as heritage partnership

programs ... and field-level partnerships, which are not necessarily
served by a formal program. Ecosystem management is best understood
as shared responsibility, and the NPS should collaborate, communicate,
cooperate, and coordinate with partners. Partnerships should be pursued
with all major players in each specific ecosystem, including other federal
agencies, state and local governments, tribal entities, private interests,
advocacy and interest groups, university and research groups, and the
general public. Partners include critics. The NPS should actively develop
ecosystem goals and work to achieve goals through consensus-building
approaches. All stakeholders in a given ecosystem should participate in
goal-setting and strategic planning to achieve the goals and should share
accountability and benefits. Partnership efforts should begin at the local
level, with ample public meetings and participation-building efforts.
Trust, openness, cooperation, and accountability takes time to develop,
and the NPS should attempt to establish equity among partners.
(National Park Service, 1994: n.p.)

The ecosystem management approach has also been influential in Canada
where, in the western provinces, Parks Canada has started to develop 'ecosystem
secretariats' in which there is usually one person who is actively involved in and
monitoring regional activities relevant to the organisation (Lovelock, 1999).
However, in the case of both the United States and Canada it should be noted that
there is a strong suspicion among staff that such measures are a way of further
cutting staff and resource funds (National Park Service, 1994; Lovelock, 1999).

Coordination and Sustainability

As the ecosystem management approach in the United States demonstrates,
the development of coordinated or integrative frameworks undoubtedly has
substantial implications for agencies which are designed to fulfil the goals of
sustainable development. Sustainable development has a primary objective of
providing lasting and secure livelihoods which minimise resource depletion,
environmental degradation, cultural disruption and social instability. The
World Commission on Environment and Development (1987) extended this
basic objective to include concerns of equity; the needs of economically marginal
populations; and the idea of technological and social limitations on the ability of
the environment to meet present and future needs. The concern for equity, in
terms of both intra- and inter-generational equity, in sustainable development
means that not only should we be concerned with the maintainance of 'environmental capital' (Jacobs, 1991) but also the maintenance and enhancement of
social capital (Healey, 1997), in terms of the rich set of social networks and relationships that exist in places, through appropriate policies and programmes of
social equality and political participation (Blowers, 1997). Such an approach has
considerable implications for the structure of tourism planning and
policy-making. To fulfil the sustainable goal of equity, decision-making
processes will need to be more inclusive of the full range of values, opinions and
interests that surround tourism developments and tourism's overall contribution to development, and provide a clearer space for public argument and debate
(Smyth, 1994). As Evans (1997: 8) argued,

if environmental planning for sustainability … is to be anywhere near effective, the political processes of public debate and controversy, both formal and informal, will need to play a much more significant role than has hitherto been the case.

In an ideal collaborative or interactive approach towards tourism planning the emphasis is on planning with as wide a set of stakeholders as possible thereby attempting to meet the public interest rather than planning for a narrow set of industry stakeholders or private interests as under a corporatist perspective (Healey, 1997; Hall, 2000). A public collaborative approach also seeks to mediate the community base of tourism destination products by recognising that the opinions, perspectives, and recommendations of non-industry stakeholders are just as legitimate as those of the planner or the 'expert' or of industry. Such an approach may well be more time-consuming than a top-down approach but the results of such a process will have a far greater likelihood of being implemented because stakeholders will likely have a greater degree of ownership of the plan and of the process. Furthermore, such a process may well establish greater cooperation or collaboration between various stakeholders in supporting the goals and objectives of tourism organisations, and also create a basis for responding more effectively to and for change (Hall & McArthur, 1998). Nevertheless, while collaboration clearly has potential to contribute to the development of more sustainable forms of tourism in that they can create social capital, it has to be emphasised that the goal of partnership as emphasised by a number of Western governments which have restructured their involvement in tourism in recent years, need not be the same as an inclusive collaborative approach (Lovelock, 1999).

In the case of the United Kingdom, for example, many of the partnerships established between government and business in the 1980s and early 1990s as part of urban and regional development programmes have been heavily criticised for their narrow stakeholder and institutional base. Goodwin (1993: 161) argued that in order to ensure that urban leisure and tourism development projects were carried out, 'local authorities have had planning and development powers removed and handed to an unelected institution. Effectively, an appointed agency is, in each case, replacing the powers of local government in order to carry out a market-led regeneration of each inner city'. Harvey (1989: 7) recognised that:

> the new entrepreneurialism of the smaller state has, as its centrepiece, the notion of a "public–private partnership" in which a traditional local boosterism is integrated with the use of local government powers to try [to] attract external sources of funding, new direct investments, or new employment sources.

In this case, partnership does not include all members of a community, those who do not have enough money, are not of the right lifestyle, or simply do not have sufficient power, are ignored. For example, in referring to Derwentside in the United Kingdom, Sadler (1993: 190) argued:

> The kind of policy which had been adopted – and which was proving increasingly ineffective even in terms of its own stated objectives … rested

not so much on a basis of rational choice, but rather was a simple reflection of the narrow political and intellectual scope for alternatives. This restricted area did not come about purely or simply by chance, but had been deliberately encouraged and fostered.

In examining issues of collaboration and partnership in relation to sustainable tourism it therefore becomes vital that the range of stakeholders involved in such arrangements is examined so as to ensure that it is as inclusive of the public interest as possible. Unfortunately, the validity of partnership arrangements between the public and private sectors in tourism has only received a limited amount of analysis (e.g. Hayes, 1981; Craik, 1990; Dombrink & Thompson, 1990; Pelissero *et al.* 1991; Lovelock, 1999). Nevertheless, these studies, along with the review by Hall and Jenkins (1995b) of the role of interest groups in the tourism policy making process, strongly suggest that business groups tend to dominate the policy process to the exclusion or detriment of other interests.

The Role of Interest Groups in Collaborative Arrangements

The role of interest groups is crucial to any discussion of collaboration in tourism. The term 'interest group' tends to be used interchangeably with the terms 'pressure group', 'lobby group', 'special interest group' or 'organised interests'. According to Hall and Jenkins (1995b), an interest group is defined as any association or organisation which makes a claim, either directly or indirectly, on government so as to influence public policy without itself being willing to exercise the formal powers of government (Matthews, 1980). Although individuals are clearly significant in tourism development, planning and policy, network and collaborative approaches have tended to focus on the organisational dimensions of development. Yet, perhaps surprisingly, the well developed literature on interest groups and organisational relationships with respect to policy formulation has been little considered in the discussion on the benefits of collaborative approaches to tourism (see Hall & Jenkins, 1995b for a brief discussion of some of this literature). Therefore, this article argues that such an approach may be of tremendous benefit to understanding the limits of collaboration, particularly within the scope of public–private arrangements and its wider contribution to the creation of effective social capital for sustainability. Within many discussions of the establishment of networks and partnership arrangements, including those in tourism and place promotion (e.g. Kotler *et al.* 1993), policy networks are typically portrayed as interdependent, coequal, patterned relationships (Klijn, 1996). However, different policy actors occupy different positions and can carry different weight within networks. Some sit in positions with extensive opportunity contexts, filling 'structural holes' (Nohria, 1992: 10), while others may be reluctant participants or may not even be able to participate at all. Organisations and actors also differ with respect to resource dependencies (Rhodes, 1981), leading to differences in their relative power to influence policy processes. As Clegg and Hardy (1996: 678) remind us, 'We cannot ignore that power can be hidden behind the facade of "trust" and the rhetoric of "collaboration", and used to promote vested interest through the manipulation of and capitulation by weaker partners'.

The Australian Situation

Despite the rapid growth of public interest, consumer, environmental and community-based organisations in Western countries since the early 1960s, 'the pressure system is tilted heavily in favour of the well-off especially business' (Schlozman, 1984: 1029). Business performance affects employment, prices, inflation, production, growth and the material standard of living, which are all items increasingly utilised by government at all levels to measure success. Indeed, in the increasingly corporatised world of government success indicators for government have almost come to be synonymous with those of the private sector (Saul, 1995). Therefore, government leadership will be strongly influenced by business leadership in order to achieve certain public policy goals. In one of the few studies of the influence of the tourism industry on government policy, Craik (1990: 29) observed that 'the private sector claims that because it takes risks, it should shape policy'. Nevertheless, as she went on to note, 'the fostering of the private sector by government inevitably leads to charges of clientelism, the coincidence between policy outcomes and the interests of key lobbyists'. Craik (1990) clearly demonstrated that the key industry association was able to influence government policy deliberations in a manner which met their specific interests. Indeed, such is the extent of the relationship between Tourism Council Australia (the key tourism industry body in Australia) and the Australian Tourist Commission (the national marketing organisation) that their head offices even share the same office building in Sydney. Such a situation can be described as a subgovernment.

The notion of subgovernment connotes a stable triangular alliance of policy specialists, including the 'triangle' of legislative committees, executive agencies, and interest groups, including other interests and actors (Cigler, 1991). If a stable relationship exists between the members of the triangle then it means that the subgovernment is relatively impervious to outside influences on policy formulation and implementation – as in the case of Craik's (1990; 1991a) analysis of tourism policy in Australia. Hall and Jenkins (1995b) argued that in many countries and regions' tourism policy-making has historically resembled the subgovernment model, given the close relationship that exists between peak industry bodies and business interests and tourism agencies. Indeed, the goals of the two may sometimes be regarded as synonymous. Yet, such a situation clearly has profound implications for the possibility of effecting sustainable tourism policies, especially when sustainability also assumes greater equity to resources and the decision-making process.

In the case of Australia, all the state and national tourist organisations presently espouse greater 'coordination', 'collaboration', and/or 'partnership' with industry in their key policy documents such as Annual Reports and Strategic Plans. For example, the Queensland Travel and Tourism Corporation's (QTTC) mission statement is 'To enhance the marketing of Queensland's destinations in partnership with industry' (QTTC, 1997a: 2). In 1997 the Queensland Government development a framework for the future of tourism in Queensland which 'aims to create a commercially attractive operating element for the tourism industry' (QTTC, 1997b: 3). The QTTC will implement in conjunction with the private sector, 'particularly in relation to effective marketing and distribution of

Queensland tourist product, and the provision of expert advice on planning and development issues' (QTTC, 1997c: 3).

Under its *Statement of Corporate Intent 1997–1999*, Tourism Tasmania's mission is 'to promote Tasmania as a premier tourism destination through strategic marketing and sustainable development in partnership with industry, in order to maximise economic and social benefits for all Tasmanians' (Tourism Tasmania, 1997: 41). The strategic directions for Tourism Tasmania are expressed in its core corporate objectives as:

> *Marketing* – influence target markets to travel to Tasmania;
>
> *Development* – facilitate development of export ready product and infrastructure to meet identified market opportunities;
>
> *Distribution* – ensure effective distribution of Tasmanian tourism products;
>
> *Coordination* – maximise existing and new partnerships with stakeholders to ensure Tasmania is marketed and developed as a premier visitor destination utilising the available resources to the maximum benefit;
>
> *Management* – ensure that Tourism Tasmania manages its business by balancing resources with priorities. (Tourism Tasmania, 1997: 41)

Similarly, according to the then South Australian Minister of Tourism, Mike Rann (1993: 1), the decision to replace a traditional government department, Tourism South Australia, with a Tourism Commission in 1993 was 'more than cosmetic. The change to a more private sector styled statutory corporation with a strong focus on tourism marketing, will have clear benefits for our tourism industry'. The private sector, commercial orientation of the SATC is also seen in the Minister's comments regarding the Commission's direction:

> The direction, administration and operation of the new Tourism Commission will be clearly and firmly in the hands of those with private sector expertise operating in partnership with the South Australian Government. This will provide the opportunity for a much greater sense of 'ownership' of the Commission's marketing and promotional direction by the tourism industry in our State, with all parties making a contribution and all being accountable. This partnership should promote greater shared commitment to tourism growth, rather than alibis and excuses or wasteful territorialism. (Rann, 1993: 1)

Such orientations may have substantial consequences for sustainable tourism. For example, the major objective of the *South Australian Tourism Plan 1987–89* was to achieve sustainable growth in the economic value of tourism in South Australia. The overall aim of the plan was to ensure a coordinated approach by government and industry to the maximisation of the State's tourism potential (South Australian Tourism Development Board, 1987a, b). The emphasis on sustainability had grown further by the time of the development of the 1991–93 tourism plan to the point where the State's tourism mission to the end of the century had been defined as 'achieve sustainable growth in the net value of tourism activity to South Australia' (Tourism South Australia, 1991: 13). Although it is important to note that Tourism South Australia recognised 'the mission of the Government and the tourism industry is essentially economic, but via the concept of qualitative growth it embraces social and environmental concerns'. Nevertheless, despite such a far-reaching approach to the overall integration of planning and marketing within the context of tourism development, this planning direction was not maintained within the restructuring of State government involvement in tourism as previously noted and the policy agenda of the State Liberal Government in the 1990s, with the Strategy for 1996–2001 aiming to:

- establish a strong marketing position and a distinctive brand;
- strengthen South Australia's appeal as a holiday destinations;
- make the tourism industry stronger (including regional tourism);
- ensure tourism is sustainable;
- identify initiatives that achieve simultaneous economic and community benefits; and
- forge partnerships between all relevant stakeholders. (South Australian Tourism Commission, 1996: 10)

This last point is critical and also typical of the corporatist approach to tourism in Australia as well as some other Western nations. A sustainable approach to tourism would state that all stakeholders are relevant because of the contribution they bring to the creation of social capital. In contrast, the dominant corporatist approach in Australian tourism tends to emphasise that in the creation of public–private partnerships only some stakeholders, primarily the tourism industry, are relevant. Indeed, an analysis of state tourist organisation annual reports over the last decade indicates that members of governing boards all come from an industry background with nearly all being tourism industry related. At one level such an observation may seem appropriate given the need for coordination between government and industry and, it could be argued, the development of a more business-like approach by government. However, such an approach also precludes the input of a wider range of stakeholders from environmental organisations, from public interest groups, and wider community interests. Thereby, leading to a narrowing of policy advice and therefore tourism policy options which may, in the longer term, actually reduce the capacities of tourism organisations to be responsive to the environment in which they operate (Mandell, 1994).

The Changing Role of Government

Changes in government's role as interest protector has major implications for tourism and sustainability. As Blowers (1997: 36) noted in the case of the United Kingdom, 'the long period of privatisation, deregulation, cuts in public expenditure and attacks on local government have resulted in a "democratic deficit" – a dispersal of power to unelected quangos and business interests – and have led to unsustainable developments'. A critique also reflected in the comments of Haughton and Hunter (1994: 272):

> The unregulated market approach, being relatively amoral, can allow individuals to be immoral. The ethical dimension is important since the market does not provide a sufficient basis for the resolution of the profound moral

issues which face us every day; it can play a part in avoiding distorted decision making by individuals and organisations, but alone it cannot reconcile all of the environmental problems facing society.

These comments highlight the need to see partnership and collaboration within the context of the public interest as opposed to the market interest. Incorporation of a wider range of inputs into the policy process would lead to the formation of issue networks as opposed to subgovernments. Issue networks are structures of interaction among participants in a policy area that are marked by their transience and the absence of established centres of control (Heclo, 1978). According to Heclo (1978: 102) the term 'issue network' describes

> a configuration of individuals concerned about a particular aspect of an issue and the term policy community is used more broadly to encompass the collection of issue networks within a jurisdiction. Both describe the voluntary and fluid configuration of people with varying degrees of commitment to a particular cause.

As Hall and Jenkins (1995b) observed, one of the great problems in examining the role of interest groups in the tourism policy-making process is deciding what the appropriate relationship between an interest group and government should be. At what point does tourism industry membership of government advisory committees or of a national, regional or local tourism agency represent a 'closing up' of the policy process to other interest groups rather than an exercise in consultation, coordination, partnership or collaboration? As Deutsch (1970: 56) recognised

> ... this co-operation between groups and bureaucrats can sometimes be a good thing. But it may sometimes be a very bad thing. These groups, used to each other's needs, may become increasingly preoccupied with each other, insensitive to the needs of outsiders, and impervious to new recruitment and to new ideas. Or the members of the various interest group elites may identify more and more with each other and less and less with the interests of the groups they represent.

The relationship between the tourism industry and government tourism agencies clearly raises questions about the extent to which established policy processes lead to outcomes which are in the 'public interest' and which contributee to sustainabilty rather than meeting just narrow sectoral interests. Mucciaroni (1991: 474) noted that 'client politics is typical of policies with diffuse costs and concentrated benefits. An identifiable group benefits from a policy, but the costs are paid by everybody or at least a large part of society'. As Hall and Jenkins (1995b) argued, tourism policy is one such area, particularly in terms of the costs of tourism promotion and marketing. However, the implications of this situation also affect the overall sustainability of tourism and of communities. The present focus by government tourism agencies on partnership and collaboration is laudable. But the linguistic niceties of partnership and collaboration need to be challenged by focusing on who is involved in tourism planning and policy processes and who is left out. The policy arguments surrounding networks and collaboration need to be examined within broader ideas of 'governance' and an examination of the appropriate role of government and changing relationships and expectations between government and communities. Unless there are attempts to provide equity of access to all stakeholders than collaboration will be one more approach consigned to the lexicon of tourism planning clichés.

Correspondence

Any correspondence should be directed to Dr C. Michael Hall, Centre for Tourism, University of Otago, Dunedin, New Zealand (cmhall@commerce.otago.ac.nz).

References

Ackoff, R.L. (1974) *Redesigning the Future*. New York: Wiley.

AusIndustry (1996) *Network News: AusIndustry Business Networks Program 6* (December) 8.

Blowers, A. (1997) Environmental planning for sustainable development: The international context. In A. Blowers and B. Evans (eds) *Town Planning Into the 21st Century* (pp. 34–53). London: Routledge.

Bonham, C. and Mak, J. (1996) Private versus public financing of state destination promotion. *Journal of Travel Research* 35 (2), 2–10.

Buhalis, D. and Cooper, C. (1998) Competition or co-operation? Small and medium sized tourism enterprises at the destination. In E. Laws, B. Faulkner and G. Moscardo (eds) *Embracing and Managing Change in Tourism: International Case Studies* (pp. 324–346). London: Routledge.

Cigler, A.J. (1991) Interest groups: A subfield in search of an identity. In W. Crotty (ed.) *Political Science: Looking to the Future Vol. 4, American Institutions*. Evanston: Northwestern University Press.

Clegg, S.R. and Hardy, C. (1996) Conclusion: Representations. In S.R. Clegg, C. Hardy and W.R. Nord (eds) *Handbook of Organization Studies* (pp. 676–708). London: Sage.

Cooke, P. and Morgan, K. (1993) The network paradigm: New departures in corporate and regional development. *Environment and Planning D: Society and Space* 11, 543–564.

Craik, J. (1990) A classic case of clientelism: The Industries Assistance Commission Inquiry into Travel and Tourism. *Culture and Policy* 2 (1), 29–45.

Craik, J. (1991a) *Resorting to Tourism: Cultural Policies for Tourist Development in Australia*. St. Leonards: Allen & Unwin.

Craik, J. (1991b) *Government Promotion of Tourism: the Role of the Queensland Tourist and Travel Corporation*. Brisbane: The Centre for Australian Public Sector Management, Griffith University.

Davidson, R. and Maitland, R. (1997) *Tourism Destinations*. London: Hodder and Stroughton.

Davis, G., Wanna, J., Warhurst, J. and Weller, P. (1993) *Public Policy in Australia* (2nd edn). St Leonards: Allen and Unwin.

Deutsch, K. (1970) *Politics and Government: How People Decide Their Fate*. Boston: Houghton Mifflin.

Dombrink, J. and Thompson, W. (1990) *The Last Resort: Success and Failure in Campaigns for Casinos*. Reno: University of Nevada Press.

Elliot, J. (1997) *Tourism: Politics and Public Sector Management*. London: Routledge.

Evans, B. (1997) From town planning to environmental planning In A. Blowers and B. Evans (eds) *Town Planning Into the 21st Century* (pp. 1–14). London and New York: Routledge.

Freeman, C. (1991) Networks of innovators: A synthesis of research issues. *Research Policy* 20, 499–514.

Friedmann, J. (1973) A conceptual model for the analysis of planning behaviour. In A. Faludi (ed.) *A Reader in Planning Theory* (pp. 344–370). Oxford: Pergamon Press.

Goodwin, M. (1993) The city as commodity: The contested spaces of urban development. In G. Kearns and C. Philo (eds) *Selling Places: The City as Cultural Capital, Past and Present* (pp. 145–162). Oxford: Pergamon Press.

Gray, B. (1985) Conditions facilitating interorganizational collaboration. *Human Relations* 38 (10), 911–936.

Gray, B. (1989) *Collaborating: Finding Common Ground for Multiparty Problems.* San Francisco: Jossey–Bass.

Hall, C.M. (1995) *Introduction to Tourism in Australia: Impacts, Planning and Development* (2nd edn). South Melbourne: Longman Australia.

Hall, C.M. (2000) *Tourism Planning.* Harlow: Prentice Hall.

Hall, C.M. and Jenkins, J. (1995a) Tourism policy in federal systems: comparisons between Australia and Canada. In B. Gidlow and C. Simpson (eds) *Leisure Connexions, Proceedings of the Second Conference of the Australian and New Zealand Association for Leisure Studies.* Lincoln: Department of Parks, Recreation and Tourism, Lincoln University.

Hall, C.M. and Jenkins, J. (1995b) *Tourism and Public Policy.* London: Routledge.

Hall, C.M. and McArthur, S. (1998) *Integrated Heritage Management.* London: Stationery Office.

Hall, P. (1992) *Urban and Regional Planning* (3rd edn). London: Routledge.

Harvey, D. (1989) From managerialism to entrepreneurialism: The transformation in urban governance in late capitalism. *Geografiska Annaler* 71B, 3–17.

Haughton, G. and Hunter, C. (1994) *Sustainable Cities.* London: Jessica Kingsley.

Hayes, B.J. (1981) The congressional travel and tourism caucus and US national tourism policy. *International Journal of Tourism Management* 2 (2), 121–137.

Healey, P. (1997) *Collaborative Planning: Shaping Places in Fragmented Societies.* Basingstoke: Macmillan Press.

Heclo, H. (1978) Issue networks and the executive establishment. In A. King (ed.) *Annual Review of Energy* (Vol. 4). Palo Alto: Annual Reviews Inc.

Heath, E. and Wall, G. (1992) *Marketing Tourism Destinations: A Strategic Planning Approach.* New York: John Wiley & Sons.

Inskeep, E. (1991) *Tourism Planning: An Integrated and Sustainable Development Approach.* New York: Van Nostrand Reinhold.

Jacobs, M. (1991) *The Green Economy.* London: Pluto Press.

Jamal, T.B. and Getz, D. (1995) Collaboration theory and community tourism planning. *Annals of Tourism Reseach* 22, 186–204.

Klijn, E. (1996) Analyzing and managing policy processes in complex networks. *Administration and Society* 28 (1), 90–119.

Kotler, P., Haider, D.H. and Rein, I. (1993) *Marketing Places: Attracting Investment, Industry, and Tourism to Cities, States, and Nations.* New York: Free Press.

Lang, R. (1986) Achieving integration in resource planning. In R. Lang (ed.) *Integrated Approaches to Resource Planning and Management* (pp. 27–50). Calgary: University of Calgary Press.

Lickorish, L.J., Jefferson, A., Bodlender, J. and Jenkins, C.L. (1991) *Developing Tourism Destinations: Policies and Perspectives.* Harlow: Longman.

Lovelock, B. (1999) Stakeholder relations in the 'national park-tourism' domain: The influence of macro-economic policies. In *Tourism Policy and Planning, Proceedings of the IGU Study Group on the Geography of Sustainable Tourism Regional Conference.* Centre for Tourism, University of Otago, Dunedin.

Mandell, M.P. (1994) Managing interdependencies through program structures: A revised paradigm. *American Review of Public Administration* 24 (1), 99–121.

Mandell, M.P. (1999) The impact of collaborative efforts: Changing the face of public policy through networks and network structures. *Policy Studies Review* 16 (1), 4–17.

Matthews, T. (1980) Australian pressure groups. In H. Mayer and H. Nelson (eds) *Australian Politics A Fifth Reader.* Melbourne: Longman Cheshire.

Milward, H.B. (1996) Symposium on the hollow state: Capacity, control and performance in interorganizational settings. *Journal of Public Administration Research and Theory* 6 (2), 193–195.

Mitchell, B. (1989) *Geography and Resource Analysis* (2nd edn). Harlow: Longman.

Mucciaroni, G. (1991) Unclogging the arteries: The defeat of client politics and the logic of collective action. *Policy Studies Journal* 19 (3–4), 474–494.

Mulford, C.L. and Rogers, D.L. (1982) Definitions and models. In D.L. Rogers and D.A. Whetten (eds) *Interorganizational Coordination*. Ames: Iowa State University Press.

Murphy, P.E. (1985) *Tourism: A Community Approach*. New York: Methuen.

Murphy, P.E. (1988) Community driven tourism planning. *Tourism Management* 9 (2), 96–104.

National Park Service (1994) *Ecosystem Management in the National Park Service, Discussion Draft, Vail Agenda: Resource Stewardship Team Ecosystem Management Working Group, September*. Washington: National Park Service, U.S. Department of the Interior.

Nohria, N. (1992) Is a network perspective a useful way of studying organizations? In N. Nohria and R.G. Eccles (eds) *Networks and Organizations: Structure, Form and Action* (pp. 1–22). Boston: Harvard Business School Press.

O'Toole, L. (1997) Treating networks seriously: Practical and research based agendas in public administration. *Public Administration Review* 57 (1), 45–52.

Pearce, D. (1990) Tourism, the regions and restructuring in New Zealand. *Journal of Tourism Studies* 1 (2), 33–42.

Pearce, D. (1992) *Tourist Organizations*. Harlow: Longman Scientific and Technical.

Pelissero, J.P., Henschen, B.M. and Sidlow, E.I. (1991) Urban regimes, sports stadiums, and the politics of economic development agendas in Chicago. *Policy Studies Review* 10 (2/3), 117–129.

Powell, W. (1990) Neither market nor hierachy: network forms of organization. In B. Straw and L. Cummings (eds) *Research in Organizational Behaviour* (Vol. 12) (pp. 295–336). Greenwich: JAI Press.

Queensland Tourist and Travel Corporation (1997a) *Annual Report 1997*. Brisbane: Queensland Tourist and Travel Corporation.

Queensland Tourist and Travel Corporation (1997b) *Queensland Tourist and Travel Corporation: Corporate Plan*. Brisbane: Queensland Tourist and Travel Corporation.

Queensland Tourist and Travel Corporation (1997c) *Queensland Tourism: A Framework for the Future*. Brisbane: Queensland Tourist and Travel Corporation.

Rann, M. (1993) *Marketing Directions for South Australia: A Statement from the Minister of Tourism, Mike Rann*. Adelaide: Office of the Minister of Tourism, Parliament House.

Rhodes, R.A.W. (1981) *Control and Power in Central-Local Relations*. Aldershot: Gower.

Rhodes, R.A.W. (1997) From marketisation to diplomacy: It's the mix that matters. *Australian Journal of Public Administration* 56 (2), 40–53.

Sadler, D. (1993) Place-marketing, competitive places and the construction of hegemony in Britain in the 1980s. In G. Kearns and C. Philo (eds) *Selling Places: The City as Cultural Capital, Past and Present* (pp. 175–192). Oxford: Pergamon Press.

Saul, J.R. (1995) *The Unconscious Civilization*. Anansi: Concord.

Schlozman, K.L. (1984) What accent and heavenly chorus? Political equality and the American pressure system. *Journal of Politics* 46, 351–377.

Selin, S. (1993) Collaborative alliances: New interorganizational forms in tourism. *Journal of Travel and Tourism Marketing* 2 (2/3), 217–227.

Selin, S. (1998) The promise and pitfalls of collaborating. *Trends* 35 (1) 9–13.

Selin, S. and Chavez, D. (1994) Characteristics of successful tourism partnerships: A multiple case study design. *Journal of Park and Recreation Administration* 12 (2), 51–62.

Smyth, H. (1994) *Marketing the City: The Role of Flagship Developments in Urban Regeneration*. London: E & FN Spon.

South Australian Tourism Commission (1996) *South Australian Tourism Plan 1996–2001*. Adelaide: South Australian Tourism Commission.

South Australian Tourism Development Board (1987a) *Tourism in South Australia. The Strategic Plan. The South Australian Tourism Plan 1987–89*. Adelaide: South Australian Tourism Development Board.

South Australian Tourism Development Board (1987b) *Tourism in South Australia. The Trends. The Challenge. The Future. A Summary of the South Australian Tourism Plan 1987–89*. Adelaide: South Australian Tourism Development Board.

Spann, R.N. (1979) *Government Administration in Australia*. Sydney: George Allen and Unwin.

Tourism South Australia (1991) *Making South Australia Special: South Australian Tourism Plan 1991–1993*. Adelaide: Tourism South Australia.

Tourism Tasmania (1997) *1996/97 Annual Report*. Hobart: Tourism Tasmania.

Wight, P.A. (1993) Sustainable ecotourism: Balancing economic, environmental and social goals within an ethical framework. *Journal of Tourism Studies* 4 (2), 54–66.

Wight, P.A. (1998) Tools for sustainability analysis in planning and managing tourism and recreation in the destination. In C.M. Hall and A. Lew (eds) *Sustainable Tourism Development: A Geographical Perspective* (pp. 75–91). Harlow: Addison-Wesley Longman.

Wood, D.J. and Gray, B. (1991) Toward a comprehensive theory of collaboration. *Journal of Applied Behavioral Science* 27 (2), 139–162.

World Commission on Environment and Development (1987) (The Brundtland Report) *Our Common Future*. London: Oxford University Press.

Zarza, A.E. (1996) The LEADER programme in the La Rioja Mountains: An example of integral tourist development. In B. Bramwell, I. Henry, G. Jackson, A.G. Prat, G. Richards and J. van der Straaten (eds) *Sustainable Tourism Management: Principles and Practice* (pp. 103–120). Tilburg: Tilburg University Press.

9. Community Roundtables for Tourism-related Conflicts: The Dialectics of Consensus and Process Structures

Tazim Jamal
Department of Recreation, Park and Tourism Sciences, Texas A&M University, College Station, TEXAS, USA 77843-2261

Donald Getz
Faculty of Management, University of Calgary, 2500 University Drive NW, Calgary, AB, Canada T2N 1N4

The article discusses research on a community-based round table process to address conflict over tourism-related development in the rapidly growing mountain town of Canmore, adjacent to Banff National Park, Canada. Business, political, environmental and resident/community stakeholders convened as the Canmore Growth Management Committee (GMC) to develop a growth management strategy, though the planners and local government stayed at arm's-length from decision-making. This interpretive study demonstrates that the collaboration space can be a contested terrain where power and legitimation interrelate with process structures and activities, influencing meaning constructions and outcomes. Process structures are paradoxical in terms of shaping, constraining or enabling meaningful stakeholder participation. 'Consensus' is a problematic construct that can be shaped through the enactment of certain process rules, structures and activities, commencing in the convening stage. Local government initiators, destination planners and facilitators/mediators also play an important role in shaping consensus. Hence, a multi-stakeholder process labelled as a consensus approach is no guarantee that interests and concerns will be considered in the decision-making process, or that implementation of participants' recommendations and plans will follow smoothly. Practical implications and suggestions are forwarded for multi-stakeholder processes for destination management and planning, under conditions of conflict and rapid growth. As this study indicates, conflict can be constructive as well as destructive – community capacity was enhanced in some aspects by the GMC process.

Introduction

The 20th century draws to a close in a culture of globalisation and modernisation, where the increased mobility of people and commodities (including capital) across nations, places and spaces greatly increases the challenge of sustaining the planet's ecological and cultural resources. While the need for a holistic and community-based approach to strategy formulation and planning for sustainable tourism has been emphasised (cf. Bramwell & Lane, 1993; Inskeep, 1991; Murphy, 1985), the task of practising sustainable tourism remains formidable, as Fyall and Garrod (1997) point out. The domain of tourism planning and development is a *political* one, where the needs, demands and values of a diverse number of stakeholders impact on the ecological, economic, and sociocultural resources of tourism destinations. It is also influenced and structured by the discourse and rhetoric of the language of tourism marketers (cf. Dann, 1996) and by the de-differentiation of the tourism product into signs and spectacles for visual consumption (cf. Rojek & Urry, 1997; Urry, 1995). Interdependence and interrelationships among the stakeholders (who may also not all be located in the same destination) further complicate the already complex planning issues in such settings.

The concept of sustainable tourism development, as related to tourists and host regions,

> is envisaged as leading to management of all resources in such a way that economic, social and aesthetic needs can be fulfilled while maintaining cultural integrity, essential ecological processes, biological diversity, and life-support systems. (WTO, 1997: 30)

This echoes the definition forwarded by the Brundtland Commission's report *Our Common Future* (WCED, 1987: 8), which emphasises the need for development which meets present needs 'without compromising the ability of future generations to meet their own needs'. While this well-cited work has incurred a gamut of criticisms on its modernist rhetoric (cf. Peterson, 1997), it also points to the need for cooperative alliances between public- and private-sector stakeholders in order to effectively address development impacts. It can be argued that this approach is particularly necessary in tourism destination areas that face intense conflict over the use and protection of fragile or vital ecological spaces. Multi-sectoral and community involvement in addressing development issues and impacts within this context is easily recommended, but the difficulties of enacting such processes for *effective* participation tend to be underestimated.

This paper focuses on process issues related to consensus in a multi-party round table initiated by local government stakeholders to deal with ongoing concern and conflict over large-scale tourism development and rapid community growth. The research on which this article is based aims to further the preliminary investigations commenced by Getz and Jamal (1994) in Canmore (Canada), a mountain community whose scenic vistas belie the historic conflict over large-scale resort development in this area. That study indicated three major areas of concern: (1) protecting the Corridor's ecological environment; (2) quality of life for Canmore residents; and (3) a lack of integrated vision and direction for the town. The authors suggested that a multi-stakeholder, collaborative approach to address these issues would be looked on favourably by the environmental and local resident organisation interests interviewed. Government and private business interests interviewed expressed some concern about adding another layer of bureaucracy to the existing decision-making structure, if such a mechanism was employed.

Subsequent to a long, drawn out provincial board hearing on a major resort development (Three Sisters Resorts, Inc.) proposed for Canmore, stakeholders were convened by the local government to develop strategic direction for the community, since controversy did not end. The Canmore Growth Management Committee (GMC) followed a process resembling multi-stakeholder round tables (cf. Cormick *et al.*, 1996), as well as the principles of 'interest-based' negotiation (Fisher & Ury, 1983; Ury, 1993). Initiation and convening participants are activities in the first stage of such a collaboration, Stage 2 is the direction setting/issues negotiation, and implementation is a key focus of Stage 3 (cf. Gray, 1989; Jamal & Getz, 1995; Bramwell & Sharman, 1999). The research described here indicates the importance of the convening stage and its influence on the notion of 'consensus'. The paper also offers insights into the dynamism and intricate interrelationships of power and legitimation in collaborations that are driven by community conflict and concern about rapid growth. After a brief summary of the research methodology, several issues and characteristics of convening in the GMC process are described, followed by examples of factors that influence the development of 'consensus' in this process. The final section presents managerial implications of community-based multi-stakeholder collaborations for addressing growth and tourism-related pressures in mountain destinations like Canmore. Some theoretical suggestions on the study of power in collaborations are also forwarded in this last section.

Methodology

This paper is based on research conducted in the community of Canmore, Alberta (Canada). Data gathering and analysis were based on: (1) in-depth interviews (shortly after the process ended in June 1995) with over 20 stakeholders in the GMC representing a broad array of interests and concerns; (2) attendance of public meetings related to the process, and (3) examination of documents related to this initiative. In addition, a few follow-up interviews were also conducted over a year and a half after the process ended. Interviews were primarily field-based and face-to-face, though a few were conducted over the telephone. Glaser and Strauss (1967) and Glaser (1992) were adapted for a method to analyse the transcribed data for themes and concepts (with the help of NUD.IST, a software program for qualitative analysis). The methodology followed a social constructionist (cf. Berger & Luckmann, 1967) and hermeneutic approach (cf. Gadamer, 1989) situated within an interpretive paradigm (cf. Denzin & Lincoln, 1994: Morgan & Smircich, 1980). The focus of an interpretive approach in this research was the everyday, lived *experience* of participants in the process and community, as well as the *meanings* associated with participation in this context. Since space constraints prevent detailed elaboration of interpretive research, readers are referred to Jamal (1997) for methodological insights into the GMC plus other community-based collaborations investigated.

The narrative approach employed in this article helps to present key issues pertaining to the lived experience of participants in the process and the community, and inscribe the rich, multi-vocal, dynamic and sometimes contradictory meanings and voices encountered along the research journey. Narrative is a powerful form of constructing meanings (cf. Bruner, 1990; Mumby, 1988), being a condition of temporal experience where events are connected in a way that enable individuals to understand themselves and others, historically and in the present (Richardson, 1990). Direct quotes from the research study are included in the write-up, hence producing a multi-vocal text. This offers the reader an opportunity to engage with the data and narrations of participants and the researchers. Such an approach helps to embody the voices of residents and other participants in the collaborative planning process and community. It recalls readers, scholars and managers to the human and ethical dimension of planning, the concerns and issues of those who are impacted by such processes, those who are studied by planning researchers and theorists, those who are 'managed' by the writings and actions of researchers, planners, politicians, destination managers and other stakeholders. Note, however, that in order to protect the identity of respondents, acronyms are sometimes used though 'Jiri' is not one – he prefers the reader to know him as Jiri. Jiri was a local Canmore resident who was strongly opposed to large-scale resort development in the town.

Convening Stakeholders – Defining and Involving Participants

The context of the study

> ... Banff and Canmore are very strongly socioeconomically interdependent and even demographically interdependent. 1000 people a day travel to Banff to work from Canmore. There are more people from Banff moving to Canmore all the time ... we are providing the human resource to a large extent that drives the Banff economy ... and we are dealing with the social costs We are providing a municipal infrastructure and we're not benefiting from the commercial tax base. We're only benefiting from the personal, from the residential tax base. And so, the more that is recognised and the more that we set up regional systems to deal with our issues ... the more we'll be truly able to spread the cost the way it should be spread. (Government initiator [Town of Canmore], interview November 1995)

Located a few kilometres outside of the east boundary of Banff National Park, Alberta (Canada), the mountain town of Canmore is a popular recreation and tourist destination, as well as a bedroom community for a significant number of workers in the town of Banff within the Park (see Getz & Jamal, 1994, for details on location and history). In addition to its attractiveness for second-home owners and retired populations, development pressures on this mountain destination are further exacerbated by the imposition of development restraints within the national park. Hence the accommodation sector is mushrooming and two major resort proposals are in various stages of development, both of these having been the source of ongoing controversy in the community. As one respondent noted, volunteer energy just prior to the GMC was exhausted, a number of citizenry having just participated in the extensive board hearing on one of these (Three Sisters Resort).

The GMC process was a community-based collaboration initiated in 1994 by the Mayor and the Town of Canmore (Table 1), accelerated by a petition of over 400 signatures gathered by Jiri, who was a local resident in this area for over 10 years and was an active protester of large-scale resort development in the community. Jiri wanted the town to vote on or reconsider the merits of the Three Sisters project, proceeding after the board hearing imposed some constraints on the original proposal. Fearing that the town would be divided further along already entrenched positions on growth and development, the local government opted for a consensus-based community process and hired two facilitators experienced in organisational and community-based stakeholder processes. Active recruitment of volunteers, in addition to local advertising, resulted in the formation of the Growth Management Committee (GMC), consisting of over 40 participants representing around 19 interest groups in the community. A closer look below at the context of convening reveals the paradoxical characteristics of rules,

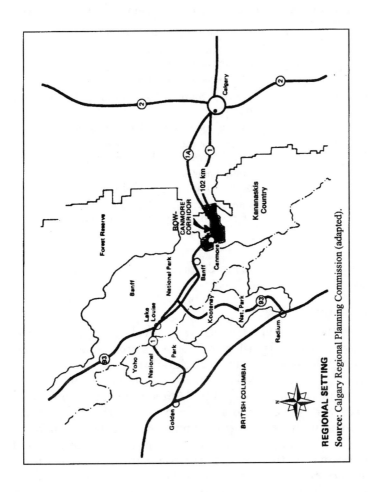

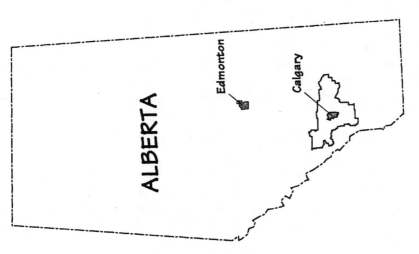

Figure 1 Location map of Canmore, Alberta (Canada)

Table 1 Overview of the Canmore Growth Management Committee process

Name	Growth Management Committee
Representation.	Approximately 19 interest groups (over 40 direct representatives/participants)
Time frame	Mid 1994–June 1, 1995
Structure	Formal ground rules established. Two local facilitators hired
Initiator	Mayor and Council (Town of Canmore)
Convenor(s)	Formal invitation to public by Town of Canmore. Also facilitators invited key participants
Public input	Public meetings/presentations. GMC meetings were not open to the community or broader public
'Product'	Canmore Growth Management Strategy (final report of the Growth Management Committee, June 1, 1995)

structures and functions in this multi-party process, particularly as related to consensus-building.

Initiating and convening

While the Mayor and the Council were involved early on in activities to publicly inform interested participants about the process (including advertising the process in the local newspaper), they chose to remain at arm's length from the rest of the process. It was hoped that this move would encourage those resident volunteers disillusioned by past political influencing of development direction, to participate with some confidence that the decision-making in the process would be a community-based one. The timing of this distancing at the early stage of the process was an important factor, for it shifted convening power from the local government to the two local facilitators appointed by the Town of Canmore. With the government initiators still in the background, the facilitators played a strong role in convening the participating groups and in setting substantive directions before and during the process. They invited specific individuals and groups or organisations to participate, particularly those who were perceived to be key stakeholders in the process (such as the Alpine Club, a large outdoor recreational non-profit organisation with a club-house on town property; the trades people; the developers; the cultural groups, etc.). In their selection process, several criteria for participating were employed by the two facilitators, which helped to set the stage for who could participate and how.

Access for the moderate voice and early entrants

> there was a primary obligation on anyone who was to be involved that as far as their involvement went, they could only participate if they were willing to compromise. There's two organisations that I know of who couldn't be part of the process because their mandate, their organisation's mandate, is no growth and that would shut out the interests of the other people being represented there. So they couldn't come, they couldn't be at the table because everything had to be done in collaborative fashion and by

consensus and you can't have consensus by someone who said there should be no development …(Resident and active community volunteer, representing non-profit organisation, interview June 1995)

This quote summarises what several respondents expressed, which was that participating in this consensus-based process required willingness to compromise, as they learned early on from the facilitator(s). Some other participants felt they were invited, not only because they represented 'legitimate' interests in the town, but also because they were perceived to be knowledgeable about certain things – for example, the environment – and/or were collaborative, i.e. experienced in participating in group or consensus-based processes. One of the organisations which could not participate was an active local environmental group, the Bow Valley Naturalists. A key member of this organisation explained that they chose not to participate when they learned from a facilitator that 'no-growth' was not on the table, not even for discussion. Considering this was supposed to be an 'interest-based' process, this omission of those with no-growth mandates is puzzling, for it could be argued that wanting growth or no-growth, like wanting limits or no limits to growth, are positions, not interests. A key purpose of interest-based processes is to enable exploration of the interests behind the positions voiced by parties. Interests relate to why you might seek a particular position or solution; for instance, fears, concerns, needs, and values help to identify interests (cf. Fisher & Ury, 1983). But, as this study of the GMC process indicated, process managers tend to face a dilemma in trying to be as inclusive as possible, yet having to control differences in a way that enables consensus to be enacted. Interestingly, a few other participants managed to find their way to the table by representing a community-related interest, even though their personal agendas were strongly positional (but mostly unvoiced). 'If we went in with anything in our minds clearly, it would've been to try and head off a no-growth scenario at the end of the day' said two respondents representing a community sector.

Imposing specific limits to growth did get into the final report of the GMC, and some discussion was finally held around this issue, upon a participant's insistence later during the process. Despite a no-growth belief and a strong environmental ethic, this persistent 'green voice' got into the process by actively assembling a group to represent a community-related interest, since the resident group she would have liked to represent was already at the table. But she did not have the radical activist image Jiri seemed to be given and did not push the issue when encountering early resistance to her desire to impose limits to growth. Instead, she insisted on a discussion many months later, when it seemed to her that the process had not yet tackled the contentious issue of growth any differently than had already been attempted before in the community. To her, Jiri was right when he said that 'no growth' was never discussed by the GMC, that some of the environmental activists who had accepted the prerequisites of the process had sold out and so 'where was the voice of the environment?'

A little of Jiri's story is described here to illustrate both the multi-vocality of interpretive research and the subtle barriers to entry in the GMC. Jiri did not join at the beginning – asking why raised a multitude of conflicting reasons which space constraints prevent us from elaborating here. But several months after the process commenced, Jiri did try to join the committee and was told that the group said no, it was too late, since they had made considerable progress and had agreed early on a process rule which did not permit late entry. He also found out too late that the process was closed to public attendance, hence he could not observe the meetings either. Nor were formal public discussions structured during the process. From time to time, updates on the GMC's progress were sent by the facilitators to the local paper. The public meetings held late in the process (April 1995) allowed the public to pass their comments on to various committee members sitting at tables laid out along topic lines around the public hall. What Jiri missed, said a resident-participant, was the opportunity to debate the strategy report, but consensus was not possible, was it, without participants coming willing to 'compromise' or 'move some distance'? However, as this respondent observed, it also meant that the process wasn't able to accommodate a solitary 'voice in the wilderness' with a firm position (like those environmental voices who wanted 'no-growth' to be on the agenda for consideration). Yet, some resident-participants noted that, over the time spent in a process that was extremely heated early on, they obtained a better understanding and tolerance of other stakeholder positions in the process. Long hours of fierce debate and dialogue in group-based activities such as the map-building and visioning exercises facilitated their learning of the potential implications of development and of 'no-growth' scenarios.

Being invited as an active community member

Even if you were involved actively with community-related issues and had heard about it somewhere, you might still have missed joining the GMC, unless you had been invited by the facilitators or someone else keenly interested in it. For one participant, it was not until he heard more about it from the facilitators that he realised it was important and worthwhile to be part of this initiative. The italics in the following and in other quotes in this paper illustrates concepts or points to support our discussion.

> ... I mean, I just heard in the background about this growth management. I thought well it's *another committee* ... I'd been involved in [XXX {local initiative}] ... *So I really wasn't ready for another committee at that time until I sort of realised what they were trying to do and I thought, Yes I'm really interested in this,* I'm concerned about it ... If [XXX {facilitator}] hadn't mentioned it and *really pushed* and said you know,[XXX], you have so much at *stake* here, you've been so *involved* in the community, you're so *good at committee work*, you like doing things and getting on with things. I'd like to see you there, come along ... (Resident participant, interview, November 1995)

In a community with a number of active voluntary initiatives and committees, it was not clear to this participant, who had just left one committee and was quite involved in other community activities, how important this process was for influencing the community's overall direction on development and growth – at least not until a facilitator informed him of it and encouraged his participation. From this resident's information, a number of conditions which facilitated getting to the table can be gathered: (a) a 'legitimate' stake in the community, as indicated by being involved in community activities; (b) being good at getting things done, plus having committee process skills; and (c) being known to the facilitators (personal invitation plus recognition of collaborative group skills by the facilitator(s) were mentioned by another participant as well). Since he was already part of a local interest group, this respondent cited above did not have to scramble around to gather a group to represent, while others did.

Similarly to this member, a number of business-related representatives did not experience the pressure of having to find ways to get into the GMC. They were already part of easily identifiable 'legitimate' stakeholder groups or organisations, such as the local Chamber of Commerce. But they had other concerns about joining the GMC. For instance, several representatives who were also active community volunteers voiced doubt about yet another process to resolve entrenched conflict over major resort development and growth. Nonetheless, the very realisation that 'so little has worked before' meant they had to continue searching, despite the lull in volunteer energy at that time. Being acquainted with one or both of the local facilitators was an added incentive to join for some such volunteers, exhausted though they were in both spirit and in body.

The entry rule of representing a 'large body of people'

A number of respondents mentioned that one of their early concerns was finding a way to get onto the GMC. Consider the following resident–participant (different than the ones previously cited), who had been in the community for eight years, was university educated and was keenly interested in getting involved and being seen as a legitimate representative of community interests. As the facilitator explained to him, he said, the process would be unmanageable if it were structured around individuals with 'general broad concerns', whereas representing a group would enable covering 'as many concerns as we possibly could, you know, and in a workable framework'. These were anxiety-filled moments, for he was uncertain about being able to find a group of people to represent. Note in the following quote, his commentary on finding a group whose interests were most closely aligned with his, though not 'identical'.

> (respondent referring to the volunteer organisation that he was a part of:) … sat down with them and said, 'Look, we're interested in being partici- pants in this process. We {respondent referring to himself and another member} think that *our concerns are generally the same as yours. They may not be specifically you know, identical* but they're generally the same and we would like to ask if we can represent you. Because basically *we need a large body of people to represent at the table and we feel that your group is the most closely aligned with us'.* And they voted that they were happy with our repre- sentation … (Resident participant, interview November 1995; the 'eager joiner')

The tension expressed here was one that we observed in several other partici- pant interviews, where representing a 'group' fulfilled an entry requirement. As a respondent explained, they were required to represent the 'valid interest' of a stakeholder group at the table, not 'personal interests'. Hence, like the partici- pants cited earlier, several other participant–respondents also scrambled to find legitimate groups to represent, or they worked to form a group. Sometimes they ended up with groups whose main interests did not include the personal concerns of the representative. Or if they did, the priorities held by each were sometimes different. For new residents in the community, the announcement of the GMC process presented both an opportunity to get involved and a concern as to whether they could find a way on to the committee. As more than one new resident participant noted, it was particularly difficult to break into the existing community network if one was new and not connected with active community members:

> My primary concerns at the beginning were about not being a participant ... It was abundantly clear to me as a newcomer that for a large segment of the population, newcomers were not welcome ... We speak the language of being a friendly community but if you haven't lived here for the last 10 years you're not really welcome ... If it was going to continue along the lines of a closed shop, you know, lock the door, don't let anybody in, shut down development ... then I would probably have had to rethink my decision to move there. (A new resident, interview June 1995)

Some people worked hard to manage their groups' interests as well as their own, and tried to keep their groups informed of developments in the process. This provided legitimacy for the representative, and enabled him/her to forward personal interests more easily, both with the constituents and at the GMC meetings. How constituent groups were kept informed by their representatives varied, for some had constituents who were not interested in being actively involved, others had constituents who were suspicious of the process and had to be brought along carefully, through conversations in the street, one at a time, or through lunch meetings at work, fax, telephone, etc. Even so, as the 'eager joiner' noted, other GMC members expressed concern as to how he was going to 'sell' results to his group when specific directions started to emerge that seemed antithetical to his group's mandate and interests.

Tensions between constituent groups and the representative's interests, like the task of 'bringing along' one's group, were thorny problems for some of the participants. This relationship between the representative(s) and the constituents was partially in the *back-stage*, not as visible, in addition to the *front-stage* of the meeting space, where the behaviour and actions of the representative could be evaluated by others against his/her 'group' interests (see Goffman, 1959, for the stage metaphors). In the process, personal interests that were hidden from the committee could be fulfilled while satisfying group interests – especially if they were able to 'bring' their constituent group on side with their personal interests, as several participants attempted to do. Selecting people *out* of the process because they had their own personal agendas and were not committed to the group or community interests was what more than one participant (and a process manager) felt was needed in this or future processes. Yet, if this was a community-based process to manage community-related growth and development issues, was it not an avenue for voicing a diversity of resident concerns and opinions about growth? How well were some of these 'other' interests or concerns being understood in the process? Or were they disregarded because they were not seen to be legitimate, hidden as they had to be behind a group front?

Citizen involvement with 'arm's-length' initiators

A local government official's comments after the process ended (with the benefit of hindsight, of course) demonstrates the difficulty of going 'arm's-length' so early in the process. For instance, 'I would have tried to get Jiri in right off the bat, perhaps harder than the others did, but I would have tried to get him to make a commitment to compromise [in] consensus ...' Just as he would have tried to make sure that there was more representation in the 'middle', between the 'left' environmental side and the development side. For instance, the 'trailer park could have been represented. There certainly wasn't anything stopping them ... but by the time we were at that stage, we had already done the arm's-length thing' (i.e. the local government decided not to get directly involved in the process). As he noted, lower-end housing or affordable housing, was identified as a big issue in the final report and would have been 'pivotal for the people living in the trailer park I think'. While this initiator said nothing was stopping the trailer park residents from participating, there were barriers to entry for several segments of the community, some less obvious than others.

More than one participant–respondent felt that some of these absent or low-income stakeholders were actually being represented in some form or another by other interest groups present, such as by the local resident organisation (BowCORD) and the Bow Valley Women's Resource Centre. But some respondents questioned how well the needs of these 'other' less affluent, less visible segments of the community were considered, to say nothing of how well they were informed about the process. For one resident–participant who was fairly new to town and seeking employment, the process was well advertised in the local paper for a couple of weeks (which is where she saw it, and took the initiative to join), but she also felt that if you did not read the paper or talk to people in town, you would have missed it. More than one dissatisfied respondent felt the process was somewhat elitist, and more than one satisfied participant thought that the general public was not as involved as they might have been. For example, she thought that holding public meetings earlier in the process, rather than toward the end, might have been more beneficial.

The challenges faced by lower-income groups and less involved or less 'connected' residents to being present in this process becomes more evident by examining both the formal and the informal, somewhat intangible but nonetheless 'real' requirements for participation. By 'connected' we mean being known in the community through active volunteer work, professional reputation, or other connections developed through long residency in the community, etc. This research study illustrates a number of factors that adversely influenced or prevented the participation of some who were not familiar with such 'consensus'-oriented public spheres. These include: (a) access to information about the process, including an understanding about the potential consequences of the process to community residents, (b) being connected to the community leaders and active volunteers, as well as (c) the complexity of the round-table process and rules, with respect to its dominant discourse of consensus, compromise, and other rules for joining. The next section demonstrates the interrelationship between consensus building and process structures.

The Dialectics of Consensus

The previous section illustrates that the context of convening has a critical and early influence in shaping consensus, through the enactment of rules and process structures, as well as the interactions among the facilitators, initiators, and participating stakeholders. Early action by the local government to stay at a distance helped to reassure participants that they 'owned' the process. It was empowering, noted a participant-respondent, to feel in charge of one's own community destiny, even though the 'shadow' of the Provincial Government (i.e. its ability to influence local level planning decisions) was not far away. Like the initiators and the facilitators, the local Town of Canmore planners took an 'arm's-length' approach to the substantive matters in the process. While government representatives from the planning and social sectors attended meetings and provided technical information, as well as acted as liaison to the Mayor and Council, they did not participate in decision-making. This is in keeping with Mintzberg's (1994) critique of strategic planning and visioning, where he argues that the planner's role should be technical support and implementing the strategic visioning developed by organisational leaders.

However, though the planners and guest speakers invited to speak on planning, growth and development in the GMC process were generally seen to be helpful, the GMC members struggled on a number of occasions with substantive issues related to growth (e.g. the issue of imposing limits to growth) and with trying to understand the meaning of their mandate, developing a growth management strategy. The sheer volume and range of information being received was overwhelming to many participants. A serendipitous suggestion by a participant wanting to see the many various aspects of the problem on a map resulted in a joint exercise in which a land base map was constructed, an activity which greatly facilitated understanding of the trade-offs to be considered in land use and allocation for different stakeholders' requirements. Finding 'common ground' and formulating consensus-based decisions among a wide number of stakeholders holding diverse opinions on growth and development, in destination domains where planning issues may be complex, interdependent and dynamic, are thus daunting tasks for process managers in such initiatives.

The facilitators in the GMC employed specific tactics to bring the group towards substantive resolutions and decisions. Of primary importance was their effort to impart conflict resolution skills to participants (related to the concept of 'interest-based' negotiation). On the one hand, this form of therapeutic mediation (cf. Bush & Folger, 1994) was very helpful in building *community capacity*; for instance many respondents commented on their own personal growth through participating in this process as they learnt valuable communication and negotiation skills and gained various kinds of knowledge. On the other hand, an instrumental approach was also employed by the facilitators, exacerbated by (a) the pressure to arrive at 'consensus' decisions under specific time constraints, (b) the rhetoric of compromise and consensus used, and coupled with (c) the process rules enacted in early meetings. This set the stage for certain consequences, decisions and outcomes for, as illustrated later, there is a dialectical and dynamic relationship between process structures, the participation context, and the actions and decisions of participants. An instrumental approach tended to sever this interaction between agency and process structures (cf. Giddens, 1984), hence stifling the emergent nature of learning and action in the participatory space. For several disillusioned resident participants, consent was manufactured coercively through the imposition of such constraints on action:

> But I would say here *what we adopted as the methodology in the beginning, was done with some of us in total ignorance of how this would work and there was no means to change it once those ground rules were set, nothing could be changed* ... I'm quite troubled now about the whole purpose of this thing because to me it's to create the perception that the community all now is happy to go ahead with what was decided in this document. ... It became a problem to me, but there were lots of people there who saw no problem ... Have you seen this video called 'Manufacturing Consent'? (Interview November 1995; 'troubled' resident–participant)

This quote reinforces what several other participants noted: that they learned a great deal from being in this process, about substantive issues as well as negotiation, conflict resolution and consensus-building skills. However, it also illustrates another point that was experienced by several committee members: as learning evolves in the process, ground rules that are accepted early in the process may change meaning later on. Does it therefore defeat the purpose of having rules for process and procedure, if some flexibility is built into the way these are used to guide round-table processes? Especially in light of the fact that there were several occasions during the GMC process when an established (formal) ground rule was contravened quietly by a member and without fuss by the rest of the group, or was invoked as a threat to achieve an outcome. For example, a participant threatened to walk away and let the process collapse after several months of hard work, if the issue of growth limits was not discussed (see shotgun rule in the next subsection). In other words, the rules are 'instantiated' (Giddens, 1984) as required by various stakeholders to legitimise and/or achieve certain objectives, interests and concerns. This concept is now described, since it pertains to the shaping of consensus.

The shotgun rule

The rules agreed early on by the participants to guide their process and procedures were enabling, in the sense of facilitating the formation of the group and other aspects of process 'management', as well as constraining (as in preventing entry into, or departure from, the GMC). In some instances, the rules that were earlier in the process perceived as constructive, later became problematic for some participants. Like the rules preventing late entrants (formal rule) and the introduction of 'no growth' voices into the process (informal rule), the 'shotgun rule' was also highly influential in shaping consensus as well as the substantive matters being agreed upon. If a participant walked away from the process, there were tremendous costs to be paid – the process was ended! While this rule was perceived to be vital to keeping the process together, and several members liked it, several others felt later in the process (but not when they first approved the rule) that it was 'just hell'. More than one participant felt compelled to stay on, for fear of repercussion from the community for terminating the process. But, staying on often meant having to 'compromise', feeling coerced or feeling that they were not listened to. The pressure exerted by the group to find agreement is expressed by the following participant – note the sense of persuasion in the quote:

> there were on numerous occasions groups who said I can't buy into this, whatever point was being made. And the *rest of the group, they became a single force, telling this group they couldn't leave* … and so we literally had to debate *issues until we got everybody to a position* where it wasn't a deal breaker issue anymore. Lots of deal breakers. That was a very, very fundamentally important point without which we would never have succeeded. (Business-participant, interview December 1995)

Hence, as the 'green voice' cited earlier noted, this rule made it even more difficult to support Jiri's entry into the process, for had he walked away, they would all have had to do the same and lose what they might consider precious gains, such as the land base map they had developed. It 'makes it really really hard and especially if you've got something that you want … To walk away and lose the map allows any other developer to buy up a hunk of land in the meantime and start building' said this 'green voice'. In addition, the influence of this rule on other aspects of the process – such as substantive outcomes – is vividly described by a long-term resident in relation to the decision-making about capping growth to a 6% limit. This same participant also characterised this process as a negotiation bull-ring, where both tenacity and alertness were required in order to succeed in having one's goals and desires met, for even when a verbal decision comes back in print form for review, oversight can occur.

> The 6% idea. I got a lot of gray hair out of that one … that's 6% reached within five years which I know, consciously I agreed to that. But the next part of it was that that 6% be maintained for the following five. I did not agree to that. I never did. *But I guess* somehow or other *it slipped by … I guess I could have said no, I won't take it and the whole thing is going to collapse* … and *I agonised* about it a lot and I thought well, that's not big enough. That's not a big enough issue to end this thing but I sure didn't like it … But on the other hand I can appreciate the fact that you can't keep continually going back over it … well, what I learned was you have to be very tenacious about what's going on. You have to really stay on top of it … (A long-term community resident, interview November 1995)

Participation through right and capacity

Being a community member and being at the table did not automatically give a resident–participant easy access to getting his/her issues addressed. Which issues were taken up were, to some extent, influenced by the perceived legitimacy of the participant's concerns, in relation to the perceived purpose of the process and to the individual's responsibilities as a group representative. It suggests that the right to be present needs to be legitimised through discussion and dialogue on a participant's concerns, desires and interests, and hence about the purpose of the process. Furthermore, the *right* to participate does not equal the *capacity* to participate, for this was an intense political arena, where stakes, issues and agendas had to be negotiated amidst constraints of time, financial, and other resources. In such a 'win–lose' setting, some lost, others compromised or backed off, intimidated by the aggressive gesturings and tactics of 'front-stage' interactions. It helped to be able to come in with arms swinging.

> *It was win–lose but there were people that lost all across the board* because they *didn't know how to bargain*, I guess or were *intimidated* when they said something and then somebody yelled at them. They backed off whereas I just, you know, rounded my shoulders and *came in swinging*. You know, maybe it's personality I guess, I don't know. (Resident participant, interview June 1995)

Tiredness and exhaustion is not surprising in a process where meetings were intense and required devotion of much time and effort. A process manager estimated that over 25,000 hours of volunteer time had been invested in this process. As some participants' energies flagged, others came forth to provide leadership and direction. One of these was mentioned by a number of participants, as being superb and instrumental in helping to get the report written and had the 'highest energy level', said one participant. However, for more than one participant, the intense pace of the final few months when the report was being drafted was really difficult to keep up, as fatigue from process demands (which were not merely physical demands) set in. Considering much of the 'meat' in the report went into it in the last few months, said the participant cited below, some items went into the report that were not agreed upon (by consensus), but it was too exhausting to 'fight every clause'. Here, in this process, the timing of events and actions, the intensity and duration of meetings, plus exhaustion played an important role in the shaping of consensus. Both the time frame and the financial resources allocated were exceeded, and the facilitators voluntarily worked without remuneration later in the process in order to enable the group to come up with a growth management strategy report. Furthermore, the interrelatedness of multiple issues, in addition to the rapidity with which these were being addressed in the waning months of the process, meant that participants had to develop substantive knowledge very quickly in order to understand and effectively make 'consensus' decisions. The need for more and timely information was mentioned by several respondents who struggled with comprehending the complex planning domain.

> and writing up the final document ... it was supposed to be a committee, [a] word-smithing committee and I said to some of the others, we've got to get on that because otherwise it will be like the Indians and white men. You know, the white men write up the treaty and the Indians just go X and they don't know what the hell is in there. So someone said, well, you go then, I'm too tired. ... And then you look at the thing and you didn't think really we agreed to saying quite that but you're too exhausted to fight every clause ... ... more and more topics got introduced and put in there and so on and most of the meat of it really got into it in the last few months. ('Troubled' resident–participant, interview, November 1995)

Implications for Community-based Round Tables

Getz and Jamal (1994), Gunn (1988), Haywood (1988), Murphy (1985) and Middleton (1997) are among those who emphasise the importance of collaborative, community-based input into destination management. We concur but add that much of this previous work has tended to focus on the functional aspects of the sustainability concern. There has been little discussion of the rhetorical, ideological and power-based aspects of partnerships and collaborations, including issues of access and capacity to participate *meaningfully* in such processes. In this article, we hope to have conveyed some insight into these latter aspects. Multi-party public spaces like that of the GMC are a form of public sphere (cf. Habermas, 1989; Taylor, 1995) whose dynamic, fluid process structures can be applied towards enabling constructive change and direction in a problem domain (cf. Gray, 1989; Trist, 1983). For instance, one outcome of the GMC was that individual and community capacity to address local level conflict over community direction and planning was increased, in the form of improved relationships between formerly warring stakeholders, the healing of tensions and recovery from historic strife, as well as better individual and group knowledge plus decision-making and communication skills. An outcome of the GMC's report has been the establishment of a threshold and monitoring committee to work with the implementation of the report. Interestingly, the report was also used as a public campaign strategy in local elections, resulting in the re-election of the Mayor and the election of three GMC members to the council.

However, the same process structures also demonstrate the potential for repressing participation in both overt and covert ways, as in the subjection (cf. Butler, 1997) of a participant by group pressure and the unspoken threat of repercussion from the community if anyone walked away and caused the process to collapse. Hence, a 'consensus' process is no guarantee that the voices and words of a participant will necessarily be heard or incorporated into the decision-making. Careful attention needs to be paid to the design and enactment of such processes, for the same process structures and rules can be both enabling and constraining, while an instrumental focus on consensus may result in 'manufacturing consent'. Similarly, conflict can be constructive and/or destructive, enabling and/or constraining. The consensus-based label attached to the GMC did not mean that the process was a warm, fuzzy, trust-based one. While tensions decreased as better understandings emerged and working relationships were created (as well as some friendships) among some participants, the early stages of the GMC were characterised by a high degree of tension, distrust and verbal battles among some participants. 'Constructive' conflict (as defined by Tjosvold, 1996) replaced 'destructive' conflict as relationships were built through the learning and application of techniques like listening and paying respect, taught and repeatedly reinforced by the facilitators. However, some other tensions and conflicts arose between different participants over time. As such, it can be argued that *'conflict in these multi-party collaborations continues to be constructive as long as spaces for change, resistance and dialogue are enabled in the mediation between structures and participation'* (Jamal, 1997: 274, emphasis in original) in community-based public spheres like the GMC.

This article has focused on the context of convening and the issue of consensus in multi-party round-table processes like the Canmore GMC. These are critical to understanding how community involvement for addressing tourism-related conflicts may be structured. Other key issues have not been covered here, such as financing and other substantive issues (e.g. imposing a numbered growth limit in the GMC, as several environmental participants wanted, versus managing impacts without numbered limits, as some business participants preferred). Similarly, we do not address methodological issues here, but note that a longitudinal study is critical in order to examine the effects of collaboration subsequent to the process. For instance, more than one participant contacted over a year and a half after the GMC process ended mentioned that their opinions had changed a great deal from the time they were first interviewed by us. For these participants, optimism and belief in the process had changed to disillusionment and the statement that the 'status quo' had prevailed in the community, despite such a major volunteer effort as the GMC. Given the parameters of the study outlined earlier, several managerial implications for enacting multi-stakeholder round-table processes ensue from this research:

(1) The importance of the convening stage should not be underestimated by the initiators and convenors of multi-party consensus-based processes. This stage is one where the process rules and structures that are enacted help to shape the form of participation and hence the consequences and outcomes of the collaboration. The role of the convenors in identifying and bringing together the stakeholders is a critical one, as is the choice of facilitators or mediators (cf. Huxham, 1996). To meaningfully involve the residents and other publics requires careful attention to advertising and raising awareness in the community and wider stakeholder domain about the nature and importance of the process. Included in this early stage should be information on various opportunities (including public meetings) for public participation, so that it is known early when or where a stakeholder can enter the process, or have the opportunity to provide input along the way. While it may be better for the schedule of such processes to be somewhat 'emergent' (Gray, 1989, Mintzberg, 1994), rather than fully planned, a 'balancing of tensions' (Huxham, 1993) is one of the process manager's challenges, such as balancing uncertainties of time and finance (hence recognising that the process may required additional time and funding later), balancing the need to enable participants to build relationships and common knowledges with allowing new entrants later in the process, as well as balancing the needs of new groups coming together for the first time versus established groups with experienced spokespeople. New groups, like representatives who may not be experienced in speaking in larger group settings – especially ones that constitute a high profile public sphere – need some assistance in developing group identities and directions.

(2) In addition, the diversity of issues, concerns and interests brought to a community round table means that stakeholders may have a variety of needs and desires, as well as differing abilities to influence the agenda and scope of the negotiations. This vastly increases the challenge of developing a 'common knowledge base' plus adequate decision-making and participation skills and capacities among the participants. As a number of authors have pointed out (cf.

Lippman, 1997; Huxham, 1996), participatory democracy is both a matter of *right* and *capacity* to participate. The Canmore GMC process indicates that careful attention needs to be paid to the development of a common purpose early in the process, recognising that issues may arise as information becomes available and shared, which may then need to be incorporated into the work schedule. In this sense, a 'common purpose' statement is also a dynamic one, evolving as the process unfolds, but a comprehensive dialogue for developing a joint purpose statement early in the process is critical, for it facilitates understanding of various concerns and issues of the different stakeholders. This is a time for legitimising the *right* of the individual or group to participate in the process. An early denial of such legitimacy can make it highly problematic for the participant to get his/her concerns addressed, as more than one representative in the GMC discovered. The exercise of jointly developing a land base map in the GMC process was seen to be very helpful in developing some common understanding of the trade-offs required to accommodate some different interests related to environmental protection and development.

(3)   The Canmore GMC's struggles also demonstrate the challenges of democratic representation, and reveal the postmodernists' concerns about representative democracy (cf. Rosenau, 1992). Our study of this process suggests that 'interests' do not have rigid, 'essential' properties with clear dualistic separations of reason and being (the Cartesian fallacy). A participant's or group's interests may be fluid and dynamic, intricately situated and woven with the place, space and structures of the collaboration (Jamal, 1997). Labelling groups as 'environmental', 'social', 'business', 'cultural', etc. may help to organise participation, but risks fragmenting, confusing and isolating highly interrelated and interdependent aspects of community and ecology. It raises questions about how to represent the natural environment and whose environment/nature is being presented (cf. Blechman *et al.* 1996; Cronon, 1996). For process managers, it becomes important to recognise that interests may be less fixed and may overlap more than expected, and that a community group may have multiple interests. Hence, attention has to be paid to overcoming the barriers that risk being enacted by labelling interest-groups or sectors at the table.

The Canmore GMC process also illustrates a related challenge to the above. The interests of both individuals and group members can be emergent, evolving and changeable, and the pressure to come to the table with a group to represent can distort a participant's ability to represent group interests in addition to individual interests. Circles of influence therefore extend between the negotiation table and the broader groups and publics being represented. What is effective representation in a community-based process? The issue of 'representation' of nature, culture and community in the face of conflicting interests that are not necessarily fully 'formed' (especially if a group has been newly formed to participate) is a difficult one. Compromise based on relativism, it can be argued, is not the answer in the face of potential trade-offs required to develop answers to such problems (Proctor, 1996). Pragmatism may have a valuable role to play here, where face-to-face dialogue and the recognition of the need to come up with solutions to pressing issues encourage putting aside metaphysical claims in order for the community and ecology to carry on and live well (cf. Jamal, 1997; Rorty, 1988, 1996; Stein & Harper, 1996).

(4) The role of technical and scientific information, as well as substantive information thus also becomes a vital one, both for the quality of decisions and the enactment of complex power relations which constitute subjects through discursive practices (Foucault, 1980, 1995; Riggins, 1997). Keeping planners at arm's-length in decision-making, but still present in the GMC meetings was viewed as helpful by participants, since it provided not only technical information but also continuity after the process, in dealing with participant concerns and implementational aspects of the strategies formulated. The GMC process also raises questions about the role of facilitators and mediators (Moore, 1995). How effective or even possible are roles of 'neutral' and 'impartial' facilitation and how much substantive expertise should facilitators and mediators possess in order to be effective? Relying on participants, invited speakers and the planners was not seen to be adequate substantive direction by several participants in the GMC.

More importantly, what about therapeutic facilitation and instrumentally driven approaches in such processes (cf. Bush & Folger, 1994)? The GMC process indicates that a therapeutic approach based on improving interpersonal and conflict-resolution skills, along with exercises that facilitated joint dialogue and understandings (e.g. the map which helped to visually orient the complicated and fragmented pieces of information), is a useful role for facilitators to undertake in conflict based processes. This helps participants to develop new frames, having come into the process with pre-existing and context-related ones (cf. Gray, 1996). As such, the role of the facilitators also becomes one of carefully balancing the process and content needs of the collaboration and the participants. The GMC exercise suggests that facilitators and mediators need to have (some) substantive knowledge of the issues, and that it would help to clarify up-front that this will be used when and where helpful, in facilitating negotiations and discussions.

(5) Similarly, the GMC demonstrates that the rules of process and procedure can be applied instrumentally to effect certain consequences and outcomes. Rules were instantiated by various participants and process managers in the GMC, such as the rules of late entry and the 'shotgun' rule, to suit particular interests and agendas. These actions and activities demonstrate a complex dialectic between agency and structure in such processes (cf. Giddens, 1979, 1984), where relations of power and subjection are enacted. Hence, labelling a process as 'consensus' is no guarantee that the voices and needs of the participating stakeholders will be included in the decision-making. Power is not merely unidimensional or ideological in the traditional Marxist sense of 'false consciousness'. Neither is it a top-down imposition through ideological state apparatuses like educational institutions (cf. Althusser, 1984). Rather, power is multi-directionally everywhere, as Foucault (1980) argues, and is closely tied to knowledge and 'truth'. As our study suggests, the same rules of process and procedure can be both enabling and constraining, and can be engaged or disabled by participants. Using rules instrumentally thus becomes a tool for ideological and power domination in a process.

This research study and discussion of the GMC initiative suggests that there were significant tensions between a round table ideology *versus* community needs and ideologies. Following Therborne (1980) and Prasad (1994), the community and round table can be described in terms of what

Table 2 Ideologies in contest – the Canmore GMC process

Stakeholder group	'What exists' (representation of social reality today)	'What is good' (better than today's reality-future vision)	'What is possible' (change actions prescribed)	'Ideological anchors'
Sociocultural (community of Canmore in GMC process)	Long-term residents versus new ones (GMC); diverse opinions on development and growth; barriers to entry into community decision-making.	Preservation and appreciation of local culture Tourism/ development integrates community way of life with environment.	Vision for community. Manage impacts on land, ecology and community (e.g. housing, sense of place, environmental impacts).	Community sense (ethos) of place. Community right to determine own future. Democratic right to reside in the town.
Process managers (of multi-party consensus process)	Multi-stakeholder conflict over development, growth and environmental protection. Conflict and loss of confidence in domain governance.	More consensus agreements (less conflict, conflict resolution), common vision and solutions.	Develop common knowledge base, vision, plus negotiate issues. Provide conflict resolution skills.	Participatory democracy and pluralism of interests. Equal opportunity for public input into decision-making.

Note: Columns 2–5: ideology dimensions based on Therborn (1980) and Prasad (1994).

exists currently, what is desirable, what is possible, and what the ideological anchors of the community and round table are (Table 2). The GMC demonstrates that convening a process under conditions of historic controversy, where stakeholder values appear to be strongly in conflict, puts a great deal of pressure on process managers (initiators, convenors, facilitators and/or mediators) to 'succeed'. Success, in this situation, is measured by the 'consensus' decisions and growth management strategies arrived at by stakeholder participants, as well as the impression that the process belonged to the public and other participants, i.e. that the decisions were not influenced unduly by political stakes. The round table ideology of consensus and multi-stakeholder participation thus offers legitimation by extolling a democratic process that has indeed involved most of the community's various segments and interests in the decision-making process. Process managers and participants need to be aware of the tensions between these two contexts, and recognise that the instrumental exercise of rules and structures can significantly affect participation in the public sphere of multi-stakeholder, community-based collaborations for addressing development and growth related conflicts.

(6) Process managers exert a great deal of influence on the direction and outcomes of consensus processes like the GMC one, through perhaps well-intentioned strategies to ensure that community-based decisions and discussions have ensued. This study indicates that much greater attention needs to be paid to the enactment and exercise of power by initiators, conveners, facilitators/mediators, resource personnel and task forces involved in such processes. The discursive structures of the process and the

context, as Foucault (1995) demonstrates, can be both enabling and constraining. Also useful in the study of power in these processes is the notion of hegemony (cf. Gramsci, 1971; Laclau & Mouffe, 1985), which enables an understanding of both the resistance demonstrated by participants in the interstitial spaces of the GMC process and the 'common-sense' domination experienced by some participants, but not by others. Creating a dialogic space which enables the construction of narrative identities (cf. Gadamer, 1989; Ricoeur,1991) and joint narratives of community and place (see Cheney,1989 for bio-regional narratives) contributes towards learning and growth through such community collaborations.

It should be noted that much of the literature on multi-stakeholder collaborative planning, conflict 'resolution and community round tables tends to be prescriptive or characterises power as an "object" or "resource" to be harnessed to "empower" participants, or to be dissipated in its negative mode, (e.g. Susskind & Cruikshank, 1987; Hoberg, 1993; Cormick *et al.* 1996). While the importance of power has been pointed out in tourism studies (cf. Hall, 1994; Richter, 1997), tourism researchers have yet to focus more closely on the dialogic and performative character of power. Hollinshead (1999) offers one theoretical point of departure for conceptualising the discursive aspect of power in the complex tourism planning domain. Power is enacted and enabled in the play of influences, relations and interactions between agent and structure, including the context of the collaboration, as has been pointed out by theoretical and empirical work in other fields of study (see, for instance, Giddens, 1984; Mumby, 1988; Westley, 1995; Darier, 1999). Hence, greater effort needs to be directed towards bringing the marginalised voices of hybridised cultures from in-between spaces (cf. Hollinshead, 1998) into the public sphere of community-based collaborations for destination planning and management. Dialogic power (Gadamer, 1989; Jamal, 1997) plays a critical role in the performative enactment of culture, people and places (cf. Bruner & Kirshenblatt-Gimblett, 1994; Selwyn, 1996) for power 'is not simply a distortion of the conversation, it is its occasion' (Calhoun, 1995: 52).

If planetary sustainability of rapidly declining natural and cultural resources (cf. Brush, 1996) is to be achieved, tourism marketers and destination managers will need to work with other stakeholders in the complex domain of travel and tourism, which is closely imbricated with the natural and sociocultural environment. Inter-organisational collaboration and round tables may not be a desirable strategy where power/knowledge structures are able to strongly influence the agenda and the outcomes of such processes. Nonetheless, in a battle for planetary sustainability, such democratic forms of partnerships and collaborations are a valuable mechanism for addressing community-based development and growth conflicts for, in addition to tangible 'products', such public spheres offer the potential of enabling improved relationships between opposed stakeholders, as well as collaborative learning. Potential pitfalls may be constructively addressed through pragmatic and dialogic approaches, aided by an awareness of the dynamic aspects of power relationships that are enacted in such spaces and places. Conflict doesn't necessarily 'end' through strategic initiatives like the

GMC, but a community-based collaborative approach to tourism-related conflicts hopefully facilitates the movement from destructive to constructive conflict, at least for some people in the process.

Acknowledgements

We thank the participants in the GMC as well as all other respondents for sharing their thoughts and insights with us. Their long voluntary hours and emotional as well as physical energy contribute towards the building of community capacity, and to the collective good of community, environment and society. We have done our best to capture the experience and meaning of participation in collaborative planning exercises like the GMC process, and hope that jointly, we can move forward in the research and practice of collaborative tourism planning and management.

Correspondence

Any correspondence should be directed to Dr Tazim Jamal, Assistant Professor, Department of Recreation, Park and Tourism Sciences, Texas A&M University, College Station, TEXAS, USA 77843-2261, USA (tjamal@rpts.tamu.edu).

References

Althusser, L. (1984) *Essays on Ideology*. London: Verso.
Berger, P. and Luckmann, T. (1967) *The Social Construction of Reality*. London: Penguin Books.
Blechman, F., Crocker, J., Docherty, J. and Garon, S. (1996) Looking back at the Northern Forest Dialogues: 1988–1995. Final draft 5/24/96 (manuscript in preparation). Institute for Conflict Analysis and Resolution, George Mason University, Fairfax, Virginia.
Bramwell, B. and Lane, B. (1993) Sustainable tourism: An evolving global approach. *Journal of Sustainable Tourism* 1 (1), 1–5.
Bramwell, B. and Sharman, A. (1999) Collaboration in local tourism policymaking. *Annals of Tourism Research* 26 (2), 392–415.
Bruner, E.M. and Kirshenblatt-Gimblett, B. (1994) Maasai on the lawn: Tourism realism in East Africa. *Cultural Anthropology* 9 (2), 435–470
Bruner, J. (1990) *Acts of Meaning*. Cambridge, MA: Harvard University Press.
Brush, S.B. (1996) Whose knowledge, whose genes, whose rights? In S.B. Brush and D. Stabinsky (eds) *Valuing Local Knowledge: Indigenous People and Intellectual Property Rights* (Chapter 1). Washington, DC: Island Press.
Bush, R.A.B. and Folger, J.P. (1994) *The Promise of Mediation: Responding to Conflict Through Empowerment and Recognition*. San Francisco: Jossey-Bass.
Butler, J. (1997) *The Psychic Life of Power: Theories in Subjection*. Stanford, CA: Stanford University Press.
Calhoun, C. (1995) *Critical Social Theory: Culture, History and the Challenge of Difference*. Cambridge, MA: Blackwell.
Cheney, J. (1989) Postmodern environmental ethics: Ethics as bioregional narrative. *Environmental Ethics* Summer (11), 117–134.
Cormick, G., Dale, N., Edmond, P., Sigurdson, S.G. and Stuart, B.D. (1996) *Building Consensus for a Sustainable Future: Putting Principles into Practice*. Ottawa, Ontario: National Round Table on the Environment and the Economy.
Cronon, W. (ed.) (1996) *Uncommon Ground: Rethinking the Human Place in Nature* (Chapter 1: Introduction). New York: W.W. Norton & Company.
Dann, G. (1996) *The Language of Tourism: A Sociolinguistic Perspective*. Wallington: CAB International.
Darier, E. (1999) *Discourses of the Environment*. Oxford: Blackwell.
Denzin, N. and Lincoln, Y. (1994) Introduction: Entering the field of qualitative research. In N. Denzin and Y. Lincoln (eds) *Handbook of Qualitative Research* (pp. 1–18). Thousand Oaks, CA: Sage.

Fisher, R. and Ury, W. (1983) *Getting to Yes: Negotiating Agreement Without Giving In.* New York: Penguin Books.

Foucault. M. (1980) *Power/Knowledge: Selected Interviews and Other Writings.* New York: Pantheon.

Foucault, M. (1995) *Discipline and Punish: The Birth of the Prison* (2nd edn). Translated from the French by A. Sheridan. New York: Vintage Books.

Fyall, A. and Garrod, B. (1997) Sustainable tourism: Towards a methodology for implementing the concept. In M.J. Stabler (ed.) *Tourism and Sustainability: Principles to Practice* (Chapter 4). Wallingford: CAB International.

Gadamer, H.G. (1989) *Truth and Method* (Translation revised by J. Weinsheimer and D. G. Marshall) (2nd edn). New York: The Continuum Publishing Company.

Getz, D. and Jamal, T. (1994) The environment-community symbiosis: A case for collaborative tourism planning. *Journal of Sustainable Tourism* 2 (3), 152–173.

Giddens, A. (1979) *Central Problems in Social Theory.* London: Macmillan.

Giddens, A. (1984) *The Constitution of Society: Outline of the Theory of Structuration.* Cambridge: Polity Press.

Glaser, B. and Strauss, A. (1967) *The Discovery of Grounded Theory: Strategies for Qualitative Research.* Chicago: Aldine.

Glaser, B. (1992) *Basics of Grounded Theory Analysis: Emergence vs. Forcing.* Mill Valley, CA: The Sociology Press.

Goffman, E. (1959) *The Presentation of Self in Everyday Life.* Garden City, NY: Doubleday.

Gramsci, A. (1971) *Selection from the Prison Notebooks.* (Edited by Q. Hoare and G. Nowell-Smith). London: Lawrence and Wishart.

Gray, B. (1989) *Collaborating: Finding Common Ground for Multiparty Problems.* San Francisco: Jossey-Bass.

Gray, B. (1996) Framing and reframing of intractable environmental disputes. Paper prepared for *Research on Negotiation in Organizations* 5, 1997.

Gunn, C.A. (1988) *Tourism Planning* (2nd edn). New York: Taylor and Francis.

Habermas, J. (1989) *The Structural Transformation of the Public Sphere: An Inquiry into a Category of Bourgeois Society* (Translated by Thomas Burger with the assistance of Frederick Lawrence). Cambridge, MA: The MIT Press.

Hall, C.M. (1994) *Tourism and Politics: Policy, Power and Place.* London: Bellhaven.

Haywood, M. (1988) Responsible and responsive planning in the community. *Tourism Management* June, 105–118.

Hoberg, G. (1993) Environmental policy: Alternative styles. In M.M. Atkinson (ed.) *Governing Canada: Institutions and Public Policy* (Chapter 10). Toronto, ONT: Harcourt Brace Jovanovich.

Hollinshead, K. (1998) Tourism, hybridity, and ambiguity: The relevance of Bhabha's 'Third Space' cultures. *Journal of Leisure Research* 30 (1), 121–156.

Hollinshead, K. (1999) Surveillance of the worlds of tourism: Foucault and the eye-of-power. *Tourism Management forthcoming.*

Huxham, C. (1993) Processes for collaborative advantage: A gentle exploration of tensions. In J. Pasquero and D. Collins (eds) *Proceedings, International Association for Business and Society* (pp. 90–95).

Huxham, C. (ed.) (1996) *Creating Collaborative Advantage.* London: Sage.

Inskeep, E. (1991) *Tourism Planning: An Integrated and Sustainable Development Approach.* New York: Van Nostrand Reinhold.

Jamal, T. (1997) Multi-party consensus processes in environmentally sensitive destinations: Paradoxes of ownership and common ground. PhD dissertation, Faculty of Management, University of Calgary, Alberta, Canada.

Jamal, T. and Getz, D. (1995) Collaboration theory and community tourism planning. *Annals of Tourism Research* 22 (1), 186–204.

Laclau, E. and Mouffe, C. (1985) *Hegemony and Socialist Strategy: Towards a Radical Democratic Politics.* London: Verso.

Lippman, W. (1997) *Public Opinion.* New York: Free Press Paperback, Simon & Schuster.

Middleton, V. (with Rebecca Hawkins) (1997) *Sustainable Tourism: A Marketing Approach.* Oxford: Butterworth Heinemann.

Mintzberg, H. (1994) *The Rise and Fall of Strategic Planning: Reconceiving Roles for Planning, Plans, Planners*. New York: The Free Press.

Morgan, G. and Smircich, L. (1980) The case for qualitative research. *Academy of Management Review* 5 (4), 491–500.

Moore, C.W. (1995) *The Mediation Process: Practical Strategies for Resolving Conflict* (2nd edn). San Francisco: Jossey-Bass Publishers.

Mumby, D.K. (1988) *Communication and Power in Organizations: Discourse, Ideology and Domination*. Norwood, NJ: Ablex Publishing Corporation.

Murphy, P.E. (1985) *Tourism: A Community Approach*. New York: Methuen.

Pearce, D.G. and Butler, R.W. (1999) *Contemporary Issues in Tourism Development*. London and New York: Routledge.

Peterson, T. (1997) *Sharing the Earth: The Rhetoric of Sustainable Development*. Columbia, SC: University of South Carolina Press.

Prasad, A. (1994) Institutional ideology and industry-level action: A macro analysis of corporate legitimation in the United States petroleum industry. PhD dissertation, School of Management, University of Massachusetts.

Proctor, J.D. (1996) Whose nature? The contested moral terrain of ancient forests. In W. Cronon (ed.) *Uncommon Ground: Rethinking the Human Place in Nature*. New York: W.W. Norton.

Richardson, L. (1990) *Writing Strategies: Reading Diverse Audiences*. Newbury Park, CA: Sage.

Richter, L. (1997) The politics of heritage tourism development: Emerging issues for the new millennium. In *Conemporary Issues in Tourism Develoment*. London: Routledge.

Ricoeur, P. (1991) Narrative identity. *Philosophy Today* 35 (1), 73–81.

Riggins, S.H. (ed.) (1997) *The Language and Politics of Exclusion: Others in Discourse*. Thousand Oaks, CA: Sage.

Rojek, C. and Urry, J. (1997) *Touring Cultures: Transformations of Travel and Theory*. London: Routledge.

Rorty, R. (1989) *Contingency, Irony and Solidarity*. Cambridge: Cambridge University Press.

Rorty, R. (1998) *Truth and Progress: Philosophical Papers*. (Vol. 3). Cambridge, UK: Cambridge University Press.

Rosenau, P.M. (1992) *Postmodernism and the Social Sciences: Insights, Inroads and Intrustions*. Princeton, NJ: Princeton University Press.

Selwyn, T. (ed.) (1996) *The Tourist Image: Myths and Myth Making in Tourism* (pp. 1–32). Chichester: John Wiley.

Stein, S.M. and Harper, T.L. (1996) Planning theory for environmentally sustainable planning. *Geography Research Forum* 16, 80–101.

Susskind, L. and Cruikshank, J. (1987) *Breaking the Impasse: Consensual Approaches to Resolving Public Disputes*. New York: Basic Books.

Taylor, C. (1995) *Philosophical Arguments*. Cambridge, MA: Harvard University Press.

Therborn, G. (1980) *The Ideology of Power and the Power of Ideology*. London: Verso.

Tjosvold, D. (1996) Conflict management in a diverse world: A review essay of Caplan's understanding disputes: The politics of argument. *Human Relations* 49 (9), 1203–1211.

Trist, E.L. (1983) Referent organizations and the development of interorganizational domains. *Human Relations* 36, 247–268.

Ury, W. (1993) *Getting Past No: Negotiating Your Way from Confrontation to Cooperation*. New York: Bantam Books.

Urry, J. (1995) *Consuming Places*. London and New York: Routledge.

WCED (The World Commission on Environment and Development) (1987) *Our Common Future*. Brundtland Commission's Report. Oxford: Oxford University Press.

Westley, F. (1995) Governing design: The management of social systems and ecosystems design. In L.H. Holling and S.S. Light (eds) *Barriers and Bridges to the Renewal of Ecosystems and Institutions* (Chapter 9). New York: Columbia University Press.

WTO (1997) *Agenda 21 for the Travel and Tourism Industry: Towards Environmentally Sustainable Development*. Published by the World Tourism Organization (WTO), the World Travel and Tourism Council, and the Earth Council.

10. Tourism Development Regimes in the Inner City Fringe: The Case of Discover Islington, London

Philip Long
Centre for Tourism, School of Leisure and Food Mangagement, Sheffield Hallam University, City Campus, Howard Street, Sheffield S1 1WB, UK

There is a growing recognition of the importance of inter-organisational collaborations, or partnerships, for tourism development at various geographical and sectoral levels. Academic studies of the phenomenon are, in part, a reflection of the increasing number and forms of partnership arrangements being established in a range of settings to develop tourism. This paper examines a particular case of inter-organisational collaboration for local tourism development for the London inner city fringe. Established in 1991, *Discover Islington* provides an illustration of an agency involving representation from diverse stakeholders with an interest in tourism within a single administrative district. The agency has been innovative in its approach to local tourism development in the inner city fringe, but it is confronted by issues that may affect its longer-term viability. The perspectives and experiences of the partners represented on the Board of *Discover Islington* are pertinent to the study of comparable collaborative arrangements for local tourism development in other urban fringe contexts. The analysis is based on interviews with Board members and their policy and strategy documents within a theoretical framework that draws on regime theory. Implications for other inner city fringe tourism development partnerships are offered in the conclusion of this paper.

Introduction

Strategies and programmes which aim for the sustainable development of tourism in British cities have in recent years increasingly been informed or devised by partnerships involving key players in an urban area's tourism. These partnerships range from informal *ad hoc* networks that lack any distinct organisational structure to more formal arrangements. In some cases agencies employing their own staff have been established with strategic marketing and development remits which are directed by a steering group or board made up of representatives from member organisations.

The focus, remit and scope of these partnership agencies varies between those that, following Waddock (1991), might be described as being:

(1) *Systemic* – where the partnership is concerned with broad, (tourism) system-wide issues across an urban area. The emphasis of such agencies is upon system benefits rather than gains for individual partners and representation tends to come from senior managers and officials across participating sectors. The Joint London Tourism Forum in the UK is an example of a systemic partnership. It brings together public and private sector tourism interests across the city to provide guidance, coordination and lobbying in support of the London Tourist Board's strategy (Bull & Church, 1996: 171)

(2) *Federational* – where the partnership comprises industry groupings and/or a district coalition within a defined area of a city. A partnership of this kind tends to adopt a proactive stance towards coalition building, issue identifi-

cation and strategy formulation within its area, which may transcend administrative boundaries.

A federational partnership will usually have a distinct organisational structure and its own strategy. Examples in the UK include Tour East (London) and Discover Islington.

(3) *Programmatic* – where the partnership is technical or operational and involves a contractual relationship between a few partners for the delivery of a specific project. The emphasis here tends to be on products or outputs and is usually a short-term arrangement. The partnerships brought together to coordinate themed festival events in cities, such as the European Cultural Capitals programmes, are examples (Long, 1997. See also Long & Arnold, 1995 for other approaches to the classification of partnerships).

Such classifications may be criticised as being too simplistic in that particular partnerships might engage in an activity that combines two or all three of these categories. However, a typology is useful as a basis for further research in an emergent field, such as the study of partnerships for tourism development.

The reasons that underlay the emergence of such partnership bodies for tourism development in British cities have included:

- Policies by successive governments to extend private sector involvement in local and regional planning, regeneration and development activity in cities, along with an array of policy instruments that *require* a partnership approach (or at least the involvement of the private sector) in urban development (including tourism) (Bailey *et al.*, 1995; Blackman, 1995; DoE, 1997; Paddison, 1997).
- The establishment during the 1980s and 1990s of a number of new institutions with extensive planning powers that impinged on the development of tourism. Many of these bodies have now been wound up following their time-limited period of existence. However, their legacy endures in successor agencies and in their influence over local government practice. Examples in urban areas in the UK included the development corporations and enterprise boards which provided the mechanisms for involving the private sector in fast-track redevelopment programmes in defined urban districts (Bailey *et al.*, 1995; Barlow, 1995; Coulson, 1993; Edwards & Deakin, 1992; Newman & Thornley, 1996).
- The associated erosion of local government powers and resources and an increased recognition by local government of the value of partnerships (ACC, 1992; CFP, 1997; DoE, 1997; Harding, 1991; Roberts *et al.*, 1995).
- The catalytic role of the national tourist boards (English, Wales, Scottish during the 1980s and 1990s in the formation of partnership agencies in local areas and the more recent reduction in their resources for this purpose (CBI, 1996).
- The increased acceptance of the concept of sustainable tourism including the notion of involving 'stakeholders' in the development process, and the emergence of a tourism 'policy community' seeking to put such ideas into practice, in part through partnership arrangements (Carpenter, 1999; Cropper, 1996; Finn, 1996; Long, 1997).

Published research on formal partnership arrangements for tourism development has, to date, been limited. Examples include studies of: collaborative alliances in tourism (Selin, 1993), evolutionary models for tourism partnerships (Selin & Chavez, 1995), partnerships for tourism planning and marketing in cities (Bramwell & Rawding, 1994), theoretical perspectives on organisational partnerships that might be applied to tourism (Long, 1994), the involvement of local communities in partnerships for sustainable tourism development (Jamal & Getz, 1994), and methodological issues in researching tourism partnerships (Long, 1997).

This paper discusses the characteristics of partnership agencies that are seeking to develop sustainable tourism in cities. It does so with reference to *Discover Islington*, a 'federational' partnership agency located in the local government district of Islington, situated on the northern fringe of London's main financial district. The paper also briefly considers the use of regime theory as a theoretical framework that may assist in guiding research on the roles and perspectives of the key actors in partnership 'regimes'.

Sustainable Urban Tourism

Strategies for the sustainable development of tourism in many urban areas in the UK and in other countries may be seen as part of a wider economic restructuring in those cities that have experienced de-industrialisation and possess limited apparent development alternatives. Presenting a city as being attractive to visitors may also be viewed as part of a re-imaging process with the broader objectives of enhancing civic pride among local communities and attracting inward investment, new industries and inward migration.

Many city authorities, in partnership with the private sector, are now promoting tourism, cultural and conference centres, together with development sites for mid- to up-market retail, arts and catering facilities, hotels, visitor attractions and luxury housing to attract executives as residents and visitors, as well as tourists and regional shoppers. However, the sustainability of some of these developments in the face of intense competition between cities and between districts within major urban areas, and by comparison with other types of investment and potential uses of resources is open to question.

Examples of a formal partnership approach dedicated to the local development of tourism in English cities date from the early 1980s and include former programmes in Leicester, Bristol, and Tyne and Wear. Other more recent partnership initiatives, most commonly conceived and constituted as Visitor and Convention Bureaux on the US model, include those located in Manchester and Birmingham (Bramwell & Rawding, 1994; Selin, 1993).

Furthermore, many urban regeneration programmes based on a partnership model have involved a tourism development dimension. These programmes are commonly centred on former industrial locations on the fringes of city centres and are often property and land assembly led (CFP, 1997; Evans & McNulty, 1995; GOL, 1996; Jewson & MacGregor, 1997; LTB, 1997). Examples include: London Docklands, Trafford (Manchester), Don Valley (Sheffield), Greenwich Waterfront, City Fringe and King's Cross (London), the latter two being directly connected with the case of Discover Islington.

Some of the issues that confront partnership agencies seeking to develop sustainable tourism in cities are addressed in two recent books on tourism in major cities (Law, 1996; Tyler *et al.*, 1998). These issues include:

- The difficulty of differentiating tourist activity and spending in cities from that of residents, making claims that tourism is developing sustainably hard to verify, a point emphasised in a recent article by the Chief Executive of Discover Islington (Carpenter, 1999).
- Reconciling the 'needs' of tourists and the tourism industry with those of (some) local residents, which may come into conflict in particular places and at certain times (Robinson & Boniface, 1999).
- Identifying the types and forms of tourism that exist in cities, with different demand patterns and market segments being more or less likely prospects upon which to base a sustainable tourism strategy.
- The sustainability of the business tourism market, including conferences and exhibitions, with the strength of this market being linked to broader business and competitive trends in global, national, regional and local economies.
- Whether tourism development in cities, focused on already attractive districts may have the effect of reinforcing social and spatial inequality.
- Physical capacities being reached or exceeded at some times and sites on city transport networks and at 'honeypot' attractions (Beioley, 1993; Bull, 1997; LTB, 1993; LTB, 1997; Thornley, 1992).
- The fragmentation and complexity of tourism supply in cities including the involvement of large numbers of agencies, authorities, businesses and communities (Bull & Church, 1996).

In these circumstances, if urban tourism is to develop sustainably, partnership is both essential and difficult to organise in practice. The prominence, political sensitivity and complexity of some of these issues suggests that any partnership seeking to develop tourism sustainably needs to be able to draw on organisations and individual board or steering group members who possess or have access to influence, networks, expertise and authority. The following section discusses the possible contribution of regime theory to an examination of the membership characteristics of partnerships for sustainable tourism development in cities.

Regime Theory

A simple description of regime theory is that it is 'a conceptual framework for understanding the variety of political responses to urban economic change' (Stoker & Mossberger, 1994: 195). These political responses have included the devising of new partnership forms, including those for sustainable urban tourism and for economic development and regeneration programmes.

Regime theory was developed in the United States by policy analysts seeking to explain and account for the characteristics and stakeholders involved in urban regeneration policies and programmes in that country (Elkin, 1987; Logan & Molotch, 1987; Stone & Sanders, 1987; Harding, 1994). It is based on the assumption that the effectiveness of local government depends greatly on the cooperation of non-governmental actors and on the combination of state capacity with non-governmental resources in a 'regime' for development.

The focus of a regime approach is on the effects of institutional structures on the decision-making behaviour of different organisational actors; the range of actors involved, formally and informally, in urban (tourism) development strategies; the importance of place to various sections of the business community; and the implications of different forms of regime for patterns of resource distribution. Regime theory may therefore contribute to an understanding of the fragmentation of institutions, the changing role of central and local government, and the emergence of new networks – both public and private – which attempt to coordinate policy areas, including that of tourism development. Regime approaches also underline the importance of human agency, inter-agency and professional relationships, and contextual factors in urban development (Harding, 1994).

Regime analysis may also involve attention to the characteristics and motivations of the members of a partnership. Contrasting motivating factors for participation may include

(1) a broad desire (either professionally or voluntarily) to achieve tangible and measurable results in terms of, for example, jobs created, land and buildings re-developed, inward investment achieved, and visitors attracted;
(2) a dependency on the locality for votes and business;
(3) the expression of a political platform in terms of, perhaps, ideology, local pride, and/or a broad concern for community welfare, quality of life, economic and environmental well-being (Stoker & Mossberger, 1994).

Such considerations can give significant substance to a comparative research agenda for the study of partnerships for sustainable urban tourism development.

For some commentators, a charge of ethnocentricity might be levelled at regime theory, constraining its applicability to non-US contexts. Harding (1994: 365), for example, suggests that

> many of the institutional and cultural characteristics underlying the formation of U.S. urban regimes ... are found less readily in the U.K. ... the instrumental business control over local political strategies is much less marked in the U.K ... U.S. cities contain higher concentrations of local resources for facilitating economic growth than do cities in the more centralized U.K. They also provide fertile environments for strong business social networks, which, in turn, create fora for discussion about urban problems and potential from a business viewpoint.

However, in spite of these criticisms,

> notwithstanding cross-national and cross-disciplinary difficulties, theoretical accounts that emphasize the importance of subnational coalition formation are likely to be of growing relevance to any understanding of the politics of comparative urban development. (Harding, 1994: 357)

It might also be suggested that the emphasis of urban policy in the UK is arguably moving towards a 'boosterist' development model drawing on US experience, and that this reduces the difficulties that may have been associated with cross-national applications of the approach. Moreover,

> U.K. (urban) policy change can be viewed as an ongoing search ... for an effective mix of interest groups whose efforts are needed to promote urban regeneration and to be involved in decision making. (Harding, 1994: 373)

A further criticism of regime theory on methodological grounds has been levelled by Harding (1994: 377), who suggests that, in relation to methodology, 'regime theory is less enlightening, primarily because the research methodologies employed by the main exponents are either under- or unspecified'. The following section briefly sets out the methodological approach adopted in this case.

Methodology

Data for this paper is drawn from interviews that were conducted between April 1997 and July 1998 with the Discover Islington Chief Executive and the members of the Board. These Board members were an Islington Borough councillor, the Head of Strategy and Policy of the London Tourist Board, a media consultant who is resident in the borough, a solicitor whose practice is located in Islington, a design consultant and former Islington resident, a property developer whose business is based in Islington, a retired Board member of the English Tourist Board, and a Transport specialist lecturer and researcher from a London university.

Other key actors in the 'regime' for tourism development in Islington and London were also interviewed. These people were the Chairman of the London Tourist Board, the Chief Executive of the London Tourist Board, the Arts and Tourism Officer for the London Borough of Camden, which neighbours Islington, the Programme Development Manager for the City of London Corporation (the local government authority for London's main financial district), and the Tourism Development Manager for another London borough, Greenwich.

The interviews were semi-structured and tape recorded, and ranged from approximately 30–90 minutes in duration. Verbatim transcripts were returned to interviewees for verification. Questions in the interview schedules were based on broad themes derived from the Gray and Wood (1991) theoretical framework on inter-organisational collaboration. These themes concerned the background to the formation of the partnership, and issues of resource dependencies, board member characteristics and involvement, the geographical focus of the partnership programme, interpretations of sustainable tourism development and programme strategy. The findings drawn from these interviews, along with partnership strategy and policy documents, are discussed here in the context of considerations that are associated with regime theory. These considerations are:

(1) The roles and motivations of Discover Islington Board members.
(2) Private sector involvement in the Discover Islington 'regime'.
(3) The advantages and disadvantages of Discover Islington being outside direct local government control.
(4) Local community and social involvement in the Discover Islington 'regime'

(5)   Relationships with neighbouring and London-wide tourism development regimes.

Some of the limitations associated with the use of qualitative interviews apply in this case. The findings relate to a particular moment in time and will be overtaken by events in a dynamic context such as that faced by a partnership such as Discover Islington. Moreover, the extent to which the views expressed reflect 'reality' in circumstances where political sensitivities may be involved and comments are 'on the record' is open to question.

Tourism in London

This section briefly sets out the broad context of tourism in London and the 'external regime' within which Discover Islington operates. Tourism is a major sector in the London economy. It is estimated to account for 8% of London's GDP and sustains around 200,000 full-time equivalent jobs, which is around 10% of total employment in the capital (Bull, 1997; Bull & Church, 1996; Evans & McNulty, 1995; LTB, 1997). Tourist Board estimates suggest that £7710 million was spent by visitors to London on goods and services in 1996, with £6775m from this total being spent by overseas visitors, which represents a significant contribution to the UK economy (LTB, 1997: 3).

The management of tourism in London (the 'external regime' for Islington) is fragmented and complex. The 32 London boroughs and City Corporation fulfil a key planning role, with guidance provided by the London Planning Advisory Committee (LPAC, 1994) and the Government Office for London (GOL, 1996). Apart from the local authorities and various partnership initiatives, other more specific bodies involved in the tourism regime for London include the London Tourist Board and Convention Bureau (the official regional tourist board for London), London Arts Board, London Regional Office of the South East Museum Service, London Tourism Manpower Project, London Voluntary Service Council and a range of transport, accommodation and attraction operators in public, private and voluntary, not-for-profit sectors.

There is also the London First Visitors Council, a consultation group that has been active since 1993 and which exists to promote London and encourage improvements in tourism product quality. There is concern that tourism in London is growing less quickly than in competing cities and the London Focus initiative, announced in 1996, aims to address this by improving the city's share of world tourism by projecting a cohesive and positive image.

London exhibits many of the issues and difficulties associated with the sustainable development of tourism in cities that were mentioned earlier. Apart from administrative complexity, tourism is concentrated in terms of attractions and accommodation, and visitors contribute to the considerable transport pressures experienced in the city. In response to these concerns there is a policy emphasis to encourage the formation of partnerships to promote the development of tourism in fringe areas of the city (LTB, 1993; LTB, 1997). An example of this attempt to spread tourism in London to fringe areas is provided by Discover Islington.

Tourism in Islington

The London Borough of Islington is situated to the north of London's main financial district ('the City') and borders the boroughs of Camden, Hackney and Haringey (Figure 1). An estimated five million people live in and within a ten mile radius of Islington and the City financial district receives a huge weekday influx of office workers and business visitors, along with a large number of tourists (four million 'visitors' estimated in 1998) (Carpenter, 1999).

Public transport connections are extensive, if often crowded and subject to delay. Four underground and three overground rail lines cross the Borough of Islington, linking Islington to the City financial district, the West End entertainment district, the rest of London and beyond. The King's Cross rail, underground and bus interchange, although located in Camden, is particularly significant as a gateway to Islington. St Paul's Cathedral is only half a mile from the Clerkenwell area of Islington and there are five visitor attractions each receiving more that one million visitors per year within two miles of the Angel underground station (a southern gateway to Islington).

Just under 60% of London's bedspaces are situated in the neighbouring boroughs of Camden and Westminster (Beioley, 1993). The visitor attractions in Islington are mainly situated in the south of the borough, and particularly in the Angel and Clerkenwell districts. They include clusters of retail and gallery outlets specialising in antiques and art and designer products, such as the Camden Passage antiques market, heritage attractions and historical associations, the architecture and ambience of parts of the borough; and sport (with Arsenal Football Club's stadium at Highbury in the north of the borough).

Parts of Islington, again most notably in the Angel and Clerkenwell districts, have become fashionable among City employees and the media as places to live, eat, drink and be entertained. There are many well-known restaurants and public houses, including the King's Head pub/theatre, and entertainment venues including the Screen on the Green art-house cinema and small-scale theatres.

Investment in accommodation has grown in recent years, including the opening in 1998 of the Stakis Hotel near the Angel and of Jury's Hotel in Pentonville Road. Budget accommodation within the borough is limited but improving, with Discover Islington's own bed and breakfast initiative encouraging local residents to offer low-cost rooms to tourists (DI, 1992). Other investments in Islington's tourism product and infrastructure in recent years include:

- the creation and refurbishment of attractions such as the Design Centre, Crafts Council and Sadler's Wells Theatre;
- the redevelopment of the Angel underground station;
- the development of tourism related regeneration strategies in the area of the King's Cross transport interchange and the City Fringe (the area immediately surrounding London's financial district).

Furthermore, tourism is receiving increased recognition from the Council as being an emerging economic sector (LBI, 1997: 7).

Set against these positive trends, some of the most important entrance points and gateways to Islington are suffering from congestion and high levels of use, and in addition there is no overall strategy for the borough to balance the needs of

Figure 1 London Borough of Islington
Source: Islington Borough Council.

the resident community and visitors (LBI, 1997: 8), a key consideration in the context of sustainable tourism development.

The Discover Islington Regime

This section presents the background to the establishment of Discover Islington and the development of its programme, notably those elements which can be linked with attempts to develop sustainable tourism in the borough. It goes on to outline the characteristics, roles and perceptions of the Board members on the work of Discover Islington, which are key considerations in the context of regime theory.

Discover Islington was launched in 1991 as one of a number of partnerships in England (the Tourism Development Action Programmes – (TDAPs) with English Tourist Board (ETB) core funding. The present Chief Executive of Discover Islington was appointed in November of that year and has therefore headed the agency since its inception. At the time of the Chief Executive's appointment, responsibility for Tourism within the borough and the staff dedicated to it resided in an Economic Development Unit (EDU). This unit was wound up soon after the establishment of the TDAP, at a time of significant cuts in Council budgets, and the Borough now no longer employs staff with specific, direct responsibility for tourism. However, the Council remains as a major funding partner of Discover Islington, and it currently reports to an Urban Regeneration Sub-committee within the Council, whose Chair is a board member of the agency.

The Action Programme set out in the initial TDAP strategy for Discover Islington (DI, 1992) was primarily concerned with marketing, public relations and promotional work to encourage a recognition of tourism as being a significant element in the local economy, as well as the development of events, packages and products based on the district's attractions.

More recently, Discover Islington has defined its strategic objectives for the period 1996–1998 as including aims that are more explicitly concerned with the sustainable development of tourism. These include securing a long-term, stable, and adequate financial base for the organisation (the sustainability of partnership agencies is in itself an issue as many of these programmes in England have operated on a time limited funding regime), the delivery of 'locally responsible' tourism and the demonstration of good practice and innovation. As Carpenter (1999) puts it, Discover Islington has a, 'commitment to high yield, low impact tourism that also benefits local people'. Discover Islington has typically had a staff of two or three plus a Chief Executive. Its budget has been in the region of £150,000–£200,000 per year.

The regime reflected in the membership of the Board of Discover Islington in 1997–1998 included representation from Islington Council (the Chair of the Urban Regeneration Sub-committee and the Leader of the Labour Group – the majority party at the time), business people whose firms are located in the borough and/or are resident in the borough (from the media, design, legal and property sectors), the Head of Strategy and Policy of the London Tourist Board (the only specialist tourism professional represented on the Board), a former senior officer from another inner-London borough, a former ETB board member known for his experience in town centre management and a local university transport specialist researcher, lecturer and consultant who was elected chair of the Board from 1997. Board members were originally appointed by the English Tourist Board after local consultation. The aim was to include a widely drawn group, reflecting business interests, the public sector and special interests. The local council held only one of the eight seats.

Regime consideration 1: The roles and motivations of Discover Islington Board members

A regime theoretical framework suggests that attention is given to the individual roles, motivations, ideologies, expertise and aspirations of the members of a regime. The characteristics of the Discover Islington Board reflect some of these considerations, as suggested in the earlier section on regime theory. These roles and motivations included broad *personal* desires to promote business, development and tourism objectives, local dependencies for votes and business, and expressions of political or voluntaristic philosophies. An example is the role of those Discover Islington Board members from the private sector who contribute because their business and/or home is located in the area and who feel a commitment to Islington. These people contribute specialist/expert advice when called upon to do so, but do not regularly attend Board meetings, nor do they concern themselves with the daily business of the agency.

Their expertise has been drawn on in the past to assist with, for example, the design and layout of Discover Islington's visitor information and retail outlet (drawing on the expertise of a Board member who was a director of a major department store chain), professional advice on legal aspects of Discover Islington's organisational arrangements, and searches for new premises, contacts with international travel writers, and student work experience placements and research projects. In all of these examples, Discover Islington benefits from specialised professional advice at low or no cost, potentially representing substantial financial savings for the agency. In the interviews, it was suggested that the relatively informal and *ad hoc* arrangement works well because the role requires limited amounts of time and because the participants have confidence in Discover Islington's Chief Executive, who has been in post since the agency's foundation. However, several interviewees suggested that were the Chief Executive to leave, it would be necessary for them to have a closer, more 'hands-on' involvement in the workings of the Board.

Regime consideration 2: Private sector involvement in the Discover Islington 'regime'

The difficulty of recruiting the owners and managers of local businesses of all types and sizes to play an active part in Discover Islington was noted by interviewees. A local business network and subscription scheme had proved difficult to develop, and the membership fee was subsequently withdrawn.

Antique traders, retailers and restauranteurs have all been hard to persuade to contribute to the agency. These businesses might be seen as 'free-riders', benefiting from the existence of Discover Islington without contributing to it. On the other hand, they might also be presented as contributing to the agency simply because their existence adds value to the tourism product of the area.

A lack of membership from large scale, locally operating national private-sector organisations was portrayed by several members as being a particular weakness of the Board. During the TDAP period, the founding Board included membership from British Waterways (a public sector agency with responsibility for the canal network in the U.K.), Arsenal Football Club, Barclays Bank and Grand Metropolitan Estates (a major hotel corporation), but this representation from major public companies has not been sustained. However, at the time of the interviews, attempts were in hand to secure involvement by the management of the recently opened Stakis Hotel.

By and large, the private sector appears to favour specific projects where benefits and returns can be readily demonstrated rather than long-term commitments to a strategic partnership. The bus company Cowie's involvement in promoting a particular service route in a partnership project with Discover Islington is a recent example.

Regime consideration 3: The advantages and disadvantages of Discover Islington being outside direct local government control

In terms of public sector professional and political representation, and in contrast with some other partnership agencies for tourism development, the Discover Islington Board is notable in its composition by a comparative lack of specialist, professional tourism or economic development officers from local government and statutory agencies. Other tourism development partnerships arguably benefit from the expert advice that might be provided by specialist tourism and economic development officers. However, there can be conflicts of interest and issues of accountability in cases where officers are involved both in defining and implementing policy. At the same time, the seniority of Council representation on the Discover Islington Board might be noted as evidence of the importance that the Council attaches to such partnerships.

Discover Islington is heavily dependent on Islington Council for core funding. This funding dependence is a major issue for the agency, with it being extremely vulnerable to cuts in Council budgets. It is notable that 'the creation of a long term, stable, and adequate financial base' is the first item on the list of the agency's strategic objectives for 1996–1998.

On the other hand, the Council has consistently supported Discover Islington since its foundation and has demonstrated an appreciation of tourism as an important sector of local economic development and of Agenda 21 strategies (LBI, 1997). During the early 1980s Islington Council had been known for left-wing politics in opposition to the national Thatcher governments, and for supporting radical causes. According to private sector Discover Islington Board members, the Council also had an image from this period of being anti-business. However, it was suggested that more recently the Council has adopted a more pragmatic stance towards working in partnership with local businesses and it now promotes and encourages joint working with the private sector, including initiatives such as Discover Islington. The significance of Discover Islington reporting to a Council Policy committee as opposed to a Service Delivery committee was also presented as being important. This position gives Discover Islington a higher political profile within the Council, and makes it less vulnerable to cuts in funding.

Uncertainties for Discover Islington in its relationship with the Council have included having to adjust to periodic departmental reorganisations. The abolition of the Economic Development Unit and of the Tourism Officer post in 1991 created uncertainty for Discover Islington on its foundation. More recently, the 1997 creation of new, broad Directorates, with Social and Economic Regeneration and Partnerships being the lead Directorate in Islington with responsibility for tourism, changed the Council structures to which Discover Islington relates.

In some cases there can be an issue over the location of responsibility for tourism within different local authority departments and their relationships and channels of communication with tourism development partnerships. However, with the Chair of the relevant Council Sub-committee on the Board and with the Urban Regeneration Officer well briefed, this appears not to be a concern for Discover Islington at the time of the interviews.

A change of governing regime after elections can, however, be a source of uncertainty for any tourism development partnership. In the case of Discover Islington, the success of the Liberal Democrats in removing overall control of Islington Council from Labour at the 1998 local government elections might result in policy changes that affect Discover Islington. The existence of a specific target in the 1996–1998 programme of achieving a higher profile for itself and a greater awareness of the value of tourism within the Council, suggests that such activity is still necessary, particularly given recent structural and political change within the authority.

Some interviewees also noted Discover Islington's ability to influence Council policy by reconciling inter-departmental and professional agenda in other domains, such as wider aspects of social and economic re-generation, leisure, arts and heritage, and environmental services.

Regime consideration 4: Local community and social involvement in the Discover Islington 'regime'

Local communities are indirectly represented on the Board of Discover Islington through an elected Council member. The agency also involves local residents in tourism development through its support for the Islington Festival and its links with amenity and voluntary associations. Furthermore, the marketing targets for 1996–1998 make specific reference to encouraging the 'tourist' activity of local residents from within the Borough. An example of such encouragement is the support given to local people wishing to start enterprises in the budget accommodation sector.

However, Discover Islington's emphasis on promoting 'honeypots' in relatively prosperous districts within the borough, as opposed to attending to the more deprived areas, was an issue for some members. At the extreme, it might be suggested that Discover Islington unintentionally serves to reinforce spatial and social inequality by concentrating attention on those areas within its boundaries with a clear and identifiable potential for tourism development. The extent to which local tourism development partnership programmes may be able to ignore less advantaged areas within their boundaries because of their quasi-independence from local government control is an issue that gives rise to questions about equity and accountability in the allocation of public funds. These organisations, for example, may arguably be solely serving the interests of already more favourably endowed areas within their boundaries.

Regime consideration 5: Relationships with neighbouring and London-wide tourism development regimes

Discover Islington's contribution to the work of the King's Cross and City Fringe partnerships (regimes) is recorded in the annual report for 1995–1996. Both of these major re-generation programmes include Islington within their boundaries, along with several other London boroughs. However, as the single major core funder of Discover Islington, Islington Council's view on the agency's involvement in programmes and projects that are, at least in part, focused elsewhere is significant. It was suggested by some interviewees that such involvement had, up to that time, not been a major distraction from the agency's core work within Islington, nor an issue for the Council.

However, there were concerns that Discover Islington, in developing its work outside the borough, might be diverted from its concentration on sustainable tourism development within Islington.

Greater attention appears to be being given to the possibility of Discover Islington assuming a consultancy and research role for other partnership organisations, based on its expertise in the development of tourism in the urban fringe. The recent appointment of an academic member to the Chair of Discover Islington is perhaps evidence of the recognition of the potential for income generation and prestige represented by this type of consultancy activity.

Conclusions

This paper has sought to apply a regime approach to the analysis of opinions expressed in key actor interviews and of strategy documents produced by the member organisations of a particular partnership for sustainable tourism development in the London city fringe.

Regime theory does appear to provide a coherent yet flexible framework for organising and analysing such data. Issues such as the characteristics, motivations and composition of board membership are comparable between partnerships, and regime theory suggests ways in which the membership might differ in their style and approach. In the case of Discover Islington, a fair degree of consensus does appear to have existed between Board members, with generally limited dissent noted from the interviews on the agency's organisation, management, aims and strategy. The role, relative autonomy and status of this partnership's Chief Executive was also significant for members.

A tourism development partnership's relations with major funding partners and their 'access to institutional resources' may also usefully be considered within a regime approach. Discover Islington's dependency on grant-in-aid from a single source, Islington Council, and its need for continuing political support from the Council is a major consideration and represents a constraint in its adopting an operational role outside the borough boundaries. At the same time, there is a widely held view that Discover Islington must tap in to other sources (and regimes), such as urban regeneration programmes, in order to secure its long-term future. This tension is unlikely to disappear entirely.

The extent to which a regime is accountable by allowing for genuine public participation in decision making, a key factor in sustainable local tourism development, is also an issue that may be subject to comparative analyses. In this case, Discover Islington aims to involve local communities in tourism development and prominent elected members serve on the Board, but reservations remain about the effects that the programme may have on reinforcing disadvantage and socioeconomic polarisation in the Borough.

Methodologically, the reliability of interpretations placed on qualitative interview findings, even if conducted with a wide range of key participants, must be taken into account. In this case, the transcripts were verified by interviewees, but they still remain a snapshot of perceptions of the circumstances that prevailed at a particular period of Discover Islington's existence. Furthermore, as in all case studies, the specific characteristics of the locality, the nature of local tourism supply and demand, the legal and administrative frameworks and the range of actors involved in local governance, place limitations on the transferability of findings from single cases to other settings and must be acknowledged. London is unique in terms of the particularly fragmented and complex set of institutions that merge, overlap and compete in the governance of the city.

Uncertainties also remain about the status and powers of the new strategic authority and Mayor that are now proposed for London and their implications for existing regimes, including those for tourism development.

As Newman and Thornley (1997: 969) put it, 'understanding the governance of London poses two additional challenges to the regime approach. First, the larger the city the less likely we are to find a single coherent regime. Secondly, the role of central government is likely to be particularly strong'. Moreover, 'one of the key areas where the London case demands some adaptation of the regime approach is in the need to focus on the metropolitan as well as the local scale'. This paper has concentrated more on the micro level of Discover Islington rather than on its place on the wider strategic stage of London's overall tourism development. Further studies of partnership regimes for sustainable urban fringe tourism development might usefully address these wider networks and relationships.

Correspondence

Any correspondence should be directed to Philip Long, Senior Lecturer in Tourism Management, Centre for Tourism, School of Leisure and Food Mangagement, Sheffield Hallam University, City Campus, Howard Street, Sheffield S1 1WB, UK (p.e.long@shu.ac.uk).

References

A.C.C. (1992) *Partnerships in Prosperity: Local Government's Role in Economic Development*. London: Association of County Councils.
Bailey, N., Barker, A. and MacDonald, K. (1995) *Partnership Agencies in British Urban Policy*. London: UCL Press.
Barlow, M. (1995) Greater Manchester: Conurbation complexity and local government structure. *Political Geography* 14 (4), 379–400.
Beioley, S. (1993) *Improving the Visitor's Experience of Islington*. London: The Tourism Company.
Blackman, T. (1995) *Urban Policy in Practice*. London: Routledge.

Bramwell, B. and Rawding, L. (1994) Tourism marketing organisations in industrial cities. *Tourism Management* 15, 425–434.

Bull, P. (1997) Tourism in London: Policy changes and planning problems. *Regional Studies* 82–85.

Bull, P. and Church, A. (1996) The London tourism complex. In C.M. Law (ed.) *Tourism in Major Cities*. London: Routledge.

Carpenter, H. (1999) Measuring the economic impact of local tourism – making the most of local resources. *Tourism – the Journal of the Tourism Society* 102, 10–11.

CBI (1996) *Visitors Welcome – Tourism in the Third Millennium*. London: Confederation of British Industry.

CFP (1997) *Building on Success: City Fringe Partnership Review 1997*. London: City Fringe Partnership.

Coulson, A. (1993) Urban development corporations, local authorities and patronage in urban policy. In R. Imrie and H. Thomas (eds) *British Urban Policy and the Urban Development Corporations*. London: Paul Chapman.

Cropper, S. (1996) Collaborative working and the issue of sustainability. In C. Huxham (ed.) *Creating Collaborative Advantage*. London: Sage.

DI (1992) *A Tourism Strategy and Programme for Islington*. London: Discover Islington Tourism Development Action Programme.

DoE (1997) *Effective Partnerships: A Handbook for Members of SRB Challenge Fund Partnerships*. London: Department of the Environment, HMSO.

Edwards, J. and Deakin, N. (1992) Privatism and partnership in urban regeneration. *Public Administration* 70, 359–368.

Elkin, S.L. (1987) *City and Regime in the American Republic*. Chicago: University of Chicago Press.

Evans, G. and McNulty, T. (1995) Planning for tourism in London: World city, whose city? A critique of local development plans and tourism policy in London. Paper presented at the Urban Environment and Tourism Conference, South Bank University, London, September.

Finn, C.B. (1996) Utilizing stakeholder strategies for positive collaborative outcomes. In C. Huxham (ed.) *Creating Collaborative Advantage*. London: Sage.

GOL (1996) *Strategic Guidance for London Planning Authorities: RPG3*. London: Government Office for London.

Gray, B. and Wood, D.J. (1991) Collaborative alliances: Moving from practice to theory. *The Journal of Behavioral Science* 27, 1.

Harding, A. (1991) The rise of urban growth coalitions, UK–style? *Environment and Planning C: Government and Policy* 9, 295–317.

Harding, A. (1994) Urban regimes and growth machines: Towards a cross-national research agenda. *Urban Affairs Quarterly* 29 (3), 356–382.

Jamal, T.B. and Getz, D. (1994) *Collaboration theory and community tourism planning. Annals of Tourism Research* (21) 3, 186–204.

Law, C.M. (ed.) (1996) *Tourism in Major Cities*. London: Routledge.

LBI (1997) *A Sustainable Tourism Strategy for Islington*. London Borough of Islington Discussion Paper.

Logan, J. and Molotch, H. (1987) *Urban Fortunes: The Political Economy of Place*. Berkeley: University of California Press.

Long, P.E. (1994) In A.V. Seaton *et al.* (eds) *Tourism – the State of the Art*. Chichester: John Wiley.

Long, P.E. (1997) Researching tourism partnership organisations: From practice to theory to methodology. In P.E. Murphy (ed.) *Quality Management in Urban Tourism*. Chichester: John Wiley.

Long, F.J. and Arnold, M.B. (1995) *The Power of Environmental Partnerships*. Dryden Press.

LPAC (1994) *Advice on Strategic Planning Guidance for London*. London: London Planning Advisory Committee.

LTB (1993) *Tourism Strategy for London 1994–1997*. London Tourist Board.

LTB (1997) *Tourism Strategy for London 1997–2000*. London Tourist Board.

Newman, P. and Thornley, A. (1996) *Urban Planning in Europe: International Competition, National Systems and Planning Projects*. London: Routledge.

Newman, P. and Thornley, A. (1997) Fragmentation and centralisation in the governance of London: Influencing the urban policy and planning agenda. *Urban Studies* 34 (7), 967–988.

Paddison, R. (1997) Politics and governance. In M. Pacione (ed.) *Britain's Cities: Geographies of Division in Urban Britain*. London: Routledge.

Roberts, V., Russell, H., Harding, M. and Parkinson, M. (1995) *Public/Private/Voluntary Partnerships in Local Government*. London: The Local Government Management Board.

Robinson, M. and Boniface, P. (eds) (1999) *Tourism and Cultural Conflicts*. Wallingford: CAB International.

Selin, W. (1993) Collaborative alliances: New interorganizational forms in tourism. *Journal of Travel and Tourism Marketing* 2, 217–227.

Selin, S. and Chavez (1995) Developing an evolutionary tourism partnership model. *Annals of Tourism Research* 22 (4), 844–856.

Stoker, G. and Mossberger, K. (1994) Urban regime theory in comparative perspective. *Environment and Planning C: Government and Policy* 12, 195–212.

Stone, C.L. and Sanders, H.T. (1987) *The Politics of Urban Development*. Lawrence: University Press of Kansas.

Thornley, A. (ed.) (1992) *The Crisis of London*. London: Routledge.

Tyler, D., Guerrier, Y. and Robertson, M. (eds) (1998) *Managing Tourism in Cities: Policy, Process and Practice*. Chichester: John Wiley.

Waddock, S.A. (1991) A typology of social partnership organisations. *Administration and Society* 22 (4), 480–515.

11. Is There a Tourism Partnership Life Cycle?

Alison Caffyn
Centre for Urban and Regional Studies, University of Birmingham, Edgbaston, Birmingham B15 2TT, UK

The paper examines how individual tourism partnerships change over time and whether there are commonalities in their dynamics and evolution. Literature on organisational evolution is reviewed and previous life cycle models are compared. A case study of the North Pennines Tourism Partnership is presented highlighting key phases in its development and partners' reflections on its nine year life. A brief comparative analysis of other tourism partnerships is presented to identify similarities and alternative life cycle trajectories. Particular attention is given to the final phases of partnerships, which by their nature are usually temporary organisations, and what happens to their role after they finish. A model tourism partnership life cycle is proposed and its implications for the planning and management of partnerships are considered. It is hoped the model will contribute to both theoretical and practical debates about partnership and collaboration.

Introduction

This paper aims to examine how individual tourism partnerships change over time and whether there are commonalities in their dynamics and evolution. A life cycle model is presented based on a review of literature from a range of disciplines, an empirical study of one particular tourism partnership and evidence from a selection of others. The approach combines elements of Long's (1997) intensive and extensive strategies, identifying key developments in the evolution of an individual partnership over time, at a local level, followed by a comparative analysis with a selection of other partnerships to develop a model with more general potential applicability.

The paper first draws together literature on organisational evolution and life cycles, particularly focusing on those applied in the public policy arena. It compares 11 previous life cycle models to identify common characteristics, in order to provide a framework for the development of a specific model for tourism partnerships. The case study of the North Pennines Tourism Partnership is then presented. Key phases in its development are highlighted along with partners' reflections on the problems which were encountered particularly in its latter years. This detailed case is then contrasted with the evolution of the comparator partnerships in an attempt to identify similarities, differences and alternative trajectories for partnership life cycles and the factors determining these.

Particular attention is given to the final phases of partnerships, a topic ignored by many authors particularly in business management literature. Partnerships are usually, though not always, temporary organisations, although some last considerably longer than others. It is vital to consider why, when and how a partnership should finish and what happens to its role after it finishes. Brown (1996) draws attention to the need to develop better exit strategies which, she says, would help in sustaining ongoing support for partnerships and avoid building up unrealistic expectations. Finally a tentative tourism partnership life cycle model is proposed and some of its implications for the planning and management of partnerships are discussed. It is hoped the model will contribute to both the theoretical and the practical debates about partnership operation and effectiveness.

The paper has a UK focus in terms of the examples of partnerships used and their external environment such as funding agencies or government policy. The theoretical sections, however, draw on literature from both the UK and North America. Whilst the model has been developed in relation to the UK context it should be possible to test its applicability in other countries to examine factors at play elsewhere.

Partnerships

The process of partnership and collaboration are key elements of sustainable development and sustainable tourism, particularly when a wide and representative range of stakeholders from the local community are able to play an active role. There have been a number of studies of inter-organisational relations and research into partnerships in the tourism field recently (Selin & Beason, 1991; Jamal & Getz, 1995; Long, 1997). This paper uses Long's definition of tourism partnerships:

> the collaborative efforts of autonomous stakeholders from organisations in two or more sectors with interests in tourism development who engage in an interactive process using shared rules, norms and structures at an agreed organisational level and over a defined geographical area to act or decide on issues related to tourism development. (Long, 1997: 239)

Tourism partnerships were first formally established in the UK in the mid 1980s. This was part of the more general trend in economic development towards collaboration between public-sector bodies. This trend was triggered by government cuts in public spending and a growing awareness of the benefits of partnership working. Whilst tourist boards, local authorities and other agencies had become accustomed to working in close collaboration, the main incentive to formalise and broaden tourism partnerships was the provision of funding from the English Tourist Board to establish Tourism Development Action Programmes (TDAPs) (Bramwell & Broom, 1989; Palmer, 1992). A range of TDAPs and other variants were set up around England in locations such as urban areas, depressed ex-industrial areas, rural areas and seaside resorts.

Initially most of these partnerships were between public-sector organisations, typically including the local authorities, the regional tourist board (membership organisations) and quangos such as the Countryside Commission (CoCo), Rural Development Commission (RDC) or the Training Agency. By the 1990s more private-sector representatives were wooed to participate in partnerships, particularly local tourism associations or chambers of commerce. This follows the trend recognised by Boyle (1993) in urban regeneration partnerships in which central government policy demanded more evenly balanced public–private involvement. In the mid 1990s there was a further shift in emphasis to widen participation to the voluntary sector and local communities to enable more multilateral partnerships to be established. Lowndes *et al.* (1997: 334) explain how these 'have emerged from local imperatives and debates about building healthy and sustainable communities, but also have been stimulated by central government funding programmes'. These programmes include City Challenge and the Single Regeneration Budget which require voluntary sector and community participation.

The Collaboration Process

Much has been written in the public policy and urban regeneration literature about collaborative approaches. Particularly useful is Wood and Gray's (1991) paper which ponders several definitions of collaboration and begins to develop a comprehensive theory of collaboration. More recently Huxham (1996) has developed the concept of collaborative advantage, i.e. those things that can be produced by partners in collaboration which would not otherwise have been achievable. She also considers the various dimensions of collaboration and hence how collaboration can be sustained over time. However little attention has been given to the dynamics of partnerships over time. Most authors focus on the processes involved in partnership and collaboration rather than how they may change as the partnership develops.

Huxham and Vangen (1994) give more emphasis to the difficulties of sustaining inter-organisational relationships long term. They present two possible routes for partnerships depending on the collaborative capability of partner organisations. Partnerships which have difficulties dealing with the process of collaboration can be overcome by inertia and frustration leading to 'collaborative fatigue' and probably the end of the partnership. Alternatively if the partners overcome most problems the partnership can develop into 'collaborative maturity' and be sustained for longer.

Several authors have addressed the processes at work within economic development partnerships. MacKintosh (1992) proposes a framework highlighting three key processes: synergy, transformation and budget enlargement. She also highlights the pressures and conflicts that can develop within partnerships. Hastings (1996) develops these ideas further, in the context of urban regeneration, and refines MacKintosh's framework to specify two different types of synergy – resource synergy and policy synergy – and two types of transformation – uni-directional, where one partner changes its ways of working under pressure from another; and mutual transformation, when all partners are changed by the process of collaboration. Both authors hint at the dynamics at play within partnerships over time, but do not consider explicitly how these factors may be more or less important at different stages of a partnership.

Life Cycle Models

The concepts of organisational evolution and life cycles have been explored by authors in the business, management and organisational studies fields (Greiner, 1979; Kimberly & Miles, 1980; Quinn & Cameron, 1983). Waddock (1989) applies the concept to partnership organisations and develops an evolutionary model. This approach was transferred to the tourism literature by Selin and Chavez (1995) with their study of tourism-related partnerships in US forests. A number of these authors stress the need for more in-depth research into how individual partnerships change over time. Long (1994) identifies the lack of discussion on how to sustain partnership programmes in the long term and Jamal and Getz (1995: 201) recommend research 'to trace the performance of collaborative planning processes and strategies over time'.

The use of a biological metaphor for studying organisations which are social constructs has been criticised. Kimberly (1980) points out that whilst biological organisms go through clear, predictable stages in their development this is not necessarily the case with organisations – there are no natural laws which govern their evolution. Similarly he points out that death is an inevitable feature of biological life, whereas there is no inevitable route towards death for organisations. This second criticism is perhaps less relevant when studying partnerships however, as whilst their lifespans vary, many do come to an end, even if they continue in another form. Thus it could be argued that the life cycle model is particularly appropriate for studying this form of organisation. Kimberly (1980: 9) concludes that:

> biological metaphors, imperfect though they most certainly are, can serve a very useful purpose in the study of organisations. By forcing theorists to think through carefully where the metaphors are appropriate and inappropriate, their use can lead to the raising of important new questions.

This section aims to bring together and briefly review previous attempts to develop life cycle models in various fields. It summarises in table format those models which have been proposed most formally and which have greatest relevance for tourism partnerships, see Table 1.

The most familiar life cycle model in the tourism literature is Butler's tourist area life cycle model first outlined in 1980 which has since been discussed, tested and criticised by numerous authors. Butler's model (see Figure 1) applies not to organisations but to tourist destinations and thus might be thought irrelevant to this discussion. However, it is included at this stage not only because of its familiarity but because it is one of the few models to focus on the final stages and possible decline of the subject to which it is applied.

A number of life cycle models have been developed in the business management and commercial fields. An early example is Greiner (1972) who outlines five phases of gradual evolution interspersed with short periods of revolution as companies grow and face operational problems. Companies reaching a crisis point have to reorganise in order to progress and continue growing. As with many business models it does not look at the decline and failure of businesses although the implication is that if a company fails to respond to one of these crises then failure may follow. A particularly interesting feature of this model is the final phase of evolution which Greiner terms 'collaboration' as a mature company builds a more flexible and behavioural approach to management using team action to solve problems. He speculates that the final crisis following the collaborative period could centre around 'psychological saturation' of employees 'who grow emotionally and physically exhausted by the intensity of teamwork and the heavy pressure for innovative solutions' (Greiner, 1972: 44). These issues may apply to the collaborative nature of partnerships.

A particularly useful study was carried out by Quinn and Cameron (1983) who themselves reviewed nine models of organisational life cycles and then

Table 1 Comparison of life-cyle models

Quinn and Cameron (1983) Summary model					
Entrepreneurial Marshalling resources, lots of ideas, entrepreneurial activities, little planning, forming a niche	*Collectivity* Informal structure, sense of collectivity and mission, high innovation and commitment	*Formalisation and control* stable structure and rules, emphasis on efficiency and procedures, conservatism	*Elaboration of structure* Decentralisation, domain expansion, adaption and renewal		
Downs (1967) Motivation for growth					
Struggle for autonomy Legitimacy and autonomy sought, stabilise resources, achieve survival threshold	*Rapid growth* Innovator control, emphasis on expansion		*Deceleration* Coordination problems, predictability emphasised, formal roles, reduced flexibility		
Lippit and Schmidt (1967) Critical managerial concerns					
Birth Short range perspective, survival, personal control	*Youth* Stability and service, efficiency planning and systematic control	*Maturity* Emphasis on adaptability, contribution to society, growth opportunities sought			
Lyden (1975) Functional problems					
First Adaption to external environment	*Second* Resources acquisition	*Third* Goal attainment	*Fourth* Pattern maintenance and institutionalisation		
Adizes (1979) Major organisational activities					
Courtship Idea formation, entrepreneurial activities	*Infant organisation* Emphasis on production, time pressures, little planning, few meetings	*Go-go organisation* Rapid expansion, personalised leadership, fast decision making	*Adolescent* Coordination and admin dominate, stability, rules, conservatism	*Prime* Loss of touch with environment, stable aspirations	*Maturity* Paternalistic, little motivation

Table 1 (cont.)

Kimberly (1979) Internal social control, structure of work and environmental relations

First	*Second*	*Third*	*Fourth*		
Marshalling resources, creation of ideology	Obtaining support, choice of leader and staff, decisions	Identity, pursuit of mission, high collectivity and commitment	Formal structure and rules, internal competition, conservative trend, personal investment questioned		

Waddock (1989) Evolutionary model of social partnership development

Context	*Initiation*	*Establishment*	*Maturity*		
Crisis, mandate, networks, vision, broker	Issue crystallisation, coalition building, forum established, trust building	Purpose formulation, work begins on agendas	Purpose re-formulation, broadening of focus	*(Death)*	

Selin and Chavez (1995) Evolutionary tourism partnership model

Antecedents	*Problem setting*	*Direction setting*	*Structuring*	*Outcomes*	
Crisis, mandate, vision, networks, leadership, incentives	Interdependence, consensus on stakeholders and benefits, problem definition	Establish goals, set ground rules explore options, organise sub-groups	Formalisation, roles assigned, tasks elaborated, monitoring	Programmes, impacts, benefits (feedback loop of cyclical re-evaluation)	

Wood (1992) The Heritage Regions Process

Entry	*Needs assessment*	*Planning*	*Doing*	*Renewal*	
Groundwork, commitment	Inventory, assessment, public acceptance	Viability of resources for development	Community action and implementation	Evaluation, rejuvenation	

Lowndes and Skelcher (1998) Partnership life cycle

Pre-partnership collaboration	*Partnership creation and consolidation*	*Delivery*	*Termination and succession*		
Network mode of governance, informality, trust, sense of common purpose	Hierarchy mode of governance, assertion of status and authority, formalisation of procedures	Market mechanisms, tendering and contracts, lower cooperation	Network mode of governance, uncertainty, new openness, community involvement		

Butler (1980) Tourism area cycle of evolution

Exploration	Involvement	Development	Consolidation	Stagnation/ stabilisation	Rejuvenation/decline

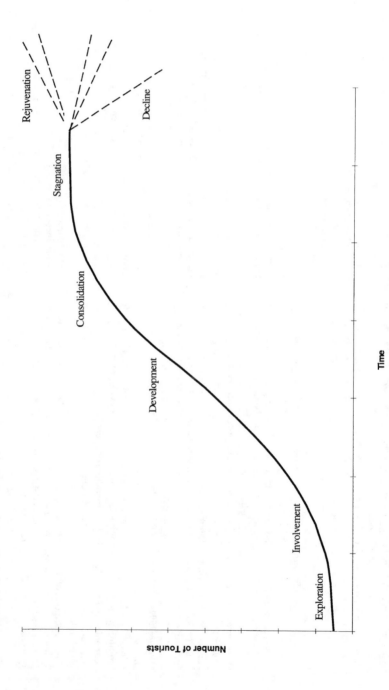

Figure 1 Butler's model of a tourist area cycle of evolution (1980)

produced their own summary model. They stress the importance of a longitudinal approach to studying organisations and criticise the tendency to focus on
fairly static, mature organisations. They point out that the most interesting
phases in organisational development are the early ones when change happens
faster. The same could apply to the final stages of an organisation which is
ending. Of the nine models they reviewed five have been chosen as most relevant
to the current discussion, some are specifically based on public or government
organisations rather than private companies. The five models and the summary
model are included in Table 1, certain points are highlighted here as being of
particular note in the context of the current study.

Downs' (1967) model focuses on government bureaux and stresses the need to
acquire both legitimacy and resources in the early stages. Lippit and Schmidt's
model, also from 1967, stresses viability in the first stage, the importance of
building a reputation in the developing stage and, in the mature stage,
responding to societal needs, which in the context of tourism partnerships could
be issues of sustainability and community development. Lyden's (1975) model,
based on public organisations, includes issues such as generating a niche;
resource acquisition; goal attainment and outputs; maintenance; and
institutionalisation in successive phases of a life cycle.

Adizes' (1979) model uses life cycle analogies of courtship, infancy, adoles-
cence and maturity. It is one of the few models to consider the decline and death
of organisations, which are attributed to an over-emphasis on stability, administration, rules and procedures. Finally, Kimberly's (1979) model stresses the early
stages of development particularly the need to first marshal resources and
develop an ideology; a second stage involving the selection of people and establishing support and a third stage of creating an identity. These are all things
which a partnership must do in its formative stages. He emphasises that most
organisations become more conservative and predictable in their later stages.

Having reviewed these models, Quinn and Cameron develop their own
summary model because, whilst the models vary significantly, all suggested
progression through similar life cycle stages. Their four summary stages are:

> an *entrepreneurial stage* (early innovation, niche formation, creativity), a
> collectivity stage (high cohesion, commitment), a *formalization and control
> stage* (stability and institutionalization), and a *structure elaboration and adap-
> tion stage* (domain expansion and decentralization). (Quinn & Cameron,
> 1983: 40)

Waddock (1989) specifically applies previous theory to partnership organisations. She develops an evolutionary model outlining four stages: first, the context
from which a partnership grows; second, the initiation phase; third, establishment; and fourth, maturity. She emphasises the importance of three processes
within the sequence: issue crystallisation – around which the partnership will
focus; coalition building – the process of assembling the appropriate partners
and balancing power between them; and thirdly purpose formulation, determining the scope, direction and goals of a partnership. Her model has a feedback
loop of 'purpose reformulation' by which a partnership in maturity can cyclically
re-evaluate its purpose in the context of a changing environment. Waddock
suggests that this re-evaluation process will lead to a broadening of focus and

that if partnerships fail to reformulate and broaden their purpose they may die. Death may of course be appropriate if the partnership's purposes have been achieved.

In the tourism literature both Jamal and Getz (1995) and Selin and Chavez (1995) have used Waddock's ideas in relation to tourism planning and partnership. Jamal and Getz (1995) suggest three broad stages in a collaboration process for community-based tourism planning. The stages include problem-setting, direction-setting and implementation. Selin and Chavez (1995) produced a more specific evolutionary model of tourism partnerships with five stages and a feedback loop: antecedents; problem-setting; direction-setting; structuring; and outcomes. They particularly stress the dynamic but fragile nature of this type of collective effort.

Wood (1992), cited in Brown (1996), gives an overview of the phases involved in the process of initiating and developing Heritage Regions in Canada (a specific government-sponsored heritage tourism programme). Wood identifies five phases: entry, needs assessment, planning, doing and renewal, plus the tasks to be undertaken at each stage.

In the urban regeneration literature Boyle (1993) outlines a series of stages through which many regeneration partnerships progress: first, a launch and need for credibility; second, the implementation of early action programmes; third, hitting a plateau of reality and deeper questioning; and fourth, longer term ambitious programmes of structural change. This emphasises evolution in terms of a work programme and differentiates between early action – often vital in developing credibility and a profile – and longer term outputs – which may have much longer lead-in times.

Finally two more recent pieces of work from the public policy field shed light on the process from a further perspective. Lowndes and Skelcher (1998) studying changing modes of governance, focus on networks and more formal partnerships and propose a four-stage life cycle: pre-partnership collaboration; partnership creation and consolidation; programme delivery; and termination and succession. They link these stages to three modes of governance which play a greater or lesser role in each stage; these are market relationships; hierarchical arrangements; and more informal and fluid networking. Networking plays an important role at the beginning and end of partnerships, but hierarchies develop in the consolidation phase and market mechanisms of tendering and contracts may play the major role in the programme delivery phase.

Deakin and Gaster's current research (1998) approaches the subject by examining the collaboration process. They propose a ladder of partnership (somewhat similar to Arnstein's (1971) ladder of participation). Partnerships, it is suggested, can move up (or down) the ladder towards greater levels of collaboration and full partnership during their lifetime.

The 11 models vary significantly as they have all been developed at different times, in different contexts and focused on different types of organisation. The number of phases also varies. However there are numerous similarities between the characteristics of various phases. A series of five summary phases has been developed containing characteristics from the models which would appear to have the most relevance to organisations such as tourism partnerships. These are presented in Table 2. Phase 5 contains the most variation in characteristics as the models identify different scenarios for organisations, some more positive than others. This forms a framework within which to assess the case study and comparative analysis, to examine which phases are apparent in reality, how the collaboration process and achievements change over time and in particular what happens in the latter stages of a partnership. The embryonic phases in Table 2 will be reassessed in the final section of the paper, in the development of a life cycle model of partnerships.

Table 2 Summary life cycle phases and characteristics

Phase 1	Phase 2	Phase 3	Phase 4	Phase 5
Responding to external environment	Problem definition	Development of identity	Full implementation	Stagnation
Exploration of ideas	Coalition building	Formulation of procedures	Stability	Commitment questioned
Vision formulation	Development of trust	Pursuit of mission	Monitoring	Uncertainty
Networking	Inventory	Explore options	Consolidation	Fewer options for innovation
Marshalling commitment	Assessment of needs	Form sub-groups	Coordination and administration	Loss of relevance
Creating a mandate	Choice of leader and staff	Personalised leadership	Decentralisation	Re-evaluation
Marshalling resources	Innovation	Build momentum	Tendering out and contracts	Purpose reformulation
Developing a common purpose	Sense of mission	Expansion of activities		Adaption and renewal
	Seeking legitimacy	High commitment		Domain expansion

The Case Study

Methodology

The case study, the North Pennines Tourism Partnership (NPTP), was chosen as a longstanding, broad partnership with an emphasis on the development and management of sustainable tourism. The partnership was in its final year and thus provided an ideal opportunity to study the latter stages of a partnership and the proposals for the continuation of its work by other means. The field research, conducted in July 1998, involved a series of semi-structured interviews with key informants. These included three past project managers, who could provide in-depth information for particular periods in the partnership's lifetime. In addition six representatives of a sample of partners were interviewed. The sample was chosen both to gather views from each type of organisation or sector involved and to give a geographical spread across the area.

Interviewees were asked about the partnership operation and outputs over time, focusing on the identification of key phases and turning points. Notes were transcribed using tapes of the interviews and the transcriptions were sent to interviewees for amendments or additional comments. The results were analysed and coded to identify common themes, opinions and attitudes about the partnership as it was established, throughout its nine year life and into the future. The first draft of the paper was widely circulated within the partnership and a number of positive and confirmatory comments were received. Members of the partnership appeared to have found the process of reflecting on the life-time of the partnership interesting and helpful, particularly as plans were being developed concurrently for a new partnership for the area. It is acknowledged that the analysis is based on a limited sample of participants in the partnership. Whilst a larger sample may have gathered additional detail the respondents were confident that the trends and phases were accurately identified.

Background

The partnership was established in 1990 as 'a Partnership to help strengthen the Rural Economy and care for the countryside in the North Pennines' (NPTP 1994: 2). The North Pennines (see Figure 2) is a bleak but beautiful upland area which has been designated as an Area of Outstanding Natural Beauty (AONB), one of the largest in the UK. Its unique and wild landscape and sparse population have led to it being dubbed 'England's Last Wilderness'. It consists of large moorland plateaux which harbour the sources of the rivers Tyne, Wear, Tees and Eden. It is a watershed area in administrative terms as well, being split between the counties of Cumbria, Northumberland and Durham and six district councils. The area has a unique industrial heritage having once been the most important lead mining area in the world. Thus it has a range of historic remains and unusual geological features in addition to being a highly valued natural environment, providing habitats for rare bird species such as merlin and black grouse and wildlife including red squirrels and otters.

The area had been the focus for tourism development previously. It was desig-nated as a Tourism Growth Point in the mid 1970s by the English Tourist Board but resources were limited and there was no project officer to implement proposals. In the 1980s the initiative was continued by the North Pennines Tourism Consultative Group involving local authorities and government agen-cies, but again progress was slow. The group commissioned a report on tourism in the area (Tym, 1988) which proposed a more coordinated and targeted approach implemented by a project officer. This period would relate to Phase 1 in Table 2. The same year the AONB designation of the area was confirmed. These two events triggered much discussion and following a public workshop to debate the best way forward, the North Pennines Tourism Partnership was launched (Phase 2).

The wide range of partners is listed in Table 3. The partnership set clear objec-tives, incorporating the principles of sustainable development, one of the first UK partnerships to do so (Table 4). The work of the partnership was carried out initially by two working groups on marketing and development, guided and coordinated by the project manager. The partnership's initial budget was about

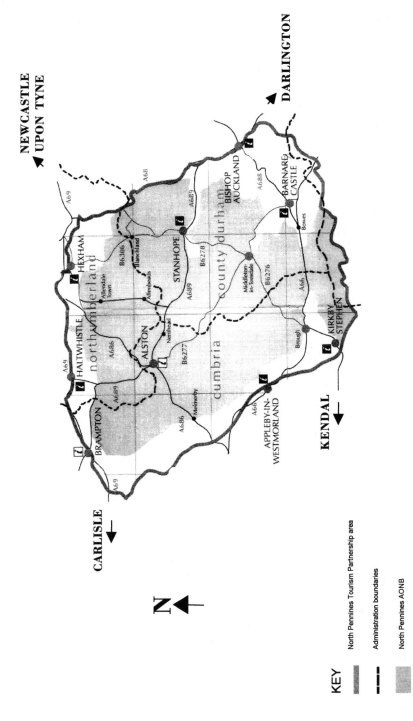

Figure 2 The North Pennines

Table 3 North Pennines Tourism Partnership Partners (as listed in the NPTP review, 1994)

Government Agencies*

- English Tourist Board (represented through the Cumbria and Northumbria Tourist Boards)
- Countryside Commission
- Rural Development Commission

Local Authorities*

- Cumbria County Council
- Durham County Council
- Northumberland County Council
- Eden District Council
- Tynedale District Council
- Wear Valley District Council
- Teeside District Council

Private Sector (including farming representative)

Voluntary Sector (the North Pennines Heritage Trust)

Note: Those marked * provide the core funding. The others give their time, energy, enthusiasm and funding, as appropriate, to individual projects.

£50,000 per year in core funding provided by the partners. The partnership generated much larger amounts for specific projects from a variety of sources.

Previous accounts give more detail of the partnership's organisation and activities (Countryside Commission, 1995; Davidson & Maitland, 1997). Two more critical accounts have also been published tackling the extent to which local communities have been involved in or benefit from tourism development in the area (Prentice, 1993; Phillips, 1991).

Results

The interviews revealed much consensus among the partners and project managers about how the NPTP developed over time. The main factors influencing its direction and success were identified as the funding available and the project managers leading the partnership. The funding arrangements for the partnership changed significantly after five years and this had a major impact on its later phases. The partnership had four project managers, and interviewees tended to link phases in the partnership's development to the managers in place at the time. The third significant internal change involved the transfer of management from Cumbria Tourist Board to Durham County Council after six years. The sequence of these changes is illustrated in Figure 3. They form the organisational context against which the other changes in the partnership must be viewed.

Table 4 North Pennines Tourism Partnership – aims and objectives (NPTP, 1994)

Overall aim:

To help strengthen the rural economy and care for the countryside in the North Pennines.

Objectives:

1. Increase awareness of the North Pennines as an area and a visitor destination by coordinating appropriate marketing opportunities.
2. Increase the range of active and informal countryside activities and promote these activities.
3. Improve existing attractions and provide quality, small to medium scale attractions based on the area's heritage and attributes.
4. Improve the quality and standards of existing accommodation and encourage modest expansions in key market sectors.
5. Promote the development of rural arts and crafts.
6. Help conserve the character of the landscape and heritage and enhance the appearance of the area's towns and villages.
7. Develop community and private sector support for tourism.
8. Improve business advice and training for the local tourism industry.

In its early stages the main challenges the partnership faced were trying to work collaboratively across a large and fragmented geographical area with a large number of partners with diverse interests. One interviewee expressed a mental image of the North Pennines being in the 'back yard' of all the partners who faced away from it towards their main areas of interest elsewhere. The partnership was making them all turn round to face the area and confront its problems together. Collaborative working was also relatively new to most partners. Another main challenge was to create and project an identity for the North Pennines externally and to build up credibility and a profile locally. The most commonly mentioned outputs from the early stages were the logo, which was rapidly taken up and used by both public and private sectors, and the newsletter which kept both partners and local communities informed of progress.

Some interviewees mentioned the early challenge of trying to win more support from the private sector. This remained problematic throughout the partnership's life. The businesses in the area are small, marginal and fragile. Only a committed few became heavily involved in the NPTP. However, after the first few years there was enough enthusiasm and momentum to establish a North Pennines Tourism Association which flourished for a few years and which in its turn developed the successful North Pennines Festival. However, interest has waned during the latter phases of the NPTP and the association is currently suspended.

The first project manager was seen as successfully setting up an operational structure, raising the profile locally, generating enthusiasm and developing momentum. Work was started on creating an identity and also monitoring and research procedures were initiated. This period would relate to Phase 3 in Table 2.

The second project manager arrived during year two and remained in post for four years. This period was seen by most as the 'golden era' of the partnership –

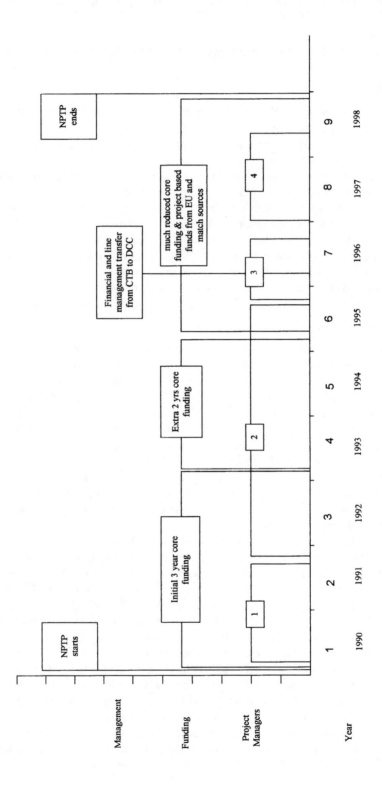

Figure 3 North Pennines Tourism Partnership – management and funding phases

the initial work had been done and the partnership concentrated on implementing the marketing and development work programmes (NPTP, 1994). The early emphasis was on marketing activity, producing basic literature for the whole area. Development projects and improvements on the ground tended to take longer to implement and came on stream later. Funding was secured for a three year Business and Training Initiative to run in parallel with the NPTP developing business advice and training opportunities for the private sector (NPTP, 1995). Most interviewees mentioned the publicity created by the PR campaign promoting 'blustery breaks'. The success of these projects and the high profile the partnership achieved enabled the partnership to secure an additional two years core funding. Thus this 'golden era' was extended into the fifth year of the partnership. It was presented nationally as good practice (English Tourist Board, 1991; Countryside Commission, 1995) and won awards. Key achievements of the partnership are summarised in Table 5. This period would relate to Phase 4 of the embryonic model in Table 2.

The main turning point came with the change in funding arrangements as the public-sector agencies withdrew from core funding leaving only the relatively small core contributions from local authorities. This coincided with the area's designation as Objective 5b status by the European Union (EU). Partners agreed that this new source of funding was the factor which enabled the partnership to continue beyond year five. However EU funding is project based and thus the partnership had to apply for funding and match funding for each of its activities individually. To complicate matters not all the area was Objective 5b; it came under two Government Office areas, under three Rural Development Commission areas and two Tourist Board areas. Thus the prospect of new funding came tied to the threat of mountains of paperwork in applications, conflicting timescales of funding sources and delays in waiting for decisions.

At the same time a new project manager took over, initially on a temporary contract. The financial situation and the time it consumed caused great frustration and a loss of morale and momentum. New staff were taken on when funds were secured for particular projects, partly because the project manager did not have capacity to do actual implementation work. The work programme was cut and consolidated to those projects that could be funded and achieved. Characteristics of Phase 4 – increasing administration and tendering out of implementation can be identified here. Whilst significant projects were completed such as the creation of a network of local information points, the partnership had fewer successful outputs and the interest of local people, businesses, the tourism association and partners themselves dropped off. A downward spiral had been triggered by the change in funding.

During this period the management of the partnership was transferred from Cumbria Tourist Board to Durham County Council. This was a point at which the partnership could have folded but Durham made a conscious decision to keep it going and a 'rescue package' of additional core funding was assembled. Partners generally still felt committed, due to the good work achieved in the past, the continuing needs of the area and their political commitment to the local population. A fourth project manager took over but again most of their energy was taken up with resolving funding crises and securing project funds.

Table 5 Key achievements of the North Pennines Tourism Partnership

---

Marketing activities:

- Created new North Pennines logo and corporate identity
- Print including visitor map, accommodation guide and leaflet
- Joint UK and overseas marketing campaigns and PR activities
- Published an outdoor activities directory and regular events listing
- Produced an annual guide to public transport services 'Across the roof of England'
- Short breaks campaigns

Development of the product:

- The Business and Training Initiative (3 year parallel project)
- Improvements to existing and development of new attractions
- Arts and crafts initiatives
- Walks development and promotion
- Assisted with development of C2C (coast to coast) cycle route and a network of camping barns
- Interpretation strategy, new interpretive information boards and local interpretive plans for individual communities
- Local information points in village shops and post offices
- Boundary signs for North Pennines AONB
- Helped set up North Pennines Farm Holiday Group
- Conducted survey of infrastructure provision
- Established cross-region working between authorities on arts, transport and the countryside
- Regular visitor surveys
- Research into tourism employment

Liaison with businesses and the community:

- Established North Pennines Tourism Association (NPTA)
- Assisted NPTA set up North Pennines Festival
- Regular newsletter and local exhibitions
- Green tourism business awards and advice

The changes in project managers would in themselves have affected momentum and implementation. Each project manager brought different expertise to the partnership and shifts in emphasis can be identified. The last two project managers were unsure of their security as long-term core funding had gone. One local authority withdrew its support when it cut its tourism budget and the future appeared ever more uncertain. The project managers' energies were concentrated on 'fire-fighting' rather than implementation and long-term planning. It was obvious to everyone that the partnership's future was in question. Elements of Phase 5 – uncertainty creeping in and partners questioning their commitment – can be identified here.

Assessment

There was considerable agreement amongst interviewees about the high and low points of the partnership and the way momentum had been lost. All identified funding as the critical factor and main turning point, which then had negative knock-on effects.

As far as the partnership process was concerned there was considerable commitment and enthusiasm from all partners to working together, tackling the problems of the area as a whole and for developing sustainable tourism. The large number of partners meant that each achieved high levels of gearing for their own relatively small financial contributions. Some interviewees thought there was a core and periphery of partners with some much more active than others. Some partners were particularly involved in certain 'pet' projects. In others the level of commitment changed as officers changed, with new personnel likely to feel less enthusiasm and ownership of the partnership. There was a sense that the partners who were least interested to start with were the first to withdraw when momentum was lost.

The private-sector involvement has been mentioned earlier. Whilst some agencies bemoaned the lack of financial input from local businesses others greatly appreciated the contributions made in time and energy, often to the detriment of their own fragile businesses, that key individuals made throughout the partnership. Both sectors faced practical problems, for example the sheer scale of the area meant that attending meetings could take the best part of a day and in winter roads could be blocked by snow. Political issues may have been important for some authorities, keen to show a presence in one of their peripheral areas. However, there were few political or power conflicts probably due to the wide spread of power amongst a large number of partners. Partners had developed significant levels of mutual trust.

Representation from the local community was never particularly strong. Local people were involved in key workshops and kept informed through newsletters, the local press and talks, but only a few parish councillors actively took part in meetings on a regular basis. Added to this was voluntary sector representation through the local heritage trust and the South Tynedale Railway, a local tourist attraction. Arguably this represents a reasonably good involvement in such a sparsely populated area. Certainly the central location of the partnership office in Alston made the project manager accessible and presented a friendly local profile.

Most of the interviewees were disappointed about the way the partnership had declined in the last few years. A formal exit strategy was never drawn up although the issues were discussed at meetings. There appears to have been a general assumption amongst most partners that the partnership would continue and that it was just going through a rough patch. One called it 'blind optimism'. No one wanted to walk away from the achievements and from the area itself which still needed considerable support. All partners felt the area needed continued input. The other key issue was that as EU funding became available until 1999, partners felt an obligation to make use of the opportunities this offered, even when the problems of administration were realised.

Interviewees felt that if partners had grasped the nettle earlier and wound the partnership up with an exit strategy earlier, then it could have finished as a success. Better communication about the ending of the partnership was needed as the private sector, locals and some partners were reportedly unclear about exactly what was happening in the last few months.

The future

Finally, pressured by the Countryside Commission's desire to tackle wider management issues in the AONB, a transition from the Tourism Partnership to a North Pennines Partnership was agreed, to start in January 1999. A new project manager will be responsible for coordinating the implementation of the AONB Management Plan (North Pennines AONB Steering Group, 1995) which focuses on environmental conservation, protection of historic remains and sustaining the economy and tourism. There appears to be a certain logic to the new arrangements, a wider, more integrated partnership, overseen by the Countryside Commission, the one agency which covers the entire area. In fact the creation of the Countryside Agency in spring 1999 (from CoCo and part of the RDC) is likely to strengthen the emphasis given to economic and social issues within a new partnership. However interviewees were still uncertain how the new partnership would work, what its priorities would be and dubious about whether one project manager could successfully coordinate such a wide range of work. It was foreseen that issues such as the production of area-wide tourism literature could fall back into the hands of individual districts and that collaboration and joint projects could begin to break up. It was not clear what private-sector representation there would be.

The NPTP was seen by some as having played a key role in influencing the proposals for the new partnership. It initiated partnership working in the North Pennines and proved it could work. It also lobbied hard for a significant focus on tourism in the new management plan. A diagrammatic representation of partnership working in the North Pennines is suggested in Figure 4. Showing the first early efforts through the Tourism Growth Point and Tourism Consultative Group resulting in the more formalised NPTP and now the broader partnership. Tourism has been used as the vehicle to mobilise the public and private sectors in the past and now a more integrated programme of environmental management and social and economic regeneration is planned.

Success

Interviewees found it difficult to pinpoint the overall impact of the NPTP. They felt the product in the area was generally stronger now and businesses were run more professionally. The creation of a new identity for the North Pennines was held up as the biggest achievement along with establishing the joint working across the area. New improvements on the ground, marketing and information literature, more events, walking and cycle trails, better networking between businesses and coordination in related areas such as arts, countryside and transport were seen as important outputs. It was also felt that the people involved had acquired a much greater understanding of the issues and problems of the area and of developing sustainable tourism. Partners' outlooks had changed through working on such an initiative.

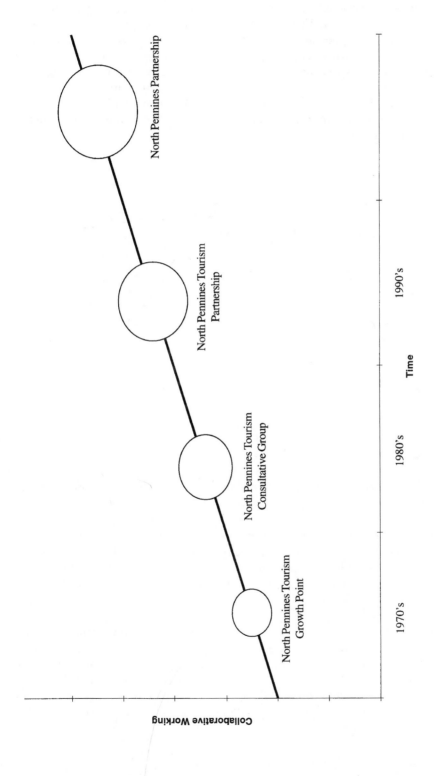

Figure 4 Representation of the development of partnership working in the North Pennines

In order to assess each interviewee's view of the partnership over its whole lifetime they were asked to chart the partnership's success on a graph. Specific indicators of success are difficult to identify for partnerships, particularly when they have not been agreed at the start. In this case a simple distinction was made between success in terms of the outputs and achievements of the partnership at different points in its lifetime, and success in terms of process and the degree of collaborative working within the partnership. The results are summarised in Figures 5 and 6. There is no specific scale on the vertical axis and thus the heights of the curves drawn by individuals have been averaged to allow the shape of the curves to be compared.

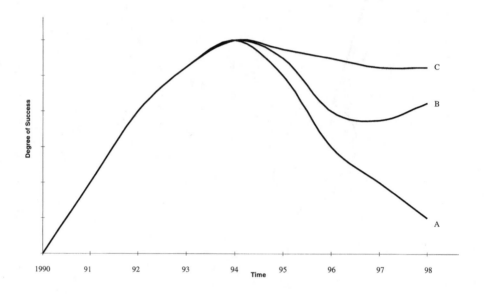

Figure 5 North Pennines Tourism Partnership – profile of success over time – outputs and achievements

The profiles drawn by interviewees were relatively consistent over the first four to five years of the partnership. In Figure 5, the pattern of achievements over time is seen to rise rapidly to a peak in 1993/4. After this most respondents drew a steep decline (A), whilst one saw a later rise in 1997/8 (B). However two respondents felt achievement levels had been maintained relatively high (C). Figure 6 reveals a flatter profile for partnership working with a start point above the bottom line indicating the collaborative efforts before the partnership was actually launched. The flatter curve represents the fact that partner relations have remained strong and joint working was maintained even through the diffi-cult times. Profiles all showed a gradual rise to 1993–5, two respondents felt efforts had increased since then while the partnership went through difficulties (A), other felt efforts had tailed away either gradually (B), or more dramatically (C).

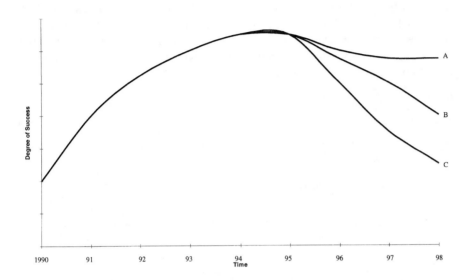

Figure 6 North Pennines Tourism Partnership – profile of success over time – partnership working

This process highlights how different individuals and organisations have differing perceptions of levels of success according to their own nature and priorities. It points to the need for a common set of evaluative criteria. Despite this there was considerable agreement over the partnership's phases and the factors affecting them. Interpretations varied, for example all agreed about the problems in the later phases, but some interpreted this as representing less collaboration and others identified higher levels of collaboration in order to try to tackle the problems.

Considerable emphasis has been given to the influence of funding over the partnership's life cycle as all interviewees stressed this factor. This is largely due to the high level of involvement of public sector organisations and lower levels of community involvement. In another partnership with a high proportion of business or community involvement the reduction in external funding might not have such a major impact. The existence of higher levels of social capital might sustain a partnership longer. In the North Pennines, however, the sheer size of the area and the dispersed nature of business and communities would make this more difficult.

Comparative Analysis

A simple comparative analysis of the lifespans of ten other partnerships was carried out in order to assess whether the results in the North Pennines were typical, whether the other partnerships followed different paths and what factors were most important in determining trajectories. The partnerships chosen were an opportunity sample utilising the knowledge of the interviewees and author of other partnerships in Cumbria and Northumbria (Eden; Carlisle; Kielder; Hadrian's Wall; Till Valley; West Cumbria) and other areas (the Peak District; 'Kite Country' in Wales; plus Stirling and the Trossachs in Scotland; Caffyn, 1998 and forthcoming). These are summarised in Table 6. Further research using a more comprehensive sample would be helpful in testing the tentative conclusions more rigorously.

Table 6 Comparator partnerships

Partnership	Location	Started	Lifespan (years)	Comment
Carlisle Tourism Development Action Programme	Cumbria	1988	4	Incorporated in strengthened district council remit
Eden Tourism Action Programme	Cumbria	1989	4	Incorporated in strengthened district council remit
Hadrian's Wall Tourism Partnership	Newcastle-Northumberland-Cumbria	1995	6	Ongoing – review scheduled for 2001
Kielder Partnership	Northumberland	1986	14	Ongoing
Kite Country Partnership	Mid Wales	1994	7	Ongoing after new funding agreed until 2001
Peak Tourism Partnership	Peak District National Park	1992	3	Split into three key initiatives each now led by a partner or as new independent sub-initiative
Stirling Initiative	Central Scotland	1993	10	Ongoing – established as 10 year initiative
Till Valley Partnership	Northumberland	1994	3	Incorporated in strengthened district council remit
Trossachs Trail Tourism Management Programme	Central Scotland	1993	5	Ongoing – possibly to be incorporated in new National Park
West Cumbria Tourism Initiative	Cumbria	1989	10	Ongoing – funding agreed until 2000

In all the cases funding sources and cycles appear to be key factors in the lifespan of the partnerships. The Till Valley and the Peak Tourism Partnerships lasted only three years, i.e. one funding cycle, and were not renewed after the initial period of pledged funding support. Both the Eden Tourism Action Programme and Carlisle TDAP continued beyond three years (due partly to changes in project manager) but were absorbed into their respective district councils not long after. The other partnerships survived into a second three year funding phase. Another significant factor may be simple geography. Each of these four partnerships falls into a specific administrative boundary and could be continued by a single authority relatively easily – either the district council or national park.

Some partnerships such as the West Cumbria Tourism Initiative and the Kielder Partnership are still going after more than ten years, with funding commitments renewed periodically. The Stirling Initiative demonstrates a different model whereby the involvement of central government, through the Scottish Office, and national agencies enabled a more ambitious tourism-led economic development initiative with an initial lifespan of ten years. While it may face some of the same problems as other partnerships it does not have to bid periodically for renewed support in the same way.

The Stirling example also demonstrates the role of political factors – as national government promoted it as a high profile initiative. In other areas partnerships demonstrate important alliances between two local authorities to tackle an issue – such as in West Cumbria. Equally if major private-sector partners see partnerships as valuable politically they are likely to continue to support them – possible factors in both West Cumbria and Kielder. Another factor may be the scope of the partnership. Those with more specific agendas such as environmental sustainability (e.g. the Trossachs and Kite Country) or heritage conservation (e.g. Hadrian's Wall) may have additional rationales for continuing. However funding is still fundamental to a decision to extend the life of a partnership.

There appears to be a range of possible options for tourism partnerships to take when they reach a certain point; either to continue, possibly in a revised format, or to bring the partnership to a close and continue its work via a different mechanism. The Scottish Tourism and the Environment Task Force Guidelines for Tourism Management Programmes identifies some strategy options and emphasises the importance of considering the long-term future of partnerships at a relatively early stage (Scotland's Tourism and Environmental Task Force, 1997).

Although examples of all were not identified in the study, there are eight possible options which suggest themselves from the earlier analysis:

(1) A partnership may finish completely with no organisation picking up its role. No examples of this have been found, but it is obviously a possibility.

(2) The work of the partnership may be taken up and continued by one partner. Eden, Till Valley and Carlisle are examples of this. It should be borne in mind that the commitment given by the local authority may diminish at a later stage, such as Carlisle's recent drastic cuts to its tourism budget.

(3) A range of partners may take up the different strands of work the partnership was involved in. These could include local authorities, tourism associations, specific agencies, voluntary groups etc.

(4) The partnership could spawn a series of independent more focused projects which continue. This is what happened in the Peak District where the initial partnership focused heavily on visitor management, interpretation and setting up an environment fund. These three main areas of work are now continuing; the visitor/traffic management led by the National Park and local authorities and the interpretation and environment fund as two independent projects. The partnership successfully developed mechanisms to continue its work after it finished.

(5) The partnership could, of course, survive in more or less its original form as West Cumbria and Kielder have to date. This may not continue indefinitely and they may still be vulnerable to local authority spending cuts or the loss of European funding. These two cases have major private-sector partners

(British Nuclear Fuels and Northumbrian Water/Forest Enterprise respectively) and this may be a factor in their longevity.

(6) The partnership could continue but in a more permanent form such as by becoming a limited company or trust.

(7) The partnership may be absorbed into broader management or partnership arrangements as with the North Pennines. This route is also an option for the Trossachs as a National Park is being established in the wider area. Similarly Hadrian's Wall Tourism Partnership which currently works alongside the English Heritage led Hadrian's Wall management programme could potentially be absorbed into a broadened format

(8) It would be feasible for the local community, businesses and/or voluntary organisations to continue a partnership independently, or with only minimal support from, the public sector. This would need considerable local commitment and organisational skills.

Various factors will determine how many of these options are available or suitable for particular partnerships. Waddock (1989) suggested that a partnership which survives must broaden it agenda periodically. This could be a crucial factor in continuing partnerships and also in those where the agenda is broadened to such an extent that it merges with a broader management framework – as with the North Pennines. If the partnership's objectives and areas of work have been very focused it may be possible to spawn new independent projects as happened in the Peak District, which can attract funding support themselves. The existence of powerful private sector partners may be crucial to continuing a partnership after early funding rounds.

Waddock (1989) describes the need to keep 're-hooking' partners with a broadening agenda – keeping them interested and committed to the work being done. This ties in with Miles (1980) description of the dangers of 'organisational drift'. He suggests that organisations need to transform themselves periodically in order to survive. Greiner (1972) and Huxham and Vangen (1994) warn of collaborative fatigue which may set in due to the pressures of ongoing partnership working. This could incorporate an element of boredom as partners' interest is taken by new, more exciting initiatives.

The most vital factor is resources – if funding sources begin to dry up and are not replaced by new sources the future for many partnership will become less viable. For example the Kite Country Partnership has recently secured just 18 months EU funding to extend its life a little longer. In the UK, as European funding is reviewed and government funding through projects such as the Single Regeneration Budget become ever tighter, the question may become: how will it be possible to sustain any form of collaborative working of this kind? An alternative would be some form of largely voluntary and community programme. At an appropriate scale, with sustained local commitment and skills, much could be achieved.

Partnerships are by nature temporary. An ending is therefore a likely outcome whether it is sooner or later. This need not normally be termed a failure as many objectives may have been achieved but it would be much more beneficial to plan a positive end to a partnership and end on a high note, rather than drifting to an uncertain conclusion, as in the North Pennines.

Tourism Partnership Life Cycle Model

This research aimed to develop a model of a typical life cycle trajectory. The model builds on the phases identified in Table 2, from the analysis of other life cycle models, but has been reformulated to incorporate the findings from the case study and the comparative analysis of other partnerships. It aims to merge the most appropriate elements of both theory and practice. The phases are now given titles and the model is expressed visually to better communicate changes in levels of success over a timescale.

The model (Figure 7) shows six phases through which a partnership may develop and the key characteristics of each phase. Firstly a *pre-partnership* phase in which the potential partners identify issues, explore ideas, formulate objectives, secure commitment and funding and develop a common purpose. The second is a relatively short *take-off* phase in which the partnership is launched formally, wider support for the partnership is sought, a project manager may be appointed, an inventory of resources and assessment of needs is carried out, there is a more precise definition of objectives, the work programme is finalised and there is a sense of mission and trust between partners. Third is a *growth* phase in which momentum builds, early projects are implemented and the partnership strives to establish its identity, both in the tourism market place and locally amongst the population and tourism businesses. The partnership explores options and expands activities and may begin to organise itself better, forming subgroups etc. At this stage there are likely to be characteristics of high partner commitment, high levels of innovation and personalised leadership.

The fourth phase is when the partnership is in its *prime* and has reached maturity and a certain stability. It has made significant achievements, achieved credibility and is held up as an example of good practice. It has often secured additional funding on the strength of this. A partnership may consolidate its activities and monitor achievements as implementation reaches its peak. Coordination and administration roles grow and activities may be decentralised or put out to tender. It would theoretically be possible to end a partnership at the end of this phase, but should the partnership continue there is likely to be a period of *deceleration* (Phase 5) and a gradual or perhaps more sudden decline, in which the partnership has stagnated or some uncertainty has entered. Partners begin to lose interest and question their commitment, project managers may have been replaced and there is a general loss of momentum and thus outputs. Partnerships would re-evaluate their objectives, and may reformulate and renew their commitment. At this point the partnership could stabilise and continue successfully for some years, perhaps at a different scale. Alternatively the decline may be terminal and a decision may be taken to formally end the partnership. The final phase proposed is a *continuation* period if the partnership survives, or the 'after-life', if it is formally brought to an close.

At this point a series of eight possible options (as previously listed) is suggested as to how the work of the partnership is continued by other mechanisms. The final phase can be 'bolted' on to the life-cycle curve after Phase 4 or 5.

The model suggests that a typical partnership may reach maturity after three years and begin to decline after six. Death or a need for some form of transformation might normally come after nine years if not before. The precise number of

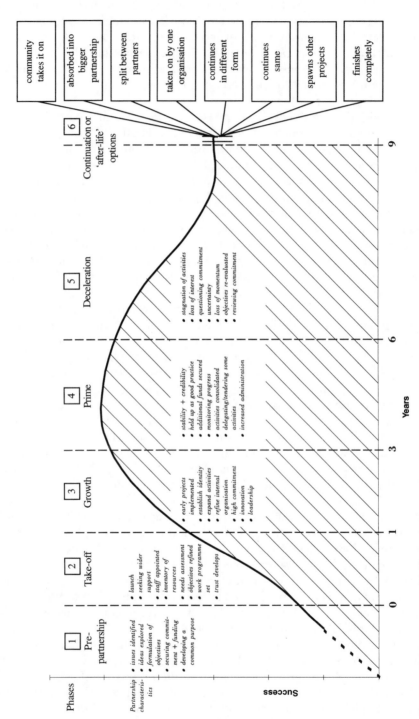

Figure 7 Tourism partnership life cycle model

years is not relevant but three year periods are suggested as these are often the cycles for agencies making funding commitments. Phase 5, the deceleration and decline, could be omitted in practice and an option from Phase 6 implemented before the partnership begins to decline. The scale on the vertical axis is left open. It is suggested that success may mean different things for different partnerships and that each should have its own measures of success. Further research is needed into indicators of success for partnerships which could be set out at the beginning of a collaboration and monitored regularly.

The North Pennines Tourism Partnership survived for nine years and broadly followed the model trajectory proposed. As in many cases there had been a longer period of pre-partnership collaboration and there were varying interpretations of how steep the decline in the last years was. The 'after-life' option in this case was being absorbed into a broader management structure.

The critical factors in determining both the trajectory and characteristics of the life cycle are the funding arrangements and also how successfully partners work collaboratively. Power struggles can influence the trajectory of a partnership enormously as they absorb energy and affect outputs. Similarly personalities in the form of project managers can be crucial. The speed at which a partnership can reach its peak of success, how high the peak is and how long it goes on for will be partly dependent on the ability of the project manager's co-ordinating role. Similarly the range of choices at the end of the partnership may be constrained by how the partnership operates during its lifetime.

The implications of the model are that decisions should be taken about the future of a partnership before decisions are forced upon it by circumstances. Partnerships need to debate pro-actively their continuation or after-life and when these should come into effect, rather than simply react to circumstances. If decisions are made in good time the transition can be planned and communicated to partners and local populations so that there is none of the uncertainty that surrounded the North Pennines for so long.

The model should also assist partnerships in visualising and managing their own development through different stages in the life cycle. It should enable a partnership to respond to change more effectively and understand the processes which influence its development. Quinn and Cameron (1983) point out how the criteria used to measure the effectiveness of an organisation should be different depending on where it is in the life cycle, as it will be trying to achieve different things in its early stages than in the mature or declining stages. This re-emphasises the importance of indicators of success. Decisions about whether and how to prolong partnerships would be made easier if clear evaluation criteria are applied regularly.

Any model will inevitably not fit all cases and it may be that just as Butler's Life Cycle Model is generally destination specific this model may be best viewed as partnership specific. While the biological metaphor of a life cycle is open to criticism the model will be useful in examining the factors which affect the development of successful partnerships. It may help partnerships plan for and manage both internal tensions and changes, and also minimise the impact of forces and changes in the external environment. It highlights the importance of evaluating progress and achievements at regular stages. Partnerships involve trying to maximise collaborative synergy between numerous partners in a dynamic environment. The life cycle model may assist a partnership to steer a course for its future and make appropriate decisions to ensure the collaborative working continues regardless of whether the partnership does itself.

Acknowledgements

I would like to thank all those interviewed in the course of the research, and Bob Prosser and Chris Skelcher for their helpful comments on the first draft of this paper.

Correspondence

Any correspondence should be directed to Alison Caffyn, Centre for Urban and Regional Studies, University of Birmingham, Edgbaston, Birmingham B15 2TT, UK (caffyna@css.bham.ac.uk).

References

Adizes, I. (1979) Organizational passages: diagnosing and treating life cycle problems in organizations. *Organizational Dynamics* (summer), 3–24.

Arnstein, S.R. (1971) A ladder of citizen participation in the USA. *Journal of the Town Planning Institute* 57, 176–182.

Boyle, R. (1993) Changing partners: The experience of urban economic policy in West Central Scotland 1980–1990. *Urban Studies* 30 (2), 309–324.

Bramwell, B. and Broom, G. (1989) Tourism development action programmes: An approach to local tourism initiatives. *Insights* A6.11-6.17.

Brown, V. (1996) Heritage, tourim and rural regeneration: The Heritage Regions Programme in Canada. *Journal of Sustainable Tourism* 4 (4), 174–182.

Butler, R.W. (1980) The concept of a tourist area cycle of evolution: Implications for management of resources. *Canadian Geographer* 24 (1), 5–12.

Caffyn, A. (1998) Tourism, heritage and urban regeneration: Community participation and power relationships in the Stirling Initiative. *The Environment Papers* 1 (3), 25–38.

Caffyn, A. (forthcoming) Developing sustainable tourism in the Trossachs, Scotland. In G. Richards and D. Hall (eds) *Tourism and Sustainable Community Development*. London: Routledge.

Countryside Commission (1995) *Sustainable Rural Tourism*. Cheltenham.

Davidson, R. and Maitland, R. (1997) *Tourism Destinations*. London: Hodder and Stoughton.

Deakin, N. and Gaster, L. (1998) Local government and the voluntary sector: Who needs whom – why and what for? Paper to the Third International Conference of the International Society for Third-Sector Research, Geneva, Switzerland, July.

Downs, A. (1967) The life cycle of bureaus. In A. Downs (ed.) *Inside Bureaucracy* (pp. 296–309). San Francisco, CA: Little, Brown and Company and Rand Corporation.

English Tourist Board (1991) *Tourism and the Environment – Maintaining the Balance*. London: ETB/Employment Department Group.

Greiner, L.E. (1972) Evolution and revolution as organizations grow. *Harvard Business Review* July/August, 37–46.

Hastings, A. (1996) Unravelling the process of 'partnership' in urban regeneration policy. *Urban Studies* 33 (2), 253–268.

Huxham, C. (ed.) (1996) *Creating Collaborative Advantage*. London: Sage.

Huxham, C. and Vangen, S. (1994) Naivety and maturity, inertia and fatigue: Are working relationships between public organisations doomed to fail? Employment Research Unit Conference, Cardiff, September.

Jamal, T.B. and Getz, D. (1995) Collaboration theory and community planning. *Annals of Tourism Research* 22 (1), 186–204.

Kimberly, J.R. (1979) Issues in the creation of organizations: Initiation innovation and institutionalization. *Academic Management Journal* 22, 437–457.

Kimberly, J.R. (1980) The life cycle analogy and the study of organizations: Introduction. In J.R. Kimberly, R.H. Miles and Associates *The Organizational Life Cycle: Issues in the Creation, Transformation and Decline of Organisations*. San Fransisco, CA: Jossey Bass.

Lippit, G.L. and Schmidt, W.H. (1967) Crises in a developing organization. *Harvard Business Review* 45, 102–112.

Long, P. (1994) Perspectives on partnership organisations as an approach to local tourism development in A.V. Seaton *et al.* (eds) *Tourism the State of the Art*. Chichester: Wiley.

Long, P. (1997) Researching tourism partnership organizations: From practice to theory to methodology. In P.E. Murphy (ed.) *Quality Management in Urban Tourism*. Chichester: Wiley.

Lowndes, V., Nanton, P., McCabe, A. and Skelcher, C. (1997) Networks, partnerships and urban regeneration. *Local Economy*, February, 333–342.

Lowndes, V. and Skelcher, C. (1998) The dynamics of multi-organisational partnerships: An analysis of changing modes of governance. *Public Administration* 76 (2), 313–333.

Lyden, F.J. (1975) Using Parsons' functional analysis in the study of public organizations. *Administrative Science Quarterly* 20, 59–70.

MacKintosh, M. (1992) Partnership: Issues of policy and negotiation. *Local Economy* 7 (3), 210–224.

Miles, R.H. (1980) Findings and implications of organizational life cycle research: A commencement. In J.R. Kimberly, R.H. Miles and Associates (eds) *The Organizational Life Cycle: Issues in the Creation, Transformation and Decline of Organizations*. San Francisco, CA: Jossey-Bass.

North Pennines AONB Steering Group (1995) *The North Pennines AONB Management Plan*.

North Pennines Tourism Partnership (1994) *1990–1993 Review*. Alston.

North Pennines Tourism Partnership (1995) *North Pennines Business and Training Initiative Report Year Three*. Alston.

Palmer, A.J. (1992) Local authority tourism development strategies: The role of tourism development action programmes. *Local Economy* 7 (4), 361–368.

Phillips, D. (1991) … In England's last wilderness. *Tourism In Focus* 2, 12–13.

Prentice, R. (1993) Community-driven tourism planning and residents' preferences. *Tourism Management* 14 (3), 218–226.

Quinn, R.E. and Cameron, K. (1983) Organizational life cycles and shifting criteria of effectiveness: Some preliminary evidence. *Management Science* 29 (1), 33–51.

Scotland's Tourism and the Environment Task Force (1997) *Guidelines for the Development of Tourism Management Programmes*. Inverness.

Selin, S. and Beason, K. (1991) Interorganizational relations in tourism. *Annals of Tourism Research* 18, 639–652.

Selin, S. and Chavez, D. (1995) Developing an evolutionary tourism partnership model. *Annals of Tourism Research* 22 (4), 844–856.

Tym, R. and Partners (1988) *Tourism in the North Pennines Action Programme*. Report for Cumbria Tourist Board, Northumbria Tourist Board, Countryside Commission, Rural Development Commission and Cumbria County Council.

Waddock, S.A. (1989) Understanding social partnerships: An evolutionary model of partnership organizations. *Administration and Society* 21 (1), 78–100.

Wood, D.J. and Gray, B. (1991) Toward a comprehensive theory of collaboration. *Journal of Applied Behavioural Science* 27 (2), 139–162.

Wood, W. (1992) *The Making of a Heritage Region Ecomuseum in the Cowichan and Chemainus Valleys*. Duncan, BC: The Cowichan and Chemainus Valleys Ecomuseum Society.

12. Developing Partnership Approaches to Tourism in Central and Eastern Europe

Lesley Roberts and Fiona Simpson
Leisure and Tourism Management Department, Scottish Agricultural College,
Auchincruive, Ayr KA6 5HV, Scotland, UK

In many of the former socialist countries of Central and Eastern Europe (CEE), the concept of developing wider involvement within decision making-processes remains inherently problematic. Prior to 1989, public participation was a limited and often ignored aspect of policy making. However, more recently throughout the region, tourist agencies, new regional organisations, a range of non-governmental organisations, and community groups have emerged in response to potential growth in new tourism industries, thus expanding the number of stakeholders involved. This paper investigates collaboration and partnership working in two rural regions of Bulgaria and Romania, countries unable to match the performance of their CEE counterparts where tourism development is concerned. It provides a reflective analysis of achievements within a framework of prerequisites to successful partnership working. Although both examples illustrate the emergence of new development practices, the paper questions their sustainability. The analysis identifies a number of elements, common to both cases, that illustrate the need to focus the evaluation of partnership working on long-term processes rather than short-term, more measurable outcomes.

Introduction

This paper evaluates the outcomes of two case studies of rural tourism development in two neighbouring countries of south-east Europe, Romania and Bulgaria. Focus is placed on the extent to which each case study approximates to what might be considered as successful collaboration and partnership working with a particular emphasis on the intangible elements of new social practices. The paper achieves its aims in three stages, by:

(1) Identifying factors critical to successful partnerships
(2) Evaluating the presented case studies in relation to these factors
(3) Analysing the outcomes of each and identifying where intangible elements of social relations may prevent sustainable practice whilst still ostensibly satisfying the requirements of development projects.

In recent decades, several influences have altered perceptions of tourism planning and perhaps none more that notions of sustainability. Planning and development processes that fit within the concept indicate a growing awareness that tourism should aim to contribute towards sustainable development (Gunn, 1994). More recently, efforts to create sustainability in tourism development have focused on social sustainability and a community development approach (Joppe, 1996) reflecting increasing recognition given to the roles played by local communities. As a result, local participation has become the cornerstone of successful tourism in many circumstances and thus 'local communities' augment the growing list of recognised stakeholders in the tourism industry.

The 'stakeholder society', largely a construct of the 1990s, may be seen as 'an increasingly necessary corrective to free-market capitalism' (Robson & Robson,

1996) providing a platform for the articulation of needs by a number of groups in the interests of consensus. This implies that stakeholders need to be identified and drawn into decision-making processes. Such a belief echoes the principles of participative planning which aim to decentralise tourism planning and integrate it into overall community objectives thus requiring greater community involvement (Simmons, 1994). In this sense, stakeholder theory existed long before its recent popularisation, being an integral part of community tourism planning. A number of characteristics have been linked with the collaboration process. The independence of stakeholder groups is paramount as is an equality, no one group holding the balance of power. It should be recognised as an 'emergent process' where groups learn to manage their changing environments, and there should be joint ownership of decisions and a collective responsibility for progress (Gray in Jamal & Getz, 1995: 189).

Partnership working and its related theoretical background have developed alongside this growing concern for stakeholder interaction. Within rural tourism, local partnerships are increasingly recognised as an appropriate policy response, particularly as a result of their ability to bring together the full range of interest groups in developing a coherent and sociopolitically inclusive planning approach (OECD, 1993: 65). Their achievement has been difficult within the international development domain, non-governmental development organisations (NGDOs) generally having shown little ability to develop partnerships amongst themselves (Fowler, 1998). Indeed, Fowler states 'there are so few NGDO partnerships around today which have the qualities of true partnership that one might expect the term to have been quietly dropped'. He cites the inability of partner organisations to strike a relational balance that empowers both as one reason for failure. Other writers also focus on power relations in community-based tourism planning (Reed, 1997; Joppe, 1996). Theories of collaboration need to focus on power relations as an explanatory variable that demonstrates why collaboration fails or succeeds (Reed, 1997). This is different from viewing them as instrumental variables which places the focus on the achievement of a balance of power within an assumed pluralism with its attendant equality of access. By following the types of consultation prescribed by pluralists, only the important and concrete decisions visible within the community will be dealt with, merely reproducing any bias that exists and excluding rather than including a wider range of stakeholder groups (Murphy, 1985; Joppe, 1996).

Although many advocate the involvement of local communities within partnerships, few evaluate the attempts made to achieve it (Simmons, 1994). Research focusing on collaborative approaches to community based tourism planning has highlighted the multiplicity of agencies involved in the tourism planning process, and the importance of understanding the interaction of institutions and stakeholders in order to ensure a successful outcome from such activities (Jamal & Getz, 1995; Reed, 1997). Much of the research to date has overlooked the potential benefits of developing partnership approaches, confining itself instead to defining and detailing the nature of collaboration and integrated community-based development in a less formal sense. Furthermore, there is little analysis that determines the factors critical to success in the community tourism development process (Joppe, 1996).

Hall (1994) states that the dynamics of interaction of the many and varied interest groups involved in tourism development, and the influence of power and values on decision-making processes have been largely neglected in the study of tourism. Similarly, whilst the World Tourism Organisation (WTO) states that 'organisational structures for tourism must be carefully established, with emphasis on coordination among government agencies and between the public and private sectors' (1994: 240), it falls short of advocating more formal interaction of 'communities of interest' (Slee & Snowden, 1997) through establishing partnership approaches. More recently, this has been confirmed by Reed, who suggests that the theoretical underpinning of community-based tourism planning remains relatively poorly developed (1997: 566). The literature on collaboration and power relations within rural tourism planning has highlighted the need to identify and discern between factors which are unique to each case, and those which can be applied to wider examples in developing practice (Reed, 1997: 588). Jamal and Getz (1995) support this, arguing for research focusing on the implementation of the theoretical constructs.

There is a clear need for empirical material that identifies practices and evaluates their effectiveness with a given context. This paper therefore compares two cases of rural development, one in Romania and the other in Bulgaria, in an effort further to explore concepts of partnership working. The post socialist setting emphasises the complex nature of partnership dynamics, and reflects the importance of intangible elements that underpin emerging working relationships and processes.

Frameworks for Analysis of Rural Partnerships

Amounting to more than ad hoc or periodic interaction between public and private sectors, partnerships establish longer-term, cross-institutional frameworks. In terms of key characteristics, partnerships are often formal, based on willingness of partners to cooperate and the identification of explicit common goals (OECD, 1990: 18). They provide access to decision making processes for all involved, thus including a range of actors in the policy-making process. In many cases, the experiences of western advanced capitalist countries have demonstrated that partnership working brings added value to development initiatives. Partnerships are widely recognised as important in promoting strategic, long-term thinking, and often their results are flexible and innovative, producing policies which are responsive to local needs (Chapman, 1998: 3). Chapman goes on to point out that despite their clear advantage in securing effective forms of governance, experiences in the west have shown that partnerships are complex; working with them can be unstructured, and is often beset with difficulties.

Examination of experiences at the local level within CEE countries provides a particularly useful insight into processes involved in establishing and developing partnership working, as a result of the relative unfamiliarity with the concepts involved. In particular, the lack of coordination within the diffuse field of tourism (Jamal & Getz, 1995) is of interest given current fragmentation of local government responsibilities (Elander, 1997; Horvath, 1997; Pickvance, 1997). In addition, the lack of identified social and cultural acceptance of collaboration may provide a further obstacle to popular participation (Brenner, 1993; Hunya,

1996; Wyzan, 1997). Similarly, the complex relationship between public and private sectors which has emerged in the region during the 1990s adds a further dimension in evaluating the role of partnership working.

Within the policy guidance and theoretical literature relating to partnerships, a wide range of criteria has been identified as critical to the success of partnership working. A number of these requirements are of particular interest in exploring the scope for partnership in rural tourism within the post-socialist context. Recognition of a shared problem, opportunity for each of the partners to benefit from its resolution, motivation and commitment are identified by the OECD (1997: 33) as primary conditions necessary for the formation and success of a partnership. Within these domains, a range of practical aspects can be identified. These must be addressed if effective partnership can be achieved.

As a framework for the comparative evaluation of the case studies, the following criteria are of particular interest (Table 1). They result from the need identified by Simmons (1994), Jamal and Getz (1995) and Reed (1997) to further our understanding of collaborative processes through analysis of practice rather than theory, and provide the structure for such analysis. They relate to the key conditions facilitating tourism planning collaborations at the community level.

Table 1 Factors critical to successful partnership working

1	Recognition of a high degree of interdependence in planning and managing the domain/project
2	Recognition of individual and/or mutual benefits to be derived from the collaborative process
3	A perception that decisions arrived at will be implemented
4	The inclusion of key stakeholder groups
5	The appointment of a legitimate convenor to initiate and facilitate community-based collaboration
6	Formulation of aims and objectives

Source: Jamal & Getz, 1995: 195–199

The following case studies explore early attempts at partnership working within rural tourism in mountain areas of Romania and Bulgaria, and the resulting analysis takes place in relation to these criteria.

Introduction to the case studies

Whilst the growth of tourism in CEE can be identified by increases in tourist arrivals, the rate of this growth is declining (WTO, 1995, 1997). The marked increase at the start of the 1990s was not sustained, and subsequent growth shows varying rates between different countries. But even accounting for the problems of data collection and analysis (Hall, 1990, 1997), it is clear that neither Romania nor Bulgaria have been able to match the performance of other CEE countries in terms of tourism growth and development, each showing falls in international tourist arrivals throughout the first half of the decade (Hunt, 1993; Hall, 1995; WTO, 1997). Neighbouring countries in south-eastern Europe, both have been beset by continued political instability throughout the 1990s.

Bulgaria's overall development was held back by a considerable foreign debt (Great Britain Foreign and Commonwealth Office, 1992), and its tourism development by the saturation of markets by other CEE tourists (Kerpel, 1990). Romania suffered the additional problem of adverse media coverage, affecting its image as a potential holiday destination.

It would be erroneous to suggest, however, that Romania and Bulgaria share common problems and potential solutions with regard to their tourism development. Both countries share similar characteristics to form the basis of a tourism experience – a common coastline, historic cities, plentiful mountain zones, and relatively unexplored cultures and religions. Each, however, has a distinctive culture resulting from, for example, different climates and geographies, relations with neighbouring countries, and responses to economic reforms of the 1980s and 1990s.

Each case study by itself provides an interesting example of partnership working. Together, they allow comparison of different experiences within similar environments thereby adding to our understanding of factors critical to success in partnership working – both in a general sense and in relation to the specifics of a case.

As with much social research, the choice of methodologies involved issues and perspectives from a number of different approaches, each of which has its roots in different disciplines and perspectives. Approaches based in *realism* influenced the researchers' choice significantly. Unlike *behaviourism*, which concentrates on cause and effect and predictive behaviour and thus focuses on the future, *realism* aims to uncover structures of social relations in order to understand existing policies and practices (May, 1993). Whilst empirical research aims to establish facts, the realism approach has helped the researchers to investigate the structures of social relations which help to explain not merely what the outcomes are, but why they may have occurred. It focuses on the subjective states of actors involved in processes, and the meanings given to social relations.

Following such principles, the information for both case studies was collected over a period of years. In Romania, visits to study the research project and to collect information spanned more than four years between 1994 and 1998. In Bulgaria, formal participation in a research and consultancy project led to four visits over a three-year period ending in September, 1999. In both cases, regular contact with key contributors to development processes was maintained throughout the duration of the studies. Findings are not based on survey data but on evaluations of formal and informal interview processes, and participant observation of partnership-building processes thus allowing the research to reveal a number of complex realities that were socially constructed. Throughout, the roles of reflective practitioner (Schon, 1991) were adopted. These methods follow directly the principles of ethnographic research (Yin, 1993).

Piloting Rural Tourism in Romania

The Romanian case study explores the extent to which the rural tourism pilot scheme has provided opportunities for collaboration, partnerships, and inclusive, community-based participation. It raises these issues in a country with a history of top-down, 'super-centralised' (Popescu, 1993) planning and control which provided local populations with little or no experience of participatory decision-making. The shaping of people's attitudes has put obstacles in the way of change (Brenner, 1993). It would therefore not be unreasonable for people used to constraint in local decision-making (Turnock, 1996) to be slow to respond positively to calls for active participation.

Romania has a wide range of natural and cultural features attractive to tourists, most of them in rural areas, and rural tourism development is now seen as a way of creating a new service industry as traditional manufacturing industries decline. Increasing numbers of rural householders now offer bed and breakfast accommodation to visitors, and entire rural communities now find themselves drawn into tourism as a potential economic future.

Early reforms created a new Ministry of Tourism in 1992, the work of which encompassed that of its predecessor, the Officul Naţional de Turism. One of the first tasks of the new ministry was the production of a 10–year tourism master plan identifying development needs at a central level, as well as decentralised measures such as the consolidation of vocational associations, the support of local initiatives in urban tourism, and the development of tourism in rural areas. Increasing recognition was given to the role of the private sector in tourism development processes as well as the need to develop a flexible and demand-led industry. Legislation in 1994 established the framework for the national development of a rural tourism industry and a sum of 900,000 ECU was provided by the European Union (EU) Phare programme.

A major donor requirement was the key involvement of non-government organisations in the development process; this established the first partnership framework. A Romanian NGO, Asociaţa Naţionala de Turism Rural, Ecologic şi Cultural (ANTREC), was quickly established to take responsibility for the coordination of an accommodation booking system, the identification of training needs and the delivery of training as appropriate, and the marketing and promotion of the rural tourism industry. Operation Villages Roumains (OVR), an international NGO familiar with rural development work in the country, was appointed with the remit of developing a rural infrastructure that would support tourism's development through, for example, the provision of waymarked footpaths, local maps and signage, and picnic and simple recreation sites. The organisations were to work together, one aim being the transfer of know-how between the two, primarily to enable ANTREC, inexperienced in decentralised capacity-building, to develop new ways of working. Figure 1 shows partnership relationships as they were established and operational from 1994 until 1997.

Bran Village, approximately 25 km south-west of the county town of Brasov, was the focus of pilot developments of both ANTREC and OVR and thus the area most likely to benefit from joint activities. The village, at the heart of Bran Zone, sits between the peaks of Mount Bucegi and the Piatra Craiului (King's Rock) on the borders of the Fagaraş Mountains, providing spectacular views throughout the year. Extremely popular with domestic tourists, Bran is also familiar with the international tourist trade as day trippers, often from the nearby ski resort, and other coach tours regularly visit the castle. Bran Castle was reputed to have links with Vlad the Impaler. Perhaps more responsible for its international fame, it is claimed to be the former residence of Bram Stoker's Count Dracula.

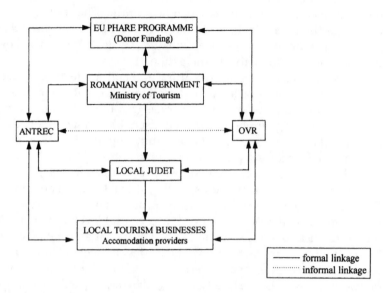

Figure 1 Romania: Extent of collaborative working as at 1997

Yet despite the area's beauty and the existence of a key visitor attraction amongst a number of interesting features, the achievements of the rural tourism development programme have been less than anticipated, perhaps reflecting the significance of the inherited difficulties in the country as a whole which serve to hinder the restructuring process. Despite the victory of a 1996 coalition government replacing earlier Iliescu governments, there remains a bureaucracy, well secured within post-socialist administrative structures, that has yet to become comfortable with ideas of transparency and accountability (Eyal, 1994; Economist, 1996; East European Newsletter, 1998; Hunya, 1998). Such a 'reform-communist' (Hunya, 1998) administration hampers processes of change and frustrates the efforts of those whose aims are decentralisation of control and wider access to decision-making processes.

Figure 1 shows the limited extent of partnerships in the early stages of the pilot programme despite the fact that tourism provision was entirely private sector led and community driven having been in existence prior to the establishment and involvement of ANTREC and OVR. Given a mistrust of centralisation, and its rejection in an emerging culture of individual enterprise, it is perhaps understandable that the interest of local people in a centralised pilot project was limited and that an existing fragmentation of activities continued. Membership of ANTREC, the national association, was always lower than anticipated and insufficient to sustain the organisation's existence in the long term. The quasi-governmental nature of the organisation and its alleged close links with the Ministry of Tourism further alienated local people. Moreover, the perception of proprietorial control of their nascent tourism businesses represented a coercion and reward system of power (French & Raven, 1959), familiar in the past but rejected now by the business community. Relationships between the two NGOs fared little better, there being limited cooperation and thus learning transfer and

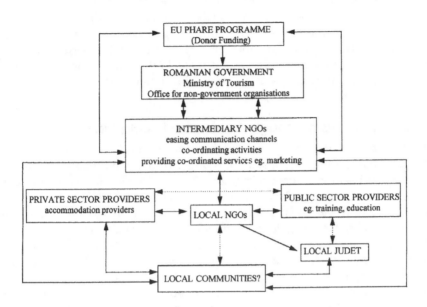

Figure 2 Romania: Proposed extension of partnership principles

it may be that the need to recognise and manage problems of competition and conflict between the two organisations was not addressed. This reflects Fowler's (1998) findings illustrating the inability to find a way of working that empowered both partners equally.

A donor-instigated review of progress, however, and an evaluation of networks and relationships has led to a recognition of the need to involve a greater number of interest groups and to work towards a decentralisation of power and of access to effective participation and collaboration, and the principles of partnership working are now being accepted by both government and the non-government organisations involved.

Figure 2 shows the projected partnerships, relationships and networks that it is hoped will revitalise rural tourism development processes in Romania. Stakeholders are clearly identified as business communities (those with a tangible stake in the programme), local government (judeţ), central government ministries, universities and training institutes, intermediate NGOs acting as an interface between local and national initiatives, grass-roots NGOs such as environmental organisations, and national and international organisations dedicated to the restructuring process. The complexities of stakeholder involvement are evident, each having different aims and objectives, unequal powers, varying administrative structures and cultures, and different levels of understanding and acceptance of the mutual benefits of collaboration. Nevertheless, there appears to be a political as well as a civic will to pursue such inclusive development practices, and importantly, a number of intermediary organisations have developed to bridge the consultation gap between work at the field level and national initiatives. On the part of government, this has manifest itself in the new Office for the Relations of Government-Non-government Organisations. This new organisation has much to learn from the Foundation for the Development of Civil Society, a US founded non-government organisation, also part funded by the EU Phare programme in Romania, which has four years' experience in developing a non-government sector in the country. Both organisations offer help in the building of partnerships and aim, in the longer term, to contribute to processes of decentralisation of power.

Sustainable Tourism through Partnership in Bulgaria

With the transition from a command to market economy, the tourism industry in Bulgaria has undergone substantial change. Tourism in Bulgaria before 1989 was characterised by group package tours, with little emphasis on attracting tourists on an individual or independent basis (Bachvarov, 1997). Since the fall of communism, however, the industry has no longer been able to rely on the traditional strength of the domestic and former eastern bloc markets, which together accounted for around 80% of the market (Bachvarov, 1997), and is looking to extend its focus in order to compete more effectively within wider European and international markets. At the same time the state-dominated institutional structures which were set in place to develop the tourist industry are no longer well placed to service the needs of the country's industry adequately (Ilieva, 1998).

The Pirin mountain range stretches between the Mesta and Struma river valleys in south-west Bulgaria. The mountains form the focus of the region, currently a UNESCO protected site and recognised as a Category 2 area within worldwide national park classification. A number of small towns are scattered along each of the river valley areas, each having a distinct identity borne out by the traditional crafts, festivals and music of the area. Pirin has a number of notable and well-visited monasteries, and to the south the vineyards produce world famous wines in and around the architectural reserve town of Melnik. Further north, close to Bansko, is a relatively well-established winter sports resort, popular with domestic tourists although relatively new to the wider international market. To date, the expansion of winter sports and in particular skiing facilities has been limited owing to the restrictions imposed by the area's national park designation. However, the Pirin National Park Authority is now under increasing pressure to approve an ever-increasing number of applications for new developments within and close to the boundaries of the protected area.

The Pirin Tourism Forum (PTF) was set up as part of a project which ran from 1993 to 1997 and was funded by the United Kingdom Environmental Know How Fund (UKEKHF). The project was known as PREST – Pirin and Rila Eco and Sustainable Tourism. Heynes (1993) outlines the objectives and achievements of the project in its earlier stages. The key aim of the forum has been to ensure that a better balance is reached between tourism development and ecological sustainability. The Forum brings together representatives of the ten municipalities of the region, to work in partnership in advancing the tourism industry in Pirin, and promote the region as an area with a distinctive and coherent traditional culture and identity. In addition, PTF involves the Pirin National Park Authority (a branch of the National Forestry Committee), and acts as an interface between the locally based municipalities and the relevant departments of central government. The role of PTF in overcoming institutional fragmentation, political polarisation and public/private sector conflict in the area, through promoting a region based on partnership, has been invaluable.

A number of specific projects has been undertaken which illustrate the collaborative emphasis promoted by the PTF. The Forum prepared a comprehensive inventory of tourism facilities in the region, upon which a common marketing approach has been based. This has resulted in production of tourism guides and associated marketing materials which relate to each of the individual municipalities but which also have a shared style of presentation, setting each locality within a region-wide context. Similarly, PTF has been responsible for the promotion of local craft products under a corporate 'labelling' system for which a regional logo and quality assurance system are currently being developed. In effecting direct contact with tour operators and the tourist as a consumer, PTF coordinated a familiarisation trip to Pirin which incorporated the diverse range of places, customs, traditions and environment which the region has to offer within a coherent, single 'package'.

The PTF has endeavoured to bring together as many members of the community as possible. In broadening the 'communities of interest' served by the partnership, the PTF recently ran a competition for schools which focused on environmental education within the area and sought to develop community involvement in the work of the partnership. Future activities include consideration of a regionally consistent signposting scheme, a waymarking path which extends across the region and passes through a number of municipalities. The PTF has been well placed to overcome entrenched inter-municipality competitiveness, primarily as a result of its perceived political impartiality, whilst it has retained close links with its founding body, the UKEKHF. Similarly, it has bridged the gap between local and central government, by being actively involved in the preparation of a new tourism law for Bulgaria, and being highlighted by the Ministry of Trade and Tourism as potential model upon which new regional tourism organisations will be developed throughout the country.

Despite these successes, the continuing need for improved cooperation in Pirin is illustrated by current proposals being promoted by a number of municipalities which fall short of recognising the need to build a coherent strategy on a region-wide basis. The municipality of Gotse Delchev, for example, plans to build an extensive new tourism village in the mountain close to the town. Similarly, the municipality of Razlog, traditionally in open competition with its neighbour Bansko, has plans to develop a new skiing village on the slopes of the Pirin mountains which encroaches on some of the most ecologically sensitive areas of the national park. Research undertaken by the University of Sofia highlighted the discrepancies arising between actual requirements of the tourism industry and development planned and being implemented by the municipalities (Marinov *et al.*, 1996). Despite much of the region's accommodation operating below capacity, public sector plans to provide additional accommodation and/or invest in improving existing stock, are being presented by virtually all of the municipalities. Whilst this situation indicates the need for further efforts to promote regional coordination of the public sector, it can also at least in part be attributed to an insufficient flow of information on the industry between public and private sectors.

As donor support expires in September 1999 (originally from the UKEKHF, and latterly from the UK government's Know How Fund), the PTF will increasingly become part of the state framework for tourism, operating as a new regional tourism authority as proposed by the 1997 law. Whether the balance within the partnership promoted by the PTF will continue within this new context remains to be seen. However, a perhaps more realistic assessment, as presented in the analysis of the shifting relations in Figures 3 and 4, underlines the influence of the new local tourism councils which will be closely associated with the municipalities. The addition of this new local tier may distance PTF from both the municipalities (which in turn have strong local business links) and the local communities. Maintaining a true partnership which is locally owned may prove difficult under these circumstances. Similarly, the growing need for PTF to become self-financing as donor support expires, questions the continuing perception locally that the organisation is neutral and apolitical. Left unchecked, this increasingly commercial orientation of the PTF is likely to undermine the achievements to date of its hitherto professional approach to a sector otherwise dominated by business and entrepreneurial interests. There is clearly scope to take the work of PTF further, but in doing so a better understanding must be developed of the criteria and mechanisms required to secure effective partnership working there.

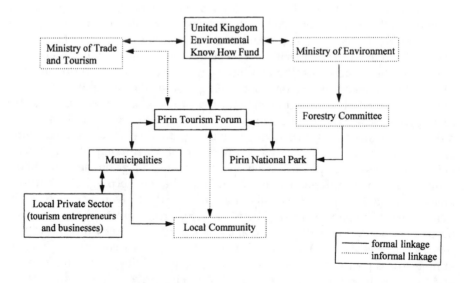

Figure 3 Current interstakeholder relationaships in Pirin

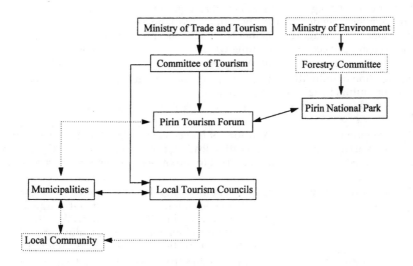

Figure 4 Emerging interstakeholder relationships in Pirin

Comparative Evaluation of the Case Studies

By revisiting the factors identified in the literature as those necessary for successful partnership working, based on Jamal and Getz's (1995) six fundamental propositions, the case studies can be analysed in a systematic way (Table 2). The analysis shows that, for two of the key criteria, clear commonalities exist between the cases. The first (proposition 2) highlights the influence of the post-socialist context on attitudes towards collaboration, through the lack of recognition of the reciprocal benefits which can be realised by such an approach. Whilst this is by no means exclusive to this context, it has been repeatedly identified as a key characteristic of it. Proposition 6, on the other hand, illustrates the influence of donor assistance on the perceived effectiveness of the partnerships. Where aims, structures and monitoring are an explicit requirement of donor organisation, they have often dominated the measurement of 'success'. This may have led to the lack of recognition of underlying, less tangible elements of collaboration, which the authors believe are the critical factors in defining sustainability in partnership working. Jamal and Getz themselves present their six propositions, as a 'starting point for further proposition development' (1995: 195). Whilst the six criteria do appear to cover the factors critical to success in partnership working, in order for them to be applied in a meaningful way, the extent to which they can be defined and measured should be taken into account. In response to this, and in order to discuss the comparative analysis in greater depth, the following prioritisation is suggested for the six propositions, in accordance with the extent of their measurability (Table 3).

It is important that the unequal nature of the propositions' measurability is taken into account within the analysis of partnership working. Taken a step

Table 2 Comparative analysis of the case studies

		Romania	*Bulgaria*
1	Recognition of a high degree of interdependence in planning and managing the domain/project	Insufficient recognition of the benefits of working together by NGOs, also precluding wider involvement	Recognition of the use of inter-agency cooperation, but with stakeholders participating to meet their respective agendas
2	Recognition of individual and/or mutual benefits to be derived from the collaborative process	Key actors saw joint and individual benefits as mutually exclusive. Competiton for scarce resources prevailed	
3	A perception that decisions arrived at will be implemented	A history of flawed communication leading to a lack of trust in 'promises'	Trust in the partnership as led by the NGO, but continuing mistrust between stakeholders
4	The inclusion of key stakeholder groups	Insufficient meaningful inclusion of communities that were already involved in tourism development prior to NGO creation	Public sector interests included, but marginalised/overtaken by municipality supported private sector interests
5	The appointment of a legitimate convenor to initiate and facilitate community-based collaboration	Clear leadership structure but legitimacy not acknowledged by local communities	Clear leadership structure exists and has been effective in steering the course of the partnership
6	Formulation of aims and objectives, and self-regulation of planning and development	Clear structure, prioritisation of aims and objectives and regular monitoring (primarily for and by external donor organisation)	

Table 3 Relative degrees of measurability of the factors critical to partnership success

Measurable

6	Formulation of aims and objectives
4	The inclusion of key stakeholder groups
5	The appointment of a legitimate convenor to initiate and facilitate community-based collaboration
1	Recognition of a high degree of interdependence in planning and managing the domain/project
2	Recognition of individual and/or mutual benefits to be derived from the collaborative process
3	A perception that decisions arrived at will be implemented

Immeasurable

further, this explicit recognition allows for the debate to be extended beyond an evaluation of formalised structures, to focus on some of the less tangible factors which are nonetheless crucial to the continued existence and further development of partnerships. In particular, the case studies illustrate where two key additional factors influence the sustainability of new working practices. These are: trust and sincerity, and the balance of power between stakeholders. Whilst the latter in particular has been referred to by others researching the subject, they remain of interest in terms of the additional dimension which can be added when these factors are layered over Jamal and Getzs' six propositions (1995).

As a result, the introduction of these concepts provides further insights into the analysis presented in Table 2 above. Whilst the Bulgarian case appears to have been relatively successful in terms of meeting most of the criteria put forward by the propositions, questions remain as to the detail and focus of the evaluation. For example, Proposition 1 accepts that there has been a recognition of interdependence between stakeholders, but does not take into account the conflicting plans which they continue to pursue alongside, and contrary to, their commitment to the partnership. Similarly, Proposition 3, identified as perhaps the least measurable factor, has been partially fulfilled, but the actual balance of power between the stakeholders is not adequately reflected in this evaluation. Trust in decisions being fulfilled is apparent, but without a full understanding of who makes the decisions, and the extent to which they represent the full common interests of the partnership. More specifically, aspects of the case study such as the dominance of municipality-based entrepreneurial interests over the objectives of the Pirin National Park Authority, also highlighted by Proposition 4, cannot be fully explored within such an analysis. Whilst the full range of stakeholders may indeed be involved (in effect, fulfilling Proposition 4), they are unlikely to maintain an equal influence on the work of the partnership and thus represent 'meaningful' participation.

A focus on the balance of power between stakeholders is also illustrated in the Romanian case, where prevalent power relations influenced, and indeed may have precluded, collaborative planning and inclusive development practices. Insufficient formal recognition has been given to the different power bases of quasi-government and non-government organisations, particularly within the post-socialist context. It should be borne in mind that the roles of such organisations are easily misunderstood even in areas where their work is well established, and it will take time for this 'third sector' to be fully appreciated in CEE. It is also important to note that the fundamental changes taking place in CEE alter working practices so significantly that they must inevitably alter the power biases that exist. These may be considered endemic to the post-socialist context where processes reinforced by opaque bureaucracies have had a tendency to operate in the interests of some stakeholders at the expense of others.

Whilst a clear leadership structure exists in both cases (proposition 5), its legitimacy and perceived sincerity is not taken into account in ascertaining whether common, political or individual interests are being met. Despite having been successful in gaining the support and trust of the local community, the PTF is likely to become more embedded within the emerging government framework in the future. This shift has the potential to undermine the benefits secured to date in terms of developing trust, which are largely attributable to the Forum's perceived impartiality. As a result, the PTF will have to pay close attention to the implications of increased government involvement if it is to maintain trust and perceived sincerity.

In contrast, whilst its leadership has hitherto lacked legitimacy owing to its central government associations, the Romanian case illustrates increasing opportunity for effective involvement at the local level. Successful partnerships are based on a legitimacy of power where the authority of a particular partner is accepted by all other groups as representative of joint interests. The likelihood of ANTREC's long-term viability is threatened by a continuing lack of legitimacy as perceived by local tourism businesses. It is possible that this situation will improve as understanding of NGOs and their central role in the support of partnership working increases. As a result, the negativity of the analysis presented in Proposition 5 for Romania obscures the fact that trust is likely to grow as local partnerships are increasingly able to distance themselves from the state and gain more direct control in their planning and decision-making processes.

Conclusion

The literature pointed to a need for empirical research and reporting on partnership working. More specifically, it called for a shift in focus towards identification of both general factors and those which are case specific. This comparative study has underlined the importance of making such a distinction, by identifying those issues shared by the cases and those which are not. Whilst many distinctions are drawn between the experiences, the common influences on their success can be attributed both to their shared post-socialist contexts and to the symptomatically complex nature of partnership working itself.

In the process of the analysis, the study identifies a need to focus further research on the intangible and immeasurable elements of collaboration and partnership working by adding a further dimension to previous discussions relating to factors critical for partnership success. The most easily measured criteria are often the most commonly used in established monitoring and evaluation processes, and contribute a great deal to the popular and politically perceived success or failure of a partnership. However, partnerships depend as much on the motivations, personalities and perceived roles of the participating stakeholders as they do on the formal structures and defined aims and objectives on which they are established. Whilst it is the very immeasurability of some factors that has led to a lack of previous attention to them, this analysis shows that they are critical to the overall sustainability of collaborative processes. Successful collaboration can exist, for example, without measurable targets, but it will fail completely without trust and sincerity. The complexities of relationships within partnerships and their environments mean that successful partnership working does not necessarily imply sustainability. Consequently, the analysis of partnerships must make a shift from a preoccupation with traditional measures of success, in order to take account of the less measurable, but more fundamental, factors critical to sustainability.

Correspondence

Any correspondence should be directed to Lesley Roberts, Leisure and Tourism Management Department, Scottish Agricultural College, Auchincruive, Ayr KA6 5HV, Scotland, UK (l.roberts@au.sac.ac.uk).

References

Bachvarov, M. (1997) End of the model? Tourism in post-Communist Bulgaria. *Tourism Management* 18 (1), 43–50.

Brenner, R. (1993) The long road from serfdom and how to shorten it. In M. Maruyama (ed.) *Management Reform in Eastern and Central Europe: Use of Pre-communist Cultures* (pp. 81–109). Aldershot: Dartmouth Press.

Chapman, M. (1998) *Effective Partnership Working.* Area Regeneration Division, Good Practice Note No. 1. Edinburgh: Scottish Office, Edinburgh.

East European Newsletter (1998) 12 (8), 7.

Economist (1996) Fingers crossed, anon, 26 October, p. 61.

Elander, I. (1997) Between centralism and localism: On the development of local self-government in post-socialist Europe. *Environment and Planning C: Government and Policy* 15, 143–159.

Eyal, J. (1994) Same old guard, same old tune. *Wall Street Journal,* New York, 7 April.

Fowler, A.F. (1998) Authentic NGDO partnerships in the new policy agenda for international aid: Dead end or light ahead. *Development and Change* 29, 137–159.

French, J. and Raven, B. (1959) The bases of social power. In D. Cartwright (ed.) *Studies in Social Power.* Michigan Institute for Social Research.

Great Britain, Foreign and Commonwealth Office, Central European Department (1992) *Current Situation in Eastern Europe.* ERIAA G/1, April.

Gunn, C.A. (1994) Emergence of effective tourism planning and development. In A.V. Seaton, C.L. Jenkins, R.C. Wood, P.U.C. Dieke, M.M. Bennett, L.R. MacLellan and R. Smith (eds) *Tourism: The State of the Art* (pp. 10–19). Chichester: John Wiley.

Hall, C.M. (1994) *Tourism and Politics: Policy, Power and Place.* Chichester: John Wiley.

Hall, D.R. (1990) Eastern Europe opens its doors. *Geographical Magazine,* April, 10–15.

Hall, D.R. (1995) Tourism change in Central and Eastern Europe. In A. Montanari and A.M. Williams (eds) *European Tourism.* Chichester: John Wiley.

Hall, D.R. (1997) Going East? *Landscape Design* April, 8–10.

Heynes, K. (1993) The environmental know how fund and conservation through sustainable development. *Revue de Tourisme* 48, 3.

Horvath, T.M. (1997) Decentralization in public administration and provision of services: An East-Central European view. *Environment and Planning C: Government and Policy* 15, 161–175.

Hunt, J. (1993) Foreign investment in Eastern Europe's travel industry. *Travel and Tourism Analyst* 3, 65–85. London: Economic Intelligence Unit.

Hunya, G. (1996) Private economy in an etatist environment: The case of Romania. In H. Brezinski (ed.) *The Economic Impact of New Firms in Post-socialist Countries. Bottom-up Transformation in Eastern Europe* (pp. 107–115). Cheltenham: Edward Elgar.

Hunya, G. (1998) *Romania 1990–2002: Stop-go Transformation, Centre for Research into Post-Communist Economies.* Austria: Vienna Institute for Comparative Economic Studies.

Ilieva, L., (1998) Development of sustainable rural tourism in Bulgaria. In *Proceedings from the Rural Tourism Management: Sustainable Options Conference.* Ayr, Scotland, September.

Jamal, T.B. and Getz D. (1995) Collaboration theory and community tourism planning. *Annals of Tourism Research* 22 (1), 186–204.

Joppe, M. (1996) Sustainable community tourism development revisited. *Tourism Management* 17 (7), 475–479.

Kerpel, E. (1990) *Tourism in Eastern Europe and the Soviet Union: Prospects for Growth and New Market Opportunities.* Special Report No 2042. London: The Economic Intelligence Unit.

Marinov, V., Vodenska, M., Atanasova, M. and Petrova, S. (1996) Tourism development research of the Bansko and Razlog municipalities. Tourist demand and the impact of tourism on the local economy. Project No. Bul/95/001. ILO/UNDP unpublished report, University of Sofia.

May, T. (1993) *Social Research: Issues, Methods, and Process*. Buckingham: Open University Press.

Murphy, P. (1985) *Tourism: A Community Approach*. London: Methuen.

Organisation for Economic Co-operation and Development (OECD) (1990) *Partnerships for Rural Development*. Paris: OECD.

Organisation for Economic Co-operation and Development (OECD) (1993) *What Future for our Countryside? A Rural Development Policy*. Paris: Paris.

Organisation for Economic Co-operation and Development (OECD) (1997) *Review of Rural Policy: Partnerships in the United States*. Paris: OECD.

Pickvance, C.G. (1997) Decentralization and democracy in Eastern Europe: A sceptical approach. *Environment and Planning C: Government and Policy* 15, 129–142.

Popescu, C. (1993) Romanian industry in transition. *GeoJournal* 29 (1), 41–48.

Reed, M.G. (1997) Power relations and community-based tourism planning. *Annals of Tourism Research* 24 (3), 566–591.

Robson, J. and Robson, I. (1996) From shareholders to stakeholders: Critical issues for tourism marketers. *Tourism Management* 17 (7), 533–540.

Schon, D.A. (1991) *The Reflective Practitioner: How Professionals Think in Action*. Aldershot: Ashgate Publishing.

Simmons, D.G. (1994) Community participation in tourism planning. *Tourism Management* 15 (2), 98–108.

Slee, B. and Snowden, P. (1997) Effective partnership working. *Good Practice in Rural Development No. 1*. Edinburgh: Scottish Office.

Turnock, D. (1996) Romania: Regional development in transition. *Reconstructing the Balkans: A Geography of the New Southeast Europe*. In D. Hall and D. Danta (eds) (pp. 157–168). Chichester: John Wiley.

World Tourism Organisation (1994) *National and Regional Tourism Planning: Methodologies and Case Studies*. London: Routledge.

World Tourism Organisation (1995) *Yearbook of Tourism Statistics* (47th edn). Madrid: WTO.

World Tourism Organisation (1997) *Yearbook of Tourism Statistics* (49th edn). Madrid: WTO.

Wyzan, M. (1997) Why is Bulgaria a land of failed reforms? *Transitions* 4 (7).

Yin, R.K. (1993) Applications of case study research. *Applied Social Research Methods Series* (Vol. 34). London: Sage Publications.

13. Collaborative Tourism Planning as Adaptive Experiments in Emergent Tourism Settings

Maureen G. Reed
Department of Geography, The University of British Columbia, 1984 West Mall, Vancouver, B.C. Canada V6T 1Z2

In this paper, the concept of adaptive management is modified from its contemporary usage in environmental management to collaborative planning in emergent tourism settings. This application is possible because both emergent tourism settings and environmental planning situations are considered turbulent, characterised by change, uncertainty, complexity and conflict. Adaptive management attempts to embrace these conditions by establishing focused interventions from which unexpected outcomes provide opportunities for learning. While adaptive management shares some features of collaboration, its focus on learning is considered more appropriate for confronting and addressing local power relations within emergent tourism settings. Yet similar problems are encountered in applying the concept. These opportunities and limitations are considered in light of a case study in Squamish, Canada.

Introduction

To scan contemporary environmental and tourism journals, it is clear that practitioners and students of sustainable tourism and sustainable development are both grappling with concerns about the content, measures, methods and implications of sustainable management systems (Butler, 1991; Wall, 1993; Robinson *et al.*, 1990; Gale & Cordray, 1994). While tourism researchers argue that planning for tourism in isolation from environmental and social considerations is a misguided approach (McKercher, 1993; see Hunter-Jones, 1997), researchers and practitioners of resource and environmental management are mounting challenges to traditional single use management systems (Barrett, 1994; Royal Commission on the Future of the Toronto Waterfront, 1992).

In addition to focusing on multi-use, multi-valued systems, researchers in both fields are examining ways in which to create successful collaborations among 'stakeholders', typically including elected and technical officials, non-governmental organisations, private economic interests and members of the general public. Mitchell (1997) argued that 'with growing complexity, interdependence and uncertainty of issues and the rapid rate at which conditions change, drawing upon many people and groups should help to achieve a balanced perspective relative to an issue ... Members of the public are also increasingly willing to accept responsibilities and risks which accompany reallocation of power or authority to them when they become partners with government agencies which have legal mandates and responsibilities' (Mitchell, 1997: 156). Collaboration in tourism planning has also been advocated because of the uncertainty, complexity and potential for conflict that characterises tourism planning in general, and emergent tourism settings in particular (Jamal & Getz, 1995). In light of common issues, Hunter (1997: 863) suggested that environmental management instruments and techniques may be appropriate in determining and managing the nature, degree and impacts of tourism development. He (1997) concluded that sustainable tourism must be regarded as an *adaptive* (emphasis in original) paradigm capable of addressing widely different situations, and articulating different goals in terms of the utilisation of natural resources.

Faced with changing conditions, complexity and uncertainty, advocates of adaptive management in environmental management have long promoted policies that encourage the development of flexible institutions capable of monitoring and evaluating change and, if necessary, taking corrective actions. To date, the details of how an adaptive paradigm might be applied in tourism development and management have yet to be articulated. The purpose of this paper is to provide a critical assessment of adaptive management to determine its merits relative to improving the practice of collaboration for emergent tourism settings.

To undertake this assessment, the paper first illustrates the similarities posed by the planning environments for environmental management and for emergent tourism settings. Both situations are characterised as turbulent, where collaboration is an emergent value. Next, an evaluative framework for adaptive planning is advanced in which requirements for adaptive planning and adaptive organisations are set out, illustrating their application to community-based tourism. While adaptive management shares values such as collaboration of interests and identification of values, it extends these to include mechanisms for continuous learning, innovation, adjustment and integration. I then use a case study of a collaborative tourism planning process in Squamish, British Columbia (BC), Canada to illustrate the framework and identify opportunities for, and constraints of, applying an adaptive approach. As I am unaware of examples where adaptive management has been explicitly attempted in a community-based tourism initiative, I have made no attempt to impose it in an exhaustive way on the case study. Instead, I use the case study to illustrate how the planning approach may have benefited from adopting the requirements for adaptive management. I then discuss important challenges of putting these requirements into practice, drawing on experiences in environmental sciences, so that researchers addressing collaboration in tourism planning need not reproduce the naive promises or the pitfalls that have befallen researchers in related fields. My overall strategy is to spark further conceptual and practical debate, rather than to undertake a detailed analysis of a particular initiative in adaptive management.

Shared Characteristics of Turbulent Planning Environments

Environmental management

For decades, students of environmental management have adapted organisational theories to their own planning situations. Environmental management situations have been characterised as turbulent, as rapidly changing ecological and social conditions contribute to their uncertainty, conflict and overall complexity (Dorcey, 1986; Mitchell, 1997 after Trist, 1980, 1983). *Change* may take several forms. For example, changes in the quality and/or quantity of resources may affect and be affected by changes in human population and preferences, changes in access to resources and environment and/or ecological changes. These changes may occur over short or long time periods, they may act alone or in combination. *Uncertainty* emerges because ecological and social systems are dynamic and our understanding of their components and interconnections is incomplete. Methods for combining the best 'scientific' knowledge and the politics of resource development are highly contested (Lemons & Brown, 1995). Uncertainty comes with even the best available data, and because management questions are fundamentally ambiguous, they do not lend themselves easily to controlled experiments, and the results of investigations are rarely unequivocal (Daniels & Walker, 1996).

Complexity characterises environmental management situations because the substantive issues become entangled in a web of biological, physical, political, financial, and social factors. Both social and natural scientists now agree that 'managing' environment or natural resources is a misnomer (Ludwig *et al.*, 1993; Mitchell, 1997). Instead, management needs to deal with conflicting human interactions with one another about the non-human environment. Rather than always being considered an obstacle to planning, conflict is now considered 'normal' by environmental management researchers because it arises from legitimate, differing values, interests, hopes, expectations, priorities of individuals or societal groups (Mitchell, 1997). Furthermore, conflict may also be productive if it provides opportunities for mutual learning (Daniels & Walker, 1996).

Emergent tourism settings

The characteristics of environmental management – change, uncertainty, complexity and conflict – also describe emergent tourism settings which are frequently affected by rapid *change*. For example, in western countries, while some rural regions are becoming de-populated, others are growing rapidly (Bryant & Johnston, 1992; Butler & Savage, 1995). The changing demographic composition of these regions has begun to combine with new public attitudes to place multiple and contradictory demands on the land base. At one time primacy was given to development of land for resource production such as forestry and agriculture. Now public demands are being made for more investments in the development of landscapes for broader objectives including the protection of biological and cultural diversity and the provision of tourism and recreational opportunities (Halfacree, 1995; Lowe *et al.*, 1993; Reed, 1997b)

As with environmental management situations, emergent tourism settings combine ecological and social systems in ways that are complex and fundamentally *uncertain* and unpredictable. Many problems such as population growth and land use patterns reflect this uncertainty. For example, often we cannot predict the outcomes or impacts of local actions on a broader scale (Cartwright, 1991). The availability and desirability of particular landscapes for particular uses cannot be known far in advance. Similarly, larger-scale social phenomena (such as a change in government and associated policies or international investment strategies) may inhibit or enhance opportunities for local tourism development.

According to Jamal and Getz (1995: 196), emergent tourism settings are characterised by 'the presence of numerous organizations [and] lack a well-defined inter-organizational process'. Interests are not collectively organised and there is a lack of institutions to support tourism. These interests render these settings *complex* and ripe for *conflict*. The various parties who become joined in tourism development bring different and often incompatible values, agendas, and strategies to these situations. Under these conditions, many and (frequently competing), individuals and organisations act independently. Outcomes are often unanticipated and discordant; yet the impacts are shared. Consequently, the tourism system is considered highly fragmented (Shaw & Williams, 1994), where, it is asserted, 'no single organization or individual can exert direct control over the destination's development process' (Jamal & Getz, 1995: 193).

Analysts of both tourism planning and environmental management have argued that these conditions make collaboration (or shared decision making) an important element of contemporary local decision making (e.g. Selin & Beason, 1991; Hunter, 1997; Jamal & Getz, 1995; Kearney, 1984; Jordan, 1989; Pinkerton, 1989; Gardner & Roseland, 1989). Collaborative decision making is defined as 'a process of joint decision-making among autonomous, key stakeholders ... to resolve planning problems ... and/or to manage issues related to the planning and development' (Jamal & Getz, 1995: 188).

Yet, mounting criticisms of collaboration in environmental management suggest that collaboration in and of itself is insufficient (e.g. Reed, 1995; Daniels & Walker, 1996; Kofinas, 1998). 'Given the complexities and uncertainties inherent in the biophysical and social systems that make up ecosystems, sustainable management can only be achieved if management institutions have strong learning capacities' (McLain, 1993 cited in Cortner *et al.*, 1996). Daniels & Walker (1996: 80) suggest that 'effective public participation must be more than simply encouraging "citizen discourse" or "good communication". It depends on *communication competence*' (emphasis in original), while Lee (1993) argues that constructive approaches to conflict include good civic dialogue. Here, emphasis is placed on treating management as a learning experience wherein management practices are considered to be a series of experiments from which new knowledge leads to continuous adjustments and modifications. Daniels and Walker (1996) offer collaborative learning, an approach which is an improvement over participatory or collaborative planning, because it focuses attention on group learning about one another. Adaptive management includes some of these goals for learning, but focuses greater attention on group learning about the development (or system) process rather than on group dynamics *per se*. This paper gives some attention to both kinds of learning.

Collaboration that includes a learning component is also important for other reasons. Collaboration alone will not be able to address unequal distributions of power that circulate within and act upon emergent tourism settings (Reed, 1997a). For example, the lack of institutions supporting tourism may allow conventional power holders in the community to retain their influence in these key decisions. This is not to suggest that cooperation and collaboration are impossible to achieve, but that structural as well as procedural conditions, within which community tourism planning is constituted, will act as constraints to collaboration. Thus, collaboration, as a means to sustainable tourism, is insufficient without specific efforts to address local power relations. By considering collaborative efforts as adaptive experiments, one can explicitly examine and address power relations within community settings, and perhaps both the explanations and the experiences of collaborative community-based tourism planning can be advanced. In the following section, I begin this task by explaining the char-acteristics of adaptive management.

The Approach and Requirements Adaptive Management

Origins of and debates within adaptive management

Adaptive management, as first developed in the environmental sciences, was conceived as a means to accept and embrace uncertainty in understanding envi-ronmental impacts of new projects or programmes and devising environmental management strategies. According to Holling (1978: 7), 'one key issue for design and evaluation of policies is how to cope with the uncertain, the unexpected, and the unknown'. It is a management approach, designed from the outset to test clearly expressed ideas or hypotheses about the behaviour of an ecosystem being changed through human use (Walters, 1986, 1997). These ideas or hypotheses usually represent predictions regarding how one or more components of the ecosystem will respond (or behave) as a result of the implementation of a policy (or intervention). When the policy is successful, the hypothesis is validated. When the policy fails, the adaptive approach is designed so that learning occurs, adjustments can be made, and future initiatives can be based on the new under-standing (Lee, 1993). Thus, surprises in outcomes provide opportunities from which to learn, rather than failures to predict and avoid.

The initial orientation of adaptive management was to understand and support the resilience of ecosystems by choosing appropriate interventions. According to its adherents, resilience is defined as the capacity to absorb and use change in a positive way (Holling, 1978; Walters & Holling, 1990). Rather than attempt to control or stabilise ecosystems, policies and practices should focus on establishing opportunities for us to learn and adapt. These practices would include providing for a range of objectives, generating indicators of change that are relevant for decisions, screening and evaluating policy alternatives and establishing appropriate communications mechanisms among relevant parties (Dearden & Mitchell, 1998).

Adaptive management has different meanings for different groups such as environmental managers, policy makers and scientists (McLain & Lee, 1996). Researchers in organisational theory and planning have modified this philos-ophy to address uncertainty in policy contexts. According to Berman (1980), implementation of programs and policies are best suited to an adaptive approach when the scope of change is large, the technology or theory guiding change is uncertain, policy or program goals and means are conflicting, the struc-ture of the institutional setting is loosely coupled, and local conditions are unstable. Emergent tourism settings share these attributes. By drawing on research in environmental management, requirements for adaptive manage-ment appropriate for emergent tourism settings are set out. They are divided according to planning procedures and to organisational characteristics.

Adaptive planning procedures

Like collaboration, adaptive planning requires *collaboration of interest groups* and *identification of shared values*. In addition, adaptive management includes the measurement of progress through structured improvements to the status quo

Table 1 Characteristics and requirements of adaptive planning processes and organisations

Characteristics of adaptive planning processes	Requirements
Collaboration of interests	Identification of stakeholders Recognises that participants are the best position to identify issues and resolutions
Identification of values	Participants must have genuine desire to build consensus and reach mutually acceptable solutions
Progress through structured improvements	Provisions of a step-wise process Establishment of checkpoints and feedback mechanisms
Continuous learning and modification	Mechanism for on-going monitoring Willingness to implement required changes
Characteristics of adaptive organisations	*Requirements*
Well defined mandates, flexible processes	Minimum critical specification Some autonomy or authority granted to planning organisation
Innovative membership	Dedicated to continuous learning and self-evaluation Members explore new approaches
Multi-participant systems	Anticipatory scanning Allow public scrutiny
Integration and co-ordination of related processes	Establish link to diverse interests and functions Implementation capability

and a commitment to continuous learning, evaluation and modification (Daniels & Walker, 1996; Dearden & Mitchell, 1998) (Table 1).

In environmental management, the first two conditions have posed serious challenges of application. Collaborative initiatives have frequently been plagued by an inability to agree on 'representative interests', power imbalances within the group, and a lack of trust and respect among group members (Reed, 1995; Wilson *et al.*, 1995). Brown (1996: 15) points out that participants may not enter into collaborative projects from a true desire to achieve an interest-based agreement. 'Traditional beliefs and patterns of relating with others, particularly others with whom there has been longstanding and acrimonious conflict' may thwart collaborative efforts. Rather, 'some parties may consider it necessary to participate as a sort of "damage control", not because they truly see a collaborative solution as their best alternative'. In emergent tourism settings where interests are not collectively organised, the identification of legitimate stakeholders may be a contestable task. It is important to consider who determines whether an individual or groups is/are affected by a development and who has sufficient capacity to participate. Particularly in emergent tourism settings, the lack of institutions supporting tourism may allow conventional power holders in the community to retain their influence in identifying local values.

Identification of shared values is also a significant challenge. To meet this challenge, participants must have a genuine desire to build consensus and reach mutually acceptable solutions. But desire is not sufficient. Power differentials among members may result in the imposition of one set of values over others. In adaptive management, alternative models or scenarios may be used to illustrate different assumptions, values and implications and help to address power differentials. McLain & Lee (1996: 445) suggest that 'With only one model, based on one set of assumptions, assumptions and values of less powerful stakeholders are bound to be submerged ... the presence of multiple models may provide an appropriate forum for debating how social and cultural values affect both the discovery of consequences and choice of corrective action'.

Beyond identifying values, adaptive planning processes emphasise generating *structured improvements* over the status quo, where results are measured in terms progress towards some ends, rather than establishing a complete solution. According to Daniels & Walker (1996: 83):

> constructing improvements rather than solutions requires parties to understand situations in terms of their complexity ... encouraging participants to focus on their concerns and interests related to the situation, thus freeing them from the more rigid task of taking positions or making demands. Suggestions for improvements grounded in these concerns are ultimately debated to determine if they represent both technically desirable and culturally feasible change.

A focus on progress also allows new information generated through the process to be used to modify actions before irreversible commitments are made. It also provides for a sense of accomplishment when sound planning products are proposed, even if full consensus is not achieved (Brown, 1996). Staged implementation allows for the generation of new information, which leads to new knowledge and understanding, which in turn become the departure point for new initiatives. This step-wise approach helps to meet a central goal of adaptive management – to develop policies and practices that result in greater resilience.

The structured process of 'learning by doing' involves much more than incremental policy making by requiring better monitoring and response to unexpected management impacts. All planned initiatives require concrete measures of performance against which anticipated outcomes can be evaluated, mistakes can be realised, and modifications made. In the context of scientific approaches, these performance criteria may take the form of hypotheses and/or predictions about the impacts of alternative actions. While such terminology may not apply to planning situations, the deliberate effort to establish indicators of change and to *continuously experiment and systematically learn* from experiences is an appropriate extension.

Adaptive organisations

When applying adaptive management to organisations, Mulvihill and Keith (1989) identified four principles: (1) mandates and processes must be well defined but not rigid; (2) innovative membership; (3) organisations must be able to operate in complex, changing and multi-participant systems; and (4) integration and coordination of related processes. The first two principles relate to the internal structure of the organisation, while the last two deal with external relations of the organisation to the broader community setting. The first principle appears to be a contradictory one. Certainly, there is a challenge between establishing minimum specification of roles to take advantage of unexpected situations and changing conditions, while simultaneously ensuring that there is sufficient power or legitimacy to bring about real changes. Organisations must be open to new ideas, willing to explore new approaches and prepared to seize opportunities through continuous learning and self-evaluation.

An innovative membership requires a diverse set of complementary skills and knowledge to apply to local situations. The ability of organisations to operate in complex, multi-participant systems must demonstrate the ability to communicate to other members of their constituency or peer group, and to the broader community. In research about environmental organisations, Reed (1997b) found that organisations that took on multiple roles (such as advisory committees, and advocacy work) were able to create innovative ideas and to gain credibility and influence within local systems. For example, innovation may be realised through the establishment of different venues and approaches for general public participation and feedback over the course of the planning period. Multiple methods may also provide for inclusion of people who respond to different kinds of learning interaction (Daniels & Walker, 1996). Innovation and integration also imply a willingness to network and cooperate with other groups in a broad range of activities including the sharing of research, information, funding, labour, and/or expertise. People involved in community-based tourism planning may have to bring in the local Chamber of Commerce, provide labour on specific projects, invite members from conventionally 'silent' groups, or share information with other organisations about how new development opportunities may benefit or hinder tourism objectives. Knowledge of, and commitment to, other formalised planning activities such as regional planning and environmental impact assessment, are also important to ensure these activities are integrated and coordinated.

Clearly, organisations that adopt these four principles do more than accommodate, collaborate, or facilitate multiple preferences. Preferences must be identified and interventions designed as experiments from which new learning can be accomplished. A commitment to implementation is also necessary. However, despite over 20 years of theoretical development and practical application in environmental management, successful application of adaptive management principles remains an elusive goal (cf. Holling, 1978; Walters, 1986; Lee, 1993; McLain & Lee, 1996; Walters, 1997). After review of longstanding and more recent adaptive management experiments, McLain and Lee (1996) suggest that implementation efforts suffer from an over-reliance on rational comprehensive planning models, a tendency to discount non-scientific forms of knowledge, and an inattention to policy processes that promote the development of shared understandings among diverse stakeholders. They attribute implementation challenges to institutional limitations. 'Under conditions of uncertainty, effective management requires that societies do more than merely acquire knowledge: they must also change their behavior in response to new understandings about how the world operates. The ability of institutions to respond to new knowledge depends on whether they have access to new information and whether they have the will and capacity to act on that information' (McLain & Lee 1996: 438). These are important cautions for tourism planning as well. Institutional capacity for change is an important issue in small-town situations where tourism is an emergent opportunity for economic diversification. The prospects for meeting the requirements as they are set out here are discussed in the next section in relation to a planning exercise in a small community in located western Canada.

Squamish: An Exercise in Collaborative Tourism Planning

The study area and approach

The discussion that follows applies the principles of adaptive management to a community-based tourism planning process involving residents and conventional stakeholders in Squamish, Canada (Figure 1). Like other communities, Squamish is confronting rapid changes in its economy, a complex set of issues and stakeholders, ripe for conflicting interests. Its efforts to consider tourism as part of its efforts to diversify its economy illustrates issues, processes and problems that are common to other small towns elsewhere in Canada. The data presented here form part of a larger research effort aimed at understanding the processes of economic and social restructuring in the region (Gill & Reed, 1997; Reed & Gill, 1997). Research in the region began in October 1992. First, the author observed the initial meetings of the citizen's tourism advisory committee and received all minutes and communication associated with its activities. Second, other documentary sources were also reviewed including Census of Canada, newspaper accounts, a draft and the final tourism development plan. Third, in 1995, the author conducted in-depth interviews with all 19 citizen participants, three of five resource people and observers, and the manager of the Chamber of Commerce. Analysis of the verbatim transcripts followed the methodology of accounts outlined by Brown and Sime (1981). The interview data were then incorporated into the other sources to form the basis for the analysis presented here. Finally, reference is made to a household survey conducted with Gill in Squamish in July 1995 where 1270 residents responded (see Gill & Reed, 1997; Reed & Gill, 1997).

Squamish, a District Municipality of approximately 13,000, is located between Vancouver and Whistler. Squamish can clearly be considered an emergent tourism setting. Until the 1980s, Squamish was a 'classical' resource-based town, dependent primarily on the forest industry relying on logging, pulp production and saw-milling. Originally, the economy of Squamish developed relatively separately from Vancouver and Whistler. However, pressures from Vancouver for port facilities, and from both Vancouver and Whistler for recreational opportunities and affordable housing within commuting range began to draw in new residents from these neighbouring municipalities. In addition, Squamish is situated in a region of the province that has experienced the highest growth rate in visitors in the past decade. Consequently, since 1991, the population of Squamish has grown more than 3% per year. New residents and public processes have begun to contribute to a broader debate over the appropriate kind and level of growth in the community. In particular, they have pointed to the physical attributes of the community which offer international calibre recreational opportunities including rock climbing, wind surfing and hiking and they have promoted and/or taken up opportunities for employment in related businesses.

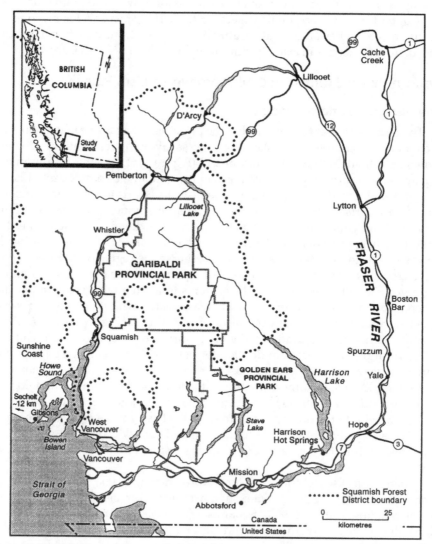

Figure 1 The location of Squamish BC, Canada

Yet, Squamish has yet to shake off its primary image as a forestry town. In 1996, the Chamber of Commerce (the Chamber) reported that 60% of local businesses are members. Of these, approximately 35 of 350 were related to tourism. This figure includes hotels, tour operators and restaurants. Since 1985, the Chamber has held a fee-for-service contract with the municipality to provide tourism information services. It also forms part of a 'joint tourism committee', composed of members of the municipal council, the Chamber and a person from the local Parks and Recreation Board to oversee the contract. The Chamber also retains the option to undertake marketing on behalf of the municipality. The marketing of Squamish as a tourist destination is currently hampered by its lack of a tourism infrastructure, the limited appeal of its town centre, restricted access to foreshore areas, and a lack of local understanding of the current and potential impact of tourism and recreation opportunities on the local economy. As will be discussed later, some members of the tourism sector would place the Chamber among those who lack understanding of contemporary tourism opportunities.

Community tourism planning in Squamish

In 1992–93, Squamish became involved in a community tourism planning exercise as a result of a proposal to develop a four seasons ski resort at Brohm Ridge located on Crown land adjacent to the municipality. For several years, the proposal had been officially endorsed by the municipal council who believed that it was necessary in order to offset the pending reduction in forestry jobs and consequent tax base. In addition, it would boost the profile of Squamish, providing a launch for a potentially lucrative tourism product. The Municipality and the proponent company had lobbied the provincial government for several years to approve the project. The Provincial government declined, stating among other reasons that the Municipality had not 'gone to the people' to determine if this were the type of tourism attraction which community residents would like to support. For some members of council, the community-based planning process remained the best means of assuring the provision of the ski hill project.

In January 1993, approximately 100 residents attended a workshop to help identify community priorities for tourism. Following the workshop, 19 volunteers met to develop a tourism development plan that ultimately incorporated a vision statement, action plan concepts and strategies for the future. After 18 months of hard work, the volunteers presented their final draft to the Municipal Council in June 1994. The plan was approved and adopted by the District of Squamish Council in December 1994 (Citizen's Advisory Committee and Howe Sound Community Futures Society, 1994).

The Municipal government appointed a tourism coordinating committee to oversee the work of the citizen's committee. Representatives from the conventional power holders such as municipal and regional government agencies, the Chamber of Commerce, and BC Rail were included (Figure 2). After an initial meeting, the Squamish (Aboriginal) First Nation, not a traditional power holder at the local level, was also appointed to the coordinating committee. The coordinating committee was charged with making recommendations to the municipal council with respect to the establishment of a comprehensive tourism plan, the setting of tourism development priorities, the allocation of local resources for assisting tourism opportunities, and the evaluation of on-going tourism initiatives. With an initial purpose that included evaluation, an opportunity for creating an adaptive approach was formed.

A citizen's advisory committee, composed of 19 on-going volunteer residents, was created to develop a local plan. An economic development officer from Community Futures, a federally sponsored community development agency, was appointed facilitator. According to the template used by Community Futures, the committee members identified priorities for specific strategies, developed action plan concepts, and created a vision statement to guide the plan. Although established under the Municipal Council, the advisory committee did not operate under the standard protocol of Council committees. For example, minutes of meetings were not provided to steering committee members on a

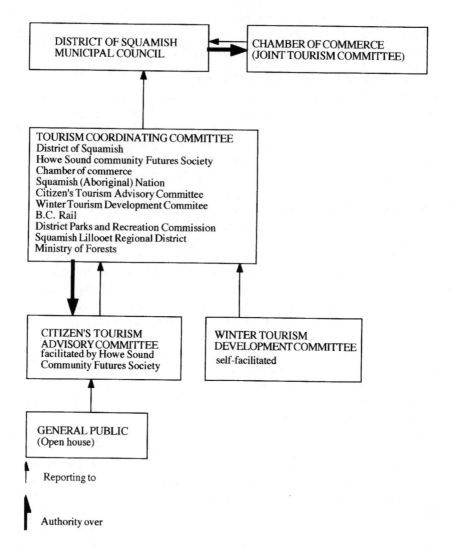

Figure 2 Reporting relationships for tourism planning in Squamish BC, Canada

regular basis and on several occasions municipal representatives were not invited to the meetings.

The community tourism plan

The citizen's advisory committee submitted its draft plan to the coordinating committee and the Municipal Council. The Chamber of Commerce, through its position on the coordinating committee, demanded that certain revisions be made. The final plan developed and ranked 30 action plan concepts for future tourism development. No effort was made to identify funding sources, although lead agencies and implementation paths were discussed. Of the 30 concepts, the first 10 related to research, planning, logistical support, training, coordination and infrastructure development.

The result of the effort was modest at best. The tourism development plan presented a much broader vision of tourism than that held by the conventional power elites, primarily the Chamber of Commerce and the Municipal Council. A diverse range of options for tourism was presented; representing a shift from the development of a solely private project towards public goods and services that would be in keeping with community needs and desires. The supporters of the ski hill got what they wanted. However, the conventional elites – the Municipality, the Chamber – along with the proponent of the ski hill development, were successful in ensuring that the plan did not threaten their interests. The ski hill proposal was, at least in general terms, endorsed. Subsequently, the ski hill proponents have continued to use the plan as an example of broad community and Municipal support and have pursued its development through Provincial requirements for environmental assessment.

While the Municipal Council approved the plan, it subsequently did little to implement it. Instead, the plan was viewed as a document that could be taken forward by members of the private sector to advance specific projects. Council initially proposed to undertake a marketing strategy which would be in keeping with conventional viewpoints of tourism. When it was discovered that even this undertaking would require a larger allocation of funds than originally anticipated, the measure was not executed. Instead, the Council passed by-laws to allow for other developments (e.g. shopping centres) that contradicted elements of the tourism plan. Thus, the interest in allocating resources and evaluating on-going activities was lost once the plan was submitted. Furthermore, following submission of the plan, the Chamber took several actions to retain its hold on the organisation and coordination of tourism for the Municipality. Despite these efforts, the Chamber has been unable to control all the players in tourism. At present, new operators continue to organise separately from the Chamber in order to promote their interests to the Municipal Council.

Elsewhere I have argued that the citizen's committee was unable to overcome systemic power relations to implement a broader vision for tourism development (Reed, 1997a). I suggested that local power relations form part of the structural conditions, within which community tourism planning is constituted, that constrain the efficacy of collaboration. Furthermore, I suggested that power relations that favour broader visions of tourism will gain ascendance as the nature and structure of the community itself changes through alterations to the demographic composition, economic base, and policies at higher tiers of government. This implies that tourism will develop through an evolutionary process, much of which is not amenable to local intervention. Here, however, I reconsider that implication, suggesting that had an adaptive approach to collaborative tourism planning been attempted, these power relations need not have resulted in stagnation. Instead, adaptive management could have been used to learn about power relations as initiatives were proposed, and the outcomes used to make adjustments and plan future initiatives. Such an approach, however, would require alterations in the structure and processes of the advisory committee. In the following section, I examine the work of the advisory committee in terms of the shortcomings and opportunities to build an adaptive approach within both planning procedures and the organisational structures set out in Squamish.

Assessing the Results

Assessing planning procedures

The procedures established in Squamish were initially geared towards the *collaboration of interests* and *identification of shared values* (Table 2). However, this initial effort broke down, resulting in a fairly limited application of collaboration. For example, the opening workshop, where 100 people attended, brought out diverse interests and exposed a broad interest in tourism that had previously been untapped. As one advisory committee member stated:

> when I found out about it [the workshop] ... I sort of started madly phoning around to all my friends in the recreation community and saying, 'listen, here's the opportunity, let's get out and see what we can do with this'. So I think that was a bit of a surprise [by council members who] were quite shocked at the number of people in fact who were there, it was 'oh, where did all these people come from, I didn't know tourism was that strong an interest in the community.

The citizen's advisory committee was drawn from workshop participants. With only one exception, the committee members had not previously been part of the local decision making hierarchy. Members included small-scale entrepreneurs, individuals with experience in tourism planning and/or marketing, and concerned citizens. Only one member was a full-time tourism operator. While a statistical comparison is not possible, a cursory review of committee members along with respondents to the community survey indicates that representation on the citizen's advisory committee was biased in favour of new residents engaged in business and professional services, 'other' employment such as the arts and retirees, and individuals employed in the public service (Table 3). Notably absent was representation from primary (e.g. forestry) and construction industries. Length of residency is also a distinctive feature of the committee members. Thirty-six per cent of all survey respondents had lived in Squamish for five years or less, compared to 63% (12 of 19) committee members. The identification of values reflected the disproportionate influence of newcomers on the committee.

Identification of values was attempted through a jointly-conceived vision statement to guide the planning process. The phrasing of the statement became one of the most problematic elements of the process. Lack of such a statement ground down the initial attempts to establish a tourism strategy. Crafting a statement took months of hard work by all members. The statement, to 'build and strengthen a diverse four season tourism sector while maintaining our small town character and preserving our heritage' (printed on every page of the report) was an obvious attempt to marry new initiatives with the traditional economic base. Heritage was interpreted as cultural and natural heritage, thus providing a link with the forest sector, the Squamish First Nation as well as the long-standing Indo-Canadian population.[1] The concern to maintain the small town character of Squamish had been raised many times in the initial public meeting and was an

Table 2 Assessing adaptive planning processes and adapative organisations in Squamish BC, Canada

Characteristics of adaptive planning processes	Summary of Squamish characteristics
Collaboration of interests	Initial collaboration included broad community interests in tourism. However, large gaps in representation (e.g. forestry) reduced the scope of collaboration. Collaboration was also reduced through heightened mistrust of other members as process endured.
Identification of values	Identifying common values became the most time-consuming task of the committee. Although a value statement was generated, factionalisation of the committee indicated that its meaning was not commonly shared.
Progress through structured improvements	No implementation steps from which 'improvements' could be determined. Initial idea to develop demonstration projects was abandoned.
Continuous learning and modification	No projects or initiatives were designed in an experimental fashion. Willingness to implement was thwarted.
Characteristics of adaptive organisations	
Well defined mandates, flexible processes	Mandate was defined but constrained to developing a plan. Template for visioning process was too general. Committee was not provided autonomy to establish its own processes.
Innovative membership	Members showed varying commitment to new ideas. Learning was concentrated on learning how local regulations and procedures worked. Committee's innovation was limited by lack of knowledge of local systems and by inability to come to coherent 'vision' of tourism.
Multi-participant systems	Committee became insular in its deliberations. Its extension activities into the broader community were not adequate to address local power relations.
Integration and co-ordination of related processes	Activities of the committee were not linked to other municipal, regional or provincial procedures.

attempt to ensure that tourism was undertaken in a way that would not compromise the traditional sense of community. The need to include this component was hotly debated, with several newcomers being much more insistent on including the term than longer-term residents.

It is not clear that all parties either began with or retained a genuine desire to build a consensus about tourism directions. There was no effort to develop alternative models or scenarios to which all members could contribute. Some individuals within the planning process became vocal on one side or another of specific issues, while others believed that their opinions were completely silenced.

Table 3 Employment and residency characteristic of the advisory committee and community respondents

Nature of employment Census categories	% of respondents resident for 0–5 years	% of respondents resident for over 5 years	% of members of citizen's advisory committee
	n = 384	n = 593	n = 19
Primary	4.4	10.5	0.0
Construction	9.9	6.7	0.0
Manufacturing	3.4	7.8	0.0
Transport	7.6	13.3	0.0
Retail	7.8	10.1	5.3
Finance	4.2	3.4	0.0
Government	8.3	7.6	21.1
Education	7.6	11.6	0.0
Health	13.3	7.4	0.0
Accommodation	6.0	5.6	0.0
Business and professional services	18.5	9.9	36.8
Sport and recreation	4.2	0.7	5.3
Other	4.9	5.4	36.8

Source: Data collected by author, Squamish Community Household Survey 1995 and interviews of committee members.

The facilitator initially had the committee's support as someone who 'gained the confidence of the group, not trying to impose his ideas, but really trying to work with the group and find solutions to the problems that were going on' (informant interview, 1995). However, as the process dragged on, he was unable to confront local power struggles in the community and gain broader public support. His attachment to the planning template, even as individuals became embroiled in conflicts about the ski hill and other specific proposals, appeared to some members as an attempt to control the process and to gain an individual profile in the town. As a newcomer to the community and to the job, he was labelled a career builder. His efforts to describe the work of the committee and write up the plan became associated with political naivety and partisanship. Writing was ultimately taken over by some of the committee volunteers.

Partly because of the continued lobbying by the proponent of individual members of the committee and partly because of the slowness of the process, five committee members broke away from the main advisory committee to focus on winter tourism activities. Two new people were asked to join this sub-committee and within a few weeks, the sub-committee endorsed the ski hill project and made other recommendations. This action was considered suspect by the remaining advisory committee members. For example, one member stated:

> How objective was this winter tourism committee? How did they go about establishing priorities, writing them through, that kind of stuff. Does it become add-ons and an apology for, like the ski area proposal. And I don't

think the main committee was ever happy with the way that process went, given that all the kinds of stuff that we went through.

In the face of objections about their procedures and plans, the winter sub-committee bypassed the citizen's committee, and submitted its recommendations directly to the coordinating committee (Figure 2). The coordinating committee required that the recommendations of the winter committee be incorporated into the main report. As one participant put it, 'that (the co-ordinating committee) was not a consensus decision-making group at all. That was strict, traditional power-base'. This splinter in the committee indicates that coming to agreement on values within a collaborative process is an enormously challenging task.

Analysis of the draft and final reports, however, does indicate an attempt to *generate improvements* in tourism (Table 2). However, in the context of adaptive management, these improvements did not contain performance criteria against which judgments and alterations could been made. While initially, there had been discussion about demonstration projects, the committee opted against developing them because it lacked the authority to implement them. Two specific recommendations contained in the draft report were that an independent tourism association or advisory body be established on an on-going basis to review tourism initiatives and to make recommendations to Council, and that a local tourism coordinator be hired to develop nascent initiatives and generate a higher profile for tourism in Squamish. These recommendations were made in light of concerns that new tourism-related businesses had been shut out from the power structure within the Chamber which consequently did not understand or address their needs. The Chamber of Commerce viewed these as direct threats to its role in the community and as a member of the coordinating committee which had ultimate approval authority, it demanded that these recommendations be rescinded. Consequently, the final plan recommended simply that the Municipality 'encourage broader-based participation in local tourism development'.

These struggles illustrate major challenges as adaptive management moves towards implementation. The Municipal Council was not willing to empower the committee by implementing recommendations, but allowed conventional power brokers (in this case the Chamber) to override the committee's work. The committee itself struggled under the limited facilitation skills provided to it. Furthermore, committee members were unable to propose demonstration projects or other initiatives that might provide incremental changes that could be monitored. As a result of these limitations – some institutional, some individual – opportunities for establishing initiatives that would provide for *continuous learning* were simply not realised.

Assessing adaptive organisations

The first two conditions for adaptive organisations relate to a *clear mandate and flexible process*, and an *innovative membership*. In this case, the mandate of the citizen's advisory committee to produce a plan was clear; yet the means to do so were limited. The process, which was initially begun in a wide open fashion, became quickly narrowed because of the template that was imposed on the committee by the facilitator. For example, the exercise in attempting to come up with a common vision statement for tourism was drawn from a community development model that had been used by Community Futures personnel in other places across the country. While it may have been successful elsewhere, the facilitator was unable to adapt it so that committee members could feel like they were making progress. In addition, the committee was not granted real power from the Municipal Council, effectively hampering its ability be a source of innovation. The two-tiered committee structure, in which traditional power brokers had authority over the citizen's committee also reduced the opportunity to promote adaptive management. Had scenarios been used to debate different values and perspectives with conventional power brokers, these power relations may have been more open to public scrutiny. This suggests that collaborative initiative, where local elites do not come face-to-face during negotiations with others, is an incomplete approach destined to failure.

Despite these shortcomings, some tentative steps in innovative directions were initiated. By moving away from considering tourism as 'products only' towards concerns for research, planning, logistical support, training, and coordination, the final plan introduced new interpretations of tourism to the municipality. Within the product and infrastructure development, recommendations reflected the heightened importance of recreation-based tourism based on improving access to internationally recognised features such as rock climbing, wind surfing and nature (particularly eagle) observation.

Innovative membership also includes the willingness to learn from within and outside the committee structure. Although the plan was modest, committee members had learned a great deal. Because there were so few people with direct experience in local planning and so many members were new to the municipality, there was a great deal of learning about how governance structures worked and the kinds of initiatives that could be attempted. In the words of the chairperson, there was a:

> ... huge learning curve. Everyone who was on the advisory committee was feeling quite overwhelmed of the amount of information that was initially coming forth from our resource people ... we had quite a few people providing a lot of information about the land holdings, First Nations, BCR [BC Rail] being land holders, provincial crown corporations holding land, municipality holding land, all these people were the major stakeholders in the community who were controlling the directions of the community as landholders ... I think the advisory committee did a commendable job just digesting the amount of information that it did.

With adaptive management, emphasis is placed on learning 'by doing'. However, this emphasis assumes that those involved in the management experience have already a baseline of knowledge about how the institutions of management operate. This quote reveals that before recommendations could be made, the committee had to wade through a morass of local regulations and institutional realities. Here, perhaps is a core difference between collaborative learning models that promote group learning (Daniels & Walker, 1996) and adaptive management which historically has been undertaken by management professionals (Walters & Holling, 1990).

Notwithstanding this observation, additional opportunities might have been realised had the committee viewed itself as part of a *multi-participant* system (Table 2). As one of the break-away participants stated, 'it took so long to do and what I felt was happening was that the world was going on outside, passing them by because they were locked into these closed doors and not listening to anything else or seeing anything that was happening'. After the first large workshop, the extension of the committee to the community at large was restricted to a specific meeting of the committee with the local Aboriginal First Nation. An obvious omission was representation from the forestry sector. This gap was noted by members of the advisory committee, yet its deliberations continued without assistance or comment by the forest sector. Indo-Canadian residents, who at the time comprised approximately 11% of the town's population, were not usually active participants in community-wide initiatives. While the tourism committee recommended a cultural festival incorporating Indo-Canadian residents, the committee members did not seek direct input from this segment of the community.

Opportunities to *integrate and coordinate* this effort with other related processes were also missed (Table 2). These may have taken the form of regular public meetings, news releases, invitations for members of the public to attend meetings regularly, links to planners in Whistler and additional public workshops. No effort was made to coordinate directly with planning initiatives of the municipality, regional district, or provincial government agencies. Instead, only a listing of potentially interested public and private agencies and non-governmental organisations was provided along with each recommendation. While more direct linkages to these agencies and planning activities may not have been in the interests defined by the Municipality, had the committee sought these opportunities, there would have been little the Municipality could have done to stop them.

Such activities could have raised the committee profile, increasing its ability to harness financial resources to carry out demonstration projects or programs. While it is arguable whether such a committee has the authority to obtain such funding, environmental advisory committees in the region have been successful in obtaining funding for planning and projects from agencies as diverse as municipal governments, the Regional Economic Development Commission, Vancouver City Savings Credit Union, Canada Trust, and the BC Ferry Corporation. In the case of one new environmental advisory committee, participants put in money from their own interest group or provided in-kind services, ranging in value from $100 to $5,000 (1996 Canadian dollars) per representative (Reed, 1997b). The purposes of providing their own funding was to allow some autonomy in setting priorities, begin undertaking inventory work, and demonstrate commitment and competence so that public funding of future projects would be more likely.

Instead, the low profile of the citizen's advisory committee allowed it to be dominated by the traditional power structures. This is evident in the ability of the ski hill operator to fragment the committee, in the problems encountered with/by the facilitator, and in the changes that the Chamber required before the Council accepted the report. In addition, Council accepted the final report without a word of acknowledgment or appreciation to the volunteers who had

spent the past year-and-a-half attempting to craft a new direction for the Municipality. Many committee members spoke of their disappointment about their
silent exit. Despite the power struggles, even the Manager of the Chamber recognised this misfortune, stating, 'volunteers are too valuable to be treated that
way'. Without implementation capability, the potential for adaptive management was severely restricted.

The problems encountered in this case support the observation by McLain and
Lee (1996) that scientific approaches used by adaptive management professionals in environmental management have assumed that the greatest challenges lie in model creation, defining parameters and/or designing alternatives.
However, for citizens involved in planning processes, it is the integration of 'scientific' (or technical) knowledge with practical concerns, learning how to
communicate competently, and understanding and overcoming institutional
hurdles that may pose more significant challenges. Within small-scale settings
such as presented here, individuals can play significant roles in meeting or
failing these challenges. A brief summary and discussion of the implications of
these challenges is provided in the final section.

Summary and Implications for Collaborative Tourism Planning

In this paper, I have extended the notion of adaptive management, illustrating
how it might be applied to collaborative planning in emergent tourism settings.
Beginning with its origins in environmental management, I demonstrated the
similarities that render it suitable for application to emergent tourism settings. In
doing so, I attempted to flesh out the characteristics and challenges of an adaptive paradigm for sustainable tourism as initially suggested by Colin Hunter
(1997). Clearly, the framework for adaptive management has not been properly
tested. Proper testing would involve the explanation of the model to all of the
stakeholders and an agreement to extend the collaborative model to include an
active learning component. Such an extension requires specialised knowledge
by at least some participants, and an ongoing commitment even in the face of
economic or political mistakes. To date, local collaborative tourism planning
efforts have not explicitly adopted requirements for adaptive management.
Notwithstanding this limitation, the framework for adaptive management
developed and applied here suggests both practical and research challenges. The
findings are not conclusive, but rather, are offered in a more general way, to
spark consideration and debate.

Theories of collaboration and adaptive management have acknowledged the
importance of the human factor in plan creation and implementation. Yet they
have not explicitly acknowledged the role that individuals can bring or the
importance of broader power relations in which individuals operate. In this case,
the facilitator was new to the community and his job. His skills as a listener were
praised, but his skills at mediating power relations locally, both within the advisory committee and between the advisory committee and other local actors (e.g.
Chamber of Commerce, Municipality, Ski Hill Developer), were minimal. In his
attempt to craft the plan according to a predetermined template, he was accused
of political naivete and power grabbing. His failure may also, in part, have been
attributed to personal conflict between himself and the Manager of the Chamber

of Commerce. This finding illustrates that despite meeting theoretical requirements, adaptive planning processes may be affected by the actions of individuals who can make or break processes and organisations.

Collaborative and adaptive approaches to community-based tourism planning share other challenges that may not be so idiosyncratic. For example, obtaining the necessary information, knowledge and expertise, and integrating it into a format that is understandable and useful for participants within reasonable time frames are tasks that can overwhelm the non-professionals who are volunteering their time over and above their work and family lives. The ability to maintain the interest of participants over the planning time frame and/or to attract new volunteers is not a simple challenge. In addition, it may prove very difficult to incorporate 'local knowledges' from residents who have pertinent experiences that may not be codified in standard, 'objective' formats. The exclusion of Indo-Canadians and the Aboriginal First Nation stems, in part, from cultural differences about how information might best be shared and used. As community-based tourism examines culturally based tourism opportunities, future research on collaboration and adaptive management should examine how local knowledges can be used in systematic and respectful ways to generate communication competence and shared learning (Daniels & Walker, 1996). Research in environmental management may offer some insights in this regard (e.g. Gadgil *et al.*, 1993; Neis, 1992).

Institutional challenges are also significant. 'Successful' implementation must confront the complexity and uncertainty that accompany planned change. Adaptive management requires building in learning objectives for each initiative, so that monitoring can lead to improvements in the future. There must be a willingness to try new initiatives in an experimental mode. Yet, users of an adaptive collaborate approach must recognise that implementation will not follow a rational comprehensive planning model. Experimentation may be viewed not only as too expensive, but also politically too risky by those in decision-making positions. Protecting self-interests by any parties within the planning process is a serious problem.

In an environmental management context, Walters (1997) pointed out that value conflicts *within* the environmental management community have become more serious than conflicts externally. He argued that there is an important role for scientists to expose these interests publicly in order to address them. Similarly with tourism planning, conflicts *within* local power structures may reduce the effectiveness of the planning effort. As the Squamish case illustrated, divisions *within* the committee were a significant barrier. Had the advisory committee been able to overcome its internal divisions about the appropriate 'vision' for sustainable tourism, the power struggles with the Municipality and the Chamber might have been easier to confront. Instead, to paraphrase an old saying, a divided committee made conquest easy.

I am not arguing that these power brokers would have been overcome by a cohesive committee. I am suggesting, however, that by forming a common front, the committee could have exposed these power struggles more effectively to public scrutiny. Attempts to build alternative scenarios and provide greater exposure to public scrutiny throughout the planning process may have helped to address the local power holders that inhibited successful application of the plan.

However, any attempts to that would add more players to the mix may, perversely, make agreement over common visions even more difficult to achieve. Notwithstanding, adaptive approaches to planning, with a deliberate focus on learning more about the power dimensions and viewing new initiatives as applied experiments, may be better able to deal with these challenges than collaboration alone.

Perhaps it is simply presumptuous to believe that our planning systems can be designed to 'manage' tourism. More realistically, we can manage our institutions and decision systems to adapt to changing conditions that tourism will inevitably bring. The complexity of the biophysical and socioeconomic systems within which tourism planning is undertaken is great, exacerbated by on-going and frequently rapid change. Uncertainty (arising from our imperfect understanding) and conflict (from different and legitimate interests) are endemic. To develop tourism within community settings, and to appraise its effectiveness of initiatives, we must recognise and deal with change, complexity, uncertainty and conflict.

In part, this requires effective citizen involvement. This includes collaboration of interests and identification of shared values. But these conditions form only part of a successful collaborative effort. We must also recognise that power relations are an integral element to understanding the characteristics and consequences of community-based planning where tourism is emergent. The stakeholders – elected, appointed, professional or volunteer – are not neutral conveners of power. If we are to understand these relations, we must combine collaborative efforts with direct opportunities for learning. Opportunities for doing so have been presented here through a discussion of adaptive management, where conditions for planning processes and organisations have been identified and discussed. The application of these conditions to the case study in Squamish illustrate that significant challenges lie ahead in the adoption of adaptive management in collaborative planning processes.

This is not an argument that adaptive management can readily overcome unequal power relations. However, aspects of collaboration, innovative membership and organising multi-participant systems can serve to expose, debate and address power relations that inhibit new initiatives. We can use adaptive management principles to learn more about how power relations affect planning and implementation by designing management strategies that explicitly address these relations.

Such processes involve large numbers of stakeholders using both formal and informal mechanisms of exchange. An adaptive approach requires logistical and financial investments in monitoring and evaluation, long-range planning horizons and willingness to make mistakes and chart new directions. These elements are easily thwarted by political decision makers and/or public servants who may serve office for short periods, who are building their careers for different purposes, and/or who are unwilling to risk political consequences of project 'failure'. Thus an adaptive approach requires good information flow and forums for generating shared understandings. For stakeholders to begin to negotiate for mutually acceptable compromises, attention must be paid to institutional structures and processes that provide greater opportunities for stakeholder participation in making *and implementing* decisions. Such opportunities may also help to generate a sense of collective responsibility that is needed to convince relatively autonomous stakeholders to engage in long-term collective action.

These are considerations to which both future research and practical efforts need to be focused. By so doing, we can move beyond the conclusion that tourism will emerge as an evolutionary process and begin to take the initiative in setting its direction and form. If we recognise that planning in emergent tourism settings is inherently uncertain and turbulent, the inevitable mistakes of application can become learning opportunities rather than implementation failures. Over the longer term, our successes can become part of a record of shared successes in collective learning as well as in sustainable tourism development.

Correspondence

Any correspondence should be directed to Professor Maureen G. Reed, Department of Geography, The University of British Columbia, 1984 West Mall, Vancouver BC, Canada V6T 1Z2 (mreed@geog.ubc.ca).

Notes

1. In Canada, the term 'First Nations' refers to Aboriginal peoples, while the term 'Indo-Canadians' refers to Canadians of East Indian origin.

References

Barrett, B. (1994) Integrated environmental management. *Journal of Environmental Management* 40, 17–32.
Berman, P. (1980) Thinking about programmed and adaptive implementation: Matching strategies to situations. In H.M. Ingram and D.E. Mann (eds) *Why Policies Succeed or Fail* (pp. 205–27). Beverly Hills, CA: Sage.
Brown, D.W. (1996) *Strategic Land Use Planning Source Book*. Victoria: Commission on Resources and Environment.
Brown, J. and Sime, J. (1981) A methodology of accounts. In M. Brenner (ed.) *Social Method and Social Life* (pp. 159–188). London: Academic Press.
Bryant, C.R. and Johnston, T.R.R. (1992) *Agriculture in the City's Countryside*. Toronto: University of Toronto Press.
Butler, R.W. (1991) Tourism, environment and sustainable development. *Environmental Conservation* 18, 201–209.
Butler, T. and Savage, M. (1995) (eds) *Social Change and the Middle Classes*. London: University College London.
Cartwright, (1991) Planning and chaos theory. *Journal of the American Planning Association* 57, 44–56.
Citizen's Advisory Committee and Howe Sound Community Futures Society (1994) *Tourism Development Plan for the District of Squamish*. Squamish, BC: Citizen's Advisory Committee and Howe Sound Community Futures Society.
Cortner, H.J., Shannon, M.A., Wallace, M.G., Burke, S. and Moote, M.A. (1996) *Institutional Barriers and Incentives for Ecosystem Management: A Problem Analysis*. General Technical Report PNW–GTR–354, Portland Oregon: Pacific Northwest Research Station, Forest Service, United States Department of Agriculture.
Daniels, S.E. and Walker, G.B. (1996) Collaborative learning: Improving public deliberation in ecosystem-based management. *Environmental Impact Assessment Review* 16, 71–102.
Dearden, P. and Mitchell, B. (1998) *Environmental Change and Challenge: A Canadian Perspective*. Toronto: Oxford University Press.
Dorcey, A.H.J. (1986) *Bargaining in the Governance of Pacific Coastal Resources: Research and Reform*. Vancouver, BC, University of British Columbia: Westwater Research Centre.

Gadgil, M., Berkes, F. and Folke, C. (1993) Indigenous knowledge for biodiversity conservation. *Ambio* 22, 151–6.

Gale, R.P. and Cordray, S.J. (1994) Making sense of sustainability: Nine answers to 'What should be sustained?' *Rural Sociology* 59, 311–332.

Gardner, J. and Roseland, M. (1989) Acting locally: Community strategies for equitable sustainable development. *Alternatives* 16, 36–48.

Gill, A. and Reed, M.G. (1997) The re-imaging of a Canadian resource town: Post-productivism in a North American context. *Applied Geographic Studies* 1, 129–142.

Halfacree, K.H. (1995) A new space or spatial effacement? Alternative futures for the post-productivist countryside. Paper presented to the American/British/Canadian Symposium on Rural Geography, Rural Systems and Geographical Scale, North Carolina, 30 July–5 August.

Holling, C.S. (1978) *Adaptive Environmental Assessment and Management.* Chichester: John Wiley and Sons.

Hunter, C. (1997) Sustainable tourism as an adaptive paradigm. *Annals of Tourism Research* 24, 850–67.

Hunter-Jones, P. (1997) Sustainable tourism. *Annals of Tourism Research* 24, 477–478.

Jamal, T.B. and Getz, D. (1995) Collaboration theory and community tourism planning. *Annals of Tourism Research* 22, 186–204.

Jordan, D. (1989) Negotiating salmon management on the Klamath River. In E. Pinkerton (ed.) *Co-operative Management of Local Fisheries: New Directions for Improvement Management and Community Development* (pp. 73–81). Vancouver: University of British Columbia Press.

Kearney, J.F. (1984) The transformation of the Bay of Fundy herring fisheries, 1976–1978: An experiment in fishermen-government co-management. In C. Lamson and A.J. Hanson (eds) *Atlantic Fisheries and Coastal Communities: Fisheries Decision Making Case Studies* (pp. 165–203). Halifax: Dalhousie Ocean Studies Programme.

Kofinas, G. (1998) The costs of power sharing: Community involvement in Canadian Porcupine Caribou co-management. PhD thesis, The University of British Columbia.

Lee, K.N. (1993) *Compass and Gyroscope: Integrating Science and Politics for the Environment.* Washington, DC: Island Press.

Lemons, J. and Brown, D.A. (1995) (eds) *Sustainable Development: Science, Ethics and Public Policy.* Dordrecht: Kluwer Academic Publishers.

Lowe, P., Murdoch, J., Marsden, T., Munton, R. and Flynn, A. (1993) Regulating the new rural spaces: The uneven development of land. *Journal of Rural Studies* 9, 205–222.

Ludwig, D., Hilborn, R. and Walters, C. (1993) Uncertainty, resource exploitation, and conservation: Lessons from history. *Science* 260, 17–18.

McLain, R.J. and Lee, R.G. (1996) Adaptive management: Promises and pitfalls. *Environmental Management* 20, 437–448.

McKercher, B. (1993) Some fundamental truths about tourism: Understanding tourism's social and environmental impacts. *Journal of Sustainable Tourism* 1, 6–16.

Mitchell, B. (1997) *Resource and Environmental Management.* Essex: Addison Wesley Longman.

Mulvihill, P.R. and Keith, R.F. (1989) Institutional requirements for adaptive EIA: The Kativik Environmental Quality Commission. *Environmental Impact Assessment Review* 9, 399–412.

Neis, B. (1992) 'Fishers' ecological knowledge and stock assessment in Newfoundland. *Newfoundland Studies* 8, 155–78.

Pinkerton, E. (1989) (ed.) *Co-operative Management of Local Fisheries: New Directions for Improvement Management and Community Development.* Vancouver: University of British Columbia Press.

Reed, M.G. (1995) Co-operative management of environmental resources: A case study from Northern Ontario, Canada. *Economic Geography* 71, 132–149.

Reed, M.G. (1997a) Power relations and community-based tourism planning. *Annals of Tourism Research* 24, 566–591.

Reed, M.G. (1997b) The provision of environmental goods and services by local non-governmental organizations: An illustration from the Squamish Forest District, Canada. *Journal of Rural Studies* 13, 177–96.

Reed, M.G. and Gill, A. (1997) Tourism, recreational and amenity values in land allocation: An analysis of institutional arrangements in the post-productivist era. *Environment and Planning* A 29, 2019–2040.

Robinson, J., Francis, G., Legge, R. and Lerner, S. (1990) Defining a sustainable society: Values, principles and definitions. *Alternatives* 17, 36–46.

Royal Commission on the Future of the Toronto Waterfront (1992) *Regeneration: Toronto's Waterfront and the Sustainable City, Final Report*. Ottawa: Minister of Supply and Services Canada; Toronto: Queen's Printer of Ontario.

Selin, S. and Beason, K. (1991) Interorganizational relations in tourism. *Annals of Tourism Research* 18, 639–52.

Shaw, G. and Williams, A.M. (1994) *Critical Issues in Tourism: A Geographical Perspective*. Oxford: Blackwell.

Trist, E. (1980) The environment and system-response capability. *Futures* 12, 113–27.

Trist, E. (1983) Referent organizations and the development of inter-organizational domains. *Human Relations* 36, 269–84.

Wall, G. (1993) International collaboration in the search for sustainable tourism in Bali, Indonesia. *Journal of Sustainable Tourism* 1, 38–47.

Walters, C. (1986) *Adaptive Management of Renewable Resources*. New York: Macmillan.

Walters, C. and Holling, C.S. (1990) Large-scale management experiments and learning by doing. *Ecology* 71, 2060–8.

Walters, C. (1997) Challenges in adaptive management of riparian and coastal ecosystems. *Conservation Ecology* 1, 1–21. or [online] http://www.consecol.org/vol1/iss2/art1

Wilson, A., Roseland, M. and Day, J.C. (1995) Shared decision-making and public land planning: An evaluation of the Vancouver Island regional core process. *Environments* 23, 69–86.

14. Stakeholder Assessment and Collaborative Tourism Planning: The Case of Brazil's Costa Dourada Project

L. Medeiros de Araujo and Bill Bramwell
Centre for Tourism, Sheffield Hallam University, Pond Street, Sheffield, S1 1WB, UK

The paper reviews approaches to identifying the stakeholders who are affected by a tourism project and who might participate in collaborative tourism planning. Two such approaches are discussed and analysed based on research carried out on stakeholders affected by the Costa Dourada project, a regional tourism planning initiative in north-east Brazil. The first approach involves assessing the stakeholders who had participated in the project planning by attending local workshops or project meetings intended to promote collaborative planning. The second involves interviewing a sample of stakeholders affected by the project and also stakeholders directly involved in the project planning, asking them for their views on stakeholders they consider relevant to the project but who were not participants in the planning process. These two approaches are used to examine whether the range of stakeholders participating in the planning process was representative of the stakeholders affected by the project and was also likely to encourage consideration of the diverse issues of sustainable development. It is found that varied stakeholders had participated in the planning process, but there was only limited participation by the private sector and environmental NGOs.

Introduction

It is seen as increasingly important for tourism planning in destinations to involve the multiple stakeholders affected by tourism, including environmental groups, business interests, public authorities and community groups (Gartner, 1996; Williams *et al.*, 1998). A stakeholder is defined here as 'any person, group, or organization that is affected by the causes or consequences of an issue' (Bryson & Crosby, 1992: 65).

Although it is often difficult and time-consuming to involve a range of stakeholders in the planning process, this involvement may have significant benefits for sustainability. In particular, participation by multiple stakeholders with differing interests and perspectives might encourage more consideration of the varied social, cultural, environmental, economic and political issues affecting sustainable development (Bramwell & Lane, 1993). Timothy (1998) argues that participation in tourism planning by many stakeholders can help to promote sustainable development by increasing efficiency, equity and harmony. For example, broad stakeholder involvement has the potential to increase the self-reliance of the stakeholders and their awareness of the issues, facilitate more equitable trade-offs between stakeholders with competing interests, and promote decisions that enjoy a greater degree of 'consensus' and shared ownership (Warner, 1997).

Assessments can be made of the stakeholders who are affected by a tourism project and who might participate in collaborative tourism planning arrangements. The identification of these stakeholders can be of critical importance for technical, political and, eventually, operational reasons. Being identified, or conversely, not being identified, as a relevant stakeholder is an essential first step that affects the whole process of involving participants in collaborative planning as well as the likely outcomes of this planning.

The first section of this paper reviews several approaches to assessing stakeholders that have potential for application in tourism planning research and practice. Subsequently, the paper illustrates the potential value of two of these approaches based on a case study examining stakeholders affected by the Costa Dourada project, a regional tourism planning initiative involving ten municipalities in Alagoas State in north-east Brazil. The project focuses on tourism development, but in the context of investment in physical and social infrastructure and of sustainable development objectives.

The first approach to stakeholder assessment used in the case study involves examining the stakeholders who had participated in the project's planning process. Some of these stakeholders had been to one of several local workshops about the project and some had attended project meetings intended to promote a collaborative approach to planning. The second approach involves interviewing a sample of stakeholders affected by the project and also stakeholders directly involved in the project planning process, asking them for their views on stakeholders they considered relevant to the project but who were not participants in the planning process.

The purpose of the paper is to illustrate the value of the application of two approaches to stakeholder assessment to examine two specific aspects of sustainable development. First, to examine whether the stakeholders involved in planning for the Costa Dourada project were representative of the stakeholders affected by the project. And, second, to evaluate whether the range of stakeholders involved in the planning process was likely to encourage consideration of the diverse issues related to sustainable development. Was the range of participating stakeholders sufficiently broad that consideration was likely to be given to the varied concerns of sustainable development, which are social, cultural, environmental, economic and political, and relate to various geographical scales? The paper reports on just one aspect of a larger research programme on collaborative planning and the Costa Dourada project, and it is beyond the scope here to consider other questions about the ultimate effectiveness of stakeholder collaboration in the project planning process.

Collaborative Tourism Planning

Collaborative planning has been defined as a 'collective process for resolving conflicts and advancing shared visions involving a set of diverse stakeholders' (Gray, 1989). Jamal and Getz (1995: 188) describe collaborative planning in a tourism context as 'a process of joint decision-making among autonomous, key stakeholders ... to resolve planning problems ... and/or to manage issues related to the planning and development'. Collaborative planning in tourist destinations is usually considered to involve direct dialogue among the participating stakeholders, including the public sector planners, and this has the potential to lead to negotiation, shared decision-making and consensus-building about planning goals and actions (Bramwell & Sharman, 1999). Much collaborative planning is made in working groups with a fairly small number of individuals, who often are representatives of organisations or stakeholder groups (Brandon, 1993). The number of individuals participating on a working group may be restricted in order to ensure the group is not unwieldly, to promote familiarity, understanding and trust among participants, and to encourage joint decision-making and consensus-building.

However, participation in tourism planning in destinations can be limited to collecting the opinions of stakeholders in order to provide fuller information for public sector planners, and this can be a largely one-way consultation process when there is little direct dialogue between the stakeholders and planners. This can occur when the opinions of stakeholders are collected using self-completion questionnaires, focus group interviews, drop-in centres and telephone surveys (Marien & Pizam, 1997). It is likely to be less complex to collect people's opinions than to involve them in direct dialogue with public sector planners or to seek negotiation and consensus-building through collaborative planning. However, the one-way collection of stakeholder opinions (often of many individuals) can provide valuable information for decision-making in collaborative working groups (often involving only a few individuals) (Simmons, 1994; Yuksel *et al.*, 1999). Stakeholders can also be consulted at several stages in the planning process so that it becomes an iterative, two-way planning process.

Approaches to Stakeholder Assessment

What approaches can be taken to assessing the stakeholders who are affected by a tourism project and who might participate in collaborative tourism planning arrangements?

A *first* potential approach is to examine whether the stakeholders who become involved in collaborative planning arrangements for a project adequately represent the affected stakeholders (Boiko *et al.*, 1996). If the collaborating stakeholders are not representative, then some needs might not be articulated and related planning alternatives could be ignored, and stakeholders who are excluded might reject the resulting planning proposals (Gregory & Keeney, 1994). Finn (1996) also suggests that problems can arise if some stakeholders are excluded from the early stages of the collaboration process. For example, it risks having to begin all over again as members joining at a later stage insist on discussing and negotiating about their understanding of the issues and about their views on planning options (Bryson, 1988; Gray, 1989). Another consideration is whether the stakeholders involved in collaborative planning includes parties with significant financial, institutional or political power and whose involvement might significantly broaden the planning options which are feasible for the other stakeholders (Warner, 1997).

A *second* approach involves passing information from assessments of relevant stakeholders to the stakeholders involved in collaborative planning arrangements in order to improve their understanding of the interests and viewpoints of other stakeholders (Finn, 1996). The information from these assessments might also assist the stakeholders to identify strategies to secure specific management or political outcomes (Bryson & Roering, 1987). For example, such information could enable stakeholders to identify parties who are supportive, opposed or neutral to their collective interests. These stakeholders might then form coalitions among supportive stakeholders in order to enhance their power and also target neutral or 'swing' stakeholders with special lobbying (Bryson, 1988; Rowe *et al.*, 1994). Such political objectives may be very contentious.

A *third* potential approach is to identify stakeholders who are considered to have legitimate and important views but need to have their capacities raised to enable them to put these views forward and to negotiate in collaborative decision-making arrangements (Carroll, 1993). For example, they may lack technical knowledge about tourism planning or skills in presenting their views in meetings, and these might be developed through education and training. Warner (1997: 418) adopts a normative position that 'stakeholder targeting' is needed to create an equitable basis for collaborative negotiations, and that 'a "consensus" model of participation should direct early effort towards those stakeholders who are most polarized from a capability to negotiate collaboratively'.

The approaches mentioned so far can be developed further by a *fourth*: asking stakeholders affected by the tourism issue or project to identify other stakeholders who could be of interest to the researcher. Stakeholders can also be asked for their opinions on which stakeholders affected by a tourism project ought to be involved in its planning. Stakeholders' opinions can be collected using such methods as focus group discussions, interviews or questionnaires. The stakeholders who are identified by other stakeholders as relevant to a tourism project will reflect the value judgements of the stakeholders themselves (Mark & Shotland, 1985).

The snowball method is a useful means of identifying relevant stakeholders based on the views of other stakeholders. This method can involve identifying a core subset of actors who are affected by an issue or project and asking them to nominate other stakeholders they consider have relevant characteristics. These nominated stakeholders then can be asked to nominate others they consider have the characteristics, with the potential to repeat this process until few new stakeholders are identified (Finn, 1996; Rowley, 1997). The snowball method can be very useful at a local level. Political rather than personal knowledge may be particularly critical in the use of the snowball method at regional and national scales.

A *fifth* approach to assess relevant stakeholders is to place them on a diagram or map according to their key relationships to the issue. A network of arrows can then be used to show existing or likely relationships between the stakeholders, such as the involvement of some of them in collaborative planning arrangements. Patterns of particularly important relationships usually emerge, and these patterns can be portrayed on a revised map. The resulting stakeholder map, usually involving a complex array of multiple relationships, can be examined using social network analysis. The purpose of this analysis is to evaluate the relational networks between stakeholders, notably to determine interdependencies between stakeholders, how their positions in the network influence their opportunities, constraints and behaviours, and how their behaviours affect the network (Marin & Mayntz, 1991; Rowley, 1997).

Stakeholders affected by an issue or project can be positioned on a map according to many relationships (Harrison & St John, 1994). Only three of these relationships are discussed here, although these three can be particularly important.

The first such relationship is the power of different stakeholders affected by an issue to influence the relationships between them (Eden, 1996). Mitchell *et al.* (1997) suggest that the power of a stakeholder in such relationships is related to the extent to which it can impose its will through coercion, through access to material or financial resources, or through normative pressure. A second relationship is the perceived legitimacy of the claims of different stakeholders. Legitimacy relates to perceptions that the interests or claims of a stakeholder are appropriate or desirable, with these perceptions being based on socially constructed values and beliefs. It has been claimed in the context of ecotourism that 'legitimacy is socially produced in the communicative interaction among stakeholders' (Lawrence *et al.*, 1997: 309). The third relationship is that of the urgency of the claims of different stakeholders. According to Mitchell, Agle and Wood (1997: 867), this urgency arises from 'the degree to which stakeholder claims call for immediate attention'. Such claims for immediate attention will be affected by views on importance, which in turn are affected by the other attributes of power and legitimacy. These three relationships are likely to be significant influences on which stakeholder groups become involved in collaborative planning arrangements around an issue.

The utility of the *first* and *fourth* of the approaches discussed above is now illustrated in an examination of the stakeholders affected by the Costa Dourada project. The two approaches are used to assess whether the range of stakeholders participating in the project planning was representative of the stakeholders affected by the project, and also likely to promote consideration of the diverse issues surrounding sustainable development. These issues are social, cultural, environmental, economic and political, and may also relate to various geographical scales. While the Costa Dourada project is a regional tourism development initiative, the analysis also considers these issues at the local and national spatial scales. This geographical hierarchy may be particularly important because government power can be highly centralised in developing or relatively newly industrialised countries (Milne, 1998; Tosun & Jenkins, 1998).

The Costa Dourada Project

The Costa Dourada project is a regional tourism development initiative covering ten municipalities in Alagoas State, in north east Brazil (Figure 1). The project area extends for about 100 km along a coastal belt about 20 km across. The ten municipalities form an economically poor region of Brazil and have a combined population of 148,080. The region's key economic sector is agriculture, notably sugar cane plantations, and the region suffers from very high unemployment, low salaries and high rates of illiteracy and endemic disease. Despite poor road access to the region, tourism has gradually intensified from a fairly low base since the second half of the 1980s (SEPLANDES, 1998). The coast is now dotted with a number of tourist facilities, such as hotels, bars, restaurants and holiday homes (Medeiros de Araujo & Power, 1993).

The Costa Dourada project forms part of a larger Programme for Tourism Development of the State of Alagoas (PRODETUR/AL). The PRODETUR/AL runs from 1994 to 2010 and in the first phase it has US $300 million funding from the Interamerican Development Bank and federal, state, municipal and private

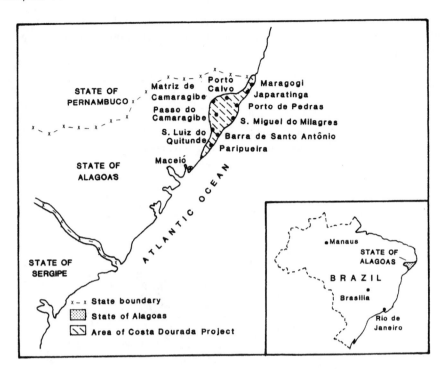

Figure 1 Location of the Costa Dourada Project

sector sources (Becker, 1995; PRODETUR, 1993; SEPLAN, 1994). This programme seeks to create the infrastructure required to exploit the tourism potential of Alagoas State, within the broader aim of 'encouraging the region's socioeconomic development, taking into account its environmental preservation and restoration' (SEPLAN, 1994: 3; CODEAL, 1993). In 1991 Alagoas State attracted 128,018 domestic and 19,127 international tourists, with the largest number of international tourists being from Argentina, Spain and Germany. In 1994 it was estimated that by 2002–2010 the PRODETUR/AL will have boosted the annual average number of domestic tourists to 265,000 and of international tourists to 172,000, compared with an annual average number without the project of 139,940 domestic tourists and 50,892 international tourists (SEPLAN, 1994). Tourism development in Alagoas will be focused on three development zones, including the Costa Dourada project on its north coast.

Key elements of the strategy for the Costa Dourada project are 'the expansion and improvement of its main product, namely "sun and beach" tourism', and also product diversification (SEPLAN, 1994: 9). The diversification includes developing visits to small, farm-based rum distilleries, ecotourism, and tourism based on raft and boat trips to the offshore coral reef. Among the tourism-related infrastructure to be built or improved in the project area are main access roads, roads within urban centres, telecommunications and electricity supplies. The project aims to address 'the serious problems of [transport] access to the north coast which, together with the deficiency in basic urban services, according to private investors, are the principal obstacles to the implementation of hotel projects in the region' (SEPLAN, 1994: 10). Investment in the project area will be concentrated in one major tourist centre, Camaragibe, and three smaller tourist centres in the municipalities of Paripueira, Porto de Pedras and Maragogi (Figure 2).

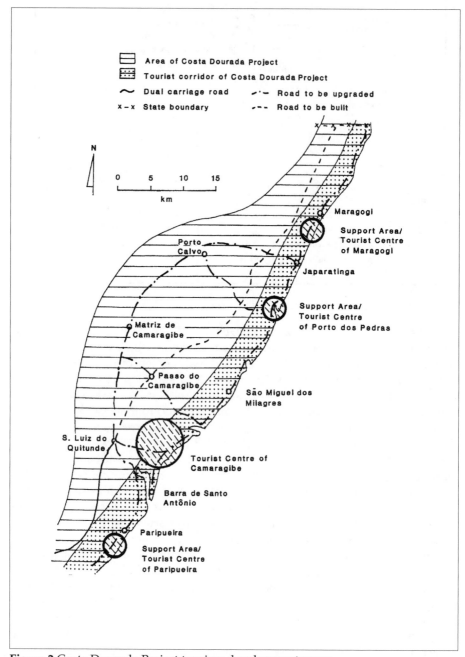

Figure 2 Costa Dourada Project tourism development areas

The Costa Dourada project uses tourism in order to promote sustainable development, and it includes investment in health care, education and social facilities, and improved access to the region. Alagoas is one of Brazil's poorest states and tourism has the potential to secure both economic and social development. In particular, it could diversify the north coast economy, which is highly dependent on sugar cane production and refining, coconut production and fishing. However, balanced growth may be illusive when there is 'economic and political control of the governmental administrative structures by a few economic groups, most of whom see conservation measures as potentially conflicting with their interests' (Medeiros de Araujo & Power, 1993: 302). Tourism development may add to environmental problems, such as urban sprawl and water pollution from untreated sewage.

One important intention of the PRODETUR/AL planners is to involve a broad range of stakeholders in the project planning process. This intention reflects a trend in Brazil towards encouraging broader participation in the shaping of public policies in various fields. Various collaborative arrangements between the government, private sector and NGOs have been established during the 1990s in north east Brazil, including in Alagoas State. A number of tourism partnerships have been developed recently in Alagoas, although collaboration is less common in this field than in education and health care (Gazeta de Alagoas 6/12/97, 6/9/99). However, the widening of participation has re-emerged only relatively recently in Brazil, with 20 years of military dictatorship only ending in the mid-1980s, during which time policy-making was highly concentrated within the national government. Because of the country's political history, there is only relatively limited recent experience of democratic structures and of broad stakeholder participation in planning (Vieira, 1995; Viola, 1987).

Stakeholder Attendance at Planning Meetings

The first approach to a stakeholder assessment of the Costa Dourada project involves examining the stakeholders who had participated in the project planning up to mid-1998. The project is scheduled to operate from 1994 to 2010. Two types of participation in the planning process are examined. The first is attendance by stakeholders at the project planning meetings organised by PRODETUR/AL that were intended to promote a collaborative approach to planning. An assessment is also made, secondly, of the stakeholders who had been to a workshop about the project in one of the municipalities.

The first of these types of participation was examined by identifying the stakeholder representatives who had often attended the project planning meetings. The number of stakeholder representatives invited to these meetings varied according to the issues being discussed and whether the meetings took place in the PRODETUR/AL offices, in a municipality or elsewhere. In these meetings PRODETUR/AL attempted to encourage collaborative planning involving discussion, negotiation and consensus-building among the participants. While there was direct dialogue in the meetings between the participants and the PRODETUR/AL planners, it is beyond the scope of the present paper to evaluate in depth the extent to which the meetings succeeded in promoting shared decision-making and consensus-building.

A preliminary list of participants who had often attended the meetings was compiled after discussion with two planners and others involved in the project and after evaluating planning documents and legislation. The Co-ordinator General of the Planning Unit for the project was then asked to indicate which of these participants, or others not on the list, were invited and often attended these meetings up to mid-1998, were accountable to their organisation, and exchanged information with the project planners. This process identified 29 stakeholder representatives who often attended these meetings.

Table 1 shows the stakeholder representatives who had often attended project planning meetings up to mid-1998, these being classified by stakeholder category and the geographical scale at which they had strongest interests. It shows that almost all the regular participants in these meetings were in the public sector. However, among these public sector organisations there is a broad spread across national, regional and local spatial scales and also between the policy areas of regional development, tourism, coastal management, transport, public utilities and environment. At the regional scale there is strong representation from the different policy areas of the Programme for Tourism Development of the State of Alagoas (PRODETUR/AL), and at the local scale there are representatives with environmental, health and tourism interests. The only organisations not wholly in the public sector are a public-private sector utility company, an NGO linking the local municipal authorities, and an environmental NGO.

Stakeholder Attendance at Workshops

The second type of participants in the planning process to be examined had attended one of the ten day-long workshops about the project organised by PRODETUR/AL, with a workshop held in each of the ten municipalities affected by the project. The workshops were designed to collect data and information, including stakeholder opinions on the project, and to identify actions to promote the development of institutions and infrastructure in the municipalities to support the project as a whole. Specific objectives for each workshop included designing a plan for public services in the municipality and identifying priority projects that need to be funded or coordinated by PRODETUR/AL (SEPLANDES, 1998).

Early in each workshop the participants were asked about their expectations and suggestions were sought on how the workshop should be conducted. A brainstorming discussion then followed, after which the participants wrote their own views on selected issues onto cards. These cards were posted on panels according to themes, these themes were then discussed and collective decisions were made to create, merge or discard some cards, and eventually various negotiated views were established. By these means the workshops were designed to promote discussion and consensus-building among the participants. However, they offered only very limited opportunities for direct dialogue between the participants and the PRODETUR/AL planners, with only one staff member and three consultants representing PRODETUR/AL attending each workshop. Instead, written summaries of the workshops were prepared to be considered subsequently by the project planners. At the same time, however, the workshops involved more than a one-way consultation process as they were used to dissem-

Table 1 Stakeholders that often attended planning meetings for the Costa Dourada Project

Geographical scale	Type of stakeholder	Stakeholder	Job title of representative
National	Government environment	Brazilian Institute for the Environment & Renewable Natural Resources (IBAMA)	Technical Director
	NGO environment	Foundation for Marine Mammals	National Director
	Government other	Service of the National Coastal Lands (DPU)	Architect
	Government other	Department for the Development of the North East (SUDENE)	Head of the Technical Department
	Private sector tourism	Brazilian Company of Airport Infrastructure (INFRAERO)	Superintendant for the State of Alagoas
Regional	Government environment	Institute for the Environment (IMA/AL)	Director of the Dept for Ecosystems
	Government environment	Coastal Management Project (GERCO/AL)	Co-ordinator for the State of Alagoas
	Government tourism	Tourist Board of the State of Alagoas (EMATUR)	Planning Co-ordinator
	Government infrastructure	Department of Roads of the State of Alagoas (DER/AL)	Assessor to Director General and President of DER/AL's Planning Unit for the Costa Dourada Project
	Government infrastructure	Water and Sewage Company of the State of Alagoas (CASAL)	Superintendant for Engineering
	Government tourism	Programme for Tourism Development of the State of Alagoas (UEE-PRODETUR/AL)	Co-ordinator for the Environment
			Co-ordinator for Administration and Finance
			Co-ordinator for Institutional Development
			Co-ordinator for Transport and Roads
			Assessor for Legislation
			Assessor for Project Development
			Assessor for Management of Partnerships and Marketing
			Co-ordinator General of the Planning Unit
	NGO other	Association of the Municipalities of the State of Alagoas (AMA)	President

Table 1 (cont.)

Geographical scale	Type of stakeholder	Stakeholder	Job title of representative
Local	Municipal government	Municip. of Barra de Santo Antônio	Secretary of Tourism
		Municip. of Japaratinga	Secretary of Health
		Municip. of Maragogi	Secretary of Tourism and Environment
		Municip. of Matriz de Camaragibe	Head of Mayor's Office
Local	Municipal government	Municip. of Paripueira	Secretary of Tourism and Environment
		Municip. of Passo do Camaragibe	Secretary of Tourism and Environment
		Municip. of Porto Calvo	Mayor
		Municip. of Porto de Pedras	Secretary of Administration
		Municip. of São Luiz do Quitunde	Secretary of Tourism
		Municip. of São Miguel dos Milagres	Secretary of Tourism and Environment

inate information and to promote coordinated local responses to the project planning. Another limitation of the workshops was that no more of them had been organised by mid-1998 to discuss more recent planning proposals.

Tables 2 and 3 analyse the workshop participants by municipality and by stakeholder category. The analysis excludes the PRODETUR/AL staff member and the three consultants.

Table 2 Stakeholders attending the workshop in each municipality

Municipality	Broad stakeholder category			Total stakeholders*	
	Alagoas State government	Municipal government	Other stakeholder	%	No.
Barra de Santo Antônio	4.6	63.6	31.8	100	22
Japaratinga	0	81.0	19.0	100	42
Maragogi	0	90.0	10.0	100	20
Matriz de Camaragibe	3.8	77.0	19.2	100	26
Paripueira	0	70.0	30.0	100	20
Passo de Camaragibe	3.6	53.6	42.8	100	28
Porto Calvo	0	87.5	12.5	100	16
Porto de Pedras	0	83.3	16.7	100	12
São Luiz do Quintunde	8.6	62.9	28.6	100	35
São Miguel dos Milagres	0	92.9	7.1	100	14

* Excludes a staff member and three consultants representing PRODETUR/AL at each workshop.

Table 3 Sectoral categories of stakeholders attending workshops in the municipalities

Broad stakeholder category*	%	Specific stakeholder category	%
Alagoas state government	2.6		
Municipal government	74.0		
		Tourism	3.0
		Public works and environmental services	2.6
		Culture and sport	1.7
		Education	20.9
		Health and social welfare	19.6
		Mayor and mayor's office	5.5
		Legislators	5.1
		Finance, legal and administration	14.0
		Other municipal government	1.6
Other stakeholders	23.4		
		Fishing	3.0
		Other business	5.1
		Rural workers	1.7
		Church and welfare organisations	4.7
		Residents' associations	3.0
		Other	5.9
Total percentage	100		
Number of stakeholders	235		

* Excludes a staff member and three consultants representing PRODETUR/AL at each workshop.

Arguably, Table 2 suggests that there was a reasonable attendance in each municipality affected by the project, with the smallest attendance being 12 in Porto de Pedras and the largest being 42 in Japaratinga. However, while it is notable that as many as 235 people participated in these workshops, this was still only a tiny fraction of the area's total population of 148,080. In addition, as many as 74% of participants were employed by municipal government, with these being in the majority in every workshop (varying from 53.6% of participants in Passo de Camaragibe municipality to 92.9% in São Miguel dos Milagres). Particularly large proportions were in local government education and social welfare sectors, suggesting either that these groups were much involved in local affairs or that the project was expected to produce improved educational and social provision. Participants outside the public sector included local representatives from the fishing and agricultural industries, the business community, church and welfare organisations, and residents' associations.

Interviews with Stakeholder Representatives

The research literature reviewed earlier suggests that stakeholders affected by a tourism project can be examined using the opinions expressed by the stakeholders themselves. The potential value of this approach is considered now for the Costa Dourada project. Its application here involves examining in interviews the opinions expressed by a sample of 38 representatives of stakeholder groups affected by the project and also by the 29 representatives of stakeholder groups who had often attended project planning meetings. The interviews are used to assess the views of these representatives about the range of stakeholders participating in the project planning process.

The sample of 38 stakeholder group representatives who were affected by the project was selected to cover a broad range of interests, including interests in the public, private and NGO or non-profit sectors, at national, regional and local geographical scales, and of small, medium and large organisations and businesses. Government representation was focused particularly on departments and organisations with statutory responsibilities for tourism planning, economic development and infrastructure development. There was also a strong representation of stakeholders from three municipalities in the project area where the first phase of tourism development is to be concentrated. The sample was also developed using the snowball method described previously. This involved asking a core of stakeholder representatives to nominate representatives of other stakeholder groups they considered were significantly affected by the project, and when several respondents mentioned a particular stakeholder group it was added to the sample. The methods used to identify the stakeholder representatives who had often attended the project planning meetings were explained previously.

The interviews with the total of 67 respondents were conducted during mid-1998 as part of a broad research programme on collaborative planning, with only selected questions focused on the specific themes of this paper. The interviews were semi-structured based on a detailed schedule of questions and conducted in Portuguese. Respondents were contacted in advance to arrange the interview and they were assured about confidentiality, although the opinions expressed may have been influenced by political sensitivities. Interviews normally took place at the place of work or home of the respondent and were tape-recorded. Ritchie and Spencer's (1994) 'framework' approach was used to analyse the interview transcripts, which involves the systematic steps of becoming familiar with the material, identifying a thematic framework, rearranging the data according to appropriate thematic references, identifying key characteristics of the data, and interpreting the overall findings.

Stakeholder opinions on differences between participants and non-participants

At the start of the interview each of the 67 respondents was shown a list of the 29 stakeholder representatives who had often attended project planning meetings, and these were described to respondents as the participants who were more directly involved in the project planning. They were then asked what they considered were the differences, if any, between these 29 participants and other

Table 4 Differences that respondents mentioned between participants and non-participants in the planning meetings

Differences	Mentioned by	
	Respondents who had often attended the planning meetings	Another respondent
Participants are mostly from government organisations or have a public mission	11	7
Non-participants are mostly from the private sector or have profit motives	12	5
Non-participants are mostly in non-governmental organisations	7	3
Participants are responsible for building infrastructure	0	7
Non-participants will invest later	0	4
Participants have technical knowledge	8	5
Non-participants lack technical knowledge	2	4
Participants have financial resources or power	4	7
Non-participants have less financial resources or power	3	3
Non-participants know the local areas better or will be affected more	5	6
Participants can take a broader or more objective view	4	0
Other distinguishing characteristic	10	21
Little difference between participants and non-participants	9	7
Total mentions	75	79

stakeholders affected by the project. Table 4 categorises the characteristics that respondents mentioned as distinguishing these two groups. To simplify explanation, the former group are identified here as 'participants' and the latter group as 'non-participants' – in fact, some 'non-participants' might occasionally have attended a project meeting. Some respondents identified several distinguishing characteristics, and there is a large 'other' category because of the diversity of responses. Responses for the 29 respondents who often attended planning meetings are shown separately from those for the other 38 respondents.

Table 4 shows that the distinguishing characteristics mentioned most often were that participants were mostly in government or had a public mission, and that non-participants were mostly in the private sector or had profit motives. Several respondents identified the non-participants as mostly in non-government organisations. Hence, many people made distinctions around the public sector being more directly involved in the planning process and the private sector not being involved in this way. A smaller number of respondents distinguished between participants and non-participants according to the former having technical knowledge, financial resources or power, and the latter lacking these attributes. Some respondents also suggested that non-participants knew the local areas better or would be more affected by the project, which suggests that they identified non-participants with interests that were focused in the municipalities.

Stakeholder opinions on the range of participants in the planning

In the interviews respondents were asked whether they considered all parties with an interest in the project were represented in the planning process. Table 5 shows that among the 29 respondents who had often attended a planning meeting, 65.5% considered that all relevant parties were represented in the project planning. By contrast, this was the opinion among only 31.6% of the 38 stakeholder representatives who were affected by the project but rarely or never attended a planning meeting. It is perhaps unsurprising that the former group considered all relevant parties were represented in the planning process, although even among this group almost a third identified other parties they considered should be represented. Some respondents who often attended planning meetings explained that the PRODETUR/AL planners had carefully selected the organisations to invite to the meetings. They had compiled an initial list of organisations, these organisations had then been invited to a meeting where they had discussed which other organisations to invite, and these other organisations were also invited to subsequent relevant meetings.

Several respondents who often attended planning meetings explained that there was scope to widen participation in later project stages. It was suggested that currently the project was focused on major infrastructure investment led by the public sector and in consequence it was premature to involve the private sector. There was a concern that the business sector would become impatient about the likely slow early pace of development if it was directly involved in planning activities from the early project stages. Some participants who often attended project meetings also suggested that additional parties could be involved once there was more evidence of physical development on the ground. A planner employed by PRODETUR/AL argued that there would be greater

Table 5 Whether respondents considered all parties with an interest in the project were represented in the planning process

Whether respondent had often attended planning meetings for the Costa Dourada Project	Whether the respondent considered all parties with an interest in the Costa Dourada Project were represented in the planning process				
	Number of respondents	Yes	No	Not sure	Total %
Had often attended planning meetings	29	65.5	34.5	0.0	100
Had not often attended planning meetings	38	31.6	60.5	7.9	100

private sector involvement during later project phases when 'we will have more financial conditions to implement the project more rapidly, to expand the scope of our actions. Nowadays our actions are limited. There is even under-utilisation of our consultants'. An airline representative who did not attend the planning meetings also suggested that airlines might become more involved in the planning when more infrastructure was in place.

A few respondents suggested that the private sector might not become involved even in the later stages of project planning. The representative of one municipality who often attended the planning meetings considered that, although commercial representation should be increased, 'They do not participate because most of them do not believe in these things [government projects] any longer ... They think that there is too much talking and too little in result'. Another representative of a municipality stated that 'They [the private sector] only work with the government when they see practical results. Normally, they don't turn up because they have been consulted various times before and nothing has been built to the present time'. A staff member of PRODETUR/AL explained in relation to the private sector that 'We have already tried to involve them but their participation was small ... what they really want is PRODETUR's resulting infrastructure'.

Later in interviews with respondents who had often attended the planning meetings they were asked for their opinions about why a wider range of parties with an interest in the project were not participating in the planning process. The most common response (six of the 29 respondents) was that some stakeholders had not participated despite having been invited to do so. Five respondents commented that it would be difficult to manage the project if more stakeholders were involved, with some noting that this applied in particular to the planning meetings. One stated that 'it would be very difficult to involve a broader number of organisations. It is already very complicated to work with the ones that had been involved so far'. The next most common response (four respondents) was that the range of parties involved is adequate for the current stage of the project and that others might be involved as necessary at a later stage. In addition, four respondents suggested that more parties might be involved if there was a stronger or more successful tradition of diverse stakeholders participating in planning activity. However, while some respondents mentioned shortcomings in the specific approach to the planning process taken by PRODETUR/AL, most suggested other explanations as to why the range of participants was not wider, such as disinterest among potential participants and the complexity of involving large numbers of people.

Stakeholder opinions on under-represented stakeholders

Respondents were also asked for their opinions about which stakeholders, if any, had not been represented in the Costa Dourada project planning but who ought to be represented. This question sought to identify the range of stakeholders that the stakeholders themselves perceived to be relevant to the project planning. The stakeholders so identified are presented in Table 6 according to whether they are in the private, public or other sectors, and in Table 7 in relation to whether their interests are focused at national, regional or local geographical

Table 6 Economic sector of stakeholders that respondents identified as under-represented in the planning process

Whether respondent had often attended planning meetings for the Costa Dourada Project	Stakeholders the respondents considered had not been represented in the planning process for the Costa Dourada Project but who ought to be represented				
	Number of mentions of such stake-holders	Percentage of mentions by economic sector			
		Private sector	Public sector	Other	Total %
Had often attended planning meetings (N = 29)	92	42.4	27.2	30.4	100
Had not often attended planning meetings (N = 38)	145	44.1	27.6	28.3	100

Table 7 The geographical scale of stakeholders that respondents identified as under-represented in the planning process

Whether respondent had often attended planning meetings for the Costa Dourada Project	Stakeholders the respondents considered had not been represented in the planning process for the Costa Dourada Project but who ought to be represented					
	Number of mentions of such stake-holders	Percentage of mentions by geographical scale				
		National	Regional	Local	Other	Total %
Had often attended planning meetings (N = 29)	92	10.9	31.5	31.5	26.1	100
Had not often attended planning meetings (N = 38)	145	4.8	45.5	29.7	20.0	100

scales. Both tables distinguish between the 29 respondents who had often attended planning meetings and the other 38 respondents.

Table 6 shows that private sector stakeholders were identified most often as under-represented in the project planning. This finding applies for respondents who had often attended planning meetings and also for those not involved in this way. Respondents gave numerous reasons as to why there should be greater private sector participation. The justification offered by one tourist accommodation owner was that 'Tourism is not made by the government. The government should provide the general direction. Tourism is made by the private sector'. A spokesperson for local hoteliers argued that the private sector should be involved to ensure that infrastructure developed by the public sector was appropriate for commercial hotel developers. He also contended that local hoteliers had prior experience of solving the infrastructure problems of water and sewage treatment and this experience would assist with the planning work. Another argument was that local tourist businesses should be more involved because skills and service levels in the sector need improving. A representative of an environmental NGO argued for greater private sector participation so there would be 'an integration of their interests with the interests of the communities affected by the project'.

Stakeholders in the 'other' category, which includes various NGOs and community organisations, were also frequently mentioned as under-represented in the project planning (Table 6). A PRODETUR/AL manager suggested that more NGOs should be involved because many existing participants see the project as bringing largely benefits, such as additional jobs, and NGO representatives may assist them to recognise and avoid negative impacts. Other respondents considered that greater NGO involvement would help to broaden the representation of social groups, capture additional resources, speed up actions, and improve the effectiveness of implementation.

Just over a quarter of the mentions of stakeholders being under-represented related to stakeholders in the public sector (Table 6). Some respondents argued for greater participation in the project by municipal legislators, known as 'vereadores'. An environmental group representative suggested that the municipal legislators often fought for local community interests, and if they were involved in the project then 'diverse types of interests can be negotiated through them'. It was argued by a representative of the 'vereadores' that municipal legislators ought to be involved in order to explain to local residents that the project will bring significant benefits only in the long-term.

In Table 7 the stakeholders considered by respondents to be under-represented in the planning process are presented according to whether their interests were focused at national, regional or local geographical scales. The 'other' category includes stakeholders for whom this geographical focus was unclear. Stakeholders with regional interests were most often identified as being under-represented, followed by stakeholders with local interests. Several respondents stressed the importance of involving local communities in the planning process. For example, a manager of tourist accommodation in Maragogi municipality asked: 'If Maragogi is going to benefit, who is Maragogi? It is its people … So they should participate in a direct way … If they live here, they know what affects them negatively and what benefits them'. A planner working for PRODETUR/AL argued that it is important to involve local people so that 'they grow with the project and they respect the project, and the project respects their culture'.

The respondents mentioned varied economic, environmental and social issues when explaining the stakeholders they considered under-represented in the project planning. For example, greater participation by fishing industry interests was advocated because fishing provides a livelihood for many people and brings substantial income to the area, and it may be affected by tourism development. Involvement by environmental groups was frequently justified in relation to specific environmental issues. Hence, one respondent wanted the Institute for the Preservation of the Atlantic Rainforest to participate in the planning as it could provide technical expertise about rainforest remnants in the region as well as an ecotourism coordinator to assist in balancing tourism and environmental concerns. A few interviewees called for navy involvement in the project to encourage off-shore reef patrols in order to reduce the volume of boats and related damage to the reef. Two respondents argued for greater participation in the project by representatives of agricultural workers so that these workers could be helped to overcome poverty by producing fruit and vegetables for the tourist industry.

Conclusions

The paper has reviewed approaches to assessing the stakeholders affected by a tourism project who might participate in collaborative tourism planning. It also sought to demonstrate the value of two of these approaches in an evaluation of stakeholders affected by the Costa Dourada project. These approaches were used in the case study to examine whether the range of stakeholders participating in the project planning was representative of the stakeholders affected by the project, thereby providing greater potential to meet the equity requirements of sustainable development. An inadequate involvement of the affected parties can heighten the potential for conflict and reinforce inequalities. Acceptance of, and support for a plan is often enhanced when those affected by it are included in designing it. Using the two approaches, an examination was also made of whether the range of stakeholder participation was likely to promote consideration being given to the diverse issues affecting sustainable development. According to Wahab and Pigram (1998: 283), sustainable tourism requires that 'the planning, development and operation of tourism should be cross-sectional and integrated, involving various government departments, public and private sector companies, community groups and experts, thus providing the widest possible safeguards for success'.

It could be argued that a relatively broad array of stakeholders was included in the project planning. Such a conclusion may be appropriate in the context of a country only emerging from a military dictatorship in the mid-1980s and only relatively recently experimenting with more inclusive or participatory approaches to planning. Indeed, some of the interview respondents noted that the Costa Dourada project was unusual in the degree to which it sought to involve diverse stakeholders in the planning process. PRODETUR/AL's use of planning meetings and workshops involved stakeholders with varied economic, cultural, social, environmental, and political interests. For example, the public sector representatives who often attended the planning meetings were involved in a broad spread of policy areas, such as regional development, transport, tourism, coastal management, and the environment.

Inputs were also encouraged from representatives of interests focused at different geographical scales, notably the state and municipal scales. For example, each municipality had a representative in the collaborative planning meetings and there was a workshop in each municipality. In regional-scale planning initiatives such as this project it is particularly important to involve stakeholders from different geographical levels of the policy hierarchy (local, regional, state and national) as well as the various interests at each of these levels of governance. The network of multiple players involved in planning for the Costa Dourada project had potential to provide the social and intellectual capital through which planning outcomes might be developed more for the common good than for narrow sectional interests (Innes, 1995; Ostrom, 1990). Similarly, it provided some possibility that varied issues of sustainable development would feature in deliberations about the direction of the project.

However, there were significant gaps in the representation in the project planning of the stakeholders affected by the project. In particular, the stakeholders who often attended the planning meetings were almost all in the public sector, and local public sector employees were in the majority in the workshops. There was also no direct commercial sector representation among those who often attended planning meetings. The interviews with stakeholder representatives show that many of them perceived there was very strong public sector involvement and relatively weak commercial sector involvement in the project planning. Some of those interviewed hoped that the private sector would become more involved once the public sector had led the way by developing the initial infrastructure.

The limited private sector participation in the project after four years of operation could reduce future support from the business sector for the project objectives of sustainable development. It might also hinder subsequent work to put planning initiatives into practice. For example, Inskeep (1994: 240) argues that with tourism development 'Public-private sector coordination is an essential ingredient in successful implementation'. The commercial sector might have been reluctant to participate because it involves time being lost that could be used to earn income or because of suspicions about strategic planning and committees. They might also have been reluctant because some government projects in Brazil have suffered from intense political competition, problems of control and accountability in the bureaucracy, scarcity of funding and other resources, and corruption (Morah, 1996). It should be noted that the business sector is a powerful influence on tourism development, and it would gain even greater influence with more involvement in the planning process.

There was also scope for greater participation in the project by environmental interests, notably by environmental NGOs. Both NGOs and community groups were mentioned as poorly represented by a number of stakeholders who were interviewed. While environmental concerns have become more prominent in Alagoas in recent years, some parties affected by the project still regard environmental conservation as a low priority because of pressures for rapid economic development. Medeiros de Araujo and Power (1993: 299–300) argue that 'This attitude is deeply rooted in the cultural heritage of Alagoas, where a kind of ruling class has been accustomed to imposing its point of view through the control of public opinion'. The interviews suggest that some people were largely concerned about economic development and new community amenities, with little mention being made of the long-term environmental impacts. Tosun and Jenkins (1998: 109) suggest that 'The struggle to overcome extreme conditions of poverty are the main source of many environmental problems in developing countries … some countries or regions have no choice but to opt to develop tourism for immediate economic benefits at the expense of sociocultural and environmental impacts'.

However, in practice the number of stakeholders involved in collaborative planning must be manageable and has to be limited in order to sustain a productive dialogue and increase the likelihood of building trust and consensus (Williams *et al.*, 1998). Involving large numbers of stakeholders can make satisfactory outcomes difficult to achieve, a point made in the interviews by some of the stakeholders affected by the Costa Dourada project. It was also suggested that some stakeholders were invited to attend and did not do so. But if legitimate stakeholders are excluded or ignored then the quality and degree of acceptance of the project plans will be questionable. In addition, it is very difficult to make definitive overall statements about whether the range of stakeholders involved in the planning process was representative of the stakeholders affected by a project. For example, how does one decide what is an appropriate balance between stakeholders with interests focused at national, regional and local geographical scales, particularly in the broader context of sustainable development? (Yuksel *et al.*, 1999). Similarly, what is an appropriate balance between stakeholders whose concerns are focused on economic and environmental issues?

Findings from this paper could be of assistance to planners involved in the Costa Dourada project. For example, the information about the under-representation of certain stakeholder groups could be used for 'stakeholder targeting' in order to broaden stakeholder representation in planning meetings. For instance, the findings of this study might encourage PRODETUR/AL to assess how the project might be affected subsequently by the limited involvement by the private sector and by environmental NGOs. The research showed that many stakeholders emphasised the economic impacts of tourism and its efficient use to create income, employment and infrastructure benefits for the region and communities. As the project is in a poor region of Brazil these priorities are perhaps unsurprising. However, these attitudes may change in the future as tourism develops in the region and the stakeholders recognise the disadvantages as well as advantages of tourism. If more environmental NGOs were to participate then the project might adopt a more cautious approach.

The case study was also intended to illustrate some aspects of stakeholder assessments that have potential value in the general field of tourism planning. Stakeholder assessments can assist planners to identify the interests, groups and individuals that are stakeholders in planning exercises, as well as their values, interests and relative power. The identification of the 'universe' of stakeholders is important for inclusive collaborative approaches to planning, such as the development of partnerships. Healey (1997: 271) also argues that such 'stakeholder analysis needs to be conducted in an explicit, dynamic and revisable way, as stakeholders may change over time in their concerns. Given the range of potential stakeholders, it is always possible that those involved in the strategy-making exercise will become aware of new stakeholders as they go along. Inclusionary strategy-making exercises need to be open to admit "new members" as work proceeds'.

Acknowledgements

The authors thank Bernard Lane and the three anonymous referees for their insightful and helpful comments on the paper, although of course the authors are responsible for their interpretation.

Correspondence

Any correspondence should be directed to Bill Bramwell, Centre for Tourism, Sheffield Hallam University, Pond Street, Sheffield, S1 1WB, UK (w.m.bramwell@shu.ac.uk).

References

Becker, B.K. (1995) *Study and Evaluation of the Federal Policy for Tourism and Its Impact on Coastal Regions (of Brazil)*. Brasilia, Brazil: Ministry of the Environment, Water Resources and of the Legal Amazon.

Boiko, P.E., Morrill, R.L., Flynn, J., Faustman, E.M., van Belle, G. and Omenn, G.S. (1996) Who holds the stakes? A case study of stakeholder identification at two nuclear weapons production sites. *Risk Analysis* 16 (2), 237–249.

Bramwell, B. and Lane, B. (1993) Sustainable tourism: An evolving global approach. *Journal of Sustainable Tourism* 1 (1), 1–5.

Bramwell, B. and Sharman, A. (1999) Collaboration in local tourism policymaking. *Annals of Tourism Research* 26 (2), 392–415.

Brandon, K. (1993) Basic steps toward encouraging local participation in nature tourism projects. In K. Lindberg and D.E. Hawkins (eds) *Ecotourism: A Guide for Planners and Managers* (pp. 134–151). North Bennington: The Ecotourism Society.

Bryson, J.M. (1988) *Strategic Planning for Public and Nonprofit Organizations. A Guide to Strengthening and Sustaining Organizational Achievement*. San Francisco: Jossey-Bass.

Bryson, J.M. and Crosby, B.C. (1992) *Leadership for the Common Good. Tackling Public Problems in a Shared-Power World*. San Francisco: Jossey-Bass.

Bryson, J.M. and Roering, W.D. (1987) Applying private-sector strategic planning in the public sector. *Journal of the American Planning Association* 53 (1), 9–22.

Caroll, A.B. (1993) *Business and Society: Ethics, and Stakeholder Management* (2nd edn). Cincinnati: South-Western.

CODEAL (Development Company for Alagoas) (1993) *Projeto Costa Dourada – 2a Etapa*. Maceió, Brazil: CODEAL.

Eden, C. (1996) The stakeholder/collaborator strategy workshop. In C. Huxham (ed.) *Creating Collaborative Advantage* (pp. 44–56). London: Sage.

Finn, C.B. (1996) Utilizing stakeholder strategies for positive collaborative outcomes. In C. Huxham (ed.) *Creating Collaborative Advantage* (pp. 152–164). London: Sage.

Gartner, W.C. (1996) *Tourism Development: Principles, Processes and Policies*. New York: Van Nostrand Reinhold.

Gazeta de Alagoas (6/12/97 and 6/9/99) Maceió, Alagoas.

Gray, B. (1989) *Collaborating. Finding Common Ground for Multi-Party Problems*. San Francisco: Jossey-Bass.

Gregory, R. and Keeney, R.L. (1994) Creating policy alternatives using stakeholder values. *Management Science* 40 (8), 1035–1048.

Harrison, J.S. and St John, C.H. (1994) *Strategic Management of Organizations and Stakeholders. Theory and Cases*. St Paul, USA: West Publishing Company.

Healey, P. (1997) *Collaborative Planning. Shaping Places in Fragmented Societies*. London: Macmillan.

Innes, J. (1995) Planning theory's emerging paradigm: communicative action and interactive practice. *Journal of Planning Education and Research* 14 (3), 183–90.

Inskeep, E. (1994) *National and Regional Tourism Planning. Methodologies and Case Studies*. London: Routledge.

Jamal, T.B. and Getz, D. (1995) Collaboration theory and community tourism planning. *Annals of Tourism Research* 22 (1), 186–204.

Lawrence, T.B., Wickins, D. and Phillips, N. (1997) Managing legitimacy in ecotourism. *Tourism Management* 18 (5), 307–316.

Marien, C. and Pizam, A. (1997) Implementing sustainable tourism development through citizen participation in the planning process. In S. Wahab and J. J. Pigram (eds) *Tourism, Development and Growth. The Challenge of Sustainability* (pp. 164–178). London: Routledge.

Marin, B. and Mayntz, R. (1991) Studying policy networks. In B. Marin and R. Mayntz (eds) *Policy Networks. Empirical Evidence and Theoretical Considerations* (pp. 11–23). Boulder, CO: Westview Press.

Mark, M.M. and Shotland, R.L. (1985) Stakeholder-based evaluation and value judgements. *Evaluation Review* 9 (5), 605–626.

Medeiros de Araujo, L. and Power, S. (1993) Nature conservation with reference to the State of Alagoas, Brazil. *The Environmentalist* 13 (4), 297–302.

Milne, S.S. (1998) Tourism and sustainable development: The global-local nexus. In C.M. Hall and A.A. Lew (eds) *Sustainable Tourism: A Geographical Perspective* (pp. 35–48). Harlow: Longman.

Mitchell, R.K., Agle, B.R. and Wood, D.J. (1997) Toward a theory of stakeholder identification and salience: Defining the principle of who and what really counts. *Academy of Management Review* 22 (4), 853–886.

Morah, E.U. (1996) Obstacles to optimal policy implementation in developing countries. *Third World Planning Review* 18 (1), 79–105.

Ostrom, E. (1990) *Governing the Commons: The Political Economy of Institutions and Decisions.* Cambridge: Cambridge University Press.

PRODETUR (Programme for Tourism Development) (1993) *Projeto PRODETUR.* Recife, Brazil: Department for the Development of the North East (SUDENE).

Ritchie, J. and Spencer, L. (1994) Qualitative data analysis for applied policy research. In A. Bryman and R.G. Burgess (eds) *Analyzing Qualitative Data* (pp. 173–194). Routledge: London.

Rowley, T.J. (1997) Moving beyond dyadic ties: A network theory of stakeholder influences. *Academy of Management Review* 22 (4), 887–910.

Rowe, A.J., Mason, R.O., Dickel, K.E., Mann, R.B. and Mockler, R.J. (1994) *Strategic Management. A Methodological Approach.* (4th edn). Reading, MA: Addison-Wesley.

SEPLAN (Secretaria de Planejamento do Estado de Alagoas) (1994) *Programa de Desenvolvimento Turístico do Estado de Alagoas – PRODETUR/AL: Estratégia e Plano de Ação.* Maceió, Brazil: SEPLAN.

SEPLANDES (Secretaria de Planejamento e Desenvolvimento do Estado de Alagoas) (1998) *Plano Estratégico dos Serviços Publicos Municipais: Município de Maragogi.* Maceió, Brazil: SEPLANDES.

Simmons, D.G. (1994) Community participation in tourism planning. *Tourism Management* 15 (2), 98–108.

Timothy, D.J. (1998) Cooperative tourism planning in a developing destination. *Journal of Sustainable Tourism* 6 (1), 52–68.

Tosun, C. and Jenkins, C.L. (1998) The evolution of tourism planning in third-world countries: A critique. *Progress in Tourism and Hospitality Research* 4, 101–114.

Vieira, P.F. (1995) Meio ambiente, desenvolvimento e planejamento. In E.J. Viola *et al.* (eds) *Meio Ambiente, Desenvolvimento e Cidadania: Desafios para as Ciências Sociais* (pp. 45–98). São Paulo: Cortez Editora.

Viola, E. (1987) O movimento ecológico no Brasil. In J.A. Pádua (ed.) *Ecologia e Política no Brasil* (pp. 63–109). Rio de Janeiro: IUPERJ.

Wahab, S. and Pigram, J.J. (1998) Tourism and sustainability. Policy considerations. In S. Wahab and J.J. Pigram (eds) *Tourism, Development and Growth. The Challenge of Sustainability* (pp. 277–290). London: Routledge.

Warner, M. (1997) 'Consensus' participation: An example for protected areas planning. *Public Administration and Development* 17 (4), 413–432.

Williams, P.W., Penrose, R.W. and Hawkes, S. (1998) Shared decision-making in tourism land use planning. *Annals of Tourism Research* 25 (4), 860–889.

Yuksel, F., Bramwell, B. and Yuksel, A. (1999) Stakeholder interviews and tourism planning at Pamukkale, Turkey. *Tourism Management* 20, 351–360.

15. Collaboration and Cultu⧸ Refocusing Sustainable

Mike Robinson
Centre for Travel & Tourism, University of Northumⁿ
Hall, Longhirst, Morpeth, Northumberland NE61

Largely reflecting the wider sustainable development debate, tnᵉ ⸗
able tourism has yet to significantly address the cultural basis that frameˢ ⸜
tives on the central environment–economy relationship. Explanations are offereᵤ ⸗
why the cultural dimension of sustainable tourism has been largely
under-emphasised. Collaboration, partnership and co-management with host communities and their cultures(s) has been an encouraging trend in the process of tourism
development over recent years though it displays, and is structured around, localised
inequalities and fundamental imbalances of power. The paper draws upon examples
of `indigenous tourism' to illustrate this. It argues that in the context of sustainable
tourism, the processes of collaboration need to be considered as part of the wider
sustainable development agenda that encourages cultural democracy as a legitimate
policy goal in itself. Through the recognition of cultural diversity and the allocation of
cultural rights, cultures should be in a stronger position not only to determine the form
and extent of tourism development, but also to say `no' to it altogether.

Introduction

Although the concept of sustainable tourism may lack precision, it is widely
accepted that it attempts to mirror the more extant framework of sustainable
development (Bramwell & Lane, 1993; Hunter, 1995; Pearce, 1995; Stabler, 1997;
Garrod & Fyall, 1998). But this too has a marked degree of contestability with
regard to its meaning, measurement and practical implementation (Lélé, 1991). It
is not the intention of this paper to enter into the lion's den of semantics which
characterise the concepts of sustainable development and sustainable tourism.
Slowly but surely, there appears to be a move away from seeking any definitive
articulation of the concepts to more pragmatic discussions regarding processes
of implementation (Fyall & Garrod, 1997).

The idea that the tourism industry, like any other sector of the economy,
should embrace the principles of sustainable development has gained currency
amongst an increasing number of businesses, regulatory bodies and governments. A central driving force behind the concept of sustainable tourism is the
concern for the destruction of the environment and thus the resource base upon
which the viability of the tourism industry depends. This, as Hunter (1995) has
pointed out, is a decidedly 'tourism-centric' approach. Though there may be
legitimate scepticism of this as a motivation for action it is no different to that
which drives the whole 'greening' of the business community (Schmidheiny,
1992).

But while we may applaud a move from principles to praxis, the down side is
that the discourse of sustainable tourism is neglecting the cultural dimension;
what Milton (1996: 64) refers to as 'an important component of
human-environment relations, perhaps the most important'. Broadly speaking,
the focus of the sustainable tourism debate has largely been upon improved

ent and regulation of the tourist/destination interface in order to ate environmental problems, better utilise natural resources, and ce the aesthetics and the overall resource context for tourists and host munities alike (Robinson & Towner, 1992). Sustainability in the tourism nse thus relates to the long-term functioning of the environment/ecosystem and to the long-term viability of business and the economy. This emphasis on management locates sustainable tourism close to the 'weak sustainability' position as identified by Turner (1992) which is defined more by managerial and market adjustments, self-regulation and the notion of the environment as substitutable capital, rather than significant intervention/regulation, major restructuring and the acceptance that the environment cannot be substituted. Thus, the thrust of 'sustainable' initiatives undertaken by the various sectors of the tourism industry, and generally endorsed by governments, chiefly relate to energy and resource efficiency gains within organisations, the refocusing of products to appeal to 'green' (high-spending) consumers and the promotion of tourist codes of practice. Such initiatives, though a welcome movement on a very steep learning curve, still fall short of the central themes of sustainable development. As Butler (1998: 28) suggests 'while some developments may have moved significantly towards sustainability, to claim that they are sustainable is clearly at best premature, and possibly completely inaccurate'.

Within this 'weak' framework, sustainable tourism has tended to overlook important, but sometimes opaque, cultural issues such as identity, belonging, spiritual meaning, and moral and legal rights. In this omission the sustainable tourism debate is failing to comprehend the cultural parameters of man–environment relationships (Bramwell *et al.*, 1996) and the fact that social justice and the central precept of cultural consent are also parts of sustainable development. At this point it is worth noting that considerations of culture in the context of sustainable development have tended to relate to indigenous communities as vulnerable, marginal and 'developing' peoples and this is borne out by the cases used in the literature. While this is understandable we should note that in every instance and locale of tourism's interface with the environment a cultural dimension is relevant to a greater or lesser degree.

This paper has three central and interrelated themes. First it reviews the discourse of sustainable tourism as being flawed along the axis of both morality and action by being slow to adequately integrate any meaningful analysis of culture and cultural relationships with an understanding of environmental issues. Second, it is argued that in attempting to address the cultural dimension of sustainable tourism, collaboration is not only a useful mechanism for problem solving, it is also a legitimate and important policy goal of sustainable development. And third, in recognition of a current lack of intragenerational equity and justice, collaboration is unlikely to be on equal terms, but it nevertheless requires the underpinning of cultural consent if it is to conform to the meaning and spirit of sustainable development.

The Centrality of Environment–Culture Relations

Tourism, as constituted by both tourists and the tourism 'industry', utilises, and to a varying extent is based upon, the natural environment and its resources.

Through the processes of both consumption and transformation, tourism in a collective sense produces varying degrees of environmental disturbance, degradation and natural resource needs which flow from resort, associated infrastructure development, day-to-day operations and tourist activity. But just as culture shapes the tourist gaze of the environment, layering upon it relatively recent values of the romantic, the exotic and the concept of the spectacular, so too does culture define the environments of host communities and help shape cultural identities.

It is well established that ideas of nature and the natural environment are culturally and humanly constructed, and exhibit, to use Parsons' (1977: 50) words 'intimate interdependencies' (see for instance Douglas, 1970; Vogel, 1988; Eder, 1996; Ellen, 1996; Milton, 1996; Urry & Macnaghten, 1998). It is the fact that tourism allows importation and exportation of different cultural constructs which is significant in the light of sustainable development as a global and globalising concept. The expansion of tourism as an ideology has been accompanied by a range of concomitant first world ideas including those which define and redefine environment/nature/culture relationships. The loss of closeness to nature and natural forms, the division of rurality from the urban, and the psychic narratives which we have developed to explain the environment in our 'developed' world culture, travel with us. Indeed, it is the search for glimpses of 'closeness' between nature and culture which is at the root of the expansion of alternative, eco and ethnic tourism; what we no longer have, or think we don't have, we seek elsewhere.

Though much attention has been given to the interconnectedness of environment and culture within non-Westernised contexts, almost as a defining quality of 'otherness', the relationships between environment and culture within a first world ideological frame do exist but as enlightened and apologetic expressions of consumerism. In Britain for instance, though we may have lost the primitive dimension of such relationships we nevertheless perpetuate the connections in the constructs of landscape, aesthetics, the rural idyll, and the ethos of preservation demonstrated by our myriad visits to the countryside (Lowenthal, 1991).

The lure of cultural difference, the attractiveness of encounters with the exotic and concentrations of the tourist gaze upon the cultural aspects of a destination are in themselves triggers for environmental disturbance and degradation. The environmental intrusions of the tourism industry, through development and volume of tourists, are frequently cultural intrusions, particularly in societies where there is an intimate relationship between the physical environment and cultural values. This is not restricted to indigenous peoples in the conventional sense. For instance, traffic congestion and its consequent pollution in, say, the English Lake District is not only an environmental problem; it is a direct challenge to those culturally defined meanings and the 'new' sacredness of the landscape which imbue tourist expectations.

Unfortunately, it appears that a majority of policy statements and actions relating to sustainable tourism are characterised as bi-polar, attempting to reconcile environmental/ecological concerns with the economic development process. Three reflections emerge. First, the environmental concerns of the tourism industry are highly selective, usually destination specific and indicative of a reactive, rather than a proactive, precautionary approach. Second, the driving forces for action chiefly emanate from the economic development extreme, which, in effect, remains committed to the economic growth paradigm – a point borne out by both advocated and objective forecasts relating to the growth of international tourism. Third, and most importantly in this context, through concentrating on attempts to integrate the two poles, sustainable tourism is neglecting the cultural context within which both operate and which provides a necessary depth to understanding fundamental people–environment relationships. Thus, what should be a dynamic, multi-dimensional and 'holistic' approach to tourism appears to have lapsed into a partial, parochial shadow of the worthy and challenging concept of sustainable development.

Sustainable Tourism Discourse: The Culture Gap

Though it may be legitimate to argue that sustainable development has under-emphasised the cultural dimension (World Commission on Culture and Development, 1995) or missed the culture mark entirely (Sachs, 1993), it nevertheless runs through the three most cogent, powerful and politically significant expressions of the concept over the last 20 years: the World Conservation Strategy (IUCN/WWF/UNEP, 1980), the 'Brundtland' Report (World Commission on Environment and Development (WCED), 1987), and the 1992 United Nations Conference on Environment and Development – the Rio 'Earth Summit' (United Nations, 1993). Not surprisingly, as global political statements they do not engage in detailed discussion of the relationships which exist between culture, cultures and the environment. However, the primacy of culture, and the explicit recognition of human rights, provides the spirit of sustainable development. For instance, WCED (1987: 116) argues that:

> Recognition of traditional rights must go hand and hand with measures to protect the local institutions that enforce responsibility in resource use … this recognition must also give local communities a decisive voice in the decisions about resource use in their area.

Similarly, Principle 22 of the Rio Declaration on Environment and Development states that:

> Indigenous people and their communities and other (my emphasis) local communities have a vital role in environmental management and development because of their knowledge and traditional practices. States should recognise and duly support their identity, culture and interests and enable their effective participation in the achievement of sustainable development. (United Nations, 1993: 7)

Though not wholly agreed upon within the environmental movement, sustainable development is decidedly anthropocentric in its aim to improve the quality of human life via the improvement and maintaining of the ecosystem (IUCN/WWF/UNEP, 1991). In other words, the conservation of the Earth's diversity and vitality is ultimately for *human* wellbeing allowing *our* development. Expressions of sustainable development and sustainable tourism as somehow being driven by a recognition of 'intrinsic' value of the environment fall into the realm of semantic twaddle. It is because of humanity and human–environment relationships that sustainable development has a strong (if not always explicit) cultural component. In addition, if we consider international tourism as having a formidable role as a vector of cultural exchange (UNESCO, 1997), why is it then that contemporary articulations of sustainable tourism give little attention to aspects of culture? We can broadly identify three reasons.

Culture is just another tradable commodity

In seeking, somewhat uncritically, to mirror the wider sustainable development paradigm, sustainable tourism discourse is showing a strong focus upon the physical environment (Cole, 1997) and how this resonates with economic wellbeing. Attempts to redirect conventional neo-classical economics and utilise market-based approaches to redress resource imbalances, regulate flows of natural capital stock and internalise externalities, have dominated discussions of sustainable development (Pearce *et al.*, 1989; Dietz & van der Straaten, 1992; Pearce, D.W., 1995). The progression of Pearce *et al.*'s (1989) view that sustainable development is a two-way interaction where 'economies affect environments – environments affect economies', has also been influential in shaping the sustainable tourism debate (Coccossis & Nijkamp, 1995; Stabler, 1997; Garrod & Fyall, 1998), encouraging the application of established methodologies of environmental economics to potential and actual cases of tourism's environmental impacts (see for instance: Dixon & Sherman, 1990; Swanson & Barbier, 1992; Bateman *et al.*, 1994).

While there is a role for such economic approaches in dealing with certain environmental issues, particularly at the planning stage prior to development, these are inadequate when dealing with the sociocultural dimension. Moreover, they fail to challenge the ways in which the international tourism industry considers culture. The tourism industry largely understands culture(s) in two ways: either as an inconsequential, and value-neutral, backdrop, or/and a product/commodity which can be packaged for the tourist. So tourism development in a first world context often takes place in a climate of apathy and acceptance. This assumption is carried into non-Westernised, developing societies where, despite having neither tradition or need of outwardly directed cultural exhibitionism, ethnic groups and practices are commodified. Indeed, indigenous societies *en masse* are often 'showcased' by developing nations for economic purposes (Walle, 1996). The exchange value of cultural and ethnic resources remains a potent argument for governments of both developing and developed nations seeking to develop tourism. In developing economies which have been stripped of their natural resource base, the only recourse may be to utilise a community's ethnocultural resources to stimulate the economy via tourism.

But though culture(s) and economy are clearly interrelated we cannot deal with culture in conventional economic terms. Attempting to do so, even allowing for an increased degree of sensitivity, endorses the view that living culture is 'just another commodity'; tradable, substitutable and separate from the natural environment. Indeed, it is the attempts to relate to cultures in terms of neo-classical economics and marketing theory that has caused problems and prevents us from recognising different ways of seeing the world, its resources, space and time (Hollinshead, 1996).

The cultural dimension is problematic to measure

In the search for a breakthrough in policy terms, sustainability 'indicators' are being developed by governments and various interest groups. These are designed to measure and monitor the goals set in relation to sustainable development and assist in understanding the change process. This approach conforms to conventional economic rationality and is self-defining, largely dealing with aspects of change that can be measured such as pollution levels, waste capacity, and energy usage. The indicators for sustainable development as adopted in the UK (Department of Environment, Transport and the Regions, 1997) do include tourism and leisure as components but measurement is strictly in terms of volume.

This approach is broadly echoed by the World Tourism Organisation which has developed 'core indicators of sustainable tourism', designed to aid the managers and decision makers in tourism development (Manning, 1996). The indicator for the social impact of tourism (there is no indicator for *cultural* impact) is based upon volume measures, i.e. what the ratio of tourists is to locals during peak periods of activity. While it is difficult to argue that this is generally a 'step in the right direction', the underlying assumptions are that tourism is value-neutral, that consensus exists and that tourism development is generally considered as a 'good thing'.

Craik (1995: 96) argues for the inclusion of a wider-ranging set of 'cultural indicators' of tourism impacts as part of the sustainable tourism agenda. As Craik herself acknowledges, more work is required to operationalise these indicators. A key issue for instance, is that cultural change, whether positive or negative, is frequently exhibited in the long, rather than the short, term and is therefore difficult to measure (Mowforth & Munt, 1998; Robinson, 1998a). What is important about the notion of cultural indicators is that the various stakeholders involved in tourism, particularly the local community, are *de facto*, in a better position than most to delineate what is culturally acceptable. However, as Craik (1995) points out, although processes of consultation to set the cultural parameters of tourism development are beginning to be adopted, particularly amongst indigenous communities, they are far from central to the sustainable debate in both developed and developing world contexts.

Culture is difficult to articulate in policy terms

In part reflecting the problems of measurement, the cultural dimension of sustainability is difficult to articulate in policy terms (Hodgson, 1997). As increasingly recognised by economists, politicians and the business community, sustainable development requires a policy framework which is both regulatory and market based. Tourism and its relationships with the environment, within a broadly liberal, first world policy context, is capable of being dealt with through limited intervention, self-regulation and market adjustments – effective management, differential pricing and in some cases restrictions on visitor access. However, such reductionist, managerial approaches do not challenge the dominant tourism ideology which sees the environment and culture as nothing more than manageable, tradable resources. As with a number of policy approaches to sustainable development, tourism policies emanate from the dominant social paradigm (Dunlap, 1983) and thus reflect first world values of materialism, consumerism, and scientific rationalism. They are also characterised by a paternalism and although able to shift resources, they are not equipped to deal with the transfer of power.

In recognising that the sustainable tourism debate has failed to make explicit the sociocultural component, Pearce (1995) argues that in the process of ecologically sustainable tourism development, emphasis should be placed upon 'cultural exchange' in order to avoid the states of 'culture shock' and 'cultural arrogance'. However, the suggested management mechanisms for improving cultural exchange would seem to illustrate an implicit paternalistic approach. These involve empowering visitors, training tourism professionals and *educating* host communities, all of which go some way to alleviate conflicts but are, nevertheless, based upon an unchallenged assumption that tourism is desirable, and problems can be solved ultimately for the benefit of the tourist.

While tourism policies have generally been successful in economic development terms they are largely inadequate to deal with issues relating to community values and the variance between value systems and traditions developed over centuries. Cultural identity, cultural democracy, and human rights within and across cultures remain areas which governments and the tourism industry have problems with. Policy goals of economic growth, and the protection of the environment are, in general, non-controversial and thus politically safe. If the cultural dimension of sustainable development is to be addressed in a meaningful manner then controversy is inevitable (World Commission on Culture and Development, 1995).

Cultural Sustainability for Tourism?

Though the processes of cultural change are normative involving some degree of evolutionary adaptation relative to the dynamic of social, economic and political change, the key issues relate to the rate of change, and the acceptability of the nature of the changes. Tourism is one of many cultural influences which can initiate dramatic and irreversible changes within the cultures of host communities (de Kadt, 1979; Smith, 1989).

From a sustainable development perspective the idea that we should respect cultures and cultural rights may be present, but the idea that we should *sustain* cultures is not fully developed, partly as a function of the reasons discussed above. Nor is there any clear indication of which cultures we are speaking of. The convention is that attention should be given to those cultures recognised as vulnerable, disempowered and under the threat of global homogenisation. The majority of the world's indigenous peoples are clearly included but then where do we draw the line, if we should draw one at all? Values, traditions and meanings provide for identity across all cultures and are reflected in the diversity of artefacts and achievements which are the very basis of tourism. Indeed, according to Mowforth and Munt (1998: 109) cultural sustainability 'refers to the ability of people or a people to retain or adapt elements of their culture which distinguish them from other people'. The notion of cultural sustainability as a positive response to the loss of identity (Arizpe, 1997) clearly challenges the negative acculturating impacts that tourism can bring, but it is only part of a much wider response to the excesses of globalisation.

However, the argument for the tourism industry seeking to minimise its environmental impacts whilst maximising the economic gains is openly expressed in functional and utilitarian terms. 'Killing the goose that lays the golden egg' is an oft used and telling epithet. Within the context of sustainable tourism one is also drawn to consider whether the notion of sustaining cultures is more about 'protection' and preservation, in the main for the benefits of the tourism industry. In this way sustainable tourism is a mere extension of the existing capitalist model of appropriation fuelled by consumption of whatever can be packaged. Cultural integrity, notions of identity and the goal of equity are thus subordinate to the uses culture(s) is put to by the tourist/tourism industry.

Reactions against rapid and uncontrolled tourism development also often hides a subtext of romantic élitism which suggests that environments should be preserved for the benefit of the tourist/tourism industry. In parallel with this, cultures and cultural traditions and rituals are cited as 'worthy' of protection and preservation for the benefit of tourism/ecotourism (Mowforth & Munt, 1998). Invariably this is a selective process which may concentrate policy and resources upon the more exotic and spectacular cultural elements in line with market demands. Hitchcock (1997), for instance, points to the dissatisfaction on behalf of some tourists to the Kalahari who thought the Bushman were not as 'traditional' as expected. Crystal (1989) and Adams (1990) provide further examples of cultures being selected to dovetail with the expectations of tourists. They both have highlighted the way in which the sacred funeral ceremonies of the Toraja people of Sulawesi, Indonesia have increasingly become directed to meet the needs of the tourists and in doing so they provoked community resentment. In 1987 this resulted in a number of Toraja communities temporarily refusing to accept tourists, but having to relent in order that they could sell tourist souvenirs upon which the community has become dependent. The idea of cultural and ethnic reconstruction is itself an attempt to sustain culture for openly commercial reasons. Unfortunately, in such cases social tensions are never far behind (see for instance Altman, 1989; Daltabuit & Pi-Sunyer, 1990; Goering, 1990).

We can, of course, be overly critical of the motivations for sustaining cultures. Tourism does have the capacity for enhancing cultural diversity and can respond to the vector of global homogenisation by encouraging what Robertson (1995) terms 'glocalisation' – the complementary heterogenising process of affirming and reaffirming local cultural identities in a global way. The key points, as we shall discuss, are those of consent and whether or not a culture will provide the tourist and the tourism industry with the necessary permission to be developed, represented and sold. Moreover, should that permission be forthcoming, does a particular culture receive its rightful reward for acceding the right to be gazed upon?

Collaboration as Mechanism for Sustainability

Following the leads given by WCED and UNEP collaboration/partnership is recognised as an essential and accepted mechanism in progress towards sustainable development. This acceptance is borne out by the burgeoning literature examining the nature and extent of collaborations between groups in seeking to address environmental and natural resource issues in various cultural contexts (see for instance Alcorn, 1993; Ghai, 1994; McNeely, 1995; Singh & Ham, 1995; Singh & Titi, 1995; Blunt & Warren, 1996; IUCN, 1997). Collaboration in this context broadly follows Getz and Jamal's (1994: 5) adaptation of Gray's (1989) definition as being:

> A process of joint decision making among autonomous and key stake-holders of an interorganisational domain to resolve problems of the domain and/or to manage issues related to the domain.

A similar interpretation is the idea of 'co-management strategies' (Berkes, 1995) which relate to power sharing between government and local communities in order to effectively manage resources.

In attempting to address the culture gap in sustainable tourism, collaboration is vital. It represents a way of giving meaning to environmental and economic imperatives by locating them in the various cultural contexts they have emerged from. However, the extent of collaboration in the quest for sustainable tourism remains decidedly narrow and almost an after-thought following environmental/economic considerations. Collaboration has tended to focus on greater community acceptance of tourism development by inviting greater involvement and representation of cultural groups. For developers and planners the consultative process itself becomes an achievement independent of the outcome and the ethics of a decision.

Getz and Jamal (1994) in their thoughtful analysis of the problems surrounding tourism planning in the Canmore community/Bow River Corridor, Alberta, Canada, highlight the need for community-based collaboration to achieve a 'model sustainable community' (p. 171). In this case tourism was recognised for the role it can play in driving the sustainable development process and thus the issues of collaboration relate to the 'how' of tourism rather than the 'why'. For while joint decision making is important in the management of tourism, tourism itself should not be seen as a *fait accompli*. Though an important form of economic development, tourism does carry associated costs and there may be other development choices which can be explored through collaboration.

At the level of rhetoric the ideas of 'co-management' and 'joint' decision making imply an ideal of equality which in reality seldom exists and is more likely to involve some form of dominant–subordinate relationship (Wall, 1996). A distinction needs to be made between active and passive stakeholders. As has been pointed out in studies of community involvement in tourism (Taylor, 1995; Getz &Jamal, 1994; Joppe, 1996; Wyllie, 1998), there are often schisms within apparently homogeneous groups centring upon differing levels of power and access to resources, which can be marked by differing cultural orientations. The impetus for tourism development and tourism inward investment frequently originates from outside, rather than inside a community. In such a case the community is drawn to a reaction which is governed by those who can speak loudest and with authority. Furthermore, to compound matters, there are seldom mechanisms in place to elicit a response based on consensus whether in a developing or developed world context.

A fundamental problem which shows itself with regard to collaboration for sustainability in tourism is that the inequalities between the interest groups involved are substantial. Even within apparently coherent stakeholder groups there exist imbalances relating to concentrations of 'elite capital' and power aspirations (Smith, 1996; Smith, 1997). In short, the expansion of tourism and its utilisation of the environment and culture as tradable commodities is largely initiated by powerful commercial concerns with the ability to set the direction and terms of reference of collaboration. Inequalities relating to access to resources and political power are inherent in tourism. Such inequalities manifest themselves most visibly in instances of cultural extremes; between developing and developed economies, urban and rural settings, indigenous and non-indigenous peoples, and between haves and have-nots.

Somewhat ironically, international tourism reflects the global economic imbalances, and the structural dependency of the developing nations upon the developed nations (Britton, 1982; Erisman, 1983; Crick, 1989). For as well as the flow of tourists being primarily from developed to developing nations, the location of ownership of tourism businesses is concentrated in the developed north, and subsequently, the flow of tourism receipts is largely in a south to north direction (Cazes, 1996).

Inequalities are exemplified in various ways. Bennett (1996) for example estimates that in 1995 Maori economic involvement in the whole of New Zealand's tourism industry amounted to less than 1%. Similarly, it is estimated that less than 1% of Canadian tourism businesses are owned or operated by indigenous peoples (Kent Stewart, 1993). And Whittaker (1997), in her account of the rapidity of tourism development in the Western Australian town of Broome with its sizeable Aboriginal community, points out the complexities of attempting to achieve 'growth by consensus', particularly when there exist fundamental imbalances of power between stakeholders.

It is this asymmetry of relations (Watson & Kopachevsky, 1994) between stakeholders, particularly those split between developed and developing nations relating to production, consumption, access to capital, credit and information, which provides the very *raison d'être* for the sustainable development concept. And yet, tourism would appear to accentuate, rather than ameliorate, these intra-generational inequities (Pleumarom, 1994).

Tourism development in/of indigenous societies demonstrates a more marked inequality between stakeholders relating to the cultural paradigms they operate in. More accurately, these are not inequalities as such, but differences of seeing the world, the role of human beings within it and differing priorities relating to the balance between social, economic and environmental goals. Sofield (1996), for instance, in his account of the development, and subsequent failure, of a resort complex on Anuha Island in the Solomon Islands by Australian developers, points to the constant tension which existed between two very different cultural paradigms. Similarly, Keelan (1996) in discussing the involvement of Maori in heritage tourism, points out that the issue for Maori tribes (*iwi*) is control rather than wealth. This highlights more than a desire to satiate Maori land claims; it points to an intrinsic and fundamental difference in the way Maori culture views the development and marketing activities of tourism, and the extent to which culture, nature and society are intertwined (Ryan, 1997).

Attempts to collaborate with indigenous communities and the promise of sustainable forms of tourism development are at least significant moves away from the indiscriminate, imperialistic forms of tourism of former years. But our notions of sustainability still fall short of those of indigenous cultures and although dialogue may take place it could well be meaningless. Laenui (1993) makes the point by illustrating indigenous Hawaiian perspectives on the environment as bound up with spiritual life where there can be no ownership, no domination and no superiority of man over nature. Laenui, after referring to the anthropocentrism of sustainable development embodied in the major international bodies promoting the concept comments, 'the attempt to relegate indigenous people's tactics and techniques of dealing with the environment to fulfil the objectives set forth in the conventional approach detailed, would surely be placing indigenous peoples in the wrong place' (p. 9). In the light of such fundamental 'mis-communication', the answer is not to attempt to make the two worldviews commensurable but to recognise and accept the diversity they represent, while empowering the indigenous culture to address sustainable development in its own way.

Interestingly, what has emerged in recent years are the makings of an inverse dependency whereby developed societies are looking towards developing and indigenous communities for guidance as to how to achieve sustainability. Many first world nations having signed up to the 1992 Rio Convention on Biodiversity and the Statement of Forest Principles (United Nations, 1993), recognise that most of the world's biodiversity is located in the developing nations of the South, and that indigenous peoples, the 'traditional knowledge' they hold and the genetic diversity they represent, are likely to provide the key to the sustainability of the planet. The discovery that the more peripheral and disadvantaged populations now hold valuable natural and intellectual resources within their cultures goes a little way to redress global inequities. At one level the preservationist dimension of the tourism industry can have a role to play in the protection and promotion of biodiversity through the protection and promotion of the cultures which own and manage it. At another level, without effective collaboration based upon consent, tourism will remain as a major catalyst in the erosion of cultural diversity.

Pathways to Cultural Consent

Collaboration, whether for more sustainable forms of tourism or as part of the broader agenda of sustainable development, thus implies a measure of intra-generational equity between stakeholders; a dimension of sustainable tourism recognisable by its absence (Williams & Shaw, 1998). There are examples whereby the redistribution and ownership of resources are being addressed in tourism. Zeppel (1998), for instance, reviews a number of examples across the world whereby indigenous peoples are beginning to move from being the providers of cultural experiences for tourists, to having an ownership and management role in tourism (see also Wall, 1998). This is scheduled to provide a more equitable distribution of the economic gains from locally orientated tourism enterprises. The Canadian National Aboriginal Tourism Association, for example, estimates that over 15,000 people are employed in approximately

2100 aboriginal tourism businesses which are worth some $250 million annually (Alberta Aboriginal Tourism Alliance, 1996).

Such examples are encouraging, though still few and far between, and are often precariously positioned against a cultural agenda shaped by dominant 'first world' value systems and exhibited by the international tourism industry. Collaboration is seldom constructed upon a level playing field in either cultural or economic terms. Indeed, the process of collaboration itself should act as a mechanism for achieving a better balance between partners. In the case of peripheral and indigenous communities (though not exclusively) the starting point may need to be an offer of atonement, reconciliation and recognition. Following the report of the Canadian Royal Commission on Aboriginal Peoples, Canada's Aboriginal Action Plan, 'Gathering Strength' (Ministry of Indian Affairs and Northern Development, 1998), provides an important lead here through its open and highly symbolic acknowledgement of, and apologies for, mistakes and injustices of the past. While yet to be tested the Statement of Reconciliation which opens the Plan and which has had various verbal airings by the Minister of Indian Affairs and Northern Development, represents a significant attempt to address both economic and cultural inequities between the Canadian Government and First Nations, Inuit, Métis and non-status Indians, by re-inventing the relationships between stakeholders. The key objectives of the Plan thus builds upon a 'fresh start'. In summary the main objectives are:

- The 'renewal' of meaningful partnerships with Aboriginal People;
- Strengthening Aboriginal Governance;
- Developing new fiscal relationships;
- Supporting strong communities, people and economies.

For indigenous peoples in Canada the Gathering Strength Plan gives political and policy substance to an approach which has been advocated by various international bodies. The IUCN for instance, has put forward the view that:

> The right to development for Indigenous Peoples includes (a) the right of access to resources on their territories, and (b) the right to seek development on their own terms. (IUCN, 1997: 83)

It is the allocation of cultural rights (as an extension of human rights) and subsequent respect for, and protection of, those rights which underpins sustainable development and should underpin the notion of sustainable tourism. Armed with land, resource and intellectual property rights, communities and cultures can not only influence the direction and pace of tourism developments, they can provide or withhold consent for tourism development *a priori*. In the tourism context, consent acts at a number of interdependent levels. It relates to ownership of the tourism object or objects, in legal and moral terms. It refers to the right to determine one's past, present and future. It also relates to a *willingness* to transfer this ownership to others based upon internal consensus, which may not mean unanimity (Carew-Reid *et al.*, 1994), but is representative of differing values. It is about assenting 'permission to gaze' to the tourist, and granting permission to 'other' stakeholders to enter into collaboration for developments commensurate with agreed cultural and community goals. It is about self-determination, capacity building and the move towards self-reliance. All of these features are not only means to an end; in sustainable development terms they are ends in themselves. The allocation and protection of rights and the promotion of 'cultural democracy' (World Commission on Culture and Development, 1995: 240), backed up by the transfer of natural, financial and intellectual resources, provides the basis for biodiversity and the health of the ecosystem. But they also provide the basis for the interconnected cultural dimension of sustainability which ultimately is concerned with the quality of human life.

Several reflections emerge. First, the tourism industry, and the governments and organisations which empower it, cannot, and arguably would not, engage in the dramatic structural and intellectual reshuffling which would put consent at the centre of the collaborative process. Locked into the self-regulatory approach to sustainability, the tourism industry can go some way to providing appropriate mechanisms for the transference of resources across cultures. Clearly, it can, through the economic development process contribute to wider environmental and cultural goals; it can encourage local community participation in the management of tourism resources; and, it can aim to include non-traditional decision-makers in the development process. The problem is that it does these things in a way that is both tourism- and ethno-centric.

Second, though much of the discussion relating to rights and cultural consent is centred upon indigenous peoples, the issues carry across to all cultures and communities. As the author has argued elsewhere (Robinson, 1998b), inequalities of power between stakeholder groups are equally apparent in a developed world context where tourism development can be thrust upon marginalised cultural groups without their consent. In such cases the right to say no may be implicit but the apparatus to obtain consent may be absent or not even considered an option. The notion of sustainable tourism in the first world faces similar sociocultural by-passes as is experienced in the third world. As Johnston (1989: 188) suggests:

> Citizens are weak when confronted with the power of the neo-corporatist state, and lack of information necessary to counter that power; and pluralism is predicated upon compromise, but the fear of scarcity encourages confrontation and in such circumstances only the powerful are satisfied.

So, whilst recognising the more substantive issue of cultural and economic asymmetry at the global scale, sustainability also needs to deal with local imbalances.

Third, in accepting the importance of cultural consent within the sustainable development framework, a pervasive and fundamental dilemma is invoked. Throughout the development of environmentalism as a first world ideology, and the subsequent evolution of sustainable development as a process for carrying this forward in global terms, a central paradox remains. How do we balance the goals of environmental quality, biodiversity and the maintenance of a healthy ecosystem with culturally determined rights and access to the benefits of economic development which have (and still are) denied to large number of the world's ethnic and cultural groups? The mechanics of moving from paternalistic dependency to postnationalist self-determination remains one of the grey areas of sustainable development.

As discussed earlier, in the case of some indigenous societies, the relationships between the environment, economy and society are so deeply interwoven that the well-being of the environment would seem assured provided there is no disturbance from 'outside'. The problem is there is usually disturbance from outside. Bennett (1992), for instance, cites a typical example of an environment/culture dilemma where the Inuit have hunted the Bowhead whale for some 3500 years for subsistence and cultural and religious reasons. And yet, because of the well-meaning world moratorium on whaling, Inuit culture is being challenged.

In ironic counterpoint to 'otherness', tourism represents 'outsiderness', a phenomenon which can disturb internal balance. One is tempted to take an eco-fascist perspective by denying the 'rights' of tourists in order to safeguard environments and cultures. The problem with this position is that not only does it deny the regenerative dimension of tourism in environmental and cultural terms; importantly it may be confining certain ethnic and cultural populations to poverty. Moreover, it is denying the rights of cultural groups to decide what *they* want. As Butcher (1997: 29) asks: 'But what is really so wrong in aspiring to own a camera and wear fashionable clothes?' The 'risk' in putting cultural consent into the sustainable tourism equation is that it may produce outcomes which do not conform to the sustainability criteria and the environmental standards developed nations expect. As Stansfield (1996) indicates, the expression of economic sovereignty on US Indian reservations has resulted in developments which seek a quick fix to the deep-rooted problems facing First Nations. Stansfield provides the example of the vast Foxwoods High Stakes Bingo and Casino complex, established in East Connecticut and providing the Mashantucket Pequot tribe with some 8400 jobs. The development is a far cry from cosy, small scale ecotourism exemplars; its eco-friendliness is debatable and its long term economic sustainability is also in question, but it would seem to be a product of consent and genuine aspiration.

Though unlikely, one of the implications of a sustainable tourism constructed around the idea of cultural consent is that tourism may be rejected outright. More likely is that via more equitable collaborations, the nature, extent and type of tourism development can be wrought to suit cultural needs. As Hitchcock (1997) illustrates in his examination of tourism's impacts upon the Kalahari Bushmen and their desire for self-determination with greater control over their natural and social environments, the important feature for many groups is the possession of rights, not necessarily the exercise of them in any automatic sense.

Conclusion: Refocusing Sustainable Tourism

Despite its nebulousness sustainable development presents humanity with an important and challenging framework for future global wellbeing. International tourism and its predicted growth is not immune from this challenge. Indeed, because of the way tourism commodifies and utilises environment and culture, its pervasiveness, and its power to influence global environmental and sociocultural change, arguably, it needs to be guided by the sustainable development paradigm more than any other sector of industrial activity. In this context attempts to create more sustainable forms of tourism are worthy.

However, moves towards sustainable tourism continually reveal a myriad of seemingly intractable issues surrounding basic tensions between economy and environment, and the developed and developing world. Such tensions amplify the need to consider tourism within the dynamics of major restructuring, the redistribution of rights and resources, and the recognition of a cultural dimension to sustainability. Indeed, we can view sustainable development as essentially a cultural construct borne of an uneasy mixture of first world angst, guilt, and a desire for the preservation of the 'quality of life'. By framing sustainable tourism between the two opposing poles of economic development and environmental quality we are following a traditional pattern of environmentalist debate and failing to penetrate the deeper and more meaningful value-systems upon which both depend. This is not to say that we should be neglecting the continued refinement of economic instruments in order to effect sustainability in tourism. There is a role for such approaches. But we should be looking for ways of handling the more intangible, and non-substitutable, cultural dimensions of sustainable tourism.

In effect this means engaging in dialogue and cultural exploration to reveal the 'unity in difference' which is at the root of both tourism and sustainable development. As well as exploring cultural diversity, tourists and the tourism industry need to understand, recognise and respect this diversity. Increasingly it seems that in attempting to progress the sustainable tourism ideal we should be focusing upon our own cultural parameters as well as those of visited destinations.

Collaboration and partnership are important elements of sustainable tourism, both as a mechanism for achieving sustainable outcomes and as symbolic of new ways of working. They represent a way of bridging cultural disparities and different paradigms. But we should be seeing them as something more than convenient (and frequently one-way) business-oriented relationships and we need to recognise that they too are culturally constructed with certain mores dominating the direction and nature of development. It may well be in some cases that the prerequisite of partnership is reconciliation and reinstatement leading to a stable and equitable baseline of agreement. In considering the present patterns of tourism flows and ownership of the tourism industry one cannot help but be pessimistic as to how such a basis could come about without a real leap of faith, or some hard-line policy lead from governments.

Building on a foundation of equity, gaining the consent of cultural groups and granting them the right to define a tourism which meets cultural, as well as economic and environmental needs, would be a highly significant development. In some cases the right to say no to tourism will be exercised. In other cases, the development outcomes may not fit with the sustainability ideal. Inevitably the dilemmas will remain. But at least, consent will have been gained and the sustainable development concept may begin to be 'owned' by a much wider cultural constituency.

Correspondence

Any correspondence should be directed to Dr Mike Robinson, Centre for Travel & Tourism, University of Northumbria at Newcastle, Longhirst Hall, Longhirst, Morpeth, Northumberland NE61 3LL, UK (mike.robinson@unn.ac.uk).

References

Adams, K.M. (1990) Cultural commoditization in Tana Toraja, Indonesia. *Cultural Survival Quarterly* 14 (1), 31–34.

Alberta Aboriginal Tourism Alliance (1996) Natives claim government and indifference hurdles to Aboriginal tourism. *Alberta Aboriginal Tourism Alliance News Report.* Calgary, 17 November.

Alcorn, J.B, (1993) Indigenous peoples and conservation. *Conservation Biology* 7 (2), 424–426.

Altman, J.C. (1989) Tourism dilemmas for Aboriginal Australians. *Annals of Tourism Research* 16, 456–476.

Arizpe, L. (1997) On cultural and social sustainability. *Development* 40 (1) Special Edition, Forty Years in Development – The Search for Social Justice, 110–117.

Bateman, I., Willis, K.G., and Garrod, G. (1994) *Consistency Between Contingent Valuation Estimates: A Comparison of Two Studies of UK National Parks* Regional Studies 28, 457–474.

Bennett, G. (1992) *Dilemmas – Coping with Environmental Problems.* London: Earthscan Ltd.

Bennett, R. (1996) *Maori Tourism Seminar; Working Papers.* Aotearoa Maori Tourism Federation.

Berkes, M. (1995) Community-based management and co-management as tools for empowerment. In N. Singh and V. Titi (eds.) *Empowerment: Towards Sustainable Development* (pp. 149–161). Halifax, NS: Fernwood Publishing.

Blunt, P., Warren, M.D. (eds) (1996) *Indigenous Organisations and Development.* London: Intermediate Technology Publications.

Bramwell, B., and Lane, B. (1993) Sustainable tourism: An evolving global approach. *Journal of Sustainable Tourism* 1 (1), 1–5.

Bramwell, B., Henry, I., Jackson, G., Prat, A.G., Richards, G., van der Straaten, J. (eds) (1996) *Sustainable Tourism Management: Principles and Practice.* Tilburg: Tilburg University Press.

Britton, S. (1982) The political economy in the third world. *Annals of Tourism Research* 9, 331–329.

Butcher, J. (1997) Sustainable development or development? In M.J. Stabler (ed.) *Tourism and Sustainability* (pp. 27–38). Wallingford: CAB International.

Butler, R. (1998) Sustainable tourism – looking backwards in order to progress? In C.M. Hall and A.A. Lew (eds) *Sustainable Tourism: A Geographical Perspective* (pp. 25–34). London: Longman.

Carew-Reid, J., Prescott-Allen, R., Bass, S. and Dalal-Clayton, B. (1994) *Strategies for National Sustainable Development – A Handbook for their Planning and Implementation.* London: UUCN/IIED/Earthscan.

Cazes, G.H. (1996) The growth of tourism in the developing countries. In *SCO/AIEST Proceedings of Round Table, Culture, Tourism, Development: Critical Issues for the XXIst Century* (pp. 15–18). Paris: NESCO/AIEST.

Coccossis, H. and Nijkamp, P. (eds) (1995) *Sustainable Tourism Development.* Aldershot: Avebury.

Cole, S. (1997) Anthropologists, local communities and sustainable tourism development. In M.J. Stabler (ed.) *Tourism and Sustainability* (pp. 219–230). Wallingford: CAB International.

Craik, J. (1995) Are there cultural limits to tourism? *Journal of Sustainable Tourism* 3 (2), 87–98.

Crick, M. (1989) Representations of international tourism in the social sciences. *Annual Review of Anthropology* 18, 307–344.

Crystal, E. (1989) Tourism in Toraja (Sulawesi, Indonesia). In V.L. Smith (ed.) *Hosts and Guests: The Anthropology of Tourism* (2nd edn) (pp. 139–168). Philadelphia: University of Pennsylvania Press.

Daltabuit, M. and Pi-Sunyer, O. (1990) Tourism development in Quintana roo, Mexico. *Cultural Survival Quarterly* 14 (1), 9–13.

de Kadt, E. (1979) Arts, crafts, and cultural manifestations. In E. de Kadt (ed.) *Tourism: Passport to Development?* (pp. 68–76). London: Oxford University Press.

Department of Environment, Transport and the Regions (1997) *Indicators of Sustainability for the UK*. London: Department of Environment, Transport and the Regions.

Dietz, F.J., van der Straaten, J. (1992) Sustainable development and the necessary integration of ecological insights into economic theory. In F.J. Dietz, U.E. Simonis and J. van der Straaten (eds) *Sustainability and Environmental Policy – Restraints and Advances* (pp. 21–54). Berlin: Edition Sigma.

Dixon, J.A. and Sherman, P.B. (1990) *Economics of Protected Areas – A New Look at Benefits and Costs*. London: Earthscan Publications Ltd.

Douglas, M. (1970) *Implicit Meanings*. London: Routledge and Kegan Paul.

Dunlap, R. (1983) Commitment to the dominant social paradigm and concern for environmental quality: An empirical examination. *Social Science Quarterly* 65, 1013–1028.

Eder, K. (1996) *The Social Construction of Nature – A Sociology of Ecological Enlightenment*. London: Sage Publications.

Ellen, R. (1996) Introduction. In R. Ellen and K. Fukui (eds) *Redefining Nature – Ecology, Culture and Domestication*. Oxford: Berg.

Erisman, M.H. (1983) Tourism and cultural dependency in the West Indies. *Annals of Tourism Research* 10, 337–361.

Fyall, A. and Garrod, B. (1997) Sustainable tourism: Towards a methodology for implementing the concept. In M.J. Stabler (ed.) *Tourism and Sustainability* (pp. 51–68). Wallingford: CAB International.

Garrod, B. and Fyall, A. (1998) Beyond the rhetoric of sustainable tourism? *Tourism Management* 19 (3), (199–212).

Getz, D., Jamal, T.B. (1994) The environment–community symbiosis: A case for collaborative tourism planning. *Journal of Sustainable Tourism* 2 (3), 152–173.

Ghai, D. (ed.) (1994) *Development and Environment: Sustaining People and Nature*. Oxford: Blackwell.

Goering, P.G. (1990) The response to tourism in Ladakh. *Cultural Survival Quarterly* 14 (1), 20–25.

Gray, B. (1989) *Collaborating: Finding Common Ground for Multiparty Problems*. San Francisco: Jossey-Bass.

Hitchcock, R.K. (1997) Cultural, economic, and environmental impacts of tourism among Kalahari bushmen. In E. Chambers (ed.) *Tourism and Culture – An Applied Perspective* (pp. 93–128). Albany: State University of New York Press.

Hodgson, G. (1997) Economic, environmental policy and the transcendence of utilitarianism. In J. Foster (ed.) *Valuing Nature? Economics, Ethics and Environment* (pp. 48–63). London: Routledge.

Hollinshead, K. (1996) Marketing and metaphysical realism: The disidentifications of Aboriginal life and traditions through tourism. In R. Butler and T. Hinch (eds) *Tourism and Indigenous Peoples* (pp. 309–348). London: Routledge.

Hunter, C.J. (1995) On the need to re-conceptualise sustainable tourism development. *Journal of Sustainable Tourism* 3 (3), 155–165.

IUCN/WWF/UNEP (1980) *World Conservation Strategy: Living Resource Conservation for Sustainable Development*. Gland, Switzerland: IUCN/WWF/UNEP.

IUCN/WWF/UNEP (1991) *Caring for the Earth. A Strategy for Sustainable Living*. Gland, Switzerland: IUCN/WWF/UNEP.

IUCN (1997) *Indigenous Peoples and Sustainability – Cases and Actions, IUCN and Inter-Commission Task Force on Indigenous Peoples*. London: International Books.

Johnston, R.J. (1989) *Environmental Problems: Nature, Economy and State*. London: Belhaven Press.

Joppe, M. (1996) Sustainable tourism development revisited. *Tourism Management* 17 (7), 475–479.

Keelan, N. (1996) Moari heritage: Visitor management and interpretation. In C.M. Hall and S. McArthur (eds) *Heritage Management in Australia and New Zealand: The Human Dimension* (pp. 195–201). Melbourne: Oxford University Press.

Kent Stewart, J. (1993) Traditional ecological knowledge. In *Travel and Tourism Research Association, 24th Annual Conference Proceedings, Expanding Responsibilities: A Blueprint for the Travel Industry* (pp. 252–257). Whistler, British Columbia, June 13–16, Travel and Tourism Research Association.

Laenui, P. (1993) An introduction to some Hawaiian perspectives on the environment. Paper presented to Conference on Indigenous Peoples and their Relationship to the Environment, California State University, Sacramento, October.

Lele, S. (1991) Sustainable development: A critical review. *World Development* 19 (6), 607–621.

Lowenthal, D. (1991) British national identity and the English landscape. *Rural History* 2, 205–230.

McNeely, J.A. (ed.) (1995) *Expanding Partnerships in Conservation*. Washington, DC: IUCN, The World Conservation Union.

Manning, E.W. (1996) Carrying capacity and environmental indicators: What tourism managers need to know. *WTO News* 2 (May/June), 9–12. World Tourism Organization, Madrid.

Milton, K. (1996) *Environmentalism and Cultural Theory – Explaining the Role of Anthropology in Environmental Discourse*. London: Routledge.

Ministry of Indian Affairs and Northern Development (1998) *Gathering Strength: Canada's Aboriginal Action Plan*. Ottawa, Canada: Ministry of Indian Affairs and Northern Development.

Mowforth, M. and Munt, I. (1998) *Tourism and Sustainability – New Tourism in the Third World*. London: Routledge.

Parsons, H.L. (1977) *Marx and Engels on Ecology*. London: Greenwood.

Pearce, D.W. (1995) *Blueprint 4 – Capturing Global Environmental Value*. London: Earthscan.

Pearce, D.W., Markandya, A. and Barbier, E.B. (1989) *Blueprint for a Green Economy*. London: Earthscan.

Pearce, P.L. (1995) From culture shock and culture arrogance to culture exchange: Ideas towards sustainable socio-cultural tourism. *Journal of Sustainable Tourism* 3 (3), 143–154.

Pleumarom, A. (1994) The political economy of tourism. *Ecologist* 24 (4), 142–147.

Robertson, R. (1995) Glocalization: Time–space and homogeneity–heterogeneity. In M. Featherstone, S. Lash and R. Robertson (eds) *Global Modernities* (pp. 25–44). London: Sage.

Robinson, M. (1998a) Cultural conflicts in tourism: Inevitability and inequality. In M. Robinson and P. Boniface (eds) *Tourism and Cultural Conflicts* (pp. 1–32). Wallingford: CAB International.

Robinson, M. (1998b) Tourism development in de-industrializing centres of the UK: Change, culture and conflict. In M. Robinson and P. Boniface (eds) *Tourism and Cultural Conflicts* (pp. 128–160). Wallingford: CAB International.

Robinson, M. and Towner, J. (1992) *Beyond Beauty – Towards a Sustainable Tourism*. Centre for Travel and Tourism Occasional Paper. Sunderland: Business Education Publishers.

Ryan, C. (1997) Maori and tourism: A relationship of history, constitutions and rites. *Journal of Sustainable Tourism* 5 (4), 257–278.

Sachs, W. (ed.) (1993) *Global Ecology: A New Arena of Political Conflict*. London: Zed Books.

Schmidheiny, S. (1992) *Changing Course – A Global Business Perspective on Development and the Environment*. Cambridge, MA: The MIT Press.

Singh, N. and Ham, L. (eds) (1995) *Community-based Resources Management and Sustainable Livelihoods: The Grass-roots of Sustainable Development*. Winnipeg, MB: International Institute of Sustainable Development.

Singh, N. and Titi, V. (eds) (1995) *Empowerment: Towards Sustainable Development*. Halifax, NS: Fernwood Publishing.

Smith, V.L. (1996) Indigenous tourism: The four Hs. In R. Butler and T. Hinch (eds) *Tourism and Indigenous Peoples*. (pp. 283–307). London: Routledge.

Smith, V.L. (ed.) (1989) *Hosts and Guests: The Anthropology of Tourism*. (2nd edn). Philadelphia: The University of Pennsylvania Press.

Smith, M.E. (1997) Hegemony and elite capital: The tools of tourism. In E. Chambers (ed.) *Tourism and Culture – An Applied Perspective* (pp. 199–214). Albany: State University of New York Press.

Sofield, T.H.B. (1996) Anuha Island resort: A case study of failure. In R. Butler and T. Hinch (eds) *Tourism and Indigenous Peoples* (pp. 176–202). London: Routledge.

Stabler, M.J. (ed.) (1997) An overview of the sustainable tourism debate and the scope and content of the book. In M.J. Stabler (ed.) *Tourism and Sustainability* (pp. 1–21). Wallingford: CAB International.

Stansfield, C. (1996) Reservations and gambling: Native Americans and the diffusion of legalized gaming. In R. Butler and T. Hinch (eds) *Tourism and Indigenous Peoples* (pp. 129–147). London: Routledge.

Swanson, T.M. and Barbier, E.B. (eds) (1992) *Economics for the Wilds – Wildlife, Wildlands, Diversity and Development*. London: Earthscan.

Taylor, G. (1995) The community approach: Does it work? *Tourism Management* 16 (7), 487–489.

Turner, R.K. (1992) *Speculations of Weak and Strong Sustainability*. CSERGE Working Paper, GEC 92–96. Norwich and London: CSERGE.

United Nations (1993) *Report of the United Conference on Environment and Development, Rio de Janeiro, 3–14 June, 1992* (Vol. 1). New York: United Nations.

UNESCO (1997) *Culture, Tourism, Development: Crucial Issues for the XXIst Century*. Paris: UNESCO.

Urry, J. and Macnaghten, P. (1998) *Contested Natures*. London: Sage Publications.

Vogel, S. (1988) Marx and alienation from nature. *Social Theory and Practice* 14 (3), 367–388.

Wall, G. (1996) Towards the involvement of indigenous peoples in the management of heritage sites. In M. Robinson, N. Evans, and P. Callaghan (eds) *Tourism and Cultural Change, Conference Proceedings, Tourism and Culture: Towards the 21st Century* (pp. 311–320). Northumberland: Centre for Travel & Tourism, Northumberland.

Wall, G. (1998) Partnerships involving indigenous peoples in the management of heritage sites. In M. Robinson and P. Boniface (eds) *Tourism and Cultural Conflicts* (pp. 269–286). Wallingford: CAB International.

Walle, A.H. (1996) Habits of thought and cultural tourism. *Annals of Tourism Research* 23, 874–890.

Watson, G.L. and Kopachevsky, J.P. (1994) Interpretations of tourism as commodity. *Annals of Tourism Research* 21, 643–660.

Whittaker, E. (1997) The town that debates tourism: Community and tourism in Broome, Australia. In E. Chambers (ed.) *Tourism and Culture – An Applied Perspective* (pp. 13–30). Albany: State University of New York Press.

Williams, A. and Shaw, G. (1998) *Tourism and the Environment: Sustainability and Economic Restructuring*. In C.M. Hall and A.A. Lew (eds) *Sustainable Tourism: A Geographical Perspective* (pp. 49–59). London: Longman.

World Commission on Environment and Development (1987) *Our Common Future*. Oxford: Oxford University Press.

World Commission on Culture and Development (1995) *Our Creative Diversity. Report of the World Commission on Culture and Development*. Paris: UNESCO Publishing.

Wyllie, R.W. (1998) Not in our backyard: Opposition to tourism development in a Hawaiian community. *Tourism Recreation Research* 23 (1), 55–64.

Zeppel, H.D. (1998) Land and Culture: Sustainable Tourism and Indigenous Peoples. In C.M. Hall, A.A. Lew (eds) *Sustainable Tourism: A Geographical Perspective* (pp. 60–74). London: Longman.

16. An Evolutionary Interpretation of the Role of Collaborative Partnerships in Sustainable Tourism

Pascal Tremblay
Faculty of Business, Northern Territory University, Darwin, NT 0909, Australia

This paper develops a theoretical rationale for the role of organisational networks and partnerships in sustainable tourism. It borrows from the evolutionary approach to social sciences to argue that inter-organisational relationships play a critical role in the process of organisational learning about the environment. This idea can be extended to the coordinating and learning needs of various stakeholders in tourism destinations or communities. The paper first reviews and criticises both the conventional market failures and the comprehensive planning approaches to dealing with environmental externalities. It is argued that tourism constitutes a complex and rapidly changing system in which participants are partially ignorant of the impacts of their actions. There is then an examination of the role of organisational and stakeholders networks in providing the basis for learning about their environment and about diverging values and beliefs. Partnerships can play a dual role in maintaining some coherence between participants' beliefs whilst being open to innovation. This is particularly important in tourism as community interest groups must constantly experiment to discover institutional arrangements to satisfy local tourism and community needs. This argument provides an alternative perspective to policy which does not rely on *laissez-faire* and yet recognises the value of destination- or community-specific solutions.

Tourism and Environmental Sustainability

In the last few decades, interesting developments in evolutionary theory have affected a number of social sciences including economics. Their general relevance for the study of complex industrial systems such as that of tourism where innovative capabilities are critical in the determination of competitive advantage has been discussed elsewhere (Tremblay, 1997, 1998). This paper argues that evolutionary thinking also can shed some light on difficulties associated with the joint concepts of tourism and environmental sustainability, as well as the capacity of alternative institutional forms such as networks to tackle tourism-related externalities. The evolutionary approach to social sciences stems from heterogenous sources but a convergent body of ideas has arisen which provides a useful framework for contrasting alternative coordinating arrangements for stakeholders connected with tourism.

The present paper aims at providing a theoretical framework capable of explaining both (1) the increasingly common claim that stakeholder alliances and partnerships play an important role in the economic coordination of tourism and (2) that they could be critical in the management of social and environmental externalities which give rise to allegations that it brings unsustainable development. Rather than proceeding by elaborating a detailed representation of the tourism system as a highly volatile system and tourism products as incompletely specified commodities preventing the smooth working of simple market transactions, this section will first address tourism in the context of environmental sustainability. It will briefly summarise the evolution of arguments supporting the view that traditional approaches to policy have been ineffective in dealing with tourism-related external effects on communities and their environments. The difficulties of existing theoretical approaches to policy will serve as a platform to advance the evolutionary perspective in the following sections.

The fundamental problem of tourism external impacts has traditionally been approached by economists as a typical case of market failure. The recognition of the public good characteristics of many tourism-related common social and natural assets and their tendency to be over-exploited led to reactions ranging from careful optimism warning against aggravating the 'goose laying the golden egg' to scenarios of self-destruction (due to free-riding over environmental resources in the case of Mishan (1967) or due to fickle tourism motivations in the case of Walter, 1982). Prescriptions usually belonged to two basic categories. First, the Pigouvian approach makes the government (or a related bureaucratic institution) responsible for introducing quantity restrictions or price distortions in theory capable of correcting behaviour. The former usually rests on specific regulations to control the behaviour of consumers or producers while the second takes the form of taxes or charges. The alternative Coasian approach relies on the establishment of property rights in an effort to show that as long as measurement and transaction costs would be reasonably low, it would be simpler to further develop required ownership institutions and allow the market mechanism to fulfil its role. In both cases, an omniscient bureaucrat would be able to proceed with the required calculations and circumvent the failure of the market. The appeal of the market failure approach to policy lies in its assumed simplicity. The use made by pro- and anti-tourism lobbying groups of the concept of market failures to either promote or condemn tourism developments testifies to its malleability (Tremblay, 1993b).

In the specific context of the connection between tourism-related commercial activities and their impacts on the natural and cultural environments, a number of issues throw some doubts on the ability of both types of mechanisms to resolve emerging resource-related conflicts (Tremblay, 1993a). Of the many difficulties with Pigouvian and Coasian solutions described summarily below, many are well documented in the recent literature on tourism impacts (Burns, 1989; Forsyth *et al.*, 1995). But they are rarely presented as fundamental problems of lack of knowledge. This interpretation is critical insofar as it clashes with the basic assumptions on which the market failure approach to policy rests. Also, a significant theoretical justification for network-based institutions must build on the realisation that conventional approaches rest on misconceptions of critical knowledge-related quandaries which they present as mere informational asymmetries.

In contrast, the evolutionary approach contends that tourism policy and planning models must deal with situations of overwhelming ignorance in which agents (tourists, businesses, communities, planners and other stakeholders) consider carefully the experiments and measurement processes which are needed to decide on the best course of action. These actions are recognised as possibly irreversible, highly uncertain and costly. Major sources of ignorance causing difficulties in the framing of policy connected with tourism externalities are discussed in Tremblay (1997) and stem in general from lack of knowledge in the following areas:

- the ability to predict tourism demand (Aislabie, 1992; Tremblay, 1997);
- the nature, link and importance of tourism technology and its impacts on various types of environments; this is due in large part to the speed and radical nature of much tourism developments as well as the multifaceted, complex and often cumulative external impacts which need to be considered (Burns, 1989). This supports a view of tourism as a chaotic and complex system in which positive feedback effects can trigger highly unpredictable results (Faulkner & Russell, 1997);
- the nature of community preferences regarding tourism development; problems with respect to the choice of spatial boundaries and lack of techniques allowing for the valuation of environmental assets considerations of irreversibility and the potential for learning about impacts and changing preferences (see Garrod & Fyall, 1998);
- the identification of a target group such as an industry or stakeholders which can be clearly connected with the incidence of externalities; which explains that charges are often levied on tourists which can be fairly arbitrary (Forsyth & Pigram, 1995; Kavallinis *et al.*, 1994).

Some of the above claims can be found scattered in the tourism literature, but usually not approached as categories of knowledge failures. Yet they together reflect our pervasive ignorance of tourism technology as a whole. In particular they should confront analysts, policy-makers and participants in the tourism system with the critical role played by partial ignorance with respect to the technical links between various forms and phases of tourism development and the degradation (and sometimes enhancement) of natural or socio-cultural resources. This ignorance extends to the actual and future valuation of the resources on which tourism actually builds its attractiveness and the conceptual difficulty to connect industrial actors with precise impacts and measure them. It also casts some doubt on the ability of tourism self-regulation or of bureaucratic planning even to start to address issues of resources deterioration and redress the situation (National Ecotourism Strategy, 1994: 29).

In the face of major difficulties regarding our ability to conceptualise and manage tourism technology, it is not surprising that individuals and groups call for new and broader concepts or perspectives on the contributions and costs of tourism development. A legitimate basis for an alternative assessment lies in the application of the concept of 'sustainability' to the tourism context. Sustainability generally refers to the preservation of the ability to consume or use (for productive purposes) a stock of common resources in the future (WCED, 1987). The concept incorporates the two fundamental notions that tourism development and exploitation rests in large part on common resources often quite remotely connected with the tourism industry and that tourist consumers and producers can damage or even deplete these assets valuable to both the resident community and themselves.

Sustainability has usually been associated with suggestions that it might be possible for communities to undertake planning activities for the sake of sorting out complex external effects (Gunn, 1988; Inskeep, 1991). This planning view of sustainability is itself highly simplistic and problematic on similar grounds but has constituted a main contender to the market failures approach in the context of tourism (Tremblay, 1993a). A number of criticisms of the abstract planning approach can be provided. As conventional planning constitutes an extreme form of direct intervention based on an assumed sufficient understanding of how tourism and the resources on which it depends unfold, it attracts similar difficulties with respect to the knowledge requirements that tourism system participants and planners are believed to hold (Haywood & Walsh, 1996):

- there are major problems regarding the definition and implementation of the concept of sustainability itself. The identification of the resources which must be considered is far from a trivial exercise when the fluidity of inter-connections between environmental, social and economic sustainability and the diversity of definition and categorisations is recognised (Khan, 1995). Moreover, the notion of a constant stock of natural and cultural capital can lead to philosophical disagreements if it is recognised that the latter are never fixed and constant, even when human interference is eliminated (Pearce *et al.*, 1989). In particular, the potential for various resources stock to be traded off against each other means more or less flexible definitions of constant resources will be associated with community groups attempting to favour or hinder the commercial development of tourism (Garrod & Fyall, 1998). The issue of the determination of a balance between natural and man-made resources can be argued to constitute an intellectual dead-end, a fact supported by the ability of both pro-development and pro-preservation interests to appropriate the concept of planning and interpret it for their own purposes (McKercher, 1993: 132). From a more practical viewpoint, there is a need to validate and document the notion of a relationship between (1) the presence of tourism and the deterioration of common capital and (2) the deterioration of that capital and the following decrease in tourism or foreign exchange receipts (Sinclair, 1992: 75);
- there are intrinsic difficulties with the operationalisation of sustainability for the sake of planning, in particular in measuring a stock of common resources connected directly with tourism development and alternative uses (Garrod & Fyall, 1998);
- the acquisition of information about the evaluation of impacts (at a point in time) is prone to rapid obsolescence due to the intrinsic endogeneity of community values (Jamal & Getz, 1996; Wall, 1996);

Knowledge difficulties with the implementation of tourism plans have started to surface in the tourism literature. Choy (1991) has argued that large-scale tourism planning attempts had been recuperated and used by developers because their lack of theoretical and empirical foundations prevented most stakeholders from taking them seriously. Choy's argument for a return to market failure approaches is symptomatic of the realisation that planning failures not only match market failures in terms of the extent and complexity of knowledge requirements but also that they seriously constrain the elaboration of innovative institutional or technological solutions and their implementation.

This forces tourism analysts to consider the question of how it is possible to propose a different approach to policy which places the focus on the fundamental knowledge limitations regarding the evolution of complex systems and their connections with incompletely specified natural and collective tourism assets. Furthermore it begs researchers to adopt a more normative definition of sustainability based on unpredictable community perceptions and valuations of those assets rather than assuming the ability to identify objective technical and economic connections.

An Evolutionary Interpretation of Sustainability

Taking into consideration weaknesses with past policy approaches, this section argues that the broad evolutionary paradigm applied to the study of organisations in the social sciences (with arguments and examples mainly stemming from the behavioural, institutional and evolutionary economics literatures) is a good candidate for an alternative viewpoint. Evolutionary thinking features agents or system participants (or groups) whose coordination requires that they adapt, consciously or not, to environments whose future shape and attributes they cannot predict. In particular it seeks to identify sources of novelty and of continuity and attempts to explain the processes of transformation accompanying unpredictable changes in environmental conditions. This constitutes a particularly valuable theoretical framework as it showcases inter-organisational networks and partnerships as an alternative coordination mechanism to conventional market failures or planning approaches when participants from various socioeconomic contexts are recognised as 'partially ignorant'.

Novelty and diversity of structures and behaviours do not constitute theoretical anomalies nor are they undesirable features in evolutionary models (Foss, 1994). Rather, they play important roles in the processes by which organisations and institutions adapt to changing circumstances. The mechanisms that generate such novelty and select the structural and behavioural forms for survival feature centrally in evolutionary thinking. The survival capabilities of various organisational systems are analysed in terms of the ability of such systems to learn about their environment and adapt. This suggests a view of sustainability articulated around the maintenance and development of the learning potential of an organisational system. Rents from productive activities are not generated solely from the exploitation of (and reinvestment in) given natural and cultural resources. They also arise from their transformation and the ability to mutate and revise the evaluation of these resources. In other words, sustainability depends on the ability to learn rather than the maintenance of an arbitrary and fixed stock of assets.

Learning in the context of sustainable tourism development and of the management of common resources is clearly multi-faceted. It involves a deliberate effort to explore the various paths which tourism development can take. It implies a certain level of experimentation with respect to the consequences of various types of tourism activities on the nature, quality and social valuation of various common resources. It needs to be accompanied by an awareness of the irreversibility of certain development paths. Such experimentation does not equate with 'chaotic' tourism development but rather supports an exploration of alternative approaches to managing the 'tourism-environment' connection. Participants in the tourism system face genuine uncertainty in the sense that they cannot comprehend, envision or predict the structure of the whole relevant sociotechnological environment as the result of any given action. But because they do recognise that uncertainty and participate endogenously in its formation, the system is best represented as one of organic interactions where some degree of structuring can temporarily take place (Khalil, 1992). Local or regional communities investing in such learning capabilities are expected to demonstrate superior survival qualities if they can achieve a balanced level of protection for long-term core natural assets without stifling local innovative potential.

Sustainability is redefined to consider the ability to maintain learning competences compatible with the level of complexity found in a given environment. Desirable organisational forms and institutions emerge when there is sufficient agreement on the nature of the problems to be tackled and sufficient divergence regarding the possible solutions. This cannot be achieved by plans to systematically preserve resources nor by blind reliance on spontaneous market forces.

Early work on the adaptability of learning socioeconomic systems point at a critical tradeoff between the need to maintain coherence and that of sustaining innovativeness (Loasby, 1976). Coherence refers to a sufficient level of agreement on core objectives, principles or beliefs. This would not be such an issue if community aspirations were homogeneous, easily defined and measurable. In systems involving diverse viewpoints and a high potential for conflicts, a minimum amount of attitudinal or ideological convergence is required to maintain organisational stability and sustain efficient and equitable use of resources. The control of fragile and common resources requires a level of cooperation which itself involves sufficient adherence to a common set of objectives, beliefs and constructs. Institutions must be designed which allow the sharing, negotiation and evolution of these common visions regarding the control of public assets and connected productive activities. Yet, their design needs to incorporate elements specific to the community concerned. It must attempt to define agreed-upon visions of acceptable development and resource utilisation without frustrating innovation or relying on given recipes. This further redefines sustainability as the ability to provide a community-specific learning approach striking a balance between coherence (convergence of visions) and flexibility (ability to either adapt, generate new ideas and follow them through) capable of transforming itself as circumstances change. The next section provides a theoretical rationale for organisational collaboration which supports the role of networks and partnerships as alternative learning institutions.

Inter-organisational Networks as Learning Capital

Evolutionary theorising has paid a great deal of attention to institutional structures capable of delivering various types of learning appropriate to different environments. These theories typically differentiate between incremental learning needed in periods of environmental stability and radical learning usually called upon to deal with environmental volatility (Loasby, 1976, 1991; Langlois & Robertson, 1995). This categorisation of learning modes allows us not only to connect learning strategy types with diverse environmental contexts, but also to establish that a sustainable organisational structure must be able to adjust with changes in environmental conditions. The main thrust of the argument in the previous section was that a sustainable system needs to cope and ensure continuity in relatively stable environments as well as incorporating mechanisms supporting adaptability and flexibility when technological considerations and values evolve rapidly. The former type of environment calls for coordination mechanisms capable of fostering converging views or visions in which socioeconomic progress is enhanced by increased coherence in the specification of developmental objectives (which applies to complex systems such as bureaucracies or communities) or strategies (which applies to profit-maximising firms). Volatile environments on the other hand call for a large diversity of viewpoint and the generation of novel ideas fitting local needs, problems and conflicts.

Evolutionary economics has recently recognised the important role of inter-organisational collaboration (thereafter equivalent to networks and partnerships) as an organisational structure allowing agents to develop high levels of interdependence and coherence promoting efficiency (Camagni, 1993; Loasby, 1994). Such inter-firm and inter-organisational partnerships need to be distinguished from arm's length or anonymous exchanges (characteristic of neoclassical economic markets) insofar as the transactions do not involve the exchange of well-identified and standardised commodities. To the contrary, networks incorporate adjustments in knowledge about the nature and quality of abstract commodities or about plans and implications of investment projects regarding the production of commodities (Richardson, 1972). Yet they are differentiated from formal planning (of a bureaucratic nature) as they involve continual investments in 'relationship capital' which transforms the parties involved rather than imposes restrictions on them.

Two main complementary roles are suggested for network relationships in such learning perspectives which might at the outset seem superficially contradictory. The first is that of 'negotiated convergence' in which collaborative linkages allow organisations to learn from each other and adopt compatible strategies. The second emphasises 'experimentation' and the generation of new, radically diverging ideas. These two representations of the learning role of networks will be discussed in turn, and a synthesis will be suggested subsequently. The main argument is that partnerships and networks allow both forms of learning to take place and make it possible to shift the balance towards one or the other. Different types of networks will dominate and become more successful as environmental change takes place.

In the first learning-based interpretation, inter-firm relationships allow organisations or stakeholders to learn about their environments and bring their own views closer to those of other network members because the continual interactions promoted by richer communication and information exchanges support such convergence. This is also efficient (in the conventional sense) because it allows collaborating agents or organisations to understand the needs and objectives of their partners and to play increasingly complementary roles in that association and fine-tune their activities accordingly (Richardson, 1972). This is the basis of socioeconomic specialisation and the network becomes a meaningful organisational entity when it acquires the ability to 'operate on shared assumptions' (Loasby, 1976: 193). The coherence of network-based learning strategies is reinforced as team members' interpretations of their environments increasingly coincide and their activities become compatible. Many authors have theorised the convergence of learning competencies enhanced by collaborative linkages and one can now find competing paradigms for that process. For instance, Antonelli (1996: 282) describes it as 'percolation' in which diffusion and absorption by close contact lead to local learning. The extent of connectivity (the number and quality of potential communication channels leading to a certain amount of redundancy) and receptivity (prior degree of closeness in interpretations) affect the degree of diffusion and the extent of knowledge sharing. Ring and Van de Ven (1994: 101) prefer to depict the process as one of positive feedback between 'congruent sense-making' and cooperation.

For the purpose of managing conflicting viewpoints, it is appropriate to represent network coordination as a learning strategy which encompasses and symbolises investments in external organisational capital of network member organisations. When the environment is stable and partnerships perform well, they foster trust which leads to network-specific interpretations or beliefs. Perceptions regarding local values and desirable development partners are allowed to converge and lead to integrated visions of the future. This does not only bring more harmony for the sake of reaching common goals, but enhances competitive advantage when an organisation (a firm, a destination or a community alike) is able to adjust to heterogenous demands and minimise disputes over resources uses and associated transaction costs. Yet if this convergence were to be pushed too far, it could lead to structures and strategies akin to centralised organisation and planning lacking the required flexibility because of bureaucratic costs and associated rigidities. Sharing a paradigm reduces short-term conflicts but eventually 'produces intellectual tunnel vision' which can be highly undesirable if the environment is changing rapidly (Loasby, 1976: 198).

How can networks or collaborative alliances maintain a balance between the need for convergence and that of flexibility? And how is it possible to sustain alternative types of learning strategies when the environment is highly unpredictable? The second interpretation of the role of networks puts the emphasis on experimentation and the creation of radically new ideas. The emphasis is this time not on the production of richer and convergent interactions, but on the ability of clashing viewpoints to generate new perspectives. As networks necessarily involve multiple and not always compatible interactions, the confrontation of ideas between differentiated partners implies that they will explicitly attempt to resolve conflicting viewpoints (Bianchi, 1995: 196–8; Ciborra, 1992; Langlois, 1992: 120). In market situations, this would most likely result in communication breakdown as actors prefer to exit conflicting situations. But when participants have invested in trust and built relationship-specific communication channels, they are more likely to explore improbable avenues and create solutions to their problems. The latter event describes the emergence of a radical innovation.

This interpretation of the role of networks and partnerships allows to overcome the notion that the generation of radically new ideas is a purely exogenous or random process. By forcing and multiplying the number of interactions with a potential for disagreement; networks allow a substantial pool of cognitive departures from *status quo*; the essence of innovation. If trust has been invested in the network, participants will be in a better position to get involved in experiments (the majority of which are bound to be unsuccessful), to observe experiments by other network members, interpret the nature of potential disagreements and possibly to be persuaded by network partners about the value of new concepts and the profitability of new ventures or institutional designs. This is equivalent to a process of 'dialogue' in which incoherence and incompatibilities are revealed and which forces interacting participants to defend their own perspectives in their own terms (Senge, 1990). It is here argued that such a process eventually drives debating parties to clarify the premises on which their positions rest. They must come to a decision as to whether their differences are due to some error in the inner logic of one (or possibly both) of the parties' argument or the result of incompatible theories or world views (a more detailed argument is provided in Tremblay, 1997).

In the first case, this would lead to the two parties agreeing on the reasons and the solution for the initial problem. Such a convergent process is what could emerge from repeated interactions in which differences are incrementally resolved but which in turn trigger new local problems at different levels in an ongoing chain of incremental steps. But the role of 'dialogue', in the context of partnership or network learning, is more often associated with the emergence of new sets of ideas (Senge, 1990: 238). The purpose of dialogue is to reveal incoherence and the possible need for an alternative framework. This differs from a 'discussion' where participants summarise a situation with a given view but might make little effort to question the participants' own thinking. The new construct or framework arises only from such dialogue which necessarily incorporates intermingled elements of cooperation and conflict. Senge argues that 'contrary to popular myth, great teams are not characterised by an absence of conflict. On the contrary, in my experience, one of the most reliable indicators of a team that is continually learning is the visible conflict of ideas. In great teams conflict becomes productive' (Senge, 1990: 249).

This section argues that the evolutionary conception of the learning process provides a compelling explanation of the rationale of networks and partnerships which adequately reflects their collaborative and competitive properties. It further supports the alternative interpretation of sustainability which was discussed in the first part of the paper and stemmed from the ability to deal with knowledge failures. Networks play a crucial role in forcing differentiated agents to contrast their beliefs, values or theories and challenge their foundations. The extent to which this will lead to convergence or to revolutionary change depends on the particular 'cognitive positions' of parties interacting at a point in time and the potential for compromise. If some coherent, common ground can be found, convergence will result, and with it the benefits from closer cooperation. Partnerships could therefore be sustained through the appropriation of 'cooperation rents' provided by repeated interactions and incremental learning. In other words, when convergence is possible it will result in a positive-sum game in which steady learning becomes a source of competitive advantage relatively to less efficient learners.

Alternatively, the interacting participants' inability to reconcile their differences might produce genuine change as it constitutes an exploration of alternative institutional mechanisms to solve resources conflicts and various development paths for given communities. From older viewpoints can emerge new creative ones as exploration is never totally blind. Creativity requires an environment which balances stability and unpredictability. Herbert Simon (1965: 97–8), an authority on the subject, argues that this is done by maintaining appropriate degrees of structure:

> People (and rats) find the most interest in situations that are neither completely strange nor entirely known – where there is novelty to be explored, but where similarities and programs remembered from past experience help guide the exploration. Nor does creativity flourish in completely unstructured situations. The almost unanimous testimony of creative artists and scientists is that the first task is to impose limits on the situation if the limits are not already given.

Experimentation and the development of creative solutions to developmental conflicts is not sustainable without a frame of reference. As for the dialogue analogy, finding mutually acceptable solutions to resources conflicts requires *both* commonality and differences in viewpoints. The presence of common grounds makes the dialogue possible and slight differences of interpretation can trigger the search for new types of solutions. New ideas emerge when the search for a solution is unsuccessful because no judgement can be made about the value of anyone's claims. Then a new paradigm which 'redefines the set of relevant problems, and the criteria for selecting problems and evaluating solutions' might appear (Loasby, 1976: 200).

Ensuring the sustainable development of both tourism and the multi-faceted community-held resources on which it depends becomes the art of maintaining the right balance between system coherence and flexibility. In the context of tourism-related resources conflicts, networks and stakeholder partnerships will work at establishing through dialogue converging positions regarding a continually evolving process. This could result in cost reductions in the form of short-run transaction and litigation costs reductions and conceivably in terms of the long-run costs of managing and preserving irreversible sociocultural and environmental resources. It can also foster destination competitive marketing advantages as far as strategic positioning and image creation are concerned. These networks will also acquire a critical and less visible function in generating new ideas and concepts when the environment will warrant a greater role for novelty. This has the potential to trigger further changes and transform the organisational and economic landscapes in which tourism development takes place. This dual learning role reflects usefully the essential and complex interrelationships between cooperation and conflict which need to intermingle when issues of sustainability arise.

Learning Institutions in Tourism

Although the interdisciplinary literature on networks is growing into a relatively elaborate paradigm with implications for strategic marketing and organisational theories, this paper aims only at demonstrating the relevance of the network approach to policy-making in the area of tourism and highlight the usefulness of an evolutionary or 'learning' perspective. Inter-organisational networks have often been conceptualised in the recent tourism literature as simple investments made for the purpose of building goodwill and relationships. This emphasises their role in smoothing the negotiation process often put in place to connect community members disagreeing over the development of tourism-related (commercial or not) activities. It is compatible with the argument that potentially conflicting stakeholders with established linkages will seek and accept more easily to compromise because their interdependence and the need to jointly address critical market failures will have been recognised. But an evolutionary perspective does not attempt to present such partnerships simply as the inescapable early steps of a comprehensive planning process. It would be mistaken to justify collaborative alliances by portraying them as efficient simply because they constitute information-rich organisational structures with a greater survival potential, or enlightened because they have discovered the virtues of collaboration. This would be circumventing the problems identified earlier when alternative forms of coordination based on government intervention or *laissez-faire* were rejected on grounds of lack of realism regarding the availability of knowledge. In particular, interpreting the role of networks as a platform to accelerate communication and to diffuse information between stakeholders is naive and dangerous. For one thing, it would replicate the mistake of portraying a world in which trivial information gaps can be filled by simple research and reorganisation. Instead it ought to recognise that decision-makers must deal with substantial holes in the available knowledge base. The evolutionary approach suggests that it is useful to identify who owns or controls (1) the common resources whose value is critical to relevant participants in the tourism planning process (community member or otherwise, as discussed below) and (2) the knowledge and technological assets which shape the developmental visions of particular locations or communities.

The idea of attempting to tackle tourism planning at the local level has emerged partially as a knowledge-based argument and suggests that control over localised resources ought to involve participants with local knowledge of community needs, industry behaviour and environmental characteristics. It has itself become a controversial theme in the recent tourism literature (Murphy, 1985; Pearce *et al.*, 1996; Simmons, 1994). The general perspective is sound in theory insofar as the specificity of destination products and the diversity of conflicts over natural resources found across various environments justify location-specific solutions. Most supporters of a community-based approach to tourism coordination aim at achieving a balance between the benefits of tourism (which itself rests on achieving long-term competitive advantage through the marketing and management of tourism supply) and the preservation of critical, identifiable physical, social and cultural resources. The value of the latter resources constitutes a central concern for the community and usually contributes to tourism development itself. This has led to claims that sustainable natural or social environments can often be confused with sustainable tourism (see Woodley, 1993; Leiper & Hunt, 1996). The somewhat naive belief that there is a fundamental connection between local resources and general impacts on local residents does suggest reasonable ethical and moral grounds for attempting to address conflicts regarding resource allocation in their specific local contexts. It is then not so surprising to encounter idealistic proposals involving planning processes combined with widespread local participation information exchanges and converging visions of development promoted through the establishment of close communication channels and shared community values.

But this view is excessively optimistic in assuming automatically increasing convergence of values and technological paths. When stakeholders hold varying mixes of private knowledge about tourism technology or environmental degradation, when they have the opportunity to strategically destabilise or manipulate negotiations or even when community members are indifferent to the implications of tourism development, reliance on idealistic community-based interactions does not constitute a realistic solution. In particular, much criticism towards the community-based focus of tourism planning has been connected with issues such as the bargaining position of given communities in the broader, regional or national tourism systems, the limited technological capital facing small communities and the constraints imposed by existing decision-making power and political structures (Long, 1991; Milne, 1998; Redclift, 1987; Taylor, 1995; Wheeller, 1991).

Although strong community-based networks linking participants in the tourism planning process might be able to overcome the negative impacts that political volatility can have on community development, the existence of appropriate linkages between stakeholders in specific locations can not be taken for granted. Networks do not simply spontaneously arise when needed and involve complex resource allocation decisions in themselves. Nor can partnerships be arbitrarily designed or imposed on poorly defined or insufficiently integrated communities as their effectiveness relies on meaningful cooperation initiated by coexisting and willing parties. It is therefore imperative to address the implications and impacts of regional tourist infrastructures, transit tourist movements and the complementarity between nearby tourist destinations to understand how to select strategically appropriate network boundaries. It must indeed be recognised that if the control over the nature and marketing of the tourism product needs to be compatible with local development visions, the latter can involve a number of differentiated positioning strategies, in particular different degrees of reliance on preservation or innovation to ensure a sustainable future. In fact, the need for moving away from planning stereotypes towards location-specific institutions and policies recognising 'geographic heterogeneity' and the central role of innovation has emerged from the tourism planning literature itself (Fagence & Craig-Smith, 1993: 145–7).

What is emphasised by the evolutionary approach to sustainability suggested in this paper is an inherent condition of partial ignorance about technology, the nature of tourism impacts and the value attached by members of the community to these impacts. Networks allow us to confront this complexity by providing a diversity of flexible and self-seeded learning strategies. While the community concept constitutes a useful model to pass judgements about the various impacts of diverse types of developments and the ability of stakeholders to control local resources that will be affected by tourism developments, the evolutionary approach does not suggest a uniform process or ideal recipe. It endorses the need for diversity when it recognises that the learning strategy suitable for a given community should be compatible with its overall positioning as far as tourism development is concerned, and with its expectations regarding the pace and nature of development (which shapes its attitudes towards public resources utilisation and management). The objective of a tourism network should not be to homogenise community values or bring them closer to those of tourism business and planning agencies, but to capitalise on diversity. This is indeed compatible with the objectives of making coherent decisions with respect to resources management when the environment deems it necessary. It can provide innovative tourism development alternatives when this becomes necessary for competitive advantage. The approach surely does not prescribe a given balance. It is compatible with the view that the democratic access to common resources needs to go beyond the acknowledgement of market failures. To that extent, it requires more sophisticated thinking about the technology of tourism impact assessment and the process of knowledge creation used in negotiating and articulating community values about tourism development.

If economists and organisational strategy analysts are to gather any generic knowledge about the process of investing in tourism-related organisational capital, it will most likely come from undertaking comparative institutional analysis. Tourism research must therefore attempt to document and contrast typical partnership and network strategies and evaluate their roles in various environments. This is starting to be undertaken from the point of view of destination marketing alliances and systems (see Palmer & Bejou, 1995; Baker *et al.* 1996) and the special issue of the Journal of Sustainable Tourism incorporates some of the latest developments in that area. The next section proposes a framework for the analysis of tourism networks which comprises destination-based networks as a distinct type of broader network designs and suggests that their viability depends on the relative learning benefits of various configurations.

An Agenda for Network Research in Sustainable Tourism

While the rationale for the existence and role of inter-organisational networks presented in previous sections emphasises that inherently diverse learning strategies ought to accompany diverse environmental contexts, this article does not deny the possibility of identifying empirical patterns connecting structural attributes of networks to categories of environmental contexts. This reiterates the view that recognising tourism as a complex and chaotic system does not imply that related market failures need to be interpreted as completely incomprehensible and their management as impossible. The paradigm supported here does not equate chaos with random events and spontaneous order; rather it connects the organic nature of organisations with intelligible processes and malleable structures (Faulkner & Russell, 1997; Khalil, 1992). Institutional experimentation by participants in the tourism system does not eliminate the possibility of learning by observing nor the possibility of imitating existing organisational models. Patterns emerge because it is possible to identify successful networks or partnerships and attempt to copy the attributes that seem to determine their success. Generic knowledge about successful collaborative arrangements can diffuse and some experiments, however transitory, can take place in different contexts and locations. Imitation remains an important learning strategy in itself.

The conventional inter-firm networks literature suggests ways to distinguish between types of industrial partnerships on the basis of their structural characteristics or their functional attributes. These generally emphasise the configuration of network participants (in terms of their locations and the nature of the links between them – such as 'who owns whom?') as well as industrial or technological leadership (Camagni, 1993). In tourism, similar endeavours have been applied to identify ownership-based corporate linkages between tourism-related firms. They have shown that inter-firm partnerships play a critical role in shaping the development of tourism markets and destinations but they have mainly emphasised conventional corporate links in visible international tourism ventures (Ascher, 1984; Cazes, 1989; Garnham, 1996;Kamann & Strijker, 1991; March, 1996; Smith & Forsyth, 1988; UNCTC, 1982).

The research agenda proposed here requires that a connection be made between network organisations and environmental characteristics. Marketing-based multi-layered networks capable of shaping products and distribution systems ought to be correlated with the attributes of various market segments, destinations, technological processes or products in general (Earl, 1995; Ioannides & Debbage, 1997; March, 1996; Poon, 1993; Tremblay, 1997). Tremblay (1998) contrasts various network designs along conventional functional designs and degrees of integration (vertical, horizontal or diagonal-local) and the types of learning advantages these provide. Tremblay (1999) undertakes an empirical exploration of linkages between the nature of various market segments (and products) and identifiable partnership configurations (characterised as mainly horizontal, vertical or local and the strength and number of linkages). In that study of networking behaviour, the propensity to participate in various types of functional networks has been found to be correlated mainly with the market segment that various private firms aim to cater for and the most valuable types of strategic knowhow they ought to gather.

This general approach could be extended usefully in efforts to map broader tourism institutional systems including public sector agencies, interest groups and other community members and stakeholders. This would allow us to delineate the ingredients as well as generic recipes for sustainable tourism partnerships. The latter networks could eventually be correlated with environmental characteristics and provide basic knowledge regarding the conditions and success factors supporting network-based learning about market failures (Tremblay, 1993a).

In recognising the need to move away from the study of networks formed exclusively for the purpose of advertising or marketing destinations, a number of partnership attributes could become relevant, if reliably documented. For instance:

- functional role of network; such as the explicit purposes or objectives;
- network structure (as in Tremblay 1998, 1999);
- the general configuration of linkages between stakeholders;
- the nature of network communication and exchanges;
- the intensity of network connections;
- participation rules and degree of integration in strategic decision-making;
- the speed and degree of change;
- openness to new members.

Innovative research designs are needed to attempt to establish and measure the existence of relationships to various local conditions or contexts. In particular, the propensity to establish partnerships ought to be connected to the following relevant environmental characteristics:

- distinguishable tourism market segments (as in Tremblay, 1999);
- the relative importance of specific types of market failures (natural environment, social, cultural …);
- the degree of homogeneity of tourism production processes or technology;
- the nature and extent of existing public sector involvement in tourism production, distribution and coordination;
- the degree of concentration (spatial or industrial) of tourism within in a community or region;
- other relevant attributes such as urban/rural/coastal environments, large versus small economies, degree of dependence on tourism …;
- the extent to which alternative horizontal and vertical networks dominate the existing tourism landscape (alternative to local, community or region-based networks).

Organisational partnerships emerge if they can create sustainable strategic rents that community members and groups can appropriate. Such comparative analysis would help uncover the relative benefits and desirability of various levels of public sector intervention in organising, supporting, triggering or simply accommodating tourism-related collaborative endeavours. The analytical and empirical identification of various, potentially appropriate forms of partnerships or networks is consistent with the view that relying on a blanket 'social responsibility' intention described sometimes as a 'stakeholder approach' might be insufficient and constitute a mere public relations exercise (Robson & Robson, 1996). Instead it suggests that the public sector can play a didactic role in uncovering the basic dimensions of learning about market and bureaucratic-planning failures and provide some support for institutional diversity (Dalum *et al.*, 1992).

Conclusion

Beyond the theoretical argument which this paper examined, it is important to set directions useful for tourism research and policy. The evolutionary argument should not be mistakenly identified with general *laissez-faire* arguments supporting a tourism development-push or status quo. Such a position is incompatible with the view that ignorance characterises socio-industrial systems and that the production and coordination of technological and industrial knowledge in tourism development matters (see Hodgson, 1991 for a more developed argument).

The present paper prescribes an alternative view on the coordination of common resources focusing on the facilitation and shaping of tourism networks (in addition to the participation of public agencies acting as managers and sometimes as stakeholders on a par with private businesses). This involves considering the possibility of having to view collaborative linkages as alternative and competing forms of investments in learning capital. From an economic opportunity cost viewpoint, investments in privileged linkages between tourism-related organisations and firms in different locations (horizontal or vertical) compete for attention, resources and loyalty with local linkages (Tremblay, 1998). Local communities need to establish strategies for the management of complementary and conflicting partnerships within and across destinations. The mix they eventually choose will involve more or less integration of objectives or centralisation of decision-making capabilities depending on particular circumstances. It will reflect their own development paths as well as their perceptions regarding their relative learning ability and their chances of appropriating rents from partnership investments.

The identification of diverse strategies connecting tourism products with their respective costs and benefits requires an examination of socioeconomic processes creating the knowledge required for decisions and implementation. The development of coordination mechanisms emphasising knowledge-creating networks (and various types and levels of planning) constitutes itself an investment that stakeholders in the broader tourism system need to consider but might overlook because of their incentives to free-ride.

The need to invest in the tourism knowledge base is justified by the reliance of tourism on common assets and the absence of typical industry institutions capable of enforcing a standardisation of technologies and product characteristics. Yet the lack of property rights associated with tourism assets and the volatility of product characteristics and identifiable externalities do not imply that most tourism-related failures ought to be approached from the extreme and divergent viewpoints of *laissez-faire* or of comprehensive planning. A network-based framework suggests that inter-organisational partnerships (including business firms, government agencies, community groups and other stakeholders) ought to play a critical role in establishing sustainable knowledge management through location-specific learning strategies. These would provide mechanisms allowing us to negotiate a policy mix involving the coherent coordination of scarce and imperfectly conceptualised pools of fragile resources. To ensure sustainability and manage conflicting values regarding resources uses, it is necessary to establish institutions capable of supporting both convergence and innovation. This would also ensure the maintenance of appropriate location-specific levels of flexibility. Arguably tourism destinations would improve their ability to adapt to erratic tourism markets and prepare local socioeconomic systems for unexpected product innovations and changing technological standards. The sustainability of both tourism development and of the public resources base on which it often depends ultimately rests on our understanding of the division of market and technological knowledge and the management of network-based learning strategies.

Correspondence

Any correspondence should be directed to Dr Pascal Tremblay, Faculty of Business, Northern Territory University, Darwin, NT 0909, Australia (pascal@business.ntu.edu.au).

References

Aislabie, C. (1992) The role of forecasting in assessing tourism benefits and costs. In P.J. Stanton (ed.) *Benefits and Costs of Tourism – Proceedings of a National Tourism Research Conference* (pp. 23–34). The Institute of Industrial Economics, Newcastle, New South Wales: The University of Newcastle.

Antonelli, C. (1996) Localized knowledge percolation processes and information networks. *Journal of Evolutionary Economics* 6, 281–95.

Ascher, F. (1984) *Tourisme, sociétés transnationales et identites culturelles.* Paris: UNESCO.

Baker, M., Hayzelden, C. and Sussmann, S. (1996) Can destination management systems provide competitive advantage? A discussion of the factors affecting the survival and success of destination management systems. *Progress in Tourism and Hospitality Research* 2, 1–13.

Bianchi, M. (1995) Markets and firms – transaction costs versus strategic innovation. *Journal of Economic Behavior and Organization* 28, 183–202.

Burns, M. (1989) *The Environmental Impacts of Travel and Tourism.* Discussion paper No. 1. Canberra: Industries Assistance Commission AGPS.

Camagni, R. (1993) Inter-firm industrial networks: The costs and benefits of cooperative behaviour. *Journal of Industry Studies* 1, 1–15.

Cazes, G. (1989) *Le tourisme international – mirage ou stratégie d'avenir?* Paris: Hatier.

Choy, D.J.L. (1991) Tourism planning – the case for 'market failure'. *Tourism Management* 12, 313–30.

Ciborra, C. (1992) Innovation, networks and organizational learning. In C. Antonelli (ed.) *The Economics of Information Networks* (pp. 91–102). Amsterdam: North–Holland.

Dalum, B., Johnson, B. and Lundvall, B.-A. (1992) Public policy in the learning society. In B.-A. Lundvall (ed.) *National Systems of Innovation – Towards a Theory of Innovation and Interactive Learning.* London: Pinter Publishers.

Earl, P.E. (1995) *Microeconomics for Business and Marketing.* Aldershot: Edward Elgar.

Fagence, M. and Craig-Smith, S.J. (1993) Challenges to orthodoxy – tourism planning in the South Pacific. In P. Hooper (ed.) *Building a Research Base in Tourism* (pp. 141–149). Proceedings of a national conference on tourism research, University of Sydney, Canberra: Bureau of Tourism Research.

Faulkner, B. and Russell, R. (1997) Chaos and complexity in tourism: A search for a new perspective. *Pacific Tourism Review* 1, 1–16.

Forsyth, P., Dwyer, L. and Clarke, H. (1995) Problems in use of economic instruments to reduce adverse environmental impacts on tourism. *Tourism Economics* 1, 265–82.

Foss, N.J. (1994) Realism and evolutionary economics. *Journal of Social and Evolutionary Systems* 17, 21–40.

Garnham, B. (1996) Alliances and liaisons in tourism: Concepts and implications. *Tourism Economics* 2, 61–77.

Garrod, B. and Fyall, A. (1998) Beyond the rhetoric of sustainable tourism? *Tourism Management* 19, 199–212.

Gunn, C. (1988) *Tourism Planning* (2nd edn). New York: Taylor & Francis.

Haywood, K.M. and Walsh, L.J. (1996) Strategic tourism planning in Fiji – an oxymoron or providing for coherence in decision making? In L.C. Harrison and W. Husbands (eds) *Practicing Responsible Tourism – International Cases in Tourism, Planning, Policy and Development* (pp. 103–25). New York: John Wiley.

Hodgson, G.M. (1991) Economic evolution: Intervention contra pangloss. *Journal of Economic Issues* 25 (2), 519–533.

Inskeep, E. (1991) *Tourism Planning: An Integrated and Sustainable Development Approach.* New York: Van Nostrand Reinhold.

Ioannides, D. and Debbage, K. (1997) Post-Fordism and flexibility: The travel industry polyglot. *Tourism Management* 18, 229–41.

Jamal, T.B. and Getz, D. (1996) Does strategic planning pay? Lessons for destinations from corporate planning experience. *Progress in Tourism and Hospitality Research* 2, 59–78.

Kamann, D.-J. and Strijker, D. (1991) The network approach: Concepts and applications. In R. Camagni (ed.) *Innovation Networks: Spatial Perspectives* (pp. 145–73). London and New York: Belhaven Press.

Kavallinis, I. and Pizam, A. (1994) The environmental impacts of tourism – whose responsibility is it anyway? The case study of Mykonos. *Journal of Travel Research* 33, 26–32.

Khalil, E.L. (1992) Hayek's spontaneous order and Varela's autopoiesis: A comment. *Human System Management* 11, 101–105.

Khan, A. (1995) Sustainable development: The key concepts, issues and implications. *Sustainable Development* 3, 63–69.

Langlois, R.N. (1992) Transaction-cost economics in real time. *Industrial and Corporate Change* 1, 99–127.

Langlois, R.N. and Robertson, P.L. (1995) *Firms, Markets and Economic Change*. London and New York: Routledge.

Leiper, N. and Hunt, S. (1996) Some new ideas on environmental sustainability and eco-tourism, and implications for strategy. In G. Prosser (ed.) *Tourism and Hospitality Research – Australian and International Perspectives* (pp. 513–518). Proceedings from the Australian tourism and hospitality research conference, Coffs Harbour, Canberra: Bureau of Tourism Research.

Loasby, B.J. (1976) *Choice, Complexity and Ignorance – an Inquiry into Economic Theory and the Practice of Decision-making*. Cambridge: Cambridge University Press.

Loasby, B.J. (1991) *Equilibrium and Evolution – An Exploration of Connecting Principles in Economics*. Manchester: Manchester University Press.

Loasby, B.J. (1994) Organisational capabilities and interfirm relations. *Metroeconomica* 45, 248–65.

Long, V.H. (1991) Nature tourism: Environmental stress or environmental salvation? Paper presented to Leisure and Tourism: Social and Environmental Change. WLRA World Congress, Sydney, 16–19 July.

March, R. (1996) Organisational linkages in Australia's Japanese inbound travel market. In G. Prosser (ed.) *Tourism and Hospitality Research – Australian and International Perspectives* (pp. 337–49). Canberra: Bureau of Tourism Research.

McKercher, B. (1993) The unrecognised threat to tourism: Can tourism survive 'sustainability'? *Tourism Management* 14 (2), 131–36.

Milne, S.S. (1998) Tourism and sustainable development: The global-local nexus. In C.M. Hall and A.A. Lew (eds) *Sustainable Tourism: A Geographical Perspective*. Harlow, Essex: Longman.

Mishan, E.J. (1967) *The Costs of Economic Growth*. London: Staples Press.

Murphy P.E. (1985) *Tourism – A Community Approach*. New York and London: Methuen.

National Ecotourism Strategy (1994) Canberra: Commonwealth of Australia.

Palmer, A. and Bejou, D. (1995) Tourism destination marketing alliances. *Annals of Tourism Research* 22 (3), 616–629.

Pearce, D.W., Markandya, A. and Barbier, E.B. (1989) *Blueprint for a Green Economy*. London: Earthscan.

Pearce, P.L., Moscardo, G. and Ross, G.F. (1996) *Tourism Community Relationships*. Oxford: Pergamon.

Poon, A. (1993) *Tourism, Technology and Competitive Strategies*. Wallingford: CAB International.

Redclift, M. (1987) *Sustainable Development: Exploring the Contradictions*. London: Methuen.

Richardson, G.B. (1972) The organization of industry. *Economic Journal* 82, 883–96.

Ring, P.S. and Van de Ven, A.H. (1994) Developmental processes of cooperative interorganizational relationships. *Academy of Management Review* 19, 90–118.

Robson, J. and Robson, I. (1996) From shareholders to stakeholders: Critical issues for tourism marketers. *Tourism Management* 17, 533–40.

Senge, P.M. (1990) *The Fifth Discipline – The Art and Practice of the Learning Organization*. Sydney: Random House.

Simmons, D.G. (1994) Community participation in tourism planning. *Tourism Management* 15 (2), 98–108.

Simon, H.A. (1965) *The Shape of Automation for Men and Management*. New York: Harper & Row.

Sinclair, T. (1992) Tourism, economic development and the environment: Problems and policies. In C.P. Cooper and A. Lockwood (eds) *Progress in Tourism, Recreation and Hospitality Management* (Vol. 4) (pp. 75–81). London: Belhaven Press.

Smith, N. and Forsyth, P. (1988) Corporate organisation in the tourism industry. Paper presented to an Australia-Japan Research Centre Conference on Japanese Corporation Organisation and International Adjustment, 19–20 September, Australian National University.

Taylor, G. (1995) The community approach: Does it really work? *Tourism Management* 16 (7), 487–489.

Tremblay, P. (1993a) The past, present and future of tourism policy in Australia. In P. Hooper (ed.) *Building a Research Base in Tourism* (pp. 193–200). Proceedings of a national conference on tourism research. University of Sydney, Canberra: Bureau of Tourism Research.

Tremblay, P. (1993b) Re-directing Australian tourism policy: Investing in local networks. *Tourism Working Paper* (pp. 1–35). Faculty of Business, Northern Territory University.

Tremblay, P. (1997) Information and coordination: The economic organization of tourism. Doctoral thesis, University of Melbourne, Victoria.

Tremblay, P. (1998) The economic organisation of tourism: A network approach. *Annals of Tourism Research* 25, 837–859.

Tremblay, P. (1999) An empirical investigation of tourism business relationships in Australia's Top End. In J. Molloy and J. Davies (eds) *Tourism and Hospitality: Delighting the Senses 1999 – Part 2* (pp. 194–206). Canberra: Bureau of Tourism Research.

United Nations Centre on Transnational Corporations (1982) *Transnational Corporations in International Tourism*. New York: United Nations.

Wall, G. (1996) Rethinking impacts of tourism. *Progress in Tourism and Hospitality Research* 2, 207–15.

Walter, J.A. (1982) Social limits to tourism. *Leisure Sciences* 1, 295–304.

Wheeller, B. (1991) Tourism's troubled times: Responsible tourism is not the answer. *Tourism Management* 12 (2), 91–6.

Woodley, S. (1993) Tourism and sustainable development in parks and protected areas. In J.G. Nelson, R. Butler and G. Wall (eds) *Tourism and Sustainable Development: Monitoring, Planning and Managing* (pp. 83–96). Waterloo: Department of Geography, University of Waterloo.

World Commission on Environment and Development (WCED – The Bruntland report) (1987) *Our Common Future*. London: Oxford University Press.

17. Collaborative Tourism Planning: Issues and Future Directions

Bill Bramwell
Centre for Tourism, Sheffield Hallam University, UK

Bernard Lane
Rural Tourism Unit, University of Bristol, UK

This book's contents present a striking picture of the complex and fragmented nature of the tourism industry, and of the ways in which tourism policies have consequences for many individuals and interest groups. They also show how progress toward the objectives of sustainable development entails consideration of varied economic, social and environmental issues and of multiple actors. The high degree of interdependence around and between tourism issues means that tourism planning can be more effective if it involves a range of stakeholders, representing the full spectrum of interests and issues. Collaboration can allow stakeholders to develop a common approach to tourism policy-making and planning. This chapter reviews some key arguments presented by the authors in this book about collaborative tourism planning and it suggests some future directions for research in the field.

Issues Affecting Collaboration

Evaluations of collaborative tourism planning in particular circumstances can enhance our understanding of why partnerships succeed or fail and may assist practitioners to learn from experiences elsewhere. What broad issues can affect the character of collaboration in tourism planning?

First, *the scope of collaborative arrangements* in different partnerships was examined in several chapters of this book. A prime consideration is that of inclusion: whether all relevant parties and interest groups become participants in the collaborative planning process. Mason *et al.* (Chapter 5) note that some groups were excluded from meetings of the World Wide Fund for Nature (WWF) Arctic Tourism Programme due to insufficient funds for travel, lack of translation services and limited access to computers. Some tourism operators may also have not participated in the meetings as they took exception to the politics of WWF, the convening organisation. Jamal and Getz (Chapter 9) show how local government and planners initially convened a growth management roundtable in the Canadian town of Canmore but then decided to remain at arms length from the process. The planners provided the participants with technical information and liaised with local government, but were not involved in decision-making. This arms-length approach helped the participants to gain a sense of 'ownership' of the process, but it might also have reduced the chances of the resulting policies being accepted and implemented by local government. The scope of collaborative arrangements is also affected by the spread of policy areas that they include. Timothy (chapter 2) illustrates this spread through his evaluation of whether cross-border partnerships established for three parks on the US-Canada border included collaborative working in their management frameworks, infrastructure development, and policies for human resources, conservation, promotion and border concessions. Timothy also emphasises the role of boundaries in determining the scope of collaborative arrangements; other contributors widened that theme to consider boundaries not just in space, but also in time, power groupings, and in abilities to pay. Boundary setting is, therefore, a key question for all partnerships.

The intensity of collaborative relations in different partnerships was also considered by several of the contributors. In Chapter 8, Hall places collaborative relations on a continuum ranging from 'loose' linkages to longer lasting coalitions where there is a broad mission and jointly conducted tasks. Parker (Chapter 4) distinguishes between institutional arrangements that are 'centred', where collaboration between organisations takes place within a highly institutionalised structure such as a task force, and 'networked' arrangements, which are more open, fluid and *ad hoc*. Roberts and Simpson (Chapter 12) highlight the importance for the long-term success of a partnership of sincerity and the building and retention of trust among participants. For example, they consider that the Pirin Tourism Forum in Bulgaria gained the trust of the local community due to its perceived impartiality, but that it will have to pay close attention to the implications that increasing government involvement may bring in the future.

The potential for partnerships to draw on 'local knowledges' in a community in systematic and respectful ways as a basis to promote shared learning is identified by Reed (Chapter 13). Mason *et al.* (Chapter 5) conclude that all participants' views were regarded as significant in the meetings organised for the World Wide Fund for Nature Arctic Tourism Programme. However, they also recognise that some participants were advantaged because the meetings were conducted in English and that sometimes the 'strong voices' dominated the 'weaker voices'. Jamal and Getz (Chapter 9) stress the need to consider how power is bound up with dominant discourses and also with the dialogical practices of a partnership. A similar point is made by Robinson (Chapter 15), who argues that there is a need to reflect on the different 'world views' of social groups that are involved as participants.

The extent to which consensus emerges among the participants in a partnership was also explored in this book. In Chapter 4 Parker suggests that the early negotiations about tourism development on the island of Bonaire faced difficulties in attempting to resolve conflicts between commercial and environmental stakeholders over deeply held values about sustainability. These difficulties were overcome subsequently by focusing more attention on common ground, and specifically on policy options that these two sides wanted separately but that the other could support. Ritchie (Chapter 3) describes how the approach taken to developing a management strategy for the Banff National Park involved focusing negotiations on the underlying motivational needs of the parties involved, rather than on stated positions. The participants were encouraged to build a consensus by moving away from fixed positions.

In Chapter 5 Mason *et al.* suggest that the World Wide Fund for Nature Arctic Tourism Programme involved a process of negotiated consensus building. In this process the participants did not agree with everything but, as most agreed that some form of project like this was necessary, they were willing to accept the majority view in order to keep the project moving. For Jamal and Getz (Chapter

9), the participants in a partnership should reach agreement by consent through such processes as paying respect, mutual learning and shared activity. They suggest that the agreement reached by a roundtable process in Canmore in Canada was partly forced on the participants by the rules established at the outset of the partnership. However, it is also suggested that the consensus-building process in Canmore led to 'destructive conflict' being replaced by 'constructive conflict'. Tremblay (Chapter 16) also suggests that if convergence and harmony between collaborating stakeholders goes too far it may lead to 'tunnel vision' and other rigidities of structure and strategies, which can reduce the ability to innovate.

The question of resources and capacity for tangible actions resulting from collaboration is also addressed by some contributors to this collection, who consider whether specific partnerships had the capacity to convert agreements about policies into practical actions. Putting initiatives into practice involves gaining access to resources and creating mechanisms or institutional abilities to accomplish the work. Caffyn (Chapter 11) identifies a range of practical outputs for the North Pennines Tourism Partnership in the UK and also reports the opinions of the participants on the partnership's achievements. She stresses the importance of resource flows from the public sector as a critical influence on the capacity of the partnership to effect changes. Most contributors noted the resource needs of partnerships, as well as issues about obtaining those resources – Long (Chapter 10) illustrates these aspects well. Resources grant political power; resources allow action; actions can be celebrated; celebrations give media exposure; and media exposure grants further political power.

Collaboration and Sustainable Development

The focus of much of the sustainability debate in tourism is that tourism must be planned and managed in a holistic way to ensure that natural and cultural resources are maintained for continuing future use. The issues involved in sustainable approaches to tourism are wide-ranging, and they are the subject of many competing interpretations. In Chapter 2, Timothy stresses four key principles behind sustainable approaches to tourism: ecological integrity, efficiency, equity, and integration-balance-harmony. Elsewhere, Timothy (1998) suggests that efficiency relates to the relative costs involved with alternative approaches, and that equity is concerned with the equality of opportunity and recognition of needs among various stakeholders, both now and in the future. He relates integration-balance-harmony to 'the struggle for integration, balance, and harmony between key factors, such as environment and economy, sectors such as agriculture and tourism, and in patterns of regional development' (p. 54). In his chapter here, Timothy uses these four principles to evaluate whether the partnerships between parks across the US-Canada border that he examined were instrumental in advancing sustainable development.

Hall (Chapter 8) argues that sustainable development should be concerned with the maintenance of 'social capital' as well as 'environmental capital'. The former involves strengthening social networks and relationships, a process that can be encouraged through participation in decision-making, helping develop shared understandings and trust. This social and intellectual capacity building can be called upon now and at future times. The educational, learning role of partnerships is emphasised by Tremblay (Chapter 16); she also notes the importance of capacity building within the business community.

While the process of collaborative working potentially can strengthen social and intellectual capital in communities and firms, the involvement of a range of stakeholders might also encourage consideration of the issues associated with environmental capital. Medeiros de Araujo and Bramwell (Chapter 14) conclude that the network of stakeholders involved in collaborative planning for Brazil's Costa Dourada Project included a relatively broad array of environmental and other interests and also provided some possibility that varied issues of sustainable development would feature in deliberations about the project's policies. However, they also note that there were gaps in the representation in the planning process, including scope for greater participation by environmental interest groups.

Collaborative working involving a range of stakeholders can also encourage the integration of tourism planning with the other sectors with which it has linkages, which is important for sustainable development given the breadth of those linkages and the diverse impacts that tourism tends to generate. In the planning process for the Banff-Bow Valley Study, Ritchie (Chapter 3) shows how a Task Force developed a broad vision for all activities affecting the area that clearly indicated a role for tourism but did not provide an explicit framework for its future. In consequence, a specific 'Tourism Destination Model' was developed that was intended to be consistent with the overall vision and elaborate on it from a tourism perspective. Participation by diverse stakeholders may also encourage coordination of various geographical scales of planning intervention in tourism, which may promote planning at each level that is complementary and consistent in direction, and hence more efficient. This coordination can be viewed as a hierarchy, with national, state, regional and local tiers. An example of such coordination is examined by Medeiros de Araujo and Bramwell (Chapter 14).

Participatory processes for addressing natural and cultural resource problems are particularly important when the challenges require cross-border coordination. Voluntary agreements are usually the primary problem-solving tool, and can be graphically illustrated across international borders. Examples of international collaborative arrangements in tourism are evaluated by Mason *et al.* (Chapter 5) and by Timothy (Chapter 2).

The Question of Evaluation

Chapter 1 noted that there can be problems as well as benefits arising from the operation of partnerships: they may, if badly managed, reduce rather than promote sustainable development. There may also be a danger that a focus on the working of partnerships could lead us to ignore the positions of the marginalised and excluded in the political process – groups and individuals who may well be unaware of the strategies resulting from collaborative tourism planning. This means it is important that partnerships are evaluated critically, including their full range of impacts on equality and other aspects of sustainability. But if partnerships consist of stakeholders with different values and goals, and there are also non-participating stakeholders, there is then a central question: whose value systems and goals should be used as criteria to evaluate partnerships?

Indeed, there are numerous difficulties involved in evaluating partnerships, with some being raised in Chapter 1. The problems are especially notable in relation to sustainability. Evaluations of the impacts of partnerships on 'environmental capital' face such difficulties as deciding how to measure changes in environmental quality, how to causally link partnership activities to environmental changes, the complexity of selecting an appropriate proxy for environmental goals, and the inability to determine the durability of environmental improvements (or deterioration). Partnership working should also be evaluated by comparison with other potential approaches to sustainable development, such as environmental regulation and legislation. Partnerships should also be assessed in relation to their effects on the wider policy system and on public attitudes. For example, does a partnership help public agencies by improving the quality of regulation, by enhancing support for regulation, and by reducing the need for regulation? Does a partnership change the attitudes of participants and non-participants, including the general public? And how does the market react to the concept of a tourism destination that is planned and managed by a partnership organisation? Does it recognise values-led organisational structures and reward destinations by increased visitation? Or is it ambivalent? Or does it react against the restrictions on visitor activity that an environmentally responsible partnership might bring? (Block, 1993; Middleton & Hawkins, 1998). Much more research is needed on specific measures for assessing the effects of partnerships in terms of their diverse outputs or impacts on equality and sustainability in general.

Potential Directions for Research on Collaborative Tourism Planning

While it has been shown that well designed and executed partnerships can help to build policies and accomplish goals in tourism planning, it is also evident that partnerships are complex and difficult and need to be evaluated critically. Collaborative working may offer important opportunities, but it will not necessarily produce less conflict, lead to improved planning or promote sustainable development. Partnerships are not panaceas, particularly when challenges require large-scale policy shifts and behavioural changes. The contributions in this book contain numerous ideas to stimulate research, discussion and practical action. Seven potential avenues for future research on collaborative tourism planning are highlighted here, but they are just seven of many.

Examination of how the processes of collaborative planning are managed in practice

According to Kickert *et al.* (1997: 43), managing collaborative relations should involve 'promoting the mutual adjustment of the behaviour of actors with diverse objectives and ambitions with regard to tackling problems within a given framework of interorganizational relationships'. Thus it is aimed at stimulating coordination through interaction in the form of mutual consultation, negotiation and consensus building between stakeholders. It involves promoting cooperation between stakeholders and preventing, bypassing or removing any block-ages to that cooperation. Managing partnerships is an important but relatively weak form of steering, with no clear hierarchies of authority and with consider-able uncertainties being inevitable. Consideration needs to be given, for example, to the role of brokers, facilitators, mediators and arbitrators and the approaches they might use to make partnerships more successful. Leadership is a related concern for partnerships. Ideally, leadership is required from all actors involved in a collaborative venture. For example, representatives of organisa-tions need to be willing to take risks during negotiations by accepting new ideas and being prepared to speak out for them to their own organisations. In practice, however, some leadership roles may be taken by a small number of actors, including the use of a broker or facilitator (Koth *et al.*, 1991; Miller *et al.*, 1992).

Examination of the relations between people and more formal structures in collaborative planning

It should be evident from this book that people make partnerships work. Roberts and Simpson (Chapter 12) stress that partnerships depend on motiva-tions and personalities as much as they do on their formal structures and defined aims and objectives. Hence, these authors and also Jamal and Getz (Chapter 9) use interpretive approaches that emphasise the everyday, lived experiences of the participants, and notably the meanings that they attach to the partnership process. More research is needed which explores the relationships between the participants in partnerships and the broader web of tourism policy networks and planning frameworks within which they operate, and which does so using theo-retically informed analyses. One potential research direction would be to draw on structuration theory, which focuses on people actively constructing their worlds, both materially and in the meanings they make, while surrounded by powerful constraints of various kinds. In Giddens' (1984) formulation of this theory, active agency interacts recursively with the containing structural forces in society. From this perspective, public sector planners not only bring power relations into being, but they also exercise delicate day-to-day choices about whether to follow the rules or change them and thus change the structural forces. While structuration theory has been influential in sociology and human geog-raphy, it has had relatively little influence on tourism research (Dann, 1999; Hall & Page, 1999).

Examination of different modes of reasoning and discourse among participants in collaborative planning

Several contributors have stressed the importance of confronting the multi-plicity of the 'needs' and 'views' of people involved in collaborative planning, while Jamal and Getz also indicate the significance of people's different forms of reasoning. Tourism research is beginning to explore the complexity of different views about tourism development using 'social representations' (Pearce *et al.*, 1996) and 'discourse' analysis (Clarke *et al.*, 1994). But there has been less consid-eration of the modes of reasoning behind the discourses of the many groups and individuals who potentially can contribute to tourism planning. The philosopher Habermas (1987) contends that there are moral and emotive forms of reasoning in addition to scientific or technical forms, and that technical reasoning often dominates public discourse, despite the importance of moral and emotional concerns for society. It can be argued that in an open society that recognises different cultural points of view, it is necessary to acknowledge these different modes of reasoning, to develop an understanding of them, and to accord them equal status. Hence, the differing modes of reasoning and discourses are important considerations for future research on collaborative tourism planning. And it will be important to recognise that cultural groups in different parts of the world may have different views about the processes and 'norms' of decision-making within a collaborative process. There is no western monopoly of good practice here, to be applied globally regardless of cultural context.

Examination of the role of government in collaborative planning

A government organisation (local, regional or national) may respond to the existence of a partnership engaged in tourism planning issues for which it has a responsibility in a number of different ways. It may decide not to join the partnership, it may join the partnership as one stakeholder among other stakeholders, it may attempt to impose its own views on the other stakeholders in the partnership, or it may take on the role of a manager, convenor or facilitator of the partnership. A case may be made that democratic legitimacy is increased by the involvement of an elected body in a partnership, with government supposed to serve the 'public interest', to safeguard certain social and democratic values, as well as being publicly accountable. Government may also bring sizeable financial and staff resources to a partnership. These arguments could also be extended to suggest that government may be well placed to act as the convenor of some tourism planning partnerships. But there are important caveats to add here. While government involvement may be valuable, the sheer power of government – legal, financial and in terms of influence – may be a danger in some situations. Financial support, for example, may lead to a weakening of entrepreneurial drive. Given the many special characteristics of government organisations, therefore, more research might usefully focus on the role of government in specific partnerships involved in tourism planning, and on the consequences of its role varying for different partnerships.

Examination of the structural conditions affecting collaborative planning in different contexts

The practices and also the rules and resources of policy and planning systems differ between nations, regions and local areas, and these systems will vary according to the extent to which they are conducive to collaborative approaches to tourism planning. More research is needed on how different policy and planning systems have affected attempts at collaborative tourism planning. Roberts and Simpson consider some of the issues in Chapter 12 in relation to collaborative planning for rural tourism in Bulgaria and Romania. It may also be that the collaborative approaches that work in highly developed, western economies may not work in countries at other stages of economic and political development.

Examination of adaptive management as an approach to collaborative planning

In Chapter 13, Reed presents a strong case for the use of an adaptive management approach to collaborative tourism planning. There is a growing interest in the tourism planning literature in adaptive, iterative or continuous approaches. Hall and Page (1999: 256) argue that 'planning systems are meant to be able to adapt and change; they *learn* how to be effective in terms of the most appropriate set of goals, objectives, actions, indicators, institutional arrangements, and practices'. Similarly, Williams (1998: 128) advocates a 'planning approach that is comprehensive yet allows for the need for regular readjustment in physical development, service delivery and visitor management'. It has also been argued that effective collaborative planning should involve a continuous learning process during the life of the collaboration, drawing on an emerging stock of social, intellectual and institutional capital among the participants as well as on changing circumstances and needs (Healey, 1997; Yuksel *et al.*, 1999). Tremblay contends in Chapter 16 that stakeholders need to engage in collaborative approaches to tourism planning in order to learn more about their environment and about their differing views. To date there is relatively little research that focuses explicitly on tourism planning conceived and conducted as an adaptive and creative learning process, and there is a clear need for more work in this direction.

Examination of the best ways of disseminating and introducing improved practice into collaborative tourism planning and management

In Chapter 1, it was claimed that there is great potential for collaboration and partnerships to promote tourism development that is more sustainable; it was also noted that partnership arrangements could be much more widespread. It follows, therefore, that ways must be found to encourage more collaborative practices, and to raise skills levels. Two research areas seem to offer potential. First, there is the question of raising awareness of the issues, advantages and problems of collaborative processes. Researchers need to assess managerial awareness of the concept, and perceived barriers to collaboration. Secondly, where staffing is considered necessary for a partnership, there are then questions of the skills levels they will need. Adequate, effective and dedicated staff can be especially important for collaborative success. Collaboration can be a great consumer of staff time; it is also a great consumer of 'people' skills as well as tourism skills. However, there are few people trained in both of these areas (OECD, 1990; National Trust for Historic Preservation, n.d.). Skills training is, therefore, a subject ripe for research. Assessments should cover the levels of training required and evaluate the types of skills required. There could be trials of varying methods of skills transfer, such as conferences, workshops, books, videos and web sites. There is also a case for post-experience training in collaborative approaches – retrofitting decision-makers and implementers with new skills – as well as for the inclusion of these issues in university tourism courses.

References

Block, P. (1993) *Stewardship: Choosing Service over Self Interest*. Chicago: Berret Koehler.

Clark, G., Darrall, J., Grove-White, R., Macnaghten, P. and Urry, J. (1994) *Key Leisure Policy Statements: A Discourse Analysis. Background Paper 7. Leisure Landscapes. Leisure, Culture and the English Countryside: Challenges and Conflicts*. London: Council for the Protection of Rural England.

Dann, G.M.S. (1999) Theoretical issues for tourism's future development. Identifying the agenda. In D.G. Pearce and R.W. Butler (eds) *Contemporary Issues in Tourism Development* (pp. 13–30). London: Routledge.

Giddens, A. (1984) *The Constitution of Society*. Cambridge: Polity Press.

Habermas, J. (1987) *The Philosophical Discourse of Modernity*. Cambridge: Polity Press.

Hall, C.M. and Page, S.J. (1999) *The Geography of Tourism and Recreation. Environment, Place and Space*. London: Routledge.

Healey, P. (1997) *Collaborative Planning. Shaping Places in Fragmented Societies*. London: Macmillan.

Kickert, W.J.M., Klijn, E.-H. and Koppenjan, J.F.M. (eds) (1997) *Managing Complex Networks: Strategies for the Public Sector*. London: Sage.

Koth, B., Kreag, G. and Sem, J. (1991) *A Training Guide for Rural Tourism Development*. Minneapolis: University of Minnesota.

Middleton, V.T.C. and Hawkins, R. (1998) *Sustainable Tourism: A Marketing Perspective*. Oxford: Butterworth-Heinemann.

Miller, L.C., Rossing, E.B. and Steele, S.M. (1992) *Partnerships: Shared Leadership Among Shareholders*. Madison: University of Wisconsin.

National Trust for Historic Preservation (NTHP) (n.d.) *Bringing Back Urban Vitality: Main Street*. Washington, DC: NTHP.

Organisation for Economic Co-operation and Development (OECD) (1990) *Partnerships for Rural Development*. Paris: OECD.

Pearce, P.L., Moscardo, G. and Ross, G.F. (1996) *Tourism Community Relationships*. Oxford: Pergamon.

Timothy, D.J. (1998) Cooperative tourism planning in a developing destination. *Journal of Sustainable Tourism* 6 (1), 52–68.

Williams, S. (1998) *Tourism Geography*. London: Routledge.

Yuksel, F., Bramwell, B. and Yuksel, A. (1999) Stakeholders interviews and tourism planning at Pamukkale, Turkey. *Tourism Management* 20, 351–360.

Index